99 DIVES

from the San Juan Islands in Washington
to the Gulf Islands and Vancouver
Island in British Columbia

TWO NEW GUIDEBOOKS . . .

99 DIVES and its companion, *101 DIVES*, are expanded and updated editions of Betty Pratt-Johnson's *141 DIVES*, which has sold more than 40,000 copies. The new books include more than 80 new dives. Of *141 DIVES*, reviewers have noted:

"This must be considered THE BIBLE for skin divers in the Pacific Northwest..."
VICTORIA TIMES

"...a must if you're going to dive in the Pacific Northwest. It has local information about wrecks, marine life, bottles..."
SKIN DIVER

"...most comprehensive reference for Northwest divers ... extensive sections on dive charters and resorts, safety information, tides, equipment and boat rentals, wrecks, bottle and junk collecting, underseas photography..."
SUNSET

"...undoubtedly the finest guidebook to local diving we have ever seen...the book will whet your appetite and look good on the coffee table."
UNDERCURRENT

The most authoritative guides to
underwater fun in Washington and British Columbia

Betty Pratt-Johnson

99 DIVES

**from the San Juan Islands in Washington
to the Gulf Islands and Vancouver
Island in British Columbia**

Heritage House Publishing Company Ltd.

FRONT COVER: Browning Wall near Port Hardy, Vancouver Island
Photograph by Jett Britnell

SPINE: The red-and-white dive flag marks an area where scuba diving is in progress and is flown from a float. It is recognized throughout North America.
    The blue-and-white dive flag is flown from a vessel when scuba divers are in the water. It is recognized throughout the world.

Canadian Cataloguing in Publication Data

Pratt-Johnson, Betty.
 99 dives from the San Juan Islands in Washington to the Gulf Islands and Vancouver Island in British Columbia

Includes index.
ISBN 1-895811-18-X

  1. Scuba diving–British Columbia–Pacific Coast–Guidebooks. 2.
Scuba diving–Washington (State)–Pacific Coast–Guidebooks. 3.
Pacific Coast (B.C.)–Guidebooks. 4. Pacific Coast (Wash.)–
Guidebooks. I. Title.
GV840.S782B75 1994   797.2'3   C94-910293-8

Library of Congress Catalog Card Number: 94-77745

First Edition 1994

Published in Canada and the United States by
HERITAGE HOUSE PUBLISHING COMPANY LTD.
Unit #8, 17921-55 Avenue, Surrey BC Canada V3S 6C4

HERITAGE HOUSE PUBLISHING COMPANY LTD.
1916 Pike Place, Suite 73, Seattle Washington 98101

Printed in Canada

To the most incredibly vital community
of people in the world

To scuba divers – thanks!

Books by Betty Pratt-Johnson

99 Dives from the San Juan Islands in Washington to the Gulf Islands and Vancouver Island in British Columbia

101 Dives from the mainland of Washington and British Columbia

Whitewater Trips and Hot Springs in the Kootenays of British Columbia: For Kayakers, Canoeists and Rafters

Whitewater Trips for Kayakers, Canoeists and Rafters in British Columbia: Greater Vancouver through Whistler, Okanagan and Thompson River Regions

Whitewater Trips for Kayakers, Canoeists and Rafters on Vancouver Island

Everybody Loves an Octopus, her popular natural-history article which was published first in the United States, was translated into French and German and reprinted in a scuba diving magazine in Switzerland. It was then made available to readers around the world in twelve additional languages as well as in big print and it was selected as an example of good writing for the college anthology *Read to Write.* It is also included in the *1979 Science Annual* of the Americana Encyclopedia.

To the islands

CONTENTS

Preface
Come Dive With Me 11

Introduction
What's Different About North Pacific Diving 14

General Conditions
Water Salinity 14
Water Temperature 15
Seasons 15
Visibility 15
Bull Kelp 16
Currents and Riptides 17
    Basic Tide and Current Information 19
    More Books on Tidal Currents 19
    Computer Aids on Tidal Currents 21
Boats and Log Booms 22
Broken Fishing Line 22
Surge and Surf 22
Marine Life 22
    Books on Fish 26
    Books on a Variety of Marine Life 26
    Marine Life Course 27
    Video Cassettes 27
Diver Traffic 28
Public Access 28
Kayak-Diving 30
Diving Regulations and Safety 31

Diving Activities
Underwater Photography 32
Marine Life Conservation 32
Spearfishing and Collecting
    of Marine Life 33
Bottle, China and Junk Collecting 33
    Books on Bottles 35
Archaeological Diving 36
Wreck Diving 37
    Computer Data Bases on Wrecks 39
    Registers of Ships 39
    Books on Ships 39
Artificial Reefs 41
Clubs and Associations 42
Night Diving 43

General Map
Key to Chapter Maps 44-45

Chapter 1
Victoria and Saanich Inlet 47
• Map 49
• Service Information 50-55
Swordfish Island 56
Race Rocks 58
Wreck of *Barnard Castle* 60

Fisgard Island 62
Saxe Point Park 64
Ogden Point Breakwater 66
Brotchie Ledge 68
Ten Mile Point 70
Spring Bay 72
Graham's Wall 74
Wreck of the *G.B. Church* 76
Arbutus Island 78
Mystery Wreck at Deep Cove 80
Setchell Point 82
Tozier Rock 84
Henderson Point 86
Tod Inlet 88
Willis Point 90
The White Lady 92
Christmas Point 94
Misery Bay 96

Chapter 2
San Juan Islands including San Juan Orcas and Lopez 99
• Map 100-101
• Service Information 102-109
Turn Island 110
Lime Kiln Point 112
Smallpox Bay 114
Reuben Tarte Park 116
Turn Point, Stuart Island 118
Lovers Cove 120
Doe Bay 122
Doe Island 124
Frost Island 126
James Island 128
Long Island 130

Chapter 3
Southern Gulf Islands including Galiano, Pender and Saltspring 133
• Map 134-135
• Service Information 136-141
Tilly Point Caves 142
Enterprise Reef 144
Retreat Cove 146
Madrona Wall 148
Pringle Park 150
Alcala Point 152
Wreck of the *Point Grey* 154
Wreck of the *Del Norte* 156
Wreck of the *Miami* 158
Beddis Beach 160
Beaver Point 162
Canoe Rock 164

First dive, 1967

Schooner Cove, 1974

Port McNeill, 1993

COME DIVE WITH ME

Scuba diving is growing and changing – it is forever new – and I feel lucky to have been involved with this remarkable recreation for so long, lucky to still be wandering around under water. I have enjoyed twenty-seven years of scuba diving in the Strait of Georgia and Puget Sound, as well as many other parts of the world.

This new *99 Dives* where-to-go guidebook is based on *141 Dives in the Protected Waters of Washington and British Columbia*, a guide I started writing in 1974 when I first became excited about diving in the North Pacific. No guide was available for the region, and the best excuse I could find to dive as much as I wanted to was to write the very book I wanted to buy, a book containing basic information about facilities and sites. The book grew as my skills increased: it was first published in 1976, and since that time has been used by beginner to expert divers. That guidebook is still growing.

More than eighty new dive sites are in two new volumes that replace it. The original guide has outgrown its binding and is now transformed into two smaller books that will easily fit in your pocket or dive bag. Forty-four new dive descriptions are in *99 Dives*, thirty-seven new sites in its companion volume *101 Dives*. Again the guide format is deliberately designed with each dive described on two opposing pages. If you don't want to take the whole book, you can photocopy it and take just the photocopy when you go for your dive. Both books contain the same type of information as in *141 Dives,* but the two new guides are fully updated and expanded, reflecting the changes in diving. The number of dive-guide and charter-boat offerings has increased. A great deal is now known about formerly difficult-to-dive sites and how to dive them. A couple of high-current dives requiring expert skills are included in each of the new guides. You will also find new, easy-but-gorgeous shore dives like Tilly Point Caves where beginning divers can go, and experts will also want to.

Wherever there is water there is a potential dive site. This endless possibility for exploration is one of the great joys of diving. It also means I could not possibly list every location. However, this book – like *141 Dives* – offers something better than a mere list. It gives clues about how to dive different types of sites. And it offers a diverse sampling of various kinds of diving available from shore, by dive-kayak and boat. It includes many of the better-known and more accessible dives sites, and some not-so-well-known spots on the Vancouver Island side of the protected inland sea stretching from Queen Charlotte Strait through the Strait of Georgia to Juan de Fuca Strait. It also includes dives from the Gulf Islands in British Columbia and the San Juan Islands in Washington.

If you like doing things with groups, you will find clubs dedicated to special interests such as wreck diving, marine life conservation, activities with physically challenged divers, creating artificial reefs. If you are a non-club-joiner type, you can go quietly with one other diver to explore. Charter boats are available for day-trips and liveaboard trips. Clues to all of these things and more are offered in this guide. I personally have dived every site described in this guidebook, some sites many times. I include information to help you find and dive these places, but I also give you the tools to go beyond the described sites.

Diving is unlimited. Use this guidebook, dive with charter operators who are constantly finding new sites, and also find your own sites. Study charts; see the important sections in the introduction with information on local conditions, wrecks, bottle collecting, kayak-diving and more; see lists of rental boats and expanded information on launching ramps included in the service information of each chapter, as well as lists of charter boats.

To obtain information for this guide, once again I talked with local divers about each site; where changes were reported I dived the sites. Many old favorites are still in it but with enhancements such as at Ogden Point Breakwater. It has been fun revisiting these sites, and a thrill to visit many new sites. A couple of places I've had minor difficulties in determining whether some properties crossed in gaining access to diving waters are public or private property. Treat with respect, therefore, any new signs advising that property is private or stating that no trespassing is allowed.

My observations of marine life are the observations of an interested layperson. I refer to all animals by common names. In the absence of an authoritative common name I have used the common name most descriptive to me.

A portion of nautical chart in the actual chart size is included in each site description. These charts are for reference only and are not to be used for navigation. All soundings are in meters unless stated otherwise. The scale varies because the charts themselves vary. Therefore I have added a small scale bar under each chart. An arrow has been added to each chart to indicate the dive-entry point described.

The tide table or current table to refer to for every site is given at the top of the page of each dive description. When a time correction is required, wherever possible, a simple rule-of-thumb figure is given. These corrections have been derived from locals. Such information is always easier to use and often more reliable than trying to pin down dive time to precisely what you find in the current tables – often currents are measured mid-channel and that is not where you are diving.

Although this is a where-to-go guidebook, I include information about possible hazards to beware of at each site. One note regarding safety: It is possible but not proven that heavy exertion after diving could bring on signs and symptoms of decompression sickness. I know of several people who suspect this problem has happened to them. Therefore I include cautions in the hazards section of some of the descriptions of dives that are most likely to require heavy physical exertion, but consider it on all dives. Each site description incorporates the best of current knowledge for your safety. All information has been checked by one or more experienced divers in addition to myself. But as noted in the disclaimer, this book is not meant to teach you how to dive. Proper training and certification are required before you can rent or purchase equipment or obtain air fills. And you must have good equipment.

All dives are rated for skill and experience required. This skill level requirement cannot be measured by the number of years you have been diving. It can only be measured by the variety of diving situations you have encountered. Any certified diver should be able to attempt the dives classified "All Divers". Beginners and visitors should have experience with a number of these dives before doing any of the more difficult ones. When a dive site has *some complications* but does not require intricate planning, I have rated it for "Intermediate Divers". I expect an intermediate to know how to use tide and current tables – and to know the difference between them – as well as to know techniques to use when diving in current. Dives that require *precision* because of current or depth or boat traffic or any other variable described in hazards, dives that present several difficult hazards, and dives that require great strength and fitness are classified for "Expert Divers".

Kayak-divers will find nineteen kayak dives, which could also be reached by larger boat, described in this guide.

Divers who use wheelchairs will find descriptions of fourteen shore dives that might be accessible to them. I say "might" because on some dives I could have misjudged suitability. Though I have dived every one of these sites, as I have dived every site in the book, not all locations have been checked out by divers using wheelchairs. Fifteen more sites described are possible for divers who use wheelchairs and who paddle dive-kayaks as well. Boat charter operations and dive resorts who welcome divers with wheelchairs are noted in the service information listings but none of them are specifically equipped for it and the capabilities differ. Wheelchair access to dive sites or boats often requires assistance from able-bodied personnel. So ask any charter boat operator or resort that you plan to use exactly what their situation is.

All dives are within sport diving limits, no dive descriptions are for greater depth than 125 feet (38 meters). Many sites are suitable for snorkeling or skin diving as well as scuba diving: when this is so, I have mentioned it. When I state that a dive is suitable for all divers, or intermediate divers "with guide", I indicate that divers who go under water with an experienced guide can enjoy a dive that is otherwise above their skill and experience level: this presupposes that the guide will have a great deal of local knowledge and will be capable of summing up the visiting diver to help him or her deal with the dive situation. Be aware that I have made no value judgments about the capabilities of any dive guides or charter operators – I simply list them. Finally, I have tried to present a balanced number of dives for divers of all skills in each locale. The greatest number are in and around cities where there are the most divers looking for places to get wet.

99 Dives is a starting point for coastal divers who have just learned to dive, dropouts who are returning to diving, and visiting divers from around the world. It contains useful service information for all divers. This book is an open invitation to enjoy some of the most varied and remarkable diving found anywhere. Producing the expanded update of *141 Dives* has been a second experience of discovery for me. I have loved repeating many dives I've enjoyed before, still seeing creatures new to me even after twenty-seven years of diving, and visiting places I never dreamed divers would ever be able to go.

Come dive with me, with this book as a guide, and we'll go on and on discovering the colorful, still world known only to North Pacific divers.

At Turn Point in the San Juans

WHAT'S DIFFERENT ABOUT NORTH PACIFIC DIVING?
WHAT'S OLD? WHAT'S NEW?

A kaleidoscope of color – hot pink, red, yellow and orange; cool blue, mauve, purple and white covers the ocean floor. The emerald sea is bursting with life.

You keep seeing things under water that you can't find in any book. Fascinating creatures, many still unnamed. It's fabulous to feel that you're on the edge of discovery on every dive. Perhaps the other most striking feature of diving in the North Pacific inland sea is the sheer magnitude of protected coastline which makes this region one of the safest and most accessible diving areas in the world. It has always been that way – so what's new?

Adventuring by going out to see wild creatures like Steller sea lions, sixgill sharks and spawning salmon is "in". Spearfishing is "out". Gone, too, are the skin-diving spearfishermen who used to hunt in competitions at depths of 60 to 100 feet (18 to 30 meters). I admired the amazing diving skill of those breath-hold divers. No more rape and pillage of wrecks and marine life. Wreck divers of today are ardent preservers of our underwater heritage. They are documenting wrecks, not tearing them apart and carrying them away, and some of them are *making* wrecks. Creating artificial reefs is a developing diving specialty. While the newest frontier of diving is exploring archaeological sites – prehistoric artifacts from 6,800 years ago have been found.

Divers have different expectations. Many divers don't want to snorkel as far as they used to. But now divers use dive-kayaks to eliminate difficult swims and to reach sites that are a much greater distance away than they could ever have snorkeled. Many people are diving – it has become mainstream, and diving facilities have increased enormously.

More features of this enormous inland sea are included in the information listed below, as well as some suggestions about how to use them to your advantage in pursuing a variety of diving activities. Details about local conditions are in the site descriptions which comprise most of the book. However, before you start selecting specific sites, read the following summary of basic information every diver will want to know. It includes a great deal of information:

General Conditions
Water Salinity
Water Temperature
Seasons
Visibility
Bull Kelp
Currents and Riptides
Boats and Log Booms
Broken Fishing Line
Surge and Surf
Marine Life
Diver Traffic
Public Access
Kayak-Diving
Diving Regulations and Safety

Diving Activities
Underwater Photography
Marine Life Conservation
Spearfishing and Shellfish Collecting
Bottle, China and Junk Collecting
Archaeological Diving
Wreck Diving
Artificial Reefs
Clubs and Associations
Night Diving

WATER SALINITY – All dives covered in this book, except one, are in salt water. Divers accustomed to diving in fresh water will find they need to wear 1 to 4 pounds (⅕ to ¾ kilograms) more weight when diving in the sea. Probably most divers should start by adding 2 pounds (1 kilogram) to compensate for the increased density of salt water. Experiment until you find the right amount.

WATER TEMPERATURE – Water temperature is affected by several factors, including depth and currents. Surface temperatures of North Pacific waters vary from 39° to 46° Fahrenheit (4° to 8° Celsius) in winter to 54° to 64° Fahrenheit (12° to 18° Celsius) in summer, depending upon location. However, below a depth of 30 to 40 feet (9 to 12 meters) the temperature varies little, winter or summer, from about 45° Fahrenheit (7° Celsius).

It is just a matter of where the temperature drop, or thermocline, comes – at 30, 40, 50 or 60 feet (9, 12, 15, or 18 meters), usually not deeper than that. If you are diving below the thermocline you will want to dress warmly year-round. Another factor for wet-suit divers to consider is that you will probably feel the cold more quickly when diving where there is a current. The current constantly forces a change of water under any gaps in your suit. And the water itself will probably be colder because shifting water never becomes warm.

Most local divers dive comfortably year-round in all locations wearing custom-fitted dry suits. Some wear custom-fitted wet suits of neoprene. Wet-suit divers usually wear the "farmer Jane" or "farmer John" style of suit which covers the trunk of the body with a double thickness. Some divers obtain extra warmth for winter by wearing an Arctic hood with a large flange around the neck, by wearing a vest under their wet-suit jacket, and/or by adding a spine pad to their suit. Others wear lightweight neoprene five-finger gloves in summer and ¼-inch (⅔-centimeter) neoprene mitts in winter. In very cold weather, wet-suit divers warm themselves for entry by pouring warm water into their gloves and hoods and down the backs of their necks.

Many wet suits manufactured in California and other warmer parts are of less than ¼-inch (⅔-centimeter) neoprene and will not be comfortably warm in winter waters of the North Pacific. Visiting divers may want to rent a dry suit or buy or rent a vest or an Arctic hood for added warmth while diving in Puget Sound and the Strait of Georgia.

SEASONS – Year-round diving is enjoyed in the Strait of Georgia and Puget Sound and a variety of diving activities is possible. Winter is best for photography since low plankton activity and low river runoff levels make visibility best then. Because summer visibility can be poor, summer is a good time to combine a dive with a picnic on an unspoiled beach, or pursue some diving activity like bottle collecting. Because much bottle collecting is done at muddy sites by touch alone, visibility does not matter. Sunny September days are considered best all-round by some, as that season can be most beautiful both above and below the surface. I opt for year-round diving, choosing sites and diving activities suitable to each season.

VISIBILITY – Water clarity is probably the most significant variable in North Pacific diving. It can vary from "faceplate" visibility when you cannot see 1 foot (⅓ meter) ahead, up to a crystal clear 100 feet (30 meters). Poor visibility may be the result of several factors: the type of bottom, river runoff, industrial pollution, and plankton growth.

• **Type of bottom** – Muddy substrates are liable to be stirred up when current is running, or when a lot of divers are swimming close to the bottom. In many locations, diving at the end of the outgoing tide will help you obtain the best possible visibility. When diving at a silty site near a wall, if possible head out at one level and back at a shallower level. A buoyancy compensation device, which gives neutral buoyancy at any depth, should be worn by all divers at all times. It is particularly useful when diving in muddy areas.

• **River runoff** – Both melting snows and rainstorms cause murky surface water, especially near river and creek mouths. In spring, early summer and after rainstorms, check your chart and avoid sites near large rivers like the Fraser or Skagit. A small, clear stream of fresh water flowing into the sea creates a shimmery appearance like scotch and water, but does not impede vision – or match the taste!

• **Industrial pollution** – Effluents, tailings and other solid wastes from mines, factories and logging operations can impair visibility. Avoid these areas.

• **Plankton growth** – Two "waves" of plankton growth, or "bloom", come to protected waters of North Pacific seas each spring and summer. Prolonged sunny weather encourages these blooms. The spring bloom invariably occurs each year throughout the Strait of Georgia and Puget Sound. It begins any time from March through April or May, and clouds the top 20 to 30 feet (6 to 9 meters) with a green growth of plankton, making the water look like pea soup. Later, the plankton aggregates in white clumps and looks like a snowstorm in the water. This condition may last only two weeks or a month. However, often just as the plankton bloom fades away, river runoff comes to cloud surface waters.

The second wave of plankton is less predictable and more localized. It may come in late summer, August through September or October, making the water look slightly red. This second bloom may come to one area and not to another, usually lasting a very short while. The water may be turbid one day and clear the next. Therefore, at easily accessible sites, it is always worth checking to see if the water is clear. The best summer visibility comes on a sunny day after a week of overcast weather.

Sometimes the only way to find good visibility in the late spring and early summer is to select a dive site deep enough that you can descend through the surface murkiness until the visibility improves. When diving in turbid water, use a compass; swim with your hands touching and extended forward to protect your head and face; and surface with a good reserve of air so that you can meet any emergency poor visibility might create.

One of the most beautiful dives I ever made was on a sunny day in May at Lookout Point in Howe Sound. Fraser River runoff and a healthy bloom of plankton had combined to make the surface almost opaque. There was only faceplate visibility until my buddy and I reached 50 feet (15 meters). Suddenly, we were in a garden of fluffy white plumose anemones shimmering with phosphorescence. Spectacular! Like a night dive, only better, because it came as such a complete surprise. Is it any wonder I advocate diving year-round?

BULL KELP – Beauty or beast? If you have never been diving in kelp you should know something about it.

The large bull kelp is beautiful on its own as it streams above you like flags in the current. I love it just for that. Experienced North Pacific divers are lured to it for many other reasons, too. For instance, it can help orient you. On the surface, bull kelp gives an indication of depth because in the Strait of Georgia it usually grows in less than 30 feet (9 meters) of water. Kelp shows you the direction the current is running. When it pops to the surface, the current is slowing down.

Under water, kelp gives a handhold in difficult current. In areas with lots of boats, if the kelp itself is not too thick to penetrate, it is a relatively traffic-free place to ascend. It provides a rich habitat for marine life. You will often find crabs hiding under it and fish swimming through it. Urchins eat it as a favorite food. Kelp is interesting on its own, too. It is a seasonal plant which nearly dies off over the winter and grows again in spring and summer. It grows very rapidly, reportedly sometimes as much as 6 inches (15 centimeters) in a day. These facts are just a start. Interested divers can find a lot of fascinating information about kelp or marine algae.

It can be a hazard, though, if you are caught in it and then panic. When diving around bull kelp, be particularly careful at the surface. Kelp is easier to swim through under water. Enter the water by surface-diving down, feet first, to avoid entanglement. Always ascend with a reserve of air so that you can descend again, if necessary, and come up at another spot where the growth is not so thick. Bull kelp has a strong stem which is very difficult to break by hand. Wear a knife you can reach with either hand, so that if caught you can calmly cut your way free. A few unprepared divers have drowned as a result of entanglement, and most of these drownings were on the surface. Do not avoid kelp because of its dangers, but use the many positive points which recommend it. Be careful when diving in it, and respect its strength.

CURRENTS AND RIPTIDES – The strongest tidal streams in the world occur in passages of the Strait of Georgia and Puget Sound. In some locations near islands and narrows there are tidal currents with massive kinetic energy – some race at the rate of 16 knots (30 kilometers/hour). You can glance at a chart and immediately predict areas in narrows where current will be a serious consideration. No person can command this element, you must work with it. However, where there is current there is also abundant marine life because the moving water provides food for many animals. It is well worth learning to dive safely in currents in order to enjoy the rich scenes that open to you:

1. Always ask local divers for advice about sites and times.

2. Wear a small-volume mask. It is less likely than a large mask to be dislodged by the current.

3. Wear a whistle.

4. Learn to use your tide and current tables, charts and other tools, and plan each dive carefully. Technical help enabling divers to determine *when to go* is burgeoning – more data, more devices are out there to help with currents.

Always think for yourself – do not rely on the expert in your crowd. Do not rely on the pickup boat, although on some dives you must also have a pickup boat standing by. And do not rely on your charter operator to put you in at the right time. All divers should learn to deal with currents and think for themselves on every dive. Ask your buddy to make a dive plan, too, then check to see if you have planned for the same time. Remember to account for daylight saving time when it is in effect. Many divers do not wear a dive watch because they calculate dive down-time using their dive computer. When diving high-current sites of the North Pacific, it is also important to know the actual time. Wear a watch.

Every year divers stretch the limits – dare more, dive where bigger, more radical tidal currents flow. Many charter operators have learned to dive their "home" big-current sites safely, and they take divers there at the right time. When you dive a big-current site on complete slack, and on one of the best days of the year for it, it feels easy. It feels like a "piece of cake". It isn't. Many operators have great skill and local knowledge. Each diver should strive to acquire those skills. And divers should ask questions, too, plumb for all the information that's out there. Use everything you can.

Diving high-current sites is also becoming more possible because of the abundance of information and aids that are available – new current tables, computer programs to calculate current time and direction, as well as hand-held computers for the same purpose. Use one or more of the new tools, carefully – use what works for you. But whatever you do, do not become complacent about current.

5. When diving in an area subject to strong currents, a fairly safe rule for timing your dive is to get wet 30 minutes before slack tide, the period when the water is still and the tide is neither coming in nor going out. Remember that tides and currents do not always fit with the tables. Depend upon your common sense. Look at the water and

sum up the situation visually before entering the water. For instance, at Campbell River be ready at the site one hour before slack, watching and waiting for the water to slow down. Then complete your dive shortly after the tide has turned.

6. When diving where the current is not too strong, you do not necessarily have to dive precisely on slack but somewhere near slack. Learn to crawl and rock climb: hold onto rocks and pull yourself along. Crawling upcurrent saves a lot of energy and air. Then when half of your air is gone, drift downcurrent until you have returned to

After-the-dive hug with boat tender

your entry point. If caught in a stronger current than expected over a sandy bottom, you could "knife it" – dig your knife in the bottom to pull yourself along. But using your knife should be avoided, if possible, to protect marine life. Even holding onto rocks should be avoided in locations with rich marine life because you are liable to damage the animals and the bottom. Try not to disturb the marine life, nor even the rocks.

7. When diving in a location with very strong currents, plan to have a "live" boat – a vessel under power and not anchored – ready to pick up all divers, if necessary. Or, you can deliberately plan a "drift" dive. A floating buoy with dive flag should mark the group of divers so that the following boat can follow easily and other boats can avoid the divers.

8. When diving from a boat in current, plan to descend at the anchor line and surface near the bow. Leave a floating line that is 200 feet (60 meters) long trailing behind. If you miss the boat you can catch onto the line. You travel 1 meter/second with a 2-knot (¾ - kilometer/hour) current. Thus 200 feet (60 meters) of line "buys" one minute to swim across the current to reach the line. Attach a float or a plastic bottle to the end of the line or use a polypropylene line which floats.

18

When diving from a charter boat, one operator offers the following rule of thumb: "Never pay operator *before* going for a boat dive! Pay *after* he finds you and picks you up."

9. If caught in a rip current, an upwelling or downwelling do not try to swim against it. Swim across it and gradually work your way out.

10. Learn to cope with current and then discover some most rewarding diving.

Finally, remember that all predictions are just that – only predictions. Whatever the source, do not accept current or tide information as infallible. No predictions are. Wind and barometric pressure can radically alter the time of the turn. According to the *Canadian Tide and Current Tables* published by the Canadian Hydrographic Service, "Currents are particularly sensitive to the effects of wind. The times of slack water can be advanced or retarded considerably by strong winds. In some instances, particularly if the following flood or ebb current is weak, the direction of current may not change and slack water may not occur."

When you reach the site check it out: look at the kelp, throw in a stick, float a bottle. If the current is not doing what you expected, trust what you see. Be prepared to watch and wait for the right moment to dive – if you have missed slack, call off the dive. And enjoy it another day.

BASIC SOURCES OF TIDE AND CURRENT INFORMATION FOR REGIONS IN THIS GUIDEBOOK ARE: the Canadian Hydrographic Service *Tide and Current Tables, Volumes 5 and 6,* and the United States NOAA National Ocean Service *Tide Tables, West Coast of North and South America*, and *Tidal Current Tables, Pacific Coast of North America and Asia North* – all published annually.

A greater number of current tables are included in the Canadian tables than used to be. It has become possible to dive with a degree of confidence at wild current sites such as Sechelt Rapids, Race Rocks and Seymour Narrows even though the "window of time" to dive is not great. The accuracy of the predictions at these sites is especially good since the dive is close to or at the current station.

At most stations in the current tables you can expect slack within 15 minutes of their predictions 80% of the time. And since you can read Reference Station times straight from the current tables, it is easy to plan a dive near a Reference Station. However, after twenty-seven years of diving I still find it difficult to make conversions and predict slack at Secondary Stations using the basic tables. I find some of the aids out there helpful. One or more of the following modes of gaining current information could make it easier to plan your dive time:

• **Books for More Information on Tidal Currents**
The following publications are an enormous help in waterways near small islands and convoluted inlets to give a concept of where the currents circle and eddy and do things that are different from simply flowing one direction when the tide floods and the other when it ebbs. Also useful in regions with straightforward ebb and flood flow.

Current Atlas: Juan de Fuca Strait to Strait of Georgia is a book of charts with arrows of varying thickness to indicate the direction and strength of current. These charts are based on theory, using a numerical model. They are of limited value near the shore and in shallow areas, but could be useful for boat diving a mile or so (a few kilometers) from the shore at the outer sides of the Gulf and San Juan islands and Vancouver Island. These charts are easy for people with visual, rather than mathematical, orientation to relate to.
• Scope: From Race Rocks in Juan de Fuca Strait north through the Strait of Georgia

to Discovery Passage at Campbell River, including the Gulf Islands and the San Juan Islands but not Howe Sound or Indian Arm. It must be used with either *Murray's Tables* or *Washburne's Tables*. The *Current Atlas* is purchased once, then you use it with new *Murray's* or *Washburne's* tables purchased annually.
• Expand its use: The *Current Atlas* can be used with the computer program *TideView*.
• Where to obtain it: The *Current Atlas,* as well as *Washburne's* and *Murray's* tables, are available wherever nautical charts are sold and from Canadian Hydrographic Service, PO Box 6000, Sidney BC V8L 4B2, (604) 363-6358; fax (604) 363-6390.

Puget Sound Current Guide is a book of charts with arrows to indicate the direction of ebb and flood currents, and with notations of time corrections to make on current table daily predictions to determine slack water. These charts are based on observations. They are easy for people with visual, rather than mathematical, orientation to relate to.
• Scope: From Juan de Fuca Strait south to Olympia, Washington. Illustrates 103 current stations in Puget Sound.
• Expand its use: This book of maps can be used on its own or to complement the *Current Master* program.
• Where to obtain it: Dive shops, marinas or contact Island Canoe, Inc., 3556 West Blakely Avenue NE, Bainbridge Island WA 98110, (206) 842-5997.

San Juan Current Guide: Including the Gulf Islands and Strait of Georgia is a book of charts with arrows to indicate the direction of ebb and flood currents, and with notations of time corrections to make on current table daily predictions to determine slack water. These charts are easy for people with visual, rather than mathematical, orientation to relate to.
• Scope: From Juan de Fuca Strait north to Dodd Narrows near Nanaimo in British Columbia. Illustrates more than 100 current stations.
• Expand its use: This book of maps can be used on its own or to complement the *Current Master* program.
• Where to obtain it: Dive shops, marinas or contact Island Canoe, Inc., 3556 West Blakely Avenue NE, Bainbridge Island WA 98110, (206) 842-5997.

Tidelog: Puget Sound Edition, daily tide graphics. A wonderful pair of waves shows the predicted high and low tides for Seattle for every day of the year. The waves give a very physical idea of the volume of tidal exchange for each day and even dip below the bottom line of the graph at minus tides. Below each wave, the time is given so divers can see when to expect high and low water. Beneath that, two lines mark the time of the predicted turn of the current at "The Narrows, north end" and "Admiralty Inlet, Bush Point". A mass of data, including tides for Port Townsend, tide corrections for other locations, currents for Rosario Strait and Deception Pass, current corrections for other locations and a set of miniaturized Tidal Current Charts are in the back of the book. *Tidelog* is an excellent source of information for divers who want quick-and-easy but abbreviated data at a glance, as well as for divers who want a great many facts.
    For added interest and fun, this popular book shows the state of the moon each day. I met a diver who uses *Tidelog* to record her dive time and experiences. Since it is apparent on the wave what the tide was supposed to be doing when she was diving, she gains a good record on which to base corrections, if required, for future dives at each site. *Tidelog* is issued annually – buy a new one each year. It is superb for people who relate to graphics.
• Scope: *Tidelog* contains information for all Washington dive sites in this guidebook.
• Where to obtain it: Dive shops or contact Pacific Publishers, PO Box 480, Bolinas CA 94924, (415) 868-2909.

• Computer Aids for More Information on Tidal Currents

TideFinder is a hand-held tide and current computer. The big advantage of this instrument is its small size. *TideFinder* and its Operations Manual can be taken onto a boat easily – you do not need a notebook computer. Information is reported on a two-line digital display. You punch in the station name, the time you want the information for and it computes. You can obtain a constant flow of information about what the tide and current are doing where you are. Current computations you can obtain are: next ebb, next flood, next slack, next current, present current speed and direction of current. Tide computations you can obtain are: next high, next low, next minus, next tide and present tide height. *TideFinder* is filled with information useful for boat divers and is suited to persons with an ability to relate to abstract numbers.
• Scope: The west coast *TideFinder* covers the entire region of this guidebook, but not all of the tide and current points in the government tables are covered: presently 1,167 tide points and 882 current points from Mexico to Alaska are included and the number is growing. Locations that relate to this guidebook are shown on nine of the sixty-two maps in the Operations Manual.
• Where to obtain it: From marinas or contact Conex Electro-Systems, Inc., 1602 Carolina Street, Bellingham WA 98226, (206) 734-4323.
   The computer is programmed to calculate tides and currents through the year 2000. After that it can be updated.

TideView is a computer program (MS-DOS/Windows) specially designed to use with the *Current Atlas.* It puts the *Current Atlas* information on the computer screen like a moving picture. You can zoom in on the area where you plan to dive and see the direction of the currents and approximate strength of predicted currents – done with arrows with tails. More tails for greater current. You can pinpoint a spot, then see and print graphs of predictions. It gives tide predictions and current predictions. It comes with a refreshingly short manual of fourteen pages, and can be used by both math-oriented persons and those who are visually-oriented.
• Scope: At the time of writing, the scope is from Race Rocks in the Strait of Juan de Fuca north to Texada Island in the Strait of Georgia. And it is increasing.
• Expand its use: Use on its own or with the *Current Atlas.*
• Where to obtain it: Channel Consulting, 2167 Guernsey Street, Victoria BC V8S 2P5, (604) 598-9500; fax (604) 595-8265. Your initial purchase gives you information for the current year plus the next year. After that, annual updates for one-third of the new-user price are available to registered users.

Current Master program (MS-DOS) provides information on both tide heights and tidal currents. It is particularly useful for obtaining current predictions. The program eliminates the need to calculate for Secondary Stations – *Current Master* makes it easy to locate the nearest station where data for currents is available, then to obtain a printed summary of corrected data for that station. Printed tide-height information too if you want it. Useful for people who are not oriented to using charts and numbers and doing calculations but who are visually oriented.
   One hitch: *Current Master* sometimes tells you it is not possible to predict slack at the place and time you request it and then you are left with no information. Always carry your basic tidal current table too.
• Scope: From Olympia, Washington, north through Puget Sound and Juan de Fuca Strait to Dodd Narrows near Nanaimo in British Columbia. It must be used with either the *Puget Sound Current Guide* or the *San Juan Current Guide: Including the Gulf Islands and Strait of Georgia,* depending on where you are diving. Buy the books of maps once, the computer program each year.
• Where to obtain it: At dive shops or contact Island Canoe, Inc., 3556 West Blakely Avenue NE, Bainbridge Island WA 98110, (206) 842-5997.

BOATS AND LOG BOOMS – Thousands of boats also use the inland sea waters described in this guide. Areas where boat traffic is particularly heavy are noted in the detailed site descriptions, and you should be especially careful at these places. But remember, a boat could appear at any time over any site. Dive defensively:

1. Dive with a dive flag – it's required. And it helps. Use it but do not count on it to protect you.
2. When ascending, spiral and look up in order to see as much of the surface as possible, and look for boats.
3. Listen for boats. Where the bottom is featureless, dive with a compass and ascend close to the contour of the bottom all the way to shore. At other sites ascend near a rock face, up your boat or dive-flag anchor line, or in a kelp bed, being careful not to become caught in the kelp. Larger vessels usually steer clear of kelp.
4. If you cannot ascend at a protected place, ascend with a reserve of air and, if you hear a power boat, stay down until it passes. If you hear a really big ship, hang onto rocks or wedge yourself between boulders on the bottom.
5. When diving near log booms, ascend with a reserve of air so that if you arrive immediately under the log boom you will have time to descend and come up again at another place. Spiral, look up, and extend one arm above you as you ascend.

BROKEN FISHING LINE – Beware of broken bits of fishing line under water. It is very strong and difficult to see. Look for it where you know there are lots of fishermen and at rocky points near heavily populated areas. Carry a diver's knife; if you become entangled you can cut yourself free.

SURGE AND SURF – Since the scope of this guide is limited to inland sea and inlets protected from the open ocean, surge and surf are not factors to consider at the sites described.

MARINE LIFE – The color and variety of marine animals living in the Strait of Georgia and Puget Sound is astonishing. I carry an underwater light on every dive in order not to miss any of that color. The sea is teeming with life, all of it fascinating, and practically none of it dangerous to the diver.

The greatest number of sea stars found in any one area of the world are here. North Pacific waters are unrivalled for colorful invertebrates – 5,000 species have been identified. Close to 400 species of fish live in the eastern North Pacific. Marine algae or kelps are abundant, as well. Over 640 species of marine algae have been recorded in British Columbia.

At shallow sandy sites you will probably find large Dungeness crabs revealed only by a pair of eyes and a slight indentation in the bottom. Moon snails that look like something from another planet. And sometimes the bottom itself takes off like a flying carpet – starry flounders in flight!

When diving deep look for yelloweye rockfish beneath ledges. You may find prawns – especially at night, or discover ancient ghostly clumps of cloud sponges with a small rockfish peeping from each tuberous appendage. No one knows how to gauge for sure, but some say a clump as tall as a man must be hundreds of years old. Some say thousands.

Among rocky reefs you will find red Irish lords, kelp greenlings skittering away spookily into crevices, tiny grunt sculpins looking like precisely painted tropical fish. Lingcod sometimes grow to 30 or 40 pounds (14 or 18 kilograms) – and more – in the rocky current-swept depths. Or you might meet a 2,000-pound (900-kilogram) Steller sea lion. Large marine mammals abound: from dolphins to harbor seals, sea lions and killer whales. Gorgeous giant red nudibranchs, delicate as tissue paper, waft through the water near newly laid eggs cascading over rocky cliffs like an intricate lace shawl. Many small nudibranchs live in these waters.

And the North Pacific is home to some of the world's largest octopuses. For many years octopuses had the reputation of being dangerous to divers, but this is a myth. The octopus can be handled quite easily. If one grabs onto you, simply tickle it and it will release you and slip away. However, if you touch one, be gentle. Octopuses are fragile and easily damaged, as well as being much more frightened of you than you are of them.

What animals *are* potentially dangerous in North Pacific waters? The following creatures are sometimes considered dangerous, or simply bothersome, by divers:

• **Dogfish Sharks** – Dogfish are not known to attack people, but most divers leave the water when dogfish start circling in a pack.

• **Jellyfish** – More of a nuisance than a hazard, the red, brown, yellow and water jellyfish can leave a painful sting. If you have seen any jellyfish, you and your buddy should check one another for stinging tentacles before removing masks and gloves. Even after removing gear be cautious as the stingers stay active on your gear for hours. I have been told that urine is an antidote, also that canned milk neutralizes the sting. Jellyfish are seasonal and appear most often in fall and early winter.

• **Killer Whales** – Killer whales are not known to attack people, but most divers leave the water when killer whales appear. Yet some divers try to meet killer whales under water.

• **Lingcod** – Though not generally considered dangerous, the lingcod has a formidable set of teeth and has been known to attack divers. Males may be aggressive when guarding eggs during winter.

• **Ratfish** – The ratfish has a poisonous spine just in front of its dorsal fin. Avoid this spine. Once a ratfish bit me in the leg on a night dive. The only attack I have heard of, yet, but beware.

• **Sea Urchins** – Urchins have sharp spines and can cause nasty puncture wounds, as well as damage dry suits. Again, one antidote I have heard of is urine, and another is meat tenderizer.

• **Seals and Sea Lions** – These animals are sometimes sought, sometimes avoided. One diver told me he saw a seal dislodge a diver's mask in play, and caused the diver to panic. Another told me of a friend whose daily dive companion is a seal. Sea lions may approach divers and some divers have reported injuries. Yet I include a write-up in the Nanaimo chapter of this book on page 210, with guidelines for a winter dive with Steller sea lions for those who choose it. Even in winter, do not dive close to haulouts, do not touch sea lions. And if you meet a bull in summer, watch out. It will be aggressive.

• **Sixgill Sharks** – Sixgills have not harmed people to date, but have been noted to be more aggressive at dawn and dusk. They are meat eaters and they have very large mouths with exceedingly sharp teeth. In spite of their sluggish appearance they can react with startling speed when annoyed. It is safer not to touch.

• **Wolf-eels** – The wolf-eel with its very strong teeth and jaws can inflict a bad bite. These fish are not known to attack without provocation, and if you avoid sticking your hands into holes and crevices you will probably never tangle with one. Be wary but not dismayed if a wolf-eel lunges out of a cave at you. Many divers hand-feed wolf-eels causing them to approach divers.

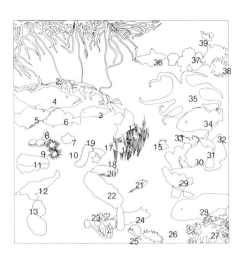

WHAT TO LOOK FOR

Rocky Reef
1. Bull kelp
2. Bottom kelp
3. Cabezon
4. Lingcod
5. Kelp greenling
6. Black rockfish
7. Red Irish lord
8. Swimming scallops
9. Abalones
10. Giant urchins
11. Rock scallop
12. Painted greenling
13. Chitons

Sand
14. Dogfish shark
15. Eelgrass
16. Seaperch
17. Striped seaperch
18. Leather star
19. Sea cucumber
20. Dungeness crab
21. Flounder
22. Sea pen
23. Plume worms
24. Orange peel nudibranch
25. Moon snail
26. Alabaster nudibranch

Rock Wall
27. Basket star
28. Wolf-eel
29. Chimney sponges
30. Grunt sculpin
31. Giant barnacles
32. Sailfin sculpin
33. Dahlia anemones
34. Copper rockfish
35. Octopus
36. Ratfish
37. Plumose anemones
38. Sunflower stars
39. Sea peaches

BOOKS ON FISH

Coastal Fishes of the Pacific Northwest by Andy Lamb and Phil Edgell, Harbour Publishing, Madeira Park BC, 1986.
(Brief facts on 174 species, easy to find. A drawing and color photograph of every fish – fish silhouettes in table of contents. Index to common and scientific names.)

Pacific Coast Inshore Fishes by Daniel W. Gotshall, Sea Challengers, Monterey CA 1989.
(User-friendly guide: covers 187 species with brief information including common and scientific names, features for identification, range and habitat; pictorial key to the fish families; 174 color photographs; index to scientific names and habitats.)

Pacific Fishes of Canada, Bulletin 180 by J.L. Hart, Fisheries Research Board of Canada, Ottawa, 1973.
(Comprehensive descriptions of 325 fishes; black-and-white drawings of every species, some color photographs. Index to common and scientific names.)

Probably More Than You Want to Know About the Fishes of the Pacific Coast by Robin Milton Love, Really Big Press, Santa Barbara CA, 1991.
(Full of facts you will find nowhere else, and it's fun! Illustrated with a drawing of each fish; index to common and scientific names.)

BOOKS ON A VARIETY OF MARINE LIFE

The Audubon Society Field Guide to North American Seashore Creatures by Norman A. Meinkoth, Alfred A. Knopf, New York, 1981.
(Pocket-sized identification guide for laypersons: filled with color photographs and well-organized data about invertebrates; a few diagrams.)

Beachwalker: Sea Life of the West Coast by Stefani Hewlett Paine, Douglas & McIntyre, Vancouver, 1992.
(Overall view for laypersons: includes fish, mammals, invertebrates. Black-and-white line drawings and photographs, some color.)

Between Pacific Tides by Edward F. Ricketts, Jack Calvin, and Joel W. Hedgpeth, revised by David W. Phillips; Stanford University Press, Stanford CA, 1985.
(Scientific classic covering marine invertebrates, organized by habitat. Black-and-white photographs and drawings.)

Exploring the Seashore in British Columbia, Washington and Oregon by Gloria Snively, Gordon Soules Book Publishers, Vancouver, 1978.
(Guide for laypersons, organized by habitat: sea stars, crabs, kelp, anemones, sea birds and more. Well illustrated with line drawings; color photographs.)

Fieldbook of Pacific Northwest Sea Creatures by Dan H. McLachlan and Jak Ayres. Naturegraph, Happy Camp CA 96039, 1979.
(User-friendly guide; contains a bit of everything from sponges to anemones to mollusks and fish. Table of contents by animal; color photographs. Index to common and scientific names.)

Guide to Common Seaweeds of British Columbia, Handbook No. 27 by R.F. Scagel, British Columbia Provincial Museum, Victoria, 1972.
(Scientific but readable by anyone; no common names used. Information for each plant includes genus and species, description, habitat, distribution, and a line drawing; with index.)

Guide to the Western Seashore: Introductory Marinelife Guide to the Pacific Coast by Rick M. Harbo, Hancock House, Surrey BC, 1988.
(Photographic guide to common invertebrates, fish, mammals and seaweeds. Brief descriptions along with 160 color photographs.)

Light's Manual: Intertidal Invertebrates of the Central California Coast, edited by Ralph I. Smith and James T. Carlton, University of California Press, Berkeley CA, 1975.
(A scientific classic. Black-and-white drawings; index to scientific names.)

Northwest Shore Dives by Stephen Fischnaller, Bio-Marine Images, Edmonds WA, 1990.
(Drawings, photographs and a great deal of information about marine life as well as dive site descriptions in this volume which is primarily a dive guidebook for Washington. Index contains common and scientific names.)

Pacific Coast Nudibranchs: A Guide to the Opisthobranchs, Alaska to Baja California by David W. Behrens, Sea Challengers, Monterey CA, 1991.
(User-friendly comprehensive guide: covers 217 species with brief information including common and scientific names, features for identification, range and habitat; 228 color photographs.)

Seashore Life of the Northern Pacific Coast: An Illustrated Guide to Northern California, Oregon, Washington, and British Columbia by Eugene N. Kozloff, University of Washington Press, Seattle, 1983.
(Scientific information organized by habitat. Lots of color photographs. Index to common and scientific names.)

Tidepool & Reef: Marinelife Guide to the Pacific Northwest Coast by Rick M. Harbo, Hancock House, Surrey BC, 1980.
(Photographic guide to invertebrates, fish and seaweeds. Brief descriptions along with 265 color photographs.)

PICTURE BOOK
The Emerald Sea by Dale Sanders (photographs) and Diane Swanson (text), Whitecap Books, North Vancouver BC, 1993.
(Elegant large-format book with fabulous color photographs of North Pacific marine life and three wrecks. Informally organized information about marine life; common and scientific names list. Index to common names.)

MARINE LIFE COURSE
Andy Lamb's Marine Life Identification Course for Divers
3171 Huntleigh Crescent
North Vancouver BC V7H 1C9
(604) 929-4131

VIDEO CASSETTES
Sub-Island Discoveries by Andrew Bell, Abel Video Productions, Victoria, 1991.
(Marine life you can see at many sites in the Strait of Georgia and Puget Sound, shot at Vancouver Island: plumose anemones, cloud sponges, wolf-eels, ratfish, painted greenlings, red Irish lords, basket star, swimming scallops, red jellyfish.)

The World Below Us by Andrew Bell, Abel Video Productions, Victoria, 1992.
(Shows marine life at Vancouver Island sites: Steller sea lions, white-sided Pacific dolphins, an octopus, a giant silver nudibranch, a sea pen and more.)

DIVER TRAFFIC – Divers have become part of the marine life scene. Diving is mainstream recreation now and there's good and bad in that. Lots of people to dive with. Lots of facilities. But diving etiquette on shore becomes more and more important. We need to be considerate when parking; be discreet when changing and not strip in the middle of the road before and after diving; take care not to trespass when walking to and from the water, and go quietly. When diving at night, it makes sense to avoid shining lights in the windows of private homes and to save wild parties for the wilds – enjoy quiet aprés-dive parties at beaches in the city.

And what about the effect of divers on the sea, the fish? Diver damage from dropping anchors on reefs and wrecks, kicking fragile cloud sponges, dragging equipment consoles on the bottom, snagging and breaking hydrocoral – it happens. Divers passing through can wreak havoc on the marine environment without the divers even being aware of it. Yet if we dive carefully we can look forward to returning again and again to pristine sites.

Also I believe we should just look, not touch, and leave the sea and fish as we find them. I still see divers with spear guns in Washington and fish are noticeably scarce – recently I met a diver with a lance who said he was hunting octopuses. I have seen no spear guns in the past few years in British Columbia and I see lots of fish, yet many divers report fewer fish. I believe that if fish are decreasing in numbers, the growing number of hook-and-line fishermen and the growing number of seals might be the reason. They eat fish. In the past 20 years, the seal population has increased tenfold.

When creating artificial reefs, we need to be careful that our additions do not harm the environment as we try to enhance it, and I do not believe in feeding fish as it alters their natural behavior. They become too trusting. Feeding a wolf-eel could result in the death of the animal. A friendly wolf-eel might lunge from its den looking for handouts, frighten a visiting diver and be killed.

When diving, we are favored guests in a special place. Let's not change that place, let's just go for a visit.

PUBLIC ACCESS – "You can't drive twenty minutes without reaching water in Washington" one dive buddy says.

Endless diving is at hand; access is only limited by our imagination. I hope readers of this guidebook will use it as a starting point, begin using these reference materials and then throw the guidebook away. Study nautical charts next to public access points. Go out and find your own sites: use everything you can to learn where to gain access to the water. For a start, you can find new sites to dive from shore by looking for parks for access. Next learn about launching ramps in each area, then use an inflatable or dive-kayak and there is no limit to where you can go. But always go carefully and honor wildlife reserves.

In Washington, whenever you see this official public access logo on a sign you may walk to the water.

Look for information on parks
- In British Columbia: federal or provincial parks, or forest service recreation sites.
- In Washington: federal, state, county or department of natural resources parks. And wherever you go, look for the official state public access sign that confirms access is permitted.

Look for information on launching ramps

Many launching ramps are listed in the service information of each chapter. In addition:

• In British Columbia: Canadian Hydrographic Service small-craft charts and many other large-scale ones show launching ramps with small black wedges. Also refer to the *BC Small Craft Guide: Vancouver Island and the Gulf Islands*, Canadian Hydrographic Service, 1989. See sections on Launching Ramps and Small Craft Facilities.

• In Washington: launching ramps are also shown by black wedges on the DeLorme *Washington Atlas & Gazetteer*.

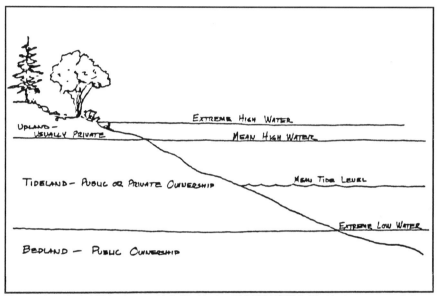

Diagram shows typical tideland ownership in Washington. PLEASE NOTE: In Washington, you cannot always land on the beach or even in shallow water. Privately owned property often extends below mean tide level to the extreme low-water mark.

Refer to lists of national wildlife refuge sites and ecological reserves so you do not inadvertently dive or land where it might be harmful to the marine life.

• For British Columbia: obtain a list of provincial ecological reserves from BC Parks, Planning and Conservation Services, 2nd Floor, 800 Johnson Street, Victoria BC V8V 1X4, (604) 387-5002; fax (604) 387-5757.

• For Washington: obtain a list of national wildlife refuge sites from San Juan Islands National Wildlife Refuge, 100 Brown Farm Road, Olympia WA 98506, (206) 753-9467.

To establish new official public access points

• In British Columbia: popular sites with entry across Crown land at road ends could be set aside as recreational reserves. To inquire, contact BC Lands, Ministry of Environment, Lands and Parks, 851 Yates Street, Victoria BC V8V 1X5, (604) 387-5011; fax (604) 356-1871.

• In Washington: refer to the *Shoreline Public Access Handbook* by James W. Scott. It contains a great deal of information about site planning, permit administrators' guidelines and how to proceed. Purchase from State of Washington Department of Ecology, Publications Department, PO Box 47600, Olympia, WA 98504-7600, (206) 407-7472; fax (206) 407-6989.

KAYAK-DIVING – Going to the site using a "sit-on-top" dive-kayak as transportation is a wonderful way to extend the scope of where you can go diving. Use a dive-kayak to eliminate a difficult swim or to reach sites as far as 2 to 3 nautical miles (4 to 5 kilometers) away. Or paddle close alongside the shore to reach a point or beach inaccessible by road. I believe every diver should try it out and consider making a dive-kayak a standard piece of diving equipment.

Find someone to teach you the basics of diving with a dive-kayak or ask how to do it where you rent or buy a dive-kayak. Remember that in both the United States and Canada every boat must be equipped with a personal flotation device (PFD) for each person on board. A guided excursion with an experienced kayak-diver is an ideal way to start. Then take it slowly.

The first time I used a dive-kayak, my buddy and I paddled for ten minutes across a short stretch of open water to a beach where it was easy to land and gear up. Next

Loading gear for Turn Island

dive I rolled off and got back on board in the shallows. Diving in open water looked like a giant step. I doubted I could climb back on, but soon found that part is easy. Once you are organized, it is also simple to roll off the kayak and get geared up in the water. First I hung a tether off my kayak to clip my weight belt to, but now have acquired a buoyancy compensator with weights in it. Makes the whole thing so easy.

The only limitations I have found with the single-person dive-kayaks I use is that the combined weight of diver plus gear must be no more than 250 to 300 pounds (115 to 135 kilograms). The dive-kayak will not float more weight. The only way to overcome that one is for a single diver to paddle a double kayak.

The second thing is that I cannot seem to avoid splashing water as I go – no problem for wet-suit divers. But on a hot day, dry-suit divers should stow their suits inside the dive-kayaks so the suits are dry to dive in and so they do not become overheated paddling to the site. If going to an open-water site or in winter, a dry-suit diver can put his or her suit halfway on and tuck the sleeves into the waist for paddling; then wriggle arms and head into the suit at the site. I've done it. But it is easier to put drip-rings on your paddle so you do not drip water into your lap. To me, this messing about to keep my dry suit dry is worth it – a dive-kayak is freedom.

DIVING REGULATIONS AND SAFETY
Dive Flag Regulations in British Columbia
• Shore divers: when diving, fly your red-and-white diver-down flag from a float. It is required under the Canada Shipping Act. This diver-down flag is recognized throughout North America as marking an area where scuba diving is in progress.

• Boat divers: whenever divers are in the water, fly your red-and-white diver-down flag from a float on the water and fly your blue-and-white international Code flag "A" – or Alpha flag – from the boat. The Alpha flag is required under the Canada Shipping Act. It is recognized throughout the world, and means "I have a diver down: keep well clear at slow speed".

Obtain the free *Safe Boating Guide* with details about dive flags from most marinas, any Coast Guard Station or from Canadian Coast Guard, 800 Burrard Street, Suite 620, Vancouver BC V6Z 2J8. In Vancouver: (604) 666-0146. In Victoria: (604) 363-3879.

Dive Flag Regulations in Washington
• Shore divers: when diving, fly your red-and-white diver-down flag from a float. It is required by law in some counties and unless you know the regulations where you are, it is simpler always to fly it. This diver-down flag is recognized throughout North America as marking an area where scuba diving is in progress.

• Boat divers: fly your blue-and-white international Code flag "A" – or Alpha flag – on all dives. The Alpha flag is required under the federal Regulations for the Prevention of Collisions, also referred to by the short titles "The Collision Regulations" or "COL REGS" – or as "The Rules of the Road". The Alpha flag is a navigational signal indicating the vessel's restricted maneuverability and does not pertain to the diver. In addition, therefore, also fly your red-and-white diver-down flag from a float.

Obtain the free *Federal Requirements and Safety Tips for Recreational Boaters* booklet with details about use of the dive flag by boaters from most marinas and boat shops or obtain from the Commander, CCGD 13(B), US Coast Guard, 915 2nd Avenue, Seattle WA 98174-1067. Send a self-addressed stamped envelope when requesting that the booklet be mailed to you.

Diving Safety in British Columbia and Washington
Divers Alert Network (DAN) is an international non-profit member-supported organization dedicated to diving safety. DAN's 24-hour diving emergency hotline number is listed at the top of the service information in each chapter of this guidebook.

Divers Alert Network (DAN)
Box 3823
Duke University Medical Center
Durham NC 27710
To join DAN: telephone 1-800-446-2671; or fax (919) 490-6630.

Membership in DAN provides
• 24-hour Diving Emergency Hotline (919) 684-8111
• Diving Medicine and Safety Infoline (919) 684-2948
• Assist America, a global emergency medical evacuation service
• Divers' medical insurance policy covering treatment expenses worldwide for any in-water diving or snorkeling accident, available to all residents of the United States and Canada
• *Alert Diver* bimonthly magazine.
• DAN credit card, and more.

UNDERWATER PHOTOGRAPHY – "If you have a camera the very worst dive site is a good one," says one enthusiastic underwater photographer. Because of an awakening of ecological awareness and conservation, and because of improved cameras and housings, underwater video- and still-photography are becoming more and more popular. Some dive boats have video players on board so you can share your dive as soon as you surface. Now when the word "shoot" is used in diving, it connotes the idea of capturing a subject on film, rather than on the end of a spear.

What's different about underwater photography in the North Pacific sea? Winter is the best season for it because visibility is then at its best. Artificial light is usually required, as available light is almost always insufficient to produce good photographs. Endless subjects are at hand, particularly to photographers interested in close-up work, as there are so many colorful invertebrates in these waters. Even after years of photography, an enthusiast may find new subjects on every dive.

MARINE LIFE CONSERVATION – In British Columbia you will be "one of the crowd" if you do not spearfish at popular sites and if you dive carefully to avoid damaging fragile marine life. Divers have been pretending and telling little white lies for years about sites they love and want to protect. Divers also make intelligent proposals to protect unique sites. They put pressure on government by way of radio and television, and they invest money to put up signs – signs saying areas are closed to the taking of marine life. Since 1980 underwater parks have existed in British Columbia and a policy defined, but the Underwater Conservancy Parks promised by the provincial parks branch have not yet happened. No regulations are in place to protect marine life at parks or ecological reserves. No waters just offshore from any coastline in British Columbia – or in Canada – are fully protected.

In Washington, the history of parks goes way back: Edmonds became the first underwater park on the west coast in 1970. In 1993, the Washington State Senate Bill 5332 was passed committing the state ". . . to conserve and protect unique marine resources of the state of Washington". To my knowledge, this new protection is not complete protection either, but it is a wonderful start of involvement on the part of government to conserve marine life.

Conservation offers divers enormous challenge and can be an important uniting activity. Historically, conservation has been big with clubs. In future it could become an even more vital common interest – a great reason for divers to meet. Contact the following organizations:

The Marine Life Sanctuaries Society of British Columbia, PO Box 48299, Bentall Centre, Vancouver BC V7X 1A1, (604) 929-4131. The objective of the society is to protect areas of the British Columbia marine environment. An example of what they are doing: in 1994, the society staged the first annual "lingcod-egg-mass count" and all interested members took part.

Canadian Marine Environment Protection Society (CMEPS), PO Box 112, 1896 West Broadway, Vancouver BC V6J 1Y9. CMEPS aids communication between conservation groups and government agencies world wide. One issue: in 1993 they researched sixgill sharks and showed that sixgills are worth more alive as an ecotourism attraction than dead as a food item. Swimming with sixgills is a dive experience unique to British Columbia waters.

Washington Scuba Alliance, 120 State Avenue NE #18, Olympia WA 98501-8212. This group promotes the study, protection, development and enhancement of the underwater environment – activities often are involved with artificial reef projects such as at Edmonds and the proposed Titlow Park Marine Preserve. The society appreciates written input from divers about where they want underwater parks.

SPEARFISHING AND SHELLFISH COLLECTING – I do not believe there is a place any longer for spearfishing at any dive site described in any diving guidebook. Scuba diving has become a mainstream recreation – too many people are doing it for it to be possible for any site to stay beautiful if each diver spears one fish or takes even just one empty shell.
• In British Columbia: Sport fishing regulations apply to collecting and spearfishing by scuba divers. At the time of writing, divers are required to obtain a license to take finned fish just as hook-and-line fishermen are. A license is not required to collect shellfish but regulations could change from year to year, and a closure on the taking of abalone by any means or from any site is in force at the time of writing. If you plan to visit remote or unusual sites and collect marine life for dinner in British Columbia, obtain a *British Columbia Tidal Waters Sport Fishing Guide* with current regulations, available free at sports stores.
• In Washington: Special sport fishing regulations apply to collecting and spearfishing by scuba divers. At the time of writing, divers in salt water may not take or fish for salmon, sturgeon, octopus or crabs with underwater spearfishing gear, and divers may not possess these fish. All license requirements related to bag limits, size, season and area restrictions for the taking of food fish and shellfish apply to divers, except that divers are limited to one lingcod per day during open season regardless of size. If you plan to visit remote or unusual sites and collect marine life for dinner in Washington, obtain a *Salmon, Shellfish, Bottomfish, Sport Fishing Guide* with current regulations, available free at sports stores.

Cautions Regarding Collecting Seafood: shellfish may be made unfit for people to eat by:
1. Feeding in waters polluted by sewage. Do not collect shellfish in highly populated areas.
2. Feeding on toxic organisms of the genus *Alexandrium* that produces a bloom commonly called "red tide". These microscopic one-celled animals may cause paralytic shellfish poisoning (PSP); high concentrations can cause illness or death. If shellfish come from red tide waters, cooking does not reduce their toxicity. The sea might take on a striking, reddish color when red tide is present or the water may be clear. Do not trust your own eyes on this one. Consult the local Fisheries Office for closed areas. Also look for posted notices and do not collect shellfish if you see a red tide sign. If you see no sign but suspect a problem, telephone.
• In British Columbia: Shellfish Infoline, recorded: (604) 666-3169.
• In Washington: Red-tide Hotline, recorded: 1-800-562-5632.

BOTTLE, CHINA AND JUNK COLLECTING – "I'm diving for history!" That is the exuberant way one diver describes his passionate pursuit of everyday relics of the past: bottles, cups and saucers, foot warmers, mining artifacts.
Try it. Diving for bottles opens a whole new world on land, stirs you to learn about pioneer days on Pacific shores, might become a wonderfully absorbing obsession! This diving specialty appeals to divers with the sleuth in them, appeals to those who like to explore, and may be lucrative for the discriminating collector. I love to explore but was still slow to catch onto the fun of diving for junk. Also, I soul searched and wondered if bottle collecting, too, is an unacceptable inclusion in a guidebook as I now believe collecting marine life to be. Are we destroying our heritage by taking old bottles buried in the muck? I think not. No one would ever have seen the bottles I found if I had not gone down to look. Those bottles could not have been photographed on the ocean floor – they were covered in silt. Any objects thrown overboard are not protected and are fair game. The only bottles and china you should not take are those within the vicinity of a shipwreck as they could be part of the wreck.
For years the general public has enjoyed the finding, trading, buying and selling of

bottles on land – the fine arts department in the public library has countless books with bottle prices on their shelves. Despite the value placed on old bottles, they are not priceless. And bottles are not irreplaceable relics of a prehistoric civilization – diving for old bottles is not like digging in a midden nor are old bottles a limited resource. Enormous numbers of bottles are out there, and they are a fun, social trading commodity that got me reading history. Having thought about it hard, I happily allowed myself to become hooked.

To really get into "diving for dishes", I believe you must take each step the dedicated artifact divers do. First, research in the library before diving. Next, have the fun or disappointment of the dive. Then research again after the dive to learn more about what you have found. For ideas to start you off, look for "bottle dives" in the index at the back of this book. When you have tried some of the known bottle sites, start finding your own. They are sure to be better, but use discretion when choosing and avoid diving where there is a shore-based historic site. The process that worked to involve me in this diving specialty is as follows:

1. In the library: look at old maps, charts and photos, and read regional histories to locate former passenger-steamer wharves, logging camps and settlements. Many easy-to-read books are available about the Mosquito Fleet in Puget Sound. And many more books on Canadian maritime history. Union Steamship Company pioneered the waterways of British Columbia. It is to British Columbia what Hudson's Bay Company is to Canada. If you want to find old artifacts, learn where the Mosquito Fleet and Union steamships called in.

It is helpful to see what a locale looked like in the old days. Photographs of old docks and wharves where the ships stopped are in some of these books, and some libraries have historic photograph files. The fine arts department of Vancouver Public Library has such a collection: it is well indexed, and most photos are dated. Buy or photocopy the old photographs and take them with you when you head out to dive.

2. At the site before diving: go to local museums, coffee shops and art galleries. Talk with people, and look for old photographs of terrain and buildings. Artifacts are often found at the base of a steep hill near an old dock; guess where objects might have rolled to. Sometimes old buildings and pilings of wharves are still there, making it easy to locate where the action was. Look for any creeks that might flood in and deposit silt which would bury artifacts. Locations at least 100 yards (90 meters) away from such a creek are less likely to be silted over, especially crucial at shallow sites. Study your charts and compare them to what you see. Before diving, make a plan with your buddy about what you will do if vision is obscured. You are almost on your own when diving for junk as usually each diver stirs up so much silt.

3. In the water: take a light. Dive on the ebb, if possible, with an extreme tidal exchange. Usually best because the tide carries away the silt that you kick up. At deeper sites that slope off rapidly on the chart, start deep and work your way up. At shallow sites, dive in a small area and gradually enlarge it. If looking for bottles thrown off a dock you can often find them in 30 to 40 feet (9 to 12 meters). Flat silty bottom is good for the determined collector who digs deep.

Fan the bottom gently with your hand to stir up silt and reveal hidden relics. If digging, wear gloves to protect yourself from broken glass. At open-water sites scan the tops of mounds. Once you've made some finds, visualize a trail and follow it.

Look for barnacles, the most obvious sign of age on china and bottles. Do an initial sort of your bottle finds while diving, and wash out as much silt as possible. Look for bottles with odd and unusual shapes and bottles with no threads for screw tops. Black shiny bottles may be old and rare and therefore most desirable. Look for bottles that do not have a seam running all the way up the neck. These are the hand-finished ones. If you find a bottle with a rough bit of glass called a "pontil" stuck to the bottom, you have found a really old collector's item. If delving for Union Steamship relics, look for logos on the china. Later you can date your finds because different logos were used at different times.

Once when diving for mining artifacts my buddy and I found a Mercedes-Benz. If you discover an unexpected item of that sort, wise to note the location and report it to the police. If you find fossils or a remarkable artifact that might be an ancient archaeological relic, do not disturb the site but note the location and report it to the appropriate government office in Washington or British Columbia on the next page.

4. At the site after diving: show-and-tell time when you and your buddy empty goodie bags and discuss what you've found is both fun and useful. You can have a closer look and put back what you decide you do not want. Or give it to your buddy. Or give it to a local resident who has expressed interest in the history of the region.

5. At home after diving: clean your finds – if you want to. I sometimes prefer my finds complete with barnacles. If you choose to clean your bottles, china, crystal and other ceramics, one method is by soaking them in a 1:16 or 1:20 solution of muriatic acid and water. Set the objects in the mixture and cover. Take out occasionally and scrub. In two or three days your "pieces of history" should be clean. However, some bottle collectors say that acid damages really old glass.

6. Go back to the library: read about each object you found. Where does it belong in history? Where did it come from? When was it made? What is its value? Identify it.

• For More Information on Bottles
Bowen Island 1872-1972 by Irene Howard, Bowen Island Historians, Bowen Island, British Columbia, 1973.
(History of places where Terminal and Union steamships called in.)

Bottles in Canada: the collectors' guide to seeking, finding, dating, pricing and researching bottles by Doris and Peter Unitt, Clock House Publishing, Markham, Ontario, 1972.
(Illustrations of more than 2,000 bottles; glossary and list of Canadian glass factories.)

Diving for Northwest Relics: Identification and Dating of Bottles, Pottery and Marine Hardware by James Seeley White, Binford & Mort, Portland, 1979.
(Well illustrated.)

The Parks Canada Glass Glossary for the Description of Containers, Table-ware, Flat Glass, and Closures by Olive Jones and Catherine Sullivan, Parks Canada, Ottawa, 1985.
(A system of recording data on glass artifacts is included. The book is illustrated with photographs and diagrams, one showing the parts of a bottle: bore, finish, lip, string rim, neck, shoulder, body, heel, resting point, push up, and base.)

Western Canadian Bottle Collecting, Volumes 1 and 2 by George Watson and Robert Skrill, The Westward Collector, Nanaimo, BC, 1971 and 1973.
(Photographs of bottles and breweries; bottle prices; a directory of early breweries.)

Unitt's Canadian Price Guides to Antiques & Collectables (Books 12 through 15) by Peter Unitt and Anne Worrall, Fitzhenry & Whiteside, Markham, Ontario, published from 1991 to 1993.
(Beer bottle photographs, breweries, prices. Also fruit jars and other collectables.)

ARCHAEOLOGICAL DIVING – Ancient relics and fossils are hidden beneath the seas. In 1992 a barbed harpoon point made of antler bone was found at Galiano Island. This tool is now being carbon-dated, it was probably crafted 6,800 years ago. Middens, petroglyphs and artifacts that were once on the surface of the earth are beneath the water today because sea level has risen as a result of the warm inter-glacial climatic period we are in now. Scuba diving makes these clues to the past available to researchers. Archaeological dive sites are becoming a major source of new evidence about prehistoric coastal plants, animals and people. At Galiano Island, marine anthropologists worked with a staff of five and fifty volunteer field workers to excavate the harpoon. It was beneath 8 feet (2½ meters) of sand submerged in 10 to 20 feet (3 to 6 meters) of water, depending on tide height. Diving was documented on video cassettes. Casual visitors at the beach were offered on-site education about the sophisticated project. These two activities took this highly technical operation out of the experts-only realm and made it a vital, living event for everyone.

Opportunities for the thrill of discovery are limitless. At the time of writing, financial reward in Canada in the form of tax incentives, as well as sale to public institutions, are also possibilities, but that day may be passing. I am told by others that chances for remuneration are zilch – in any event, cultural treasures are priceless. In British Columbia, such objects as the harpoon point are protected under the provincial Heritage Conservation Act and under the federal Cultural Property Export and Import Act. In Washington, they are protected under the state Archaeological Sites and Resources Act. It is important that scuba divers become aware of and honor invaluable heritage material hidden beneath the sea.

The most important thing to do, if you make a find, is leave it where it is and contact the appropriate agency. They want to work with divers – archaeology can become a whole new purposeful diving activity.

If you discover any old or new underwater shipwrecks, wrecked aircraft, artifacts or underwater fossils that are not well known, avoid any disturbance of the site, note the location and report your finds to the following agencies:

• In British Columbia: Director, Archaeology Branch, Ministry of Small Business, Tourism and Culture, 800 Johnson Street, 5th Floor, Victoria BC V8V 1X4, (604) 356-1045; fax (604) 387-4420. They are interested in any underwater fossils and relics, as well as any old wrecks with possible heritage value that are found in British Columbia that are not well known.

• In Washington: State Historic Preservation Officer, Office of Archaeology and Historic Preservation, Department of Community, Trade and Economic Development, 111 West 21st Avenue, Olympia WA 98504, (206) 753-4011. They are interested in any underwater fossils and relics, as well as any shipwrecks and submerged aircraft with possible heritage value that are found in Washington. If you wish to remove any fossil or artifact from any site, a permit may be required from this office and from the Department of Natural Resources (DNR).

If you wish to export any cultural material or finds from British Columbia to Washington or elsewhere, contact: Movable Cultural Property Office, Department of Canadian Heritage, 300 Slater Street, Room 500, Ottawa Ontario K1A 0C8, (613) 990-4161. A permit is required for the export of all cultural property on the *Control List* which includes fossils, old arrowheads, airplane wrecks and other such finds – no permit required for objects less than 50 years old or made by a person still living.

If you wish to import cultural material into the United States, contact: United States Customs Service, 1301 Constitution Avenue NW, Room 4345, Washington DC 20229, (202) 927-0440; fax (202) 927-0391 or (202) 927-6892. Import controls restricting transfer of cultural property might be in effect, so check. This control is in accordance with the Cultural Property Implementation Act of the UNESCO Convention and is to prevent pillage of invaluable heritage cultural property.

• **For More Information on Archaeological Diving**
Culture Department Library
Ministry of Small Business, Tourism and Culture
800 Johnson Street, Room 101
Victoria BC V8V 1X4
(604) 356-1440; fax (604) 356-7796
(This library contains archaeology reports and research material, including information about shipwrecks, fossils and ancient artifacts. The library is available for use by the public.)

WRECK DIVING – If you've ever seen the gleam in the eye of a diver who's discovered a wreck, you know what "wreck fever" means. I experienced the thrill of discovery when we found the wreck of the steamship *Ravalli* in Lowe Inlet off Grenville Channel in 1976. The surprise of seeing compacted salmon-can paper wrappers still intact from 1918 was unbeatable. Despite being under water for so long, the paper wrappers still had color on them and you could read the fine print.

Vast possibilities for exploration are available to insatiable wreck divers. A brochure of The Underwater Archaeological Society of British Columbia notes that more than 2,000 wrecks in 200 years are known to have sunk off the shores of British Columbia. Thousands of historic shipwrecks, both known and unknown, litter the North Pacific. Many have never been dived on. But even artificial reefs that have been created or sunk on purpose, and well-known wrecks that have been dived on again and again, provide a special diving interest or thrill. Heaps of ballast rocks are on the seabed, as are bricks used as ballast in many ships sailing from England to Canada. Shipwrecks, "fake wrecks" and brick and rock ballast – all harbor quantities of marine life and have varied, fascinating histories. Wreck diving is exciting. It can also be dangerous. But like all other areas of diving, if you start slowly, build your experience and observe a few basic rules, wreck diving can be a safe and satisfying sport. Some suggestions and resources for wreck divers in Washington and British Columbia:

1. As always, dive with a buddy, and know your buddy very well. The two of you should review and practice "ditch-and-don" procedures and emergency ascents before diving on wrecks.

2. Start with easy wreck dives and progress gradually to more difficult ones. On all wreck dives, watch for cables and other appendages which you might snag your equipment on.

3. If diving on a wreck from a boat, be careful not to damage the wreck by dropping your anchor on it.

4. Be extremely wary of penetrating or entering the interior of any wreck. Be sure it is stable and is not going to collapse on you. Be particularly cautious when diving on a rotting timber vessel. Check surfaces in the way you check handholds when rock climbing to be sure they are solid. Take two good lights and use a return line to follow out if silt becomes stirred up or if both lights should fail. When entering, check the entry to be sure it will still be open when you are ready to exit.

Diving the 473-foot (144-meter) freighter *Vanlene* on the surf-washed west coast of Vancouver Island, my buddies and I entered the wreck and were startled to hear the door slam as the ship heaved in the surge. We were happy it did not latch when it slammed, we did get out – no problem. But that was good luck, not good planning.

Surf conditions are not encountered in the region covered by this guidebook, I include this example just to say – plan carefully.

5. Always ascend with an adequate reserve of air in the event you encounter poor visibility, become caught on anything or must use a return line to find your way out.

6. Do not touch or disturb any underwater wrecks or artifacts unless you have applied for and have become a salvor or unless you are part of an official research team. Removing any artifacts from any shipwrecks is prohibited in Canada by the Canada Shipping Act, and in Washington by the Archaeological Sites and Resources Act.

7. If you discover any old or new underwater shipwrecks, wrecked aircraft or artifacts that are not well known, avoid any disturbance of the site, note the location and report your finds.

• In Washington report finds to
Commander
13th Coast Guard District (oan)
US Coast Guard
915 Second Avenue
Seattle WA 98174
(206) 220-7270
(Salvage laws in the United States require that you report the find of any shipwreck or wrecked aircraft that is not well known.)

Whatcom Maritime Historical Society
Underwater Archaeological Branch
PO Box 5157
Bellingham WA 98227-5157
(206) 647-8947; fax (206) 671-6572
(Purpose: to catalog, record, preserve and restore the past and present elements of our local maritime heritage.)

State Historic Preservation Officer
Office of Archaeology and Historic
    Preservation
Department of Community, Trade and
    Economic Development
111 West 21st Avenue
Olympia WA 98504
(206) 753-4011
(Shipwrecks and submerged aircraft, as well as other archaeological materials, are protected in Washington under the state Archaeological Sites and Resources Act. If you wish to remove any artifact from any site, a permit may be required from this office and from the Department of Natural Resources [DNR].)

• In British Columbia report finds to
Receiver of Wreck
Canadian Coast Guard
25 Huron Street
Victoria BC V8V 4V9
(604) 363-3303; fax (604) 363-0270
(Salvage laws in Canada require that you report the find of any shipwreck or wrecked aircraft that is not well known. Ask for the pamphlet A Guide to Reporting Wreck.)

Underwater Archaeological Society of British Columbia (UASBC)
c/o Vancouver Maritime Museum
1905 Ogden Avenue
Vancouver BC V6J 1A3
(This organization is dedicated to preserving and protecting all shipwrecks discovered in the waters of British Columbia.)

- **For More Information on Ships and Shipwrecks**

COMPUTER DATA BASE LISTINGS

Automated Wreck and Obstruction Information System (AWOIS) (constantly updated), and the **User's Guide: Automated Wreck and Obstruction Information System (AWOIS)** booklet (usually updated annually) – both compiled by N/CG241, Station 6705, SSMC3, National Ocean Service (NOAA), 1315 East-West Highway, Silver Spring MD 20910-3282, (301) 713-2702; fax (301) 713-4533.
(AWOIS is a file with information on more than 9,500 wrecks in US waters. File entries may be complete with Loran-C ratings, or may contain little more than the reported position of an "unknown" wreck. Fees charged for every search.)

Marine Data Bulletin Board which is updated intermittently, compiled by National Ocean Service (NOAA), Hydrographic Technology Program, 1315 East-West Highway, Silver Spring MD 20910-3282, (301) 713-4574, available 24 hours a day.
(Information on wrecks; also aerial photographs, chart sales, tide gauge locations. Users log on with IBM-compatible PC, a modem, and an ordinary telephone line. Information is free via the bulletin board; pay only for the phone call.)

Shipwrecks! Washington State, Set 2, compiled by Kent M. Barnard, Argonaut Resources, PO Box 743, Mukilteo WA 98275, telephone and fax (206) 355-6324, 1993.
(IBM-compatible database file covering 271 shipwrecks in six counties, including 52 wrecks in San Juan County. It contains details on known shipwrecks, with directions to dive them. It is also a tool to help divers locate undiscovered wrecks.)

REGISTERS OF SHIPS

List of Ships, Volumes I and II, Ministry of Transport, Ottawa, published under various titles since 1874. Annual list.
(List of vessels on the register in Canada. Name of ship, material of hull, when built and length are some of the details provided.)

Lloyd's Register of Shipping, Lloyd's register of Shipping, London, published from 1726 under various titles: *Lloyd's list; New Lloyd's list; Shipping gazette and Lloyd's list; Lloyd's list; Shipping and mercantile gazette;* again as *Lloyd's list;* then *Lloyd's Register of Shipping.* Published annually since 1778.
(Lists over 78,000 ships. Details included are ship's name, length, material of hull and more.)

Merchant Vessels of the United States, US Department of Transportation, US Coast Guard. Published annually since 1867, obtainable from Superintendent of Documents, US Government Printing Office, Washington DC.
(List of merchant ships: includes information on name, length, material of hull, year built and more.)

STORIES AND HISTORIES OF SHIPS

Canadian Pacific Afloat 1883-1968: A Short History and Fleet List by George Musk, Canadian Pacific, London, 1969.
(Canadian Pacific steamship history with illustrations and maps.)

Disaster Log of Ships by Jim Gibbs, Superior Publishing Co., Seattle, 1971.
(Covers shipwrecks in British Columbia. Fabulous illustrations.)

Echoes of the Whistle: An Illustrated History of the Union Steamship Company by Gerald Rushton, Douglas & McIntyre, Vancouver, 1980.
(Rich in photographs; useful to see locations where old docks were.)

Ferryboats: A Legend on Puget Sound by M.S. Kline and G.A. Bayless, Bayless Books, Seattle, 1983.
(A large-format story book and photographic record from the first ferry boat to publication; superbly indexed.)

Historic Shipwrecks of Southern Vancouver Island by Jacques F. Marc, Underwater Archaeological Society of British Columbia, Vancouver, 1990.
(A shipwreck location map, site-survey diagrams, photographs and a great many details covering 12 shipwrecks including the Barnard Castle *and* San Pedro.*)*

The H.W. McCurdy Marine History of the Pacific Northwest edited by Gordon Newell, The Superior Publishing Co., Seattle, 1966.
(A classic: this book is a companion volume to Lewis and Dryden's Marine History of the Northwest. *Every one of its 706 pages is a very good read! The book is rich with photographs of ships and men, and superbly indexed. It covers the history of the growth and development of the maritime industry from 1895 to 1965.)*

The H.W. McCurdy Marine History of the Pacific Northwest, 1966 to 1976 edited by Gordon Newell, The Superior Publishing Co., Seattle, 1977.
(A classic: this book follows up on the marine histories of Lewis and Dryden and H.W. McCurdy, again, with wonderful accounts and photographs of ships and men; well indexed. For an example of what is in it, see details on the large cargo vessel Vanlene *which went aground in 1972. This book covers the growth and development of the maritime industry from 1966 to 1976.)*

Lewis and Dryden's Marine History of the Pacific Northwest edited by E.W. Wright, The Lewis and Dryden Printing Company, Portland, 1895.
(A classic: detailed stories of ships and men, well illustrated and indexed. This 494-page review is a treasure, and you will be extremely lucky if you find it in a library. It covers the history of the growth and development of the maritime industry from the advent of the earliest navigators to 1895.)

Maritime Archaeology: New Studies in Archaeology by Keith Muckelroy, Cambridge University Press, Cambridge/London/New York/Melbourne, 1978.
(An overall view of shipwrecks around the world, including photographs of a shipwreck from the 4th century, and shipwrecks that were excavated instead of being dived on. It contains how-to tips on wreck diving, and is well illustrated with diagrams and photographs.)

More Shipwrecks of British Columbia by Fred Rogers, Douglas & McIntyre, Vancouver, 1992.
(Tales of shipwrecks, and rescues – rich with detail. With indices of wrecks and captains. Includes mention of the Del Norte *and* Robert Kerr. *Also see* Shipwrecks of British Columbia *by the same author.)*

Pacific Coastal Liners by Gordon Newell and Joe Williamson, Superior Publishing Co., Seattle, 1959.
(The foreword states ". . .this volume is designed for the reader's pleasure rather than his education. It seeks to convey the flavor of an era . . ." – another good read. Index of photographs.)

Pacific Steamboats: from Sidewheeler to Motor Ferry by Gordon Newell, Superior Publishing Company, Seattle, 1958.
(A pictorial history of the Puget Sound Mosquito Fleet.)

Pacific Tugboats by Gordon Newell and Joe Williamson, Superior Publishing Co., Seattle, 1957.
(A sampling of tugboats along with the human side of boating; drama, comedy, tragedy. Many photographs, well indexed.)

The Princess Story: A Century and a Half of West Coast Shipping by Norman R. Hacking and W. Kaye Lamb, Mitchell Press Ltd., Vancouver, 1974.
(History and photographs of the Princess ships and their Hudson's Bay and CPN company forerunners. The book covers from 1827 to 1974. Detailed fleet lists.)

Ships of the Inland Sea: The Story of The Puget Sound Steamboats by Gordon R. Newell, Binfords & Mort, Portland, 1951.
(Lively stories of the Mosquito Fleet. Contains a lengthy partial roster of ships from the 1800s.)

Shipwrecks of British Columbia by Fred Rogers, Douglas & McIntyre, Vancouver, 1980.
(Adventurous stories of 100 wrecks and diving on them, with indices of wrecks and captains. Includes details of Barnard Castle, Miami, Point Grey, Robert Kerr, Del Norte and Thrasher.)

Shipwrecks of the Pacific Coast by James A. Gibbs, Binfords and Mort, Portland, 1957.
(Stories of shipwrecks, with a chronological appendix list of all major shipwrecks on coastal, offshore and inland waters from 1500 to 1962.)

SOS North Pacific: Tales of Shipwrecks off the Washington, British Columbia and Alaska Coasts by Gordon R. Newell, Binfords & Mort, Portland, 1955.
(Covers Mosquito Fleet disasters – a very good read. Illustrated with a few drawings.)

Steamships and Motorships of the West Coast by Richard M. Benson, Superior Publishing Co., Seattle, 1968.
(A story in pictures and words about some famous and unusual motor-powered vessels, including the SS Beaver, first steamship to arrive in the North Pacific in 1836.)

Whistle Up the Inlet: The Union Steamship Story by Gerald A. Rushton, J.J. Douglas Ltd., Vancouver, 1974.
(History and photographs of the Union fleet, the men who sailed the ships, and the places where the ships called in: from 1889 to 1959.)

The Wreck Diver's Guide to Sailing Ship Artifacts of the 19th Century by David Leigh Stone, Underwater Archaeological Society of British Columbia, Vancouver, 1993.
(A unique addition to shipwreck literature: definitions, photographs and detailed drawings of what a sailing ship consists of, then the author breaks it down from ship to shipwreck.)

ARTIFICIAL REEFS – Preparing artificial reefs for diving is providing a fascinating new diving specialty for many recreational divers. Every year the reefs are becoming more sophisticated, more important.

Edmonds Underwater Park has unleashed the creative fancy of a myriad divers. The concrete-block-and-steel dinosaur at Edmonds is a far cry from the early days when most artificial reefs were made of heaps of tires. The sinking of the *G.B. Church* and *Chaudiere* by the Artificial Reef Society of British Columbia demanded imagination, research, organization and dedication of another sort. Making the ships environmentally safe for sinking in the ocean by removing insulation, making them safe for diving by removing projections from them and providing openings for light, entry and exit are two challenges they met with these projects. Members of the society stress that artificial reef sites and materials be carefully evaluated and say artificial reefs should not be used as an excuse for dumping.

Fisheries personnel in Washington warn that artificial reefs must not become an excuse or justification for solid waste disposal in the marine environment. They are researching and brainstorming to gain more knowledge about appropriate habitats to attract specific marine life while not damaging the natural habitat. This research is an important professional specialty for marine biologists and all divers will want to think about it.

Diving the wonderful variety of artificial reefs is fun but artificial reefs are sometimes wrecks. Take the same precautions when diving them as when wreck diving, especially if entering the interior of a vessel.

• For More Information on Artificial Reefs

Washington State Department of
  Fisheries
PO Box 43135
Olympia WA 98504-3135
(206) 753-6600
Located at Natural Resources Building,
1111 Washington Street.

Artificial Reef Society of
  British Columbia
c/o The Vancouver Maritime Museum
1905 Ogden Avenue
Vancouver BC V6J 1A3

Video Cassette
Reefs of Steel: Artificial Reefs in British Columbia by Neil McDaniel and Gary Bridges, Wet Film Productions, Vancouver, 1992.
(Artificial reefs and wrecks in Porteau Cove Underwater Park and wreck of the G.B. Church.)

CLUBS AND ASSOCIATIONS – From time to time, formal associations of commercial operations that provide services to divers have been active in Washington and British Columbia. At the time of writing, no active industry groups exist but recreational diving clubs are numerous and vital.
• In Washington: recreational diving clubs are united by the Washington Scuba Alliance which speaks with one voice for the sport. This vigorous group represents special diving interests as well as the interests of recreational divers (see page 32). Names of a few of the active clubs in Washington are the Atomic Ducks Dive Club, Hood Canal Aquanuts, Boeing Seahorses, Emerald Sea Dive Club, Kelp Crawlers, Kitsap Diving Association, Marker Buoys, Nor'west Divers, Pacific Northwest Dive Club, South Sound Divers and the Tentacle Gang. For more names and information about clubs, ask at your local dive shop or contact the Washington Scuba Alliance, 120 State Avenue NE, #18, Olympia WA 98501-8212, (206) 373-5367.
• In British Columbia: recreational diving clubs are lively groups in many communities but, at the time of writing, are not united by a council. Names of some old-timer clubs still meeting and diving are Aqua Soc, Aqua Addicts, Coquitlam Scuba Club, Deep Breathers, Nanaimo Dive Club, Pescaderos and Tide Rippers. I will not try to list every club as there are so many and new ones are formed all the time. Ask about clubs at your local dive shop.

Energetic societies of divers with special interests are numerous – see under Conservation, Artificial Reefs and Wreck Diving. Another vital special interest group is an association for divers with disabilities.

Pacific Northwest Scuba Challenge Association – or Scuba Challenge – offers membership and diving activities to all divers. The association makes diving accessible to handicapped persons and promotes their integration into the community. This dynamic group offers scuba instruction, publishes a newsletter and sponsors dives. In addition, they go on day- and weekend-trips. More activities are demonstrations and slide presentations at rehabilitation centers and handicapped awareness events, distribution of video cassettes and materials regarding their activities to hospitals, schools and service clubs. Membership is open to able-bodied divers – ABs – as well as to divers with disabilities. For more information, contact Pacific Northwest Scuba Challenge Association, 4447 West 16th Avenue, Vancouver BC V6R 3E7, (604) 525-7149.

Barnacles exposed at low tide, Wall Beach

NIGHT DIVING – If you've been disappointed in the marine life in an area, or by the diving in any way, or if you're just looking for an extra thrill – a new dimension – then try a night dive. In autumn, you'll see underwater fireworks.

Nothing else can match it for me. Many more animals come out at night. Some, like prawns, come up shallower and can be seen more easily then. And the old, familiar life takes on a new look. The eyes of ratfish glow like sapphires. When you switch off your light the smallest crab is magical in the fabulous phosphorescent night sea. While orange sea pens shimmer neon green in the dark; and you might find an octopus – fantastic in the phosphorescence – coiling and uncoiling in a sparkle of light. Some practical notes on night diving:

1. Dive with a buddy you have dived with in the day, and stay right with your buddy.
2. Both divers carry an underwater light, but sometimes also try turning off both to savor the beauty of the phosphorescence.
3. Wear a chemical glow-tube light.
4. Use a compass.
5. Do not dive in currents at night in rocky areas, for the rocks come past too fast.
6. Surface with a reserve of air.
7. Leave a light on shore or on your boat so you can find your way back.
8. Don't wait – do it now. Why not tonight?

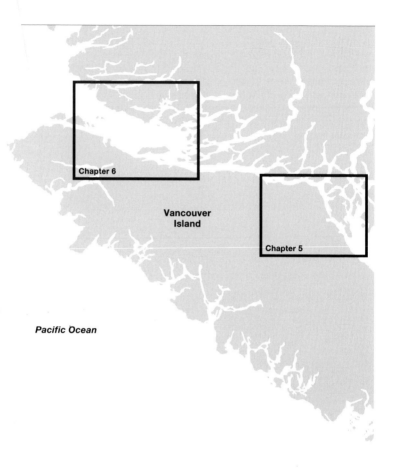

Chapter 6

Vancouver
Island

Chapter 5

Pacific Ocean

KEY TO CHAPTER MAPS

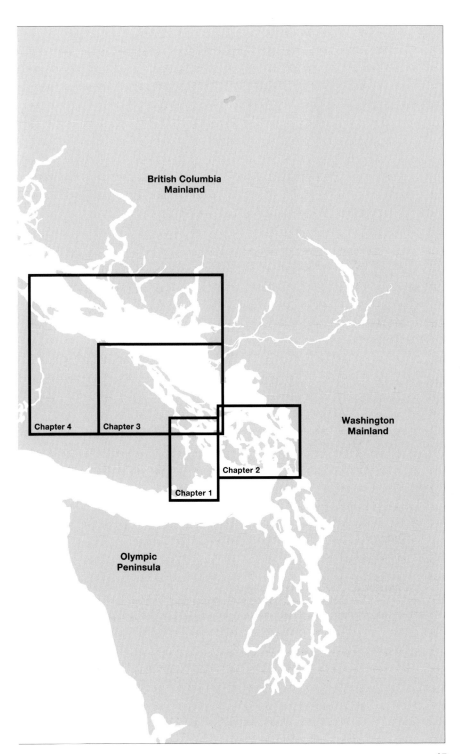

British Columbia
Mainland

Chapter 4   Chapter 3

Washington
Mainland

Chapter 2

Chapter 1

Olympic
Peninsula

Parliament Buildings at night

Shallon anchored off Metchosin, with dive flags flying

CHAPTER 1
Victoria and Saanich Inlet

At Race Rocks in thicket of kelp, photographing basket star

VICTORIA AND SAANICH INLET

Dives

1. Swordfish Island
2. Race Rocks
3. Wreck of the *Barnard Castle*
4. Fisgard Island
5. Saxe Point Park
6. Ogden Point Breakwater
7. Brotchie Ledge
8. Ten Mile Point
9. Spring Bay
10. Graham's Wall
11. Wreck of the *G. B. Church*
12. Arbutus Island
13. Mystery Wreck at Deep Cove
14. Setchell Point
15. Tozier Rock
16. Henderson Point
17. Tod Inlet
18. Willis Point
19. The White Lady
20. Christmas Point
21. Misery Bay

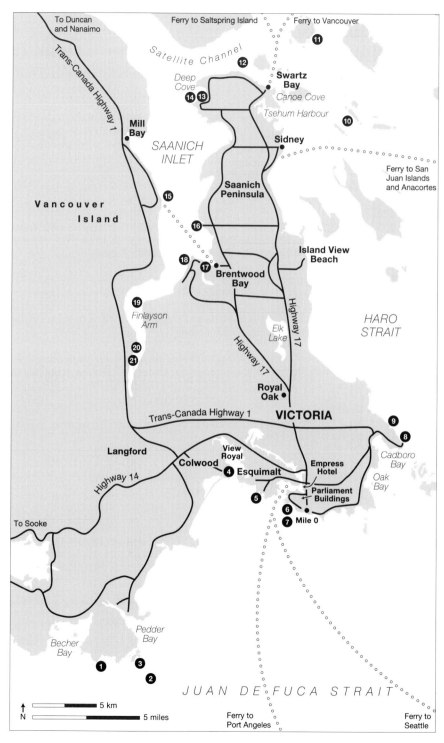

To Duncan
and Nanaimo

Ferry to Saltspring Island

Ferry to Vancouver

11

Satellite Channel

12

Deep Cove

Swartz Bay

14 **13**

Canoe Cove

Tsehum Harbour

10

Mill Bay

SAANICH INLET

Sidney

Ferry to San Juan Islands and Anacortes

Trans-Canada Highway 1

Saanich Peninsula

Vancouver Island

15

16

Island View Beach

18

17

Brentwood Bay

Highway 17

HARO STRAIT

19

Finlayson Arm

Elk Lake

Highway 17

20

21

Highway 17

Royal Oak

VICTORIA

9

Trans-Canada Highway 1

8

Langford

View Royal

Cadboro Bay

Colwood

4 **Esquimalt**

Empress Hotel

Oak Bay

Highway 14

5

Parliament Buildings

6

7 Mile 0

To Sooke

Pedder Bay

Becher Bay

1 **3**

2

5 km

N

5 miles

JUAN DE FUCA STRAIT

Ferry to Port Angeles

Ferry to Seattle

SERVICE INFORMATION *
Victoria and Saanich Inlet

Charts: Canadian Hydrographic Service
- 3310 Gulf Islands–Victoria Harbour to Nanaimo Harbour
- 3415 Victoria Harbour
- 3419 Esquimalt Harbour
- 3424 Approaches to Oak Bay
- 3430 Plans–Juan de Fuca Strait
- 3440 Race Rocks to D'Arcy Island
- 3441 Haro Strait, Boundary Pass and Satellite Channel
- L/C-3461 Juan de Fuca Strait, Eastern Portion
- L/C-3462 Juan de Fuca Strait to Strait of Georgia
- 3476 Approaches to Tsehum Harbour
- L/C-3606 Juan de Fuca Strait

Tide and Current Tables: Canadian Hydrographic Service *Tide and Current Table, Volume 5* and Canadian Hydrographic Service *Current Atlas: Juan de Fuca Strait to Strait of Georgia* (use with *Murray's Tables* or *Washburne's Tables*)

Diving Emergency Telephone Numbers
Dial 911: Say "I have a scuba diving emergency".

Vancouver General Hospital: Dial (604) 875-4111 and say "I have a scuba diving emergency. I want the hyperbaric physician on call".

If medical personnel are unfamiliar with scuba diving emergencies, ask them to telephone DAN (Divers Alert Network): (919) 684-8111, then say "I have a scuba diving emergency".

Other Useful Numbers
Continuous Marine Broadcast (CMB) recorded, 24 hours; listen for weather in Haro Strait or Juan de Fuca Strait, telephone
- Victoria: (604) 474-7998
Shellfish Infoline, recorded: (604) 666-3169
Sportfishing Information Line, recorded: 1-800-663-9333

• Dive Shops
Victoria
Frank White's Scuba Shop
1855 Blanshard Street
Victoria BC V8T 4H9
(604) 385-4713

PSD Underwater Sports
2519 Douglas Street
Victoria BC V8T 4L9
(604) 386-3483; fax (604) 386-2412

Deep Cove, Saanich Inlet
Deep Cove Ocean Sports
10992 Madrona Drive, RR 1
Sidney BC V8L 3R9
(604) 656-0060; fax (604) 656-8144
(Waterfront and roadside air fills.)

Ocean Centre
800 Cloverdale Avenue
Victoria BC V8X 2S8
(604) 475-2202; fax (604) 475-2209

Scuba Land
102B-1830 Old Island Highway
Victoria BC V9B 1J2
(604) 474-1134

Sidney, East Saanich
Frank White's Scuba Shop
2537 Beacon Avenue (in Sidney Hotel)
Sidney BC V8L 1Y3
(604) 656-9202
(Waterfront and roadside air fills.)

• Boat Charters and Rentals
Out of Victoria
Shallon
Shallon Marine Service
2853 Graham Street
Victoria BC V8T 3Z3
(604) 479-4276; fax (604) 386-2286
(Day charters out of Victoria, May through October; out of Sidney, November through April. Custom liveaboard trips throughout British Columbia. Also inflatable charters.)

Out of Sidney, East Saanich
Merganser I
Sea Island Divers
Unit #10, 7240 Moffatt Road
Richmond BC V6Y 3N7
(604) 278-3496
(Day charters out of Canoe Cove, in Sidney.)

Richardson Point
Arrawac Marine Services Ltd.
240 Meadowbrook Road
Victoria BC V8K 3X3
(604) 479-5098 – fax and phone.
(Day charters out of Tsehum [Shoal] Harbour, Sidney; and custom liveaboard trips.)

Shallon
Shallon Marine Service
2853 Graham Street
Victoria BC V8T 3Z3
(604) 479-4276; fax (604) 386-2286
(Day charters out of Port Sidney Breakwater, November through April; out of Victoria Harbour, May through October. Also inflatable charters.)

Out of Mill Bay, Saanich Inlet
Mill Bay Marina
740 Handy Road, PO Box 231
Mill Bay BC V0R 2P0
(604) 743-4112 – fax and telephone.
Telephone to arrange to fax.
(Boat rentals – telephone to reserve. Also launching. Restrooms, hot showers and bed-and-breakfast accommodation year-round. Telephone at top of ramp outside restroom.)

Out of Pedder Bay
Dinomite
Atlantis Diving
1385 Clun Place, RR 1
Sooke BC V0S 1N0
(604) 642-4845
(Day charters and liveaboard charters out of Pedder Bay; wheelchair divers welcome.)

Rose Bay
Frank White's Scuba Shop Ltd.
2537 Beacon Avenue (in Sidney Hotel)
Sidney BC V8L 1Y3
(604) 656-9202
(Day charters out of Tsehum [Shoal] Harbour, Sidney.)

Sea Dancer
Ocean Centre
800 Cloverdale Avenue
Victoria BC V8X 2S8
(604) 475-2202; fax (604) 475-2209
(Day charters out of Tsehum [Shoal] Harbour, Sidney.)

Wave Dancer
Advance Yachts Diving & Fishing
   Charters
2060 White Birch Road
Sidney BC V8L 2R1
(604) 656-5653; fax (604) 656-2106
(Day charters out of Tsehum [Shoal] Harbour, Sidney.)

Out of Deep Cove, Saanich Inlet
Class Act
Deep Cove Ocean Sports
10992 Madrona Drive, RR 1
Sidney BC V8L 3R9
(604) 656-0060; fax (604) 656-8144
(Day charters and boat rentals out of Deep Cove. Also air fills.)

• Launching for Juan de Fuca Strait
James Bay Anglers' Association Boat Ramp.
75 Dallas Road
Victoria BC V8V 1A1
(Launching for Juan de Fuca Strait: in heart of city west of The Breakwater. Concrete ramp; good at all tides. Also some parking. Telephone at top of ramp at roadside. Restrooms when ramp office open; also restrooms 1 mile (1½ kilometers) east on Dallas Road.)
Off Trans-Canada Highway 1: from Mile 0 at foot of Douglas Street go west almost 1½ miles (2 kilometers) on Dallas Road to James Bay Ramp. Five minutes from heart of Victoria.

Pedder Bay Marina
925 Pedder Bay Drive, RR 2
Victoria BC V9B 5B4
(604) 478-1771
(Launching for Juan de Fuca Strait: concrete ramp, good at all tides. Boat rentals for passengers only – not for diving. Restrooms; telephone outside marina.)
Off Highway 14: when almost through Colwood heading west, you will see a large sign to Metchosin, Pearson College, William Head and Pedder Bay. Turn left into Metchosin Road, following signs to Pedder Bay. Go to Happy Valley Road. Turn right and go to Rocky Point Road, then left and continue to Pedder Bay Marina turnoff. Turn left and go to the end of it. From Victoria, 40 minutes. From Swartz Bay, 1 hour. From Highway 1, it takes 30 minutes to Pedder Bay.

Cheanuh Marina
4901 East Sooke Road, RR 1
Sooke BC V0S 1N0
(604) 478-4880
(Launching at Becher Bay for Juan de Fuca Strait: concrete ramp, good at all except extreme low tides. Toilets. Telephone at marina office.)
Off Highway 14: when almost through Colwood heading west, you will see a large sign to Metchosin, Pearson College, William Head and Pedder Bay. Turn left into Metchosin Road, following signs to Pedder Bay. Go to Happy Valley Road. Turn right and go to Rocky Point Road, then left. Continue past Pedder Bay Road, jog right and immediately left onto East Sooke Road and go 1½ miles (2½ kilometers) more to Cheanuh Marina. From Victoria, 45 minutes. From Swartz Bay, just over 1 hour. From Highway 1, 35 minutes to Becher Bay.

Pacific Lions Marina & Campground
241 Becher Bay Road, RR 1
Sooke BC V0S 1N0
(604) 642-3816
(Launching at Becher Bay for Juan de Fuca Strait, open May to October only: concrete ramp, good at all except extreme low tides. Toilets and telephone at top of ramp.)
Off Highway 14: when almost through Colwood heading west, you will see a large sign to Metchosin, Pearson College, William Head and Pedder Bay. Turn left into Metchosin Road, following signs to Pedder Bay. Go to Happy Valley Road. Turn right and go to Rocky Point Road, then left. Continue past Pedder Bay Road, jog right and immediately left onto East Sooke Road and go 3 miles (4¾ kilometers) more to Becher Bay Road. Turn left and go 1 mile (1½ kilometers) to the water. From Victoria, 50 minutes. From Swartz Bay, 70 minutes. From Highway 1, 40 minutes to Becher Bay.

• **Launching for Haro Strait and Satellite Channel**
Van Isle Marina Ramp
2320 Harbour Road
Sidney BC V8L 2P6
(604) 656-1138; fax (604) 656-0182
(Launching at Tsehum [Shoal] Harbour for Haro Strait and Satellite Channel: concrete ramp, good at all tides. Restrooms and hot showers. Telephone on fuel dock and at parking lot.)
Off Highway 17: located north of Beacon Avenue in Sidney. From downtown Victoria, 40 minutes; from Swartz Bay or Sidney, 5 minutes to Tsehum Harbour.

Roberts Bay Public Ramp
Foot of Ardwell Avenue
Sidney BC
(Hand-launching only at Roberts Bay, Sidney. No toilet. No telephone.)
Off Highway 17: take Sidney Exit. Go on Beacon Avenue to Resthaven Drive. Turn right on Ardwell and go to the foot of it. From downtown Victoria, 35 minutes; from Swartz Bay or Sidney, 5 minutes to Roberts Bay.

Hotel Sidney Boat Ramp
2537 Beacon Avenue
Sidney BC V8L 1X7
(604) 656-1131
(Hand-launching only at Sidney Channel for Haro Strait: concrete and gravel ramp. Restrooms in hotel. Telephone in hotel lobby.)
Off Highway 17: take Sidney Exit. Go to the end of Beacon Avenue. From downtown Victoria, 40 minutes; from Swartz Bay, 5 minutes to Hotel Sidney.

Sidney Public Boat Ramp
Tulista Park, Sidney BC
(Launching for a nominal fee at Sidney Channel for Haro Strait; concrete ramp, good at medium and high tides. Restrooms in park. Telephone north of Park at ferry terminal and farther north on waterfront in lobby at Sidney Hotel, available 24 hours.)
Off Highway 17: take McTavish Road Exit and follow signs to Anacortes and San Juan ferry. It is 1 mile (1½ kilometers) off Highway 17. From downtown Victoria, 40 minutes; from Swartz Bay, 5 minutes to Tulista Park.

Island View Beach Public Ramp
Foot of Island View Road
Sidney BC
(Launching at Cordova Channel for Haro Strait; concrete ramp, good at high tide only. Restrooms and telephone at top of ramp.)
Off Highway 17: the turnoff is at a traffic light 3 miles (4½ kilometers) north of Elk Lake and 6 miles (9½ kilometers) south of the main turnoff to Sidney. Exit at Island View Road, directly opposite Keating Cross Road. Go east on Island View Road to the water – 5 minutes off Highway 17. From downtown Victoria, 30 minutes.

• **Launching for Saanich Inlet**
Goldstream Boathouse Ramp
3540 Trans-Canada Highway 1, RR 6
Victoria BC V9B 5T9
(604) 478-4407
(Launching at head of Saanich Inlet; concrete ramp, good at all tides. Parking. Restrooms; telephone by office.)
Off Trans-Canada Highway 1: start at Goldstream picnic site and go north on

Highway 1 for 1 mile (2 kilometers) to the turnoff marked with a marina sign. Turn off the highway and head downhill – do not take the first small road, go on the *second* small road to the marina. From downtown Victoria, 35 minutes.

At Brentwood Bay
Tsartlip Boat Ramp
800 Stellys Cross Road
Brentwood Bay BC VOS 1A0
(604) 652-3988
(Launching at Brentwood Bay: concrete ramp, good at all tides. Launching year-round, camping in summer only. No toilets at ramp. Telephone at office south of store; another one south toward ferry at Peden Lane and Verdier Avenue.)

Off Highway 17: follow signs to Mill Bay ferry; go to West Saanich Road (or Peden Lane) and go one block north of Verdier Avenue to Stellys Cross Road and drive to the foot of it. From downtown Victoria or off the ferry from Port Angeles, 35 minutes; from Swartz Bay or Sidney, 25 minutes; from Ferries Exit on Highway 1, it takes 25 minutes to Brentwood Bay.

At Mill Bay
Handy Road Public Ramp
Foot of Handy Road
Mill Bay BC
(Launching at Mill Bay: concrete ramp, good for larger boats at low tides. Parking space for 10 or 12 cars. No toilets; telephone south outside restroom at top of privately owned ramp.)

Off Trans-Canada Highway 1 south of Cowichan Bay Road and north of Malahat Drive: follow signs toward Brentwood ferry and go ⅓ mile (½ kilometer) to Handy Road. Past the shopping center, go down Handy Road to the foot of it.

Mill Bay Marina
740 Handy Road, PO Box 231
Mill Bay BC V0R 2P0
(604) 743-4112 – fax and telephone. Telephone to arrange to fax.
(Launching at Mill Bay: concrete ramp, good with 4-foot [1¼-meter] tides and greater. Restrooms, hot showers and bed-and-breakfast accommodations year-round; telephone at top of ramp outside restroom. Also boat rentals.)

• **More Services for Victoria Region:** see service information for Gulf Islands on page 139.

• **Ferry Information**
British Columbia Ferry Corporation
Swartz Bay Terminal
Victoria BC
(604) 656-0757: Recorded schedules available 24 hours.
Toll-free in BC: 1-800-663-7600, "live" – a person answers.
Telephoning from outside British Columbia, (604) 386-3431: "live".
(Ferries between Swartz Bay [north of Victoria], Gulf Islands and Tsawwassen [south of Vancouver].)

Victoria Line Ltd.
185 Dallas Road
Victoria, BC V8V 1A1
(604) 480-5555; fax (604) 480-5222
Toll free in western USA and western Canada, for information only: 1-800-668-1167.
(Summer sailings between downtown Victoria and downtown Seattle from mid-May through mid-September.)

Black Ball Transport, Inc.
430 Belleville Street
Victoria BC V8V 1W9
Victoria: (604) 386-2202
Port Angeles: (206) 457-4491
(Ferries between Victoria and Port Angeles WA.)

Washington State Ferries
2499 Ocean Avenue
Sidney BC V8L 1T3
Sidney: (604) 381-1551 or 656-1531
Anacortes: (206) 293-8166
(Ferries from Sidney [north of Victoria] to San Juan Islands and Anacortes.)

British Columbia Ferry Corporation
Brentwood Bay Terminal
Foot of Verdier Avenue
Brentwood Bay BC
Toll-free in BC: 1-800-663-7600
Telephoning from outside British Columbia, (604) 386-3431.
(Ferries from Brentwood to Mill Bay.)

British Columbia Ferry Corporation
Mill Bay Terminal
Foot of Mill Bay Road
Mill Bay BC
Toll-free in BC: 1-800-663-7600
Telephoning from outside British Columbia, (604) 386-3431.
(Ferries from Mill Bay to Brentwood.)

• **Tourist Information**
Discover British Columbia
1117 Wharf Street
Victoria BC V8W 2Z2
1-800-663-6000: Toll-free throughout Canada and the USA, including Hawaii and parts of Alaska.

Pat-Bay Tourist Infocentre
10382 Patricia Bay Highway, west
   side of Highway 17,
   near Swartz Bay ferry terminal
PO Box 2014
Sidney BC V8L 3S3
(604) 656-0525; fax (604) 656-7111

Tourism Victoria (Travel Infocentre)
812 Wharf Street
Victoria BC V8W 1T3
(604) 382-2127; fax (604) 382-6539

Juan de Fuca Travel Infocentre
697 Goldstream Avenue
Victoria BC V9B 2X2
(604) 478-1130; fax (604) 478-1584

South Cowichan Travel Infocentre
Frayne Centre, RR 1
Mill Bay BC V0R 2P0
(604) 743-3566

How to go – Victoria is at the southern tip of Saanich Peninsula on Vancouver Island. The Parliament Buildings and Empress Hotel are at the heart of this provincial capital. Mile 0 of Trans-Canada Highway is nearby in Beacon Hill Park. These are the landmarks that provide a focus point for me, help me sort out the tangle of roads and ferries that converge on this city which is nearly surrounded by water. What a city for divers!
• Reach Victoria by road: Drive south through Nanaimo, Ladysmith and Duncan on Trans-Canada Highway 1. From Nanaimo, 2 hours to the Empress Hotel – from Duncan, 1 hour by road to the heart of Victoria.
• Reach Victoria by water: Travel by car ferry from one of four different directions. You could sail from Tsawwassen (south of Vancouver) to Swartz Bay at the top of Saanich Peninsula. Sail from Anacortes, Washington, by way of the San Juan Islands to Sidney on the east side of Saanich Peninsula. Peel off Highway 1 at the Mill Bay turnoff, when driving south on Vancouver Island, and sail across Saanich Inlet to Brentwood Bay on the west side of Saanich Peninsula. Then, from Swartz Bay, Sidney or Brentwood Bay drive south on Patricia Bay Highway 17 for 40 minutes to Victoria.
   Or sail from Port Angeles, Washington, across Juan de Fuca Strait into the heart of Victoria. I love to arrive at the Inner Harbour at night when the Parliament Buildings are hung with lights – a magical sight.

*All of this service information is subject to change.

SWORDFISH ISLAND
Boat Dive

Skill: Intermediate and expert divers. All divers with guide.

Why go: To swim through Swordfish Island. White plumose anemones fluff out from the ceiling and walls of the tunnel. Soft pink corals frame its entry and exit. You can swim in one side of Swordfish and out the other.

On the Juan de Fuca side of Swordfish, we met a juvenile wolf-eel, an octopus and kelp greenlings you can hand feed. We saw nudibranchs, purple urchins, a giant mussel, a red Irish lord that sits in your hand – plus very "west coast" life: China rockfish and surf-washed green anemones.

Heading back to Victoria after the dive we saw killer whales recognized by our charter operator. The whales were from a resident pod: a male with a calf, and a female. They crossed over, met, split again. Swam close beside the boat, turned their white bellies up to us. One whale spy-hopped – that was a "first" for me. It leapt straight up out of the water to look around, exposing one-third of its body. Fabulous to see its picturesque black-and-white markings.

Bottom and Depths: Swordfish Island is oval shaped and a tunnel runs right through it near the eastern end of the island. The tunnel floor is 15 to 25 feet (4½ to 7½ meters) deep. On the northern side of Swordfish, the bottom is rocky with some silt and is 25 to 30 feet (7½ to 9 meters) deep. It slopes gradually to the southern Juan de Fuca side. The outside wall is indented with crevices: The base of the outside wall of Swordfish bottoms out to sand and rock at 70 to 80 feet (21 to 24 meters). Bull kelp year-round.

Hazards: Current and surge caused by wind or passing ships – both destroy visibility in the tunnel. Shallow depth and bull kelp. If a ship is passing in Juan de Fuca, go into the tunnel quickly before surge stirs up silt. Wear enough weight so you can stay down. Carry a knife; if caught in the kelp you can cut your way free.

Telephones: • Becher Bay at Cheanuh Marina, outside office. • Becher Bay, top of ramp at Pacific Lions Marina. • Pedder Bay Marina, outside office.

Facilities: None at Swordfish Island. Camping year-round with hot showers, in summer and fall, at Goldstream Provincial Park. Charters out of Victoria. Launching at Becher Bay and Pedder Bay.

Access: Swordfish Island is in Juan de Fuca Strait. It is 2½ nautical miles (4½ kilometers) southeast of the Becher Bay and 6 nautical miles (11 kilometers) southwest of Pedder Bay. At high tides, Swordfish Island is 20 yards (18 meters) offshore from Church Point, Vancouver Island. At low tides, it is connected to Church Point.

Charter out of Victoria or launch at Becher Bay or Pedder Bay and go southeast from Becher Bay for 2½ nautical miles (4½ kilometers) or southwest from Pedder Bay for 6 nautical miles (11 kilometers) to Swordfish. Early morning is best before the wind gets up. Anchor between Swordfish and Vancouver Island near a notch at the east end of the island. The easiest way to find the tunnel is to descend at this notch in the northeastern side of Swordfish Island and swim through it to the outside. However, when diving in this direction you stir up silt which follows you. No matter what the current direction, the flow in the tunnel is always southeasterly.

With a guide who knows the way, you can approach from the Juan de Fuca side, dive northwest through the tunnel toward Vancouver Island and the silt is carried away behind you. We did it this way: Dropped down the anchor line, swam through bull kelp around the eastern end of the island, cruised the outside of the island. Then followed our guide north through a thick kelp curtain into the tunnel, through the tunnel and to our boat.

Comments: An unforgettable jewel.

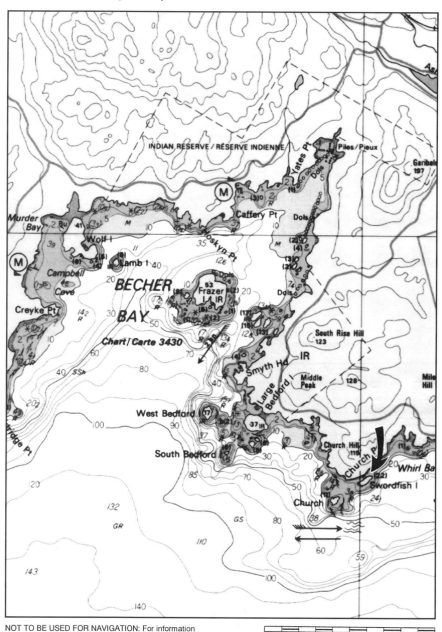

1 Nautical Mile

RACE ROCKS
Boat Dive

Current Table: Race Passage

Skill: Expert divers and snorkelers. All divers with guide.

Why go: "Animals!" one diver exclaimed after his first dive at Race Rocks.

The most marine life I've seen anywhere lives around these infamous current-swept rocks. It's a magnificent mix of protected-water sea life and outer-west-coast wildlife – much of it in shallows. I saw big lacy basket stars in only 30 feet (9 meters) of water. Abalones all over the bright white rocks; jagged giant red urchins; and thick, thick bull kelp. Black serpent stars snake from hot pink hydrocoral more brilliant than tropical coral. In "The Great Race", a plush carpet of brooding anemones like pink, pale green and lavender bonbons completely covers the sea floor. Dahlia anemones, Puget Sound king crabs, pale yellow staghorn bryozoans, black rockfish, orange solitary cup corals, and harbor seals live at Race Rocks. Wintering Steller sea lions and California sea lions haul out here from the end of September until May. We saw sea lions resting on the outermost rocks and scudding down the waves.

Race Rocks area also has its share of wrecks. This is probably the most densely wreck-ridden part in all of British Columbia.

Whatever your diving interest – you will love Race Rocks!

Bottom and Depths: South of Great Race Rock, bright white rocky bottom tiers gradually to a depth of 50 to 60 feet (15 to 18 meters) through a thicket of bull kelp. North of Great Race Rock in The Great Race, the bottom slopes gradually to a depth of 30 to 40 feet (9 to 12 meters). Some bull kelp. You will find a 100- to 110-foot (30- to 34-meter) drop-off into Race Passage at the northwest corner of the westernmost of the Race Rocks.

Hazards: Current, wind, fog, bull kelp and sea lions. Current up to 7 knots (13 kilometers/hour) can rush through Race Passage, more when wind whips it up; but slows to ½ knot (1 kilometer/hour). Dive all locations on slack. Dive The Great Race and Race Passage with a "live" boat. Wear a whistle for fog and wind. Carry a knife for kelp – use in emergency only, this is an ecological reserve. Also, do not pull yourself along on the kelp. Sea lions may approach divers and some injuries have occurred because of playful animals. They become more aggressive with familiarity. Do not stay in the water long with sea lions.

Telephones: • Race Rocks Light Station: You can use your calling card to telephone.
• Pedder Bay Marina, outside office.

Facilities: None. Between dives we enjoyed a tour of the light station; you might gain permission to tour it too. This light station has operated continuously since 1860.

Access: The Race Rocks dive is 3 nautical miles (6 kilometers) offshore from the entrance to Pedder Bay in Juan de Fuca Strait. It is 18 miles (30 kilometers) southwest of Victoria. Charter out of Victoria or launch at Pedder Bay or Becher Bay and go to Race Rocks. Approach the reserve slowly and carefully with respect for privacy of the persons at the light station and respect for the mammals and sea birds. Always leave at least 100 yards (90 meters) between your boat and killer whales. Anchor in the reserve only in emergencies – anchors damage the delicate marine life. Ask for permission to tie up at the lighthouse dock at Great Race Rock but be aware that it is a privately owned working dock. Visitors might gain permission to tie up on arrival but it is on a first-come, first-served basis – you cannot reserve. And sometimes as many as ten boaters are waiting to tie up. In any event, on all but the most minimal tidal exchanges have a "live" boat follow you.

The best time to approach the dock at Race Rocks is when wind is no greater than 20 knots (35 kilometers/hour) and not with too low a tide. The end of the dock is at zero feet (zero meters); refer to tide table for Victoria.

The best time to dive is on low slack tide that is changing to a flood. Current predictions are usually not "out" more than 15 minutes from the predictions, but the time can vary with the size of the tide and with wind. There is almost always some place to dive around Race Rocks on most days of the year. The south point of Great Race Rock usually has less current. But always dive The Great Race and Race Passage with a "live" boat following you in case you are swept away by the current. Wind and fog can make reaching Race Rocks impossible. For weather information, telephone Victoria Continuous Marine Weather Broadcast at (604) 474-7998 for a recorded weather report. For an up-to-the minute "live" report, telephone the light station, using a touch-tone telephone: dial (604) 474-4701. Listen several seconds for a clear line with no conversation. If not busy, dial 625 but not too quickly.

Comments: In 1980, Race Rocks was designated a provincial marine ecological reserve protecting sea birds as well as underwater life. The reserve surrounds Great Race Rock extending from Race Passage to Rosedale Rock. Be careful when diving: weight yourself appropriately and kick your fins carefully so you do not damage any marine life. Do not take or disturb any marine life – do not even move it for a photograph. And do not take dogs onto Race Rocks at any time. Be careful not to disturb the nesting sea birds, especially during May through September; harbor seals pup during June to September.

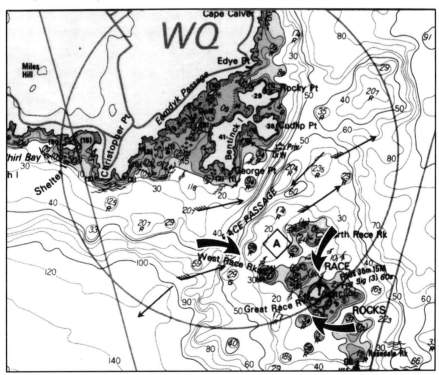

NOT TO BE USED FOR NAVIGATION: For information on obtaining navigational charts see page 318. This is a portion of 3440.

1 Nautical Mile

WRECK OF BARNARD CASTLE
Boat Dive

Current Table: Race Passage

Skill: Intermediate and expert divers. All divers with guide.

Why go: The *Barnard Castle* is a superb wreck for novice wreck divers to explore as features of the turn-of-the-century steamship are marked by an underwater interpretive trail. The wreck is shallow, easy to find and surrounded with scenic marine life.
The *Barnard Castle* hit Rosedale Reef, part of the Race Rocks chain, in 1886. The large ship – it was 260 feet (79 meters) long – made a run for Pilot Bay at Bentinck Island. The bow was beached and the stern sank at the entry to the bay. About half of the hull, the part from stern to amidships, still retains somewhat the shape of a ship. In 1992 eight plaques were placed on the wreck by the Underwater Archaeological Society of British Columbia (UASBC) marking its highlights: two large boilers, three crankshafts, the stern tube, a collapsed starboard hull piece and a coal pile. This trail makes it easy for people who have not done a great deal of wreck diving to know what they are looking at.
It is also supremely easy to find the wreck – a "you are here" buoy marks the port side of the amidship bulkhead. The wreckage is encrusted with lots of life, including graceful plumose anemones and, in summer, a jungle of bull kelp. I saw the biggest abalone I've seen in British Columbia clinging to one of the boilers. We saw a couple of large black rockfish, too. Schools of these fish live around the wreck.
Do not take anything from this wreck (or any other wreck), including the cargo of coal – do not disturb it. Leave it as it is for others to appreciate.

Bottom and Depths: The *Barnard Castle* rests on silty sand, the bow in 15 to 25 feet (6 to 7 meters), the stern in 35 to 45 feet (11 to 14 meters). Eelgrass around it.

Hazards: Bull kelp, current, and silt causing poor visibility around the wreck. Carry a knife. On large tidal exchanges dive on slack. Dive carefully so you do not stir up silt.

Telephones: • Pedder Bay Marina, outside office. • Becher Bay at Cheanuh Marina, outside office. • Becher Bay, top of ramp at Pacific Lions Marina.

Facilities: None.

Access: The *Barnard Castle* lies in the center of Pilot Bay at Bentinck Island next to Race Passage. It is 3 nautical miles (6 kilometers) south of the launching ramp at Pedder Bay; 5 nautical miles (9 kilometers) southeast of launching ramps at Becher Bay; and 10 nautical miles (18 kilometers) southwest of Victoria.
Charter out of Victoria or launch at Pedder Bay or Becher Bay and go to Pilot Bay on the south side of Bentinck Island looking out toward Race Rocks. The ship lies on a 325-degree bearing (magnetic), nearly north to south, with the bow pointing toward shore and the stern angled toward Race Rocks. Do not drop anchor on the wreck – tie onto the mooring buoy that marks the west side of the wreck. Then follow the anchor chain to the bottom. The wreck lies 20 to 30 feet (6 to 9 meters) east of the buoy anchor blocks.
Do not land at Bentinck Island; it is owned by the Department of National Defence and is used as an explosives disposal site.

Comments: A *Diver's Guide to the* Barnard Castle *Interpretive Trail* can be obtained from the UASBC, c/o Vancouver Maritime Museum, 1905 Ogden Avenue, Vancouver BC V6J 1A3.

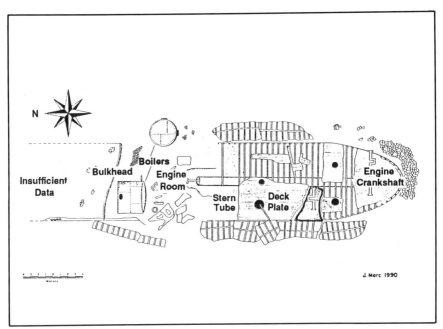

Remains of *Barnard Castle*

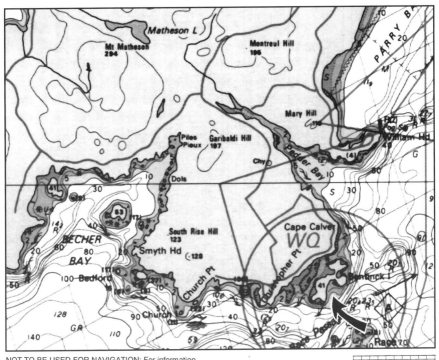

1 Nautical Mile

FISGARD ISLAND
Shore Dive

Skill: All divers and snorkelers

Why go: Fisgard Island is a beautiful place for new divers and snorkelers to see a colorful mixture of life in the shallows.

Everything from crimson sunflower stars to feather duster worms, to lacy white plumose anemones, sea lemons, prickly giant red urchins and little green urchins live here. Delicate jellyfish with red eye-spots drift through the kelp. Schools of pale green tube-snouts move along in small jerks. Kelp greenlings and schools of black rockfish swim past. Dungeness crabs and red rock crabs scramble along the bottom. We saw ratfish. I was even lucky enough to see the silvery flash of two salmon while ascending.

All in all, the waters around Fisgard Island have a feeling of luxuriant life.

Bottom and Depths: Tumbled rocks covered with thick broadleaf bottom kelp slope to white sand scattered with small rocks at 20 to 30 feet (6 to 9 meters). Some big boulders. A thicket of bull kelp in summer.

Hazards: Bull kelp and wind. Carry a knife for kelp. Southeast wind can blow up surf and make entry difficult.

Telephone: Fort Rodd Hill parking lot entrance.

Facilities: Grassy park and picnic tables; restrooms open only in summer.

Access: Fisgard Island is on the body of water called Royal Roads where Fisgard Lighthouse guards the entrance to Esquimalt Harbour. The dive is 7 miles (11 kilometers) west of Victoria off Craigflower Road (Highway 1A) at Fort Rodd Hill.

From Craigflower Road in Colwood, head uphill on Ocean Boulevard following signs to Fort Rodd. Park at the historic site parking lot. From here walk on a well-graded service road, about 450 to 500 yards (400 to 450 meters) to Fisgard Island. Bring a hand cart for gear. If you talk nicely with the commissioner and, if lucky, you might gain permission to drive down the service road to drop off gear. It's a long way. Walk to the left of the old fortifications and across a causeway to the lighthouse. Dive all around Fisgard Island.

To get to Craigflower Road and Ocean Boulevard
• From the Parliament Buildings in Victoria – and from the Port Angeles ferry which lands at the Inner Harbour in front of the Parliament Buildings, it takes 20 minutes to Fort Rodd. Follow the Inner Harbour around on Wharf Street and turn left onto Johnson Street Bridge. Cross the bridge, go under an overpass and turn right into Tyee Road. At Bay Street traffic light continue straight on Tyee. It becomes Skinner Street, then Craigflower. Go along Craigflower Road, which becomes Highway 1A to Colwood. Past Six Mile Pub you are nearing Ocean Boulevard. At the light, turn left.
• From Swartz Bay or Sidney to Fort Rodd takes 35 minutes. Head south on Patricia Bay Highway (Highway 17) toward Victoria. Past Elk Lake where signs point to the University of Victoria at McKenzie Avenue, do not turn left to the university but turn right following signs toward Highway 1. Turn right onto Highway 1 and go on it past Helmcken Road. Take Colwood and Sooke Exit "To 1A/14". Go beneath an underpass to Craigflower and continue west to Ocean Boulevard and turn left.
• Heading south from Duncan on Highway 1, leave the highway when just past the turnoff to Goldstream Provincial Park campground. From here, 10 minutes to Fort

Rodd. Follow signs toward Langford, Colwood and Sooke. Go on Highway 1A which is Goldstream Avenue through Langford. At the junction of Highways 14 and 1A in Colwood, turn left and almost immediately right onto Ocean Boulevard.

Comments: Fisgard Lighthouse was the first lighthouse on Canada's west coast and has been in continuous use since 1860. Fort Rodd Hill is a classic example of early means of defense; maps and signs tell about the fortifications. Twenty-five tame deer wander the grounds of Fort Rodd Hill National Historic Site between the well-preserved remains of three turn-of-the-century coast artillery guns. Fort Rodd Hill area offers something for everybody: for divers, snorkelers, and non-divers.

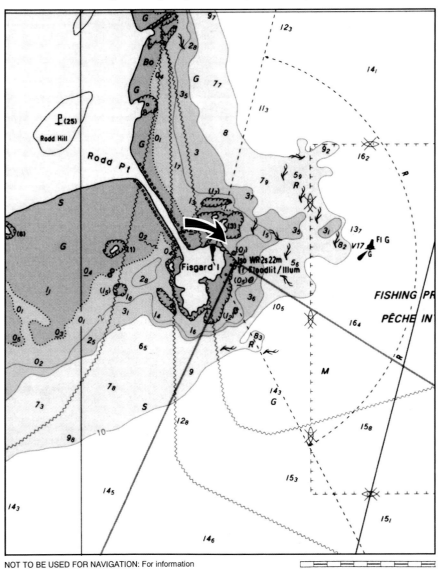

NOT TO BE USED FOR NAVIGATION: For information
on obtaining navigational charts see page 318.
This is a portion of 3419.

200 Yards

SAXE POINT PARK
Shore Dive

Skill: All divers and snorkelers

Why go: Saxe Point offers a sample of west coast underwater life without the difficulties of surf diving that usually go with it.

A fabulous place to snorkel or dive, to see thick, thick shrub-like algae, big black leather stars, gooseneck barnacles, and small colorful pastel anemones. Purple plume worms flourish under rocky overhangs in only 5 feet (1½ meters) of water. Immense sunflower stars, small chitons and green urchins cling to the rocks. We saw kelp greenlings, small decorator crabs and pale pink nudibranchs with brown spots. Delicate jellyfish with red eye-spots drift between the kelp. Geoduck clams, shrimp and burrowing cucumbers are in the silty sand.

Because this has been a favorite picnic site of Victorians for years, you may find old bottles.

Bottom and Depths: Rocky bottom thick with bushy green algae and bull kelp tiers off in shallow ledges to coarse sand at 30 feet (9 meters). Silty sand on the right.

Hazards: Thick bull kelp, especially in summer. Carry a knife; if caught in kelp you can cut your way free. Southeast wind can blow up surf and make entry difficult.

Telephone: Esquimalt Plaza, 1 block east of Fraser Street and Esquimalt Road.

Facilities: Grassy park with beach, picnic tables, restrooms and parking lot.

Access: Saxe Point Park is on the body of water named Royal Roads. It is next to Juan de Fuca Strait, and 4 miles (6 kilometers) west of Victoria in Esquimalt.

From Esquimalt Road and Fraser Street, go south ½ mile (1 kilometer) on Fraser to Saxe Point. Park near the plaque, and walk down a short curving trail on your right to the small bay.

To get to Fraser Street and Esquimalt Road
• From the Empress Hotel in Victoria – and from the Port Angeles ferry which lands at the Inner Harbour in front of the Empress, it takes 15 minutes to Saxe Point. Follow the Inner Harbour around on Wharf Street and turn left onto Johnson Street Bridge. Cross it and go west 2 miles (3 kilometers) on Esquimalt Road. Past the Sports Centre, you reach Fraser Street. Turn left.
• From Swartz Bay or Sidney to Saxe Point takes 55 minutes. Head south on Patricia Bay Highway (Highway 17) to Victoria. In the city: turn right into Herald Street or Fisgard which lead onto Johnson Street Bridge. Cross it and go 2 miles (3 kilometers) west on Esquimalt Road. Past the Sports Centre, turn left at Fraser Street.
• Heading south on Trans-Canada Highway 1, past Goldstream Park look for the turnoff to Helmcken Road; from here, 15 minutes to Saxe Point. To find Helmcken: go past Highway 1 exit to Thetis Lake Park and, at an overpass, you will see signs to Highway 1A and to Esquimalt. This is Helmcken. Turn right and follow Helmcken to a traffic light at Highway 1A. Turn left following a sign to Esquimalt. Go on Highway 1A to Admirals Road and turn right. Follow Admirals, winding around to Esquimalt Road. Turn left and almost immediately right into Fraser Street.

Comments: The plaque by the parking lot commemorates the landing here on July 8, 1955 of Bert Owen Thomas of Tacoma, Washington, the first known person to swim Juan de Fuca Strait – 11 hours and 17 minutes.

Jellyfish with red eye-spots

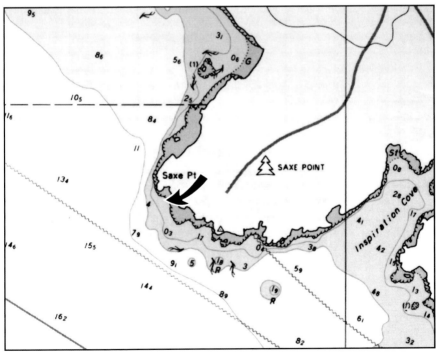

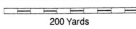

200 Yards

OGDEN POINT BREAKWATER
Shore Dive

Skill: All divers

Why go: Going to Ogden Point Breakwater is a Sunday "thing to do" in Victoria. It's a popular open-water certification site, a favorite for sightseeing and photography, excellent for practicing underwater navigation. It's a three-ring circus. The Breakwater is also a marine sanctuary – rich with life. The marine trail of five underwater plaques is unique in that the plaques are so easy to find: each plaque is located on the surface by a dive flag painted on the outside of the Breakwater. At the shallowest plaque that features shallow eelgrass reef animals, we saw leafy horn-mouth whelks laying eggs, six lingcod – one huge "ling", kelp greenlings, a swimming scallop, flounders and ghost shrimp on the sand. As we went deeper we saw abalones, gum boot chitons, red urchins. Christmas, dahlia and plumose anemones. China rockfish, seaperch, tiger rockfish, schools of black rockfish. In the riprap, look for penpoint gunnels, octopuses, wolf-eels. At night, look for sailfin sculpins. At the deepest plaque, hordes of swimming scallops.

The first half of the Breakwater is a great place for new divers to see a variety of marine life and meet other divers. Intermediate and expert divers who are experienced with current will find the most peaceful diving on the last half of the outside of the Breakwater where fewer divers disturb the scene.

Bottom and Depths: Broken rock, or riprap, is heaped along the base of the Breakwater which is 5 feet (1½ meters) deep, sloping to a depth of 80 to 90 feet (24 to 27 meters) at the end. Sand stretches out from the riprap. Thick beds of bull kelp rim the Breakwater which extends ½ mile (¾ kilometer) into the sea. The farther out the Breakwater you go, the more demanding the dive becomes because of increased current and depth. The plaques are from 5 to 50 feet (1½ to 15 meters) deep at low tide.

Hazards: Bull kelp, fishing line, wind, wash from passing boats, and current. Carry a knife; if caught in kelp or transparent fishing line you can cut your way free. Southeast wind can blow up surf which makes it difficult to swim through the kelp and climb from the water. On the surface, pay attention to wash from passing boats. Dive the last half of the Breakwater on the slack.

Telephones: • James Bay Anglers' Association Boat Ramp, 75 Dallas Road ⅓ mile (½ kilometer) west of the Breakwater. • Niagara and Douglas Streets, 2 blocks north of Mile 0. Go east on Dallas Road to Mile 0, then north.

Facilities: Parking near the Breakwater for sixteen cars in the 200 block Dallas Road; more roadside parking east along the waterfront. Toilets in the waterfront park ½ mile (1 kilometer) east of the Breakwater.

Access: The Breakwater protects Victoria Harbour, which is in the heart of Victoria, from weather off Juan de Fuca Strait. The dive is in the heart of Victoria. From the conference center behind the Empress Hotel, go 1 mile (2 kilometers) to the Breakwater. Drive south on Douglas Street bordering Beacon Hill Park to the water at Dallas Road. You are now at Mile 0 of Trans-Canada Highway 1. Turn right and go ¾ mile (1⅓ kilometers) to the Breakwater.

Look for dive flags painted on the outside of the Breakwater that locate the plaques. The flags are above water line. You could start shallow or deep. We started with the plaque that is farthest out, as diving it is dependent on current and we were there at the right time. First we walked out to view it from the surface without gear.

That took 15 minutes. Next we carried weight belts, fins and masks and dropped them. Then geared up in suits and tanks, walked out and jumped in. We saw what was at #5, enjoyed it, surfaced, snorkeled to the next flag. Dived to see what was at #4, surfaced and snorkeled again. It took us a couple of days to visit each plaque. However, so much information is on each plaque as well as so much marine life around each one, you could take a week over it.

Comments: Using the plaques, you could practice underwater navigation skills and go from one plaque to the other, staying under water all the way. The distance and compass bearings for adjacent plaques are given on each plaque.

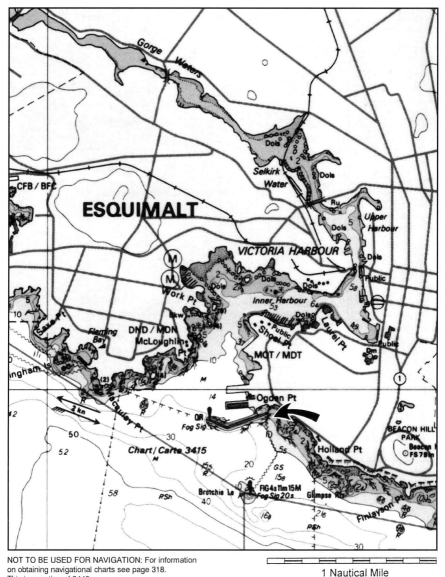

NOT TO BE USED FOR NAVIGATION: For information
on obtaining navigational charts see page 318.
This is a portion of 3440.

1 Nautical Mile

Skill: Intermediate and expert divers. All divers with guide.

Why go: Brotchie Ledge – part of Ogden Point area which is closed to spearfishing – is an endless source of gorgeous junk.
You can't take marine life or any artifact that might be connected with a wreck, but you can collect valuable old bottles, crockery and the other old "things" which are everywhere. Fifty to 100 years ago, garbage barges regularly came from Victoria's Inner Harbour and deposited their load in this area. On one dive at Brotchie Ledge three of us found two tiger whiskey bottles, two Chinese bean pots, a large flower planter and one crockery marmalade pot. From the size of the barnacles on all of them we guessed they must be at least fifty years old. Investigate anything with giant barnacles growing on it, dig in the silty sand among the swimming scallops, and you will probably find some intriguing relics.
We also stumbled onto something big which might have been a boiler from the 331-foot (100-meter) metal-hulled *San Pedro*. In 1891 the *San Pedro* went down on Brotchie Ledge. Two salvage companies went bankrupt trying to salvage the wreck before it was declared a navigational hazard and blown up. Fragments of the *San Pedro* are flung over Brotchie Ledge. Look for a plaque on the wreck.

Bottom and Depths: Silt-covered giant barnacles are attached to everything solid on the mucky bottom which ranges from very shallow at the marker to a depth of 80 to 90 feet (24 to 27 meters) deep. The ledge is located 120 feet (37 meters) toward the Breakwater from the marker in 25 to 55 feet (8 to 17 meters). It extends almost ½ mile (¾ kilometer) east and west from the marker.

Hazards: Wind, current, poor visibility and sailboats. Currents are not always as predicted. Dive at Brotchie Ledge in early morning when the water is calm, on the slack, on a small tidal exchange. If you cannot coordinate all these factors, dive in the early morning when the water is calm and the pickup person can easily see your bubbles. For best visibility, try to disturb the bottom as little as possible when delving in the muck. Sailboats approach silently; spiral, look up and ascend cautiously when you have seen sailboats at Brotchie Ledge.

Telephones: • The James Bay Anglers' Association Boat Ramp, at 75 Dallas Road.
• Niagara and Douglas Streets, 2 blocks north of Mile 0.

Facilities: None.

Access: Brotchie Ledge is just outside Victoria Harbour in Juan de Fuca Strait. It is less than ½ nautical mile (1 kilometer) offshore from the Breakwater at Ogden Point.
Charter out of Victoria, launch an inflatable at the Breakwater, or launch at James Bay. Go less than ½ nautical mile (1 kilometer) offshore from the Breakwater: a marker indicates the ledge. Before diving, look at the water. If a back eddy at Brotchie Ledge, do not dive. If the kelp is not on the surface, the current is too great to dive. The waters around the ledge itself are too deep and too current-ridden to anchor. Leave someone on the boat to follow you and pick you up when you ascend.

Comments: Remember that Brotchie Ledge is closed to spearfishing; do not disturb any marine life. And do not disturb wreckage of ships. If you find a shipwreck, surface, note the location, and report your "finds" to the Underwater Archaeological Society of British Columbia. It could start you off on a whole new specialized aspect of diving. And there is so much of interest, apart from wrecks, for the treasure hunter to take home from this site. One diver collects nothing here but foot-warmers, sometimes called "pigs".

Barnacled Chinese bean pot

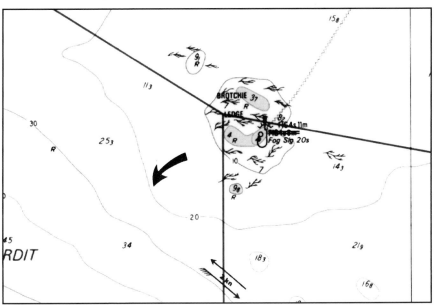

200 Yards

TEN MILE POINT
Shore Dive

Current Table: Race Passage
Subtract 15 minutes

Skill: Intermediate and expert divers. All divers with guide.

Why go: "Filter-feeder city" is the way one diver describes Ten Mile Point where the current carries food to hungry marine creatures.
Swimming scallops would be enough to lure me to this site. All creatures which feed from the current flourish here. Particularly animals like burrowing cucumbers which put out tentacles to feed. "Suspension-feeder city" is a more accurate description. The wall is a colorful tapestry. Heaps of white burrowing cucumbers look like organ pipe cacti when their tendrils are retracted. We saw orange cucumbers. A forest of white plumose anemones, some rock scallops, quillback rockfish and other rockfish in the crevices. Small black rockfish swim past in schools. At the base of the wall, abalone shells, giant urchins, massive beds of giant barnacles, thousands of swimming scallops clapping up around us from the sand. You may meet a seal in the kelp.
In 1975 Ten Mile Point was declared a provincial marine ecological reserve for scientific research. Recreational use is allowed as long as it is not damaging. A photographer's special – no taking of marine life at this reserve.

Bottom and Depths: Rocky bottom, with lettuce kelp, slopes gently to a bed of bull kelp at 30 to 40 feet (9 to 12 meters). The crevice-filled rock wall drops off quickly to a depth of 80 to 90 feet (24 to 27 meters), a sea floor of almost flat sand.

Hazards: Current, bull kelp and broken fishing line. Dive on the slack. Current up to 5 to 6 knots (9 to 11 kilometers/hour) can run past this point. Be careful on large tidal exchanges. Refer to Race Passage current table, subtracting 15 minutes to correct for Baynes Channel location; in summer, also correct for daylight saving time (add one hour). Carry a knife for kelp or fishing line.

Telephone: Cadboro Bay village, 2 miles (3 kilometers) back.

Facilities: Space for four cars to park.

Access: Ten Mile Point is on Haro Strait north of Baynes Channel. Reach it via the village of Cadboro Bay, a northern suburb of Victoria. It is 7½ miles (12 kilometers) from the heart of Victoria.
From the village of Cadboro Bay, go north on Cadboro Bay Road; the road name changes to Telegraph Bay Road. From the village go ½ mile (¾ kilometer) to Seaview Road. Turn right. Then, almost immediately, left into Tudor Avenue. Continue on Tudor for 1 mile (1½ kilometers). Tudor makes a right-angle turn to the left. Just past that sharp corner, turn right into Baynes Road. Go almost to the end of Baynes and turn left into White Rock Street to the water. Park by the small turnaround, suit up, and climb a few feet down over the rocks to the sea.

To get to village of Cadboro Bay
• From the Empress Hotel in Victoria – and from the Port Angeles ferry which lands at the Inner Harbour in front of the Empress, 20 minutes to Cadboro Bay. Go east on Fort Street which becomes Cadboro Bay Road. When the road dips close to the water you are at the village of Cadboro Bay.
• From Swartz Bay or Sidney, head south on Patricia Bay Highway (Highway 17) for 30 minutes to Cadboro Bay. Go past Elk Lake to McKenzie Avenue. Turn left and go along McKenzie through the University of Victoria. At the Finnerty traffic light, do not

turn. Continue straight on Sinclair Road which goes into the village of Cadboro Bay.
• From Duncan heading south on Highway 1: past Helmcken Road, exit Highway 1, following signs to "Ferries, Sidney, 17 North and University of Victoria". From this exit, 15 minutes to Cadboro Bay. Go to Highway 17; cross it and continue on McKenzie Avenue. At Finnerty, continue straight on Sinclair to the village of Cadboro Bay.
• From Mill Bay ferry at Brentwood Bay, 25 minutes to Cadboro Bay. Head south on West Saanich Road. When it ends at Highway 17, turn right. Go to McKenzie Avenue which is the next one; then go east on McKenzie through the University of Victoria. At Finnerty, continue straight on Sinclair to the village of Cadboro Bay.

Comments: If the current is too great at Ten Mile Point or if rough water because of wind, go nearby to Spring Bay.

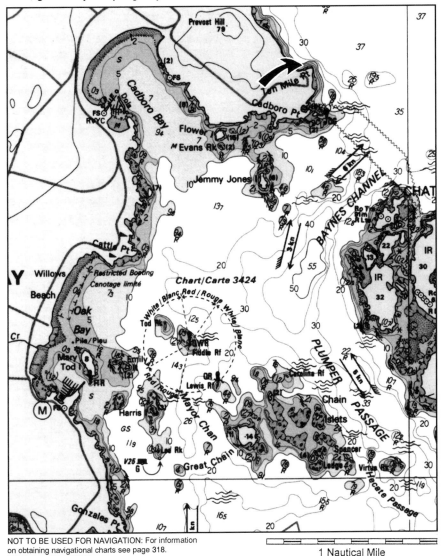

NOT TO BE USED FOR NAVIGATION: For information on obtaining navigational charts see page 318. This is a portion of 3440.

1 Nautical Mile

SPRING BAY
Shore Dive

Skill: All divers and snorkelers

Why go: Easy entry, gently terraced bottom, in-the-city dive. Excellent for new divers. Fun for veterans too.

Everybody loves an octopus – lots of them here. Hiding in dens in the valleys of rock. A jungle of orange burrowing cucumbers lights up the brown bottom kelp. Snails scramble all over the place. We saw blood stars, purple stars; kelp greenlings, lingcod, quillback rockfish; a sea lemon, shrimp, a single swimming scallop, giant barnacles, clam shells and leafy hornmouth whelks. A few plumose anemones, gum boot chitons, urchins. Spider crabs. A red-and-transparent striped gunnel with a yellow spot. And three harbor seals.

Bottom and Depths: Gradually sloping rock bottom with mini-canyons covered in leafy brown bottom kelp. Giant purple urchins between. In summer, bull kelp. You will find most of the life in 60 to 65 feet (18 to 20 meters)

Hazards: Bull kelp. Carry a knife.

Telephone: Cadboro Bay village, 2 miles (3 kilometers) back.

Facilities: Crescent of beach with a view of Mount Baker. Great place for a picnic. Air fills in Victoria, Sidney and Deep Cove.

Access: Spring Bay is located in the village of Cadboro Bay, an elegant northern suburb of Victoria. It is 7½ miles (12 kilometers) from the heart of Victoria.

From the village of Cadboro Bay, go north along Cadboro Bay Road; the road name changes to Telegraph Bay Road. From the village, go ½ mile (¾ kilometer) and turn right at Seaview Road. Then, almost immediately, turn left into Tudor Avenue. Continue on Tudor to the end of it. Room for two or three cars to park. A few steps to the gravelly beach, then head around the point on your left and explore along the rocky ridge.

To get to village of Cadboro Bay
• From the Empress Hotel in Victoria – and from the Port Angeles ferry which lands at the Inner Harbour in front of the Empress, 20 minutes to Cadboro Bay. Head east on Fort Street which becomes Cadboro Bay Road. When the road dips close to the water you are at the village of Cadboro Bay.
• From Swartz Bay or Sidney, head south on Patricia Bay Highway (Highway 17) to Cadboro Bay; it takes 30 minutes. Go past Elk Lake to McKenzie Avenue. Turn left and drive through the University of Victoria. At the Finnerty traffic light, do not turn. Continue straight on Sinclair Road which goes into the village of Cadboro Bay.
• From Duncan heading south on Highway 1: past Helmcken Road, exit Highway 1 following signs to "Ferries, Sidney, 17 North and University of Victoria". From this exit, 15 minutes to Cadboro Bay. Go to Highway 17; cross it and continue on McKenzie Avenue. At Finnerty, continue straight on Sinclair to the village of Cadboro Bay.
• From Mill Bay ferry at Brentwood Bay, 25 minutes to Cadboro Bay. Head south on West Saanich Road; when West Saanich Road ends at Highway 17, turn right. Go south on Highway 17 to McKenzie Avenue which is the next one. Then turn east to the village of Cadboro Bay.

Comments: When a southwesterly is blowing, come to Spring Bay where it is calm.

After dive at Spring Bay

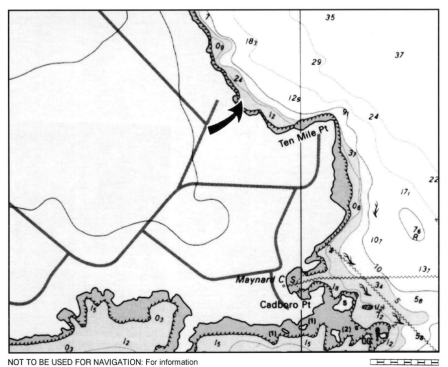

NOT TO BE USED FOR NAVIGATION: For information
on obtaining navigational charts see page 318.
This is a portion of 3424.

200 Yards

GRAHAM'S WALL
Boat Dive

Current Table: Race Passage
Add 1 hour, turn to flood
Add 1½ hours, turn to ebb

Skill: Intermediate and expert divers. All divers with guide.

Why go: Graham's Wall is covered with life – much of it new to me. It is packed with exotica. As our guide exclaimed after our dive, "You gotta go back to your books after this one"!

Huge plumose anemones billow beneath the undercut wall. Yellow encrusting sponge flames the rock. A few orange cucumbers are in crevices. Pink soft corals too. Staghorn bryozoans twist from the rocks. Pink colonial anemones are beneath the overhangs. We saw tiny sculpins with red markings, large lingcod, giant barnacles, decorator crabs, rock scallops, an octopus den. An orange-spotted clown nudibranch, an alabaster nudibranch, an orange peel nudibranch and nudibranch eggs. Orange cup corals. Crystal clear tunicates and a deep red sea peach. We saw heart crabs. A tiny porcelain crab held up its delicate, mauve colored claws to us, not fearful at all when gently pushed. Stood its ground. This little crab stretched to its full height was 1 inch (2½ centimeters) tall. I don't think any divers could identify every creature they saw on one dive here without looking at several marine identification books.

Just go to the maximum depth you want to dive and weave back and forth up the wall. You do not even have to move – just stay in one place and look. So much to see.

Bottom and Depths: A rocky wall with overhangs but you cannot touch rock nor even see it because of so much life on the wall. The wall does not drop straight down. It undercuts and bottoms out to sand at 90 to 100 feet (27 to 30 meters). East of the wall, rocky bottom with brown bottom kelp and bull kelp, especially in summer, at a depth of 25 to 35 feet (7½ to 11 meters). It ledges down gently to the wall.

Hazards: Current, small boats, transparent fishing line and bull kelp. The current correction used is for Sidney Channel. Dive on slack or during flood, except for the largest floods; on small ebbs, dive with a pickup boat. If the kelp is on the surface it is divable. Listen for boats and ascend in the bull kelp out of the way of boats. Carry a knife.

Telephones: • Port Sidney Marina, outside pub. • Beacon Avenue government wharf, Sidney.

Facilities: None. Air fills, charters – even inflatable charters, launching and hot showers at Sidney.

Access: Graham's Wall is in Haro Strait off Domville Island. Domville Island is 3 nautical miles (6 kilometers) east/northeast of Sidney on the east side of Saanich Peninsula north of Victoria.

Charter or launch out of Sidney, Deep Cove or Saltspring Island. Go to the middle of the west side of Domville Island. At low tides look for a rock with bull kelp all around and often harbor seals on it. It dries at 3-foot (1-meter) tides. If no rock is visible, look for the kelp. In summer, it is a thicket. Anchor between Domville Island and the kelp.

To find the wall: swim west to the kelp, but do not go to the rock. Descend on the east side of the kelp and head north under water. As you go deeper, stay close to the wall and go left around the corner of the rock to the west-facing wall. The wall is short. Start diving deep and work your way up, zigzagging back and forth. We saw the full length of the wall at three depths on our way up. Different life each pass we made.

Comments: Magical names of dives I've heard of are all around this site – places like North Cod Reef and Reay Island. Lots more I've seen on the chart that look inviting to explore: Rum Island, Joan Rock and Arachne Reef. Oh – it's hard to stop!

Off Domville Island, rock with seals on it

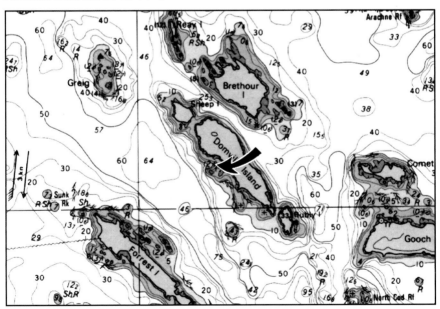

1 Nautical Mile

WRECK OF THE G.B. CHURCH
Boat Dive

Tide Table: Fulford Harbour

Skill: Intermediate and expert divers. All divers with guide.

Why go: Frills of nudibranch eggs cover the barnacled hull of the *G.B. Church* which sits upright on the bottom. This munitions carrier turned herring packer looks ready to sail away. A ghost ship. Burgeoning with new life.

Look for the giant octopus in the hollowed out mud beneath the bow – when we dived, ribbons of brilliant green bull kelp brought by the timid octopus curtained its den. We chuckled. Bull kelp does not grow at this depth. Moving up the side we saw *G.B. Church* painted on the bow. We went into the wheelhouse, saw the control panel and gauges. If you dive early in the morning before others arrive, you will probably find rockfish crowding the wheelhouse – some quillbacks but mostly canary and copper rockfish.

We swam along the length of the ship, saw a sign saying "Only One Person on the Stairs at a Time", saw a plaque placed on the front of the superstructure by the provincial parks that commemorates the sinking of this ship on August 10, 1991. It is the first vessel sunk by the Artificial Reef Society of British Columbia in conjunction with BC Parks. Diver access holes have been cut throughout the ship at a depth of 55 to 65 feet (15 to 20 meters). You can always see light wherever you go in the *G.B. Church*. Experienced wreck divers can penetrate the forecastle, engine room and galley.

The *G.B. Church* was built in 1943. It was first named *Cerium*, then *G.R. Velie*, then *G.B. Church*. Its steel hull is 175 feet (53 meters) long. Designed as a munitions carrier with a flattish keel and hull, the ship saw action on D-day in the Second World War, June 6, 1944. A crew member from those days turned up on the day of sinking when the vessel started its new life beneath the sea.

Bottom and Depths: The keel rests on featureless mud bottom at 75 to 85 feet (23 to 26 meters), depending on tide height. The top of the forward mast is the shallowest point of the ship at a depth of 13 to 23 feet (4 to 7 meters). It is marked by the westernmost marker buoy. The forepeak of the bow is at 50 to 60 feet (15 to 18 meters).

Hazards: Current, small boats and the temptation to penetrate the wreck. On large tidal exchanges, dive near slack. Listen for boats and ascend up one of the marker buoy chains attached to each mast all the way to the surface, well out of the way of boats. Only divers trained in penetration techniques as taught in a wreck diving course should enter the wreck, particularly the forecastle and engine room.

Telephones: • Canoe Cove Marina, south of Swartz Bay. • Tsehum Harbour, Van Isle Marina. • Port Sidney Marina, beside pub. • Deep Cove, outside dive shop.

Facilities: Camping at Princess Margaret Marine Park on Portland Island. Charters out of Sidney, Victoria and Pender Island; launching at Sidney and boat rentals in Deep Cove.

Access: The *G.B. Church* is beside Moresby Passage. It is in Princess Margaret Provincial Marine Park, 550 yards (500 meters) off southeast corner of Portland Island, 4 nautical miles (7 kilometers) northeast of Sidney. Charter out of Sidney, Deep Cove, Victoria, Pender Island or Saltspring Island. Or rent a boat or launch your own boat at one of many ramps in Sidney and go to the wreck.

At the time of writing, the forward mast (to the west) is marked with a yellow buoy that has a site description on it. The aft mast is marked with a red-and-black "isolated danger" buoy. Do not tie onto either of these markers. It is a federal offense to make fast to a marker or tamper with any aid to navigation. Four mooring buoys are around the markers; tie onto one of them. It's a popular site. You'll probably see more dive boats too. Go early for silt-free uncrowded diving and for the mooring buoy of your choice.

Look at the water – consider current direction when choosing which *mooring buoy* to tie up to; then swim to the closest *marker buoy* and descend on the chain. Work your way around the wreck. When diving, be aware of current direction so you can ascend the chain to the marker buoy that is upcurrent from where your boat is tied up.

Comments: You can see the *G.B. Church* plunging to its watery grave on the video cassette "Reefs of Steel: Artificial Reefs in British Columbia".

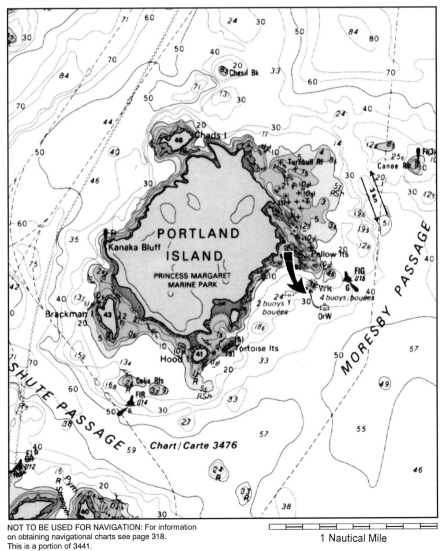

NOT TO BE USED FOR NAVIGATION: For information on obtaining navigational charts see page 318. This is a portion of 3441.

1 Nautical Mile

ARBUTUS ISLAND
Boat Dive

Skill: Intermediate and expert divers. All divers with guide.

Why go: Arbutus Island is a perfect little gem of an island. Here you can see unusual, brown cemented tube worms that form small reefs or mounds all over the bottom. And in one easy circuit you can see a cross-section of most of the life typical to the Strait of Georgia.

Sea pens, kelp greenlings, gorgeous orange spotted nudibranchs, rock scallops, octopuses, small abalones and schools of black rockfish all live at Arbutus Island. Tiger rockfish, sailfin sculpins and decorated warbonnets inhabit crevices in the wall on the west end. Overhangs are thick with white plumose anemones. We also saw small clumps of hard yellow staghorn bryozoans.

Arbutus Island: an easy dive with an outstanding variety of life. Beautiful by day or night.

Bottom and Depths: A variety of substrates surrounds this one small island. Thick bull kelp in 15 to 25 feet (5 to 8 meters), a vertical rock wall to a depth of 45 to 55 feet (12 to 17 meters), caves and arches of rock at 30 to 40 feet (9 to 12 meters), flat sand and large boulders.

Hazards: Current, small boats and, particularly in summer, bull kelp. Watch for abandoned gill nets in the late fall. Dive on the slack or during a rising tide. Many small boats stop at Arbutus Island. Listen for boats and ascend close to the bottom all the way to shore, well out of the way of those boats. Carry a knife.

Telephones: • Canoe Cove Marina, south of Swartz Bay ferry terminal. • Tsehum Harbour, Van Isle Marina. • Deep Cove, outside dive shop.

Facilities: None at Arbutus Island. Air fills, charters, launching and hot showers at Sidney. Air fills, charters and boat rentals at Deep Cove. Boat rentals at Mill Bay. Camping in summer at McDonald Provincial Park near Swartz Bay ferry terminal.

Access: Arbutus Island is in Satellite Channel. It is ½ nautical mile (1 kilometer) off the northern tip of Saanich Peninsula and ½ nautical mile (1 kilometer) west of Piers Island. Charter out of Sidney, Deep Cove, Pender Island or Saltspring Island. Rent a boat in Victoria or Deep Cove or launch at Sidney. Go to the northern tip of Saanich Peninsula, and look for a small uninhabited island with two or three skeletons of dead arbutus trees on it. Anchor or land, and dive all around the island. A good place to start is at the caves on the southwest corner of the island.

Comments: Treat this perfect little island like a reserve and keep it intact as a living display of almost everything in the Strait of Georgia.

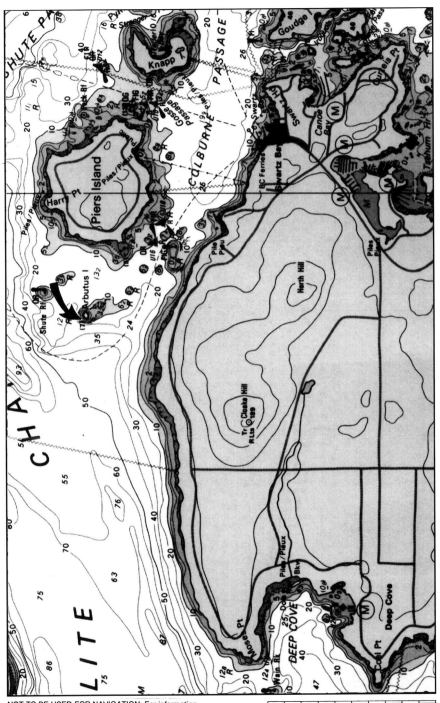

NOT TO BE USED FOR NAVIGATION: For information
on obtaining navigational charts see page 318.
This is a portion of 3441.

1 Nautical Mile

MYSTERY WRECK AT DEEP COVE
Shore Dive

Skill: All divers

Why go: Fragile spires rise row upon row like a New York cityscape – that's the vision I came up from this dive with. The wreck is shallow, current-free, excellent for sightseers and photographers.

Light shines through the skeleton of the hull. Partially rotted, the wreck is better than intact. Its spooky shape provides hiding places for a variety of life. Orange plumose anemones and white ones. We saw a cluster of lingcod eggs between two ribs, a very black male lingcod standing guard; another large "ling" at the north end of the wreck. Schools of silvery pile perch and blue perch, a solitary quillback rockfish. An alabaster nudibranch, a decorator crab, a hairy crab, a white sea star. Rose stars scattered over the wreck like giant red-white-and-gray snowflakes.

This wreck is a mystery. You might solve it. Start by looking for the railway tracks; find the cleat at the northwest corner. Look for more clues. Many stories are told about the wreck but no one knows. The story I like best is that the barge was brought to Deep Cove to be a breakwater. The Coast Guard could not tow it away because it was a registered vessel with a number and was lit at night as a vessel at anchor must be. One night a storm sank it. Voila! A wreck. Until late 1992, the most believable story was that this barge broke its back on Wain Rock: half the wreck was supposed to be there, the other half at Deep Cove. Now it has been determined that this wooden hull in Deep Cove is the whole thing: the wreck is 203 feet (62 meters) long and 29 feet (9 meters) wide.

At Deep Cove, look also for Oriental bottles from the 1920s.

Bottom and Depths: The hull rests on the gently sloping muddy bottom scattered with eelgrass at 40 to 50 feet (12 to 15 meters), depending on tide height – best for photographers on weekdays when fewer divers stir up the silt. The wreck lies parallel to the dock.

Hazards: The wreck itself, boats, silt and wind. The wreck is unstable, do not enter. Listen for boats; ascend up the buoy line out of the way of boats but be careful of the life on it – when I dived, the buoy line was smothered in orange sea cucumbers and purple feather duster worms. Try to stay off the bottom so you do not stir up the silt. Usually calm but check for northwest wind.

Telephone: Deep Cove, outside dive shop.

Facilities: Air fills, charters and boat rentals at the dive entry at Deep Cove.

Access: Deep Cove is on Saanich Inlet near the top of Saanich Peninsula, west of Swartz Bay ferry terminal. Reach it by way of Wain Road and Madrona Drive. It is 40 minutes from the Empress Hotel in Victoria.

From Patricia Bay Highway (Highway 17) just south of Swartz Bay ferry terminal or from West Saanich Road (Highway 17A) just north of Brentwood Bay near the top of the inlet, go west on Wain Road to Madrona Drive. Turn right onto Madrona, and go ⅓ mile (½ kilometer) to Admirals Walk and turn left downhill to the dive shop. If you obtain an air fill, rent a boat or charter a boat at the dive shop, the wreck dive is free. Or pay a nominal fee to enter from the privately owned dock. Walk to the end of the dock. Look northwest – a buoy marks the wreck at tides up to 5 feet (1½ meters). Jump off the end of the dock. If the buoy is visible, swim for 5 to 10 minutes to it and go down. If higher tide and the buoy is not visible, descend and follow a 270-degree compass bearing. When you reach a reef, go over it and almost immediately you will reach the wreck. The marina dock is wheelchair accessible.

If you prefer snorkeling to walking – or if you do not wish to pay the fee for the dive, you can also reach the wreck from Setchell Point (see Setchell Point on page 82.)

Comments: Sitting on the dock after the dive, we saw two white swans.

From float, to mystery wreck

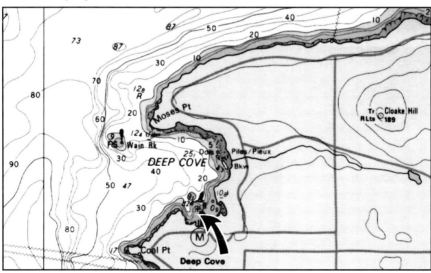

NOT TO BE USED FOR NAVIGATION: For information on obtaining navigational charts see page 318. This is a portion of 3441.

1 Nautical Mile

SETCHELL POINT
Shore Dive

Tide Table: Fulford Harbour

Skill: All divers

Why go: Current-free dive with easy access. A wreck too if you want to snorkel to it.
   One winter day at Setchell Point we saw a sailfin sculpin, a painted greenling, quill-back rockfish, a small alabaster nudibranch, a giant silver nudibranch. Golf balls. Red rock crabs, green lettuce kelp, sea cucumbers, orange plumose anemones, sunflower and leather stars, small chitons, beaded anemones – gray with pink dots on short arms, tube-dwelling anemones in the soft muddy sand, blackeye gobies darting beneath the ledges.
   The 203-foot (62-meter) long wooden hull is at 40 to 50 feet (12 to 15 meters). See Mystery Wreck at Deep Cove on the previous page for more detail. The wreck is crumbling but scenic and it shelters lots of marine life.

Bottom and Depths: Muddy bottom scattered with eelgrass and golf balls. Slopes very gently to 40 to 50 feet (12 to 15 meters).

Hazards: Small boats, silt and wind. While diving, listen for boats and stay down, yet off the bottom so you do not stir up silt. Dive with a compass: when ascending, follow it to shore, staying close to the bottom all the way. Weight yourself for shallow depth. Usually calm but check for northwest wind.

Telephone: Deep Cove, outside dive shop. Go north on Madrona Drive for ⅕ mile (⅓ kilometer) to Admirals Walk and down to the cove.

Facilities: Air fills in Deep Cove, Sidney and Victoria. Camping in summer at Brent-wood Bay, and at McDonald Provincial Park.

Access: Setchell Point is on Saanich Inlet near the top of Saanich Peninsula west of Swartz Bay ferry terminal. Reach it by way of Wain Road and Madrona Drive off West Saanich Road (Highway 17A). It is 40 minutes from the Empress Hotel in Victoria.
   From Patricia Bay Highway (Highway 17) just south of Swartz Bay ferry terminal or from West Saanich Road (Highway 17A) just north of Brentwood Bay near the top of the inlet, go west on Wain Road to Madrona Drive. Turn right on Madrona, and go ⅕ mile (⅓ kilometer) to Setchell Road, and turn left to the end of the road. Room for two or three cars to park. Walk down a short rocky path to the water. After rain, the moss-covered rocks and tree roots are slippery.
• For a golf ball and marine life dive, head straight out from the point and to the left.
• For the wreck at Deep Cove, look to the right. On lower tides – up to 5 feet (1½ meters) – a buoy marks the wreck. The wreck is on a line from Setchell Point to a Tudor-style home on the opposite side of the cove. It is closer to shore than the red navigational marker and slightly off the end of the dock and float. If higher tide and the marker buoy is not visible, follow a 75-degree compass bearing from the rocks at the bottom of the trail at Setchell Point to the wreck. Swim about 500 feet (150 meters); it takes 10 to 15 minutes.

Comments: Blackeye gobies, tiny fish commonly seen at this site, start life as females; then when they reach 2½ to 3 inches (6 to 7½ centimeters) they become males.

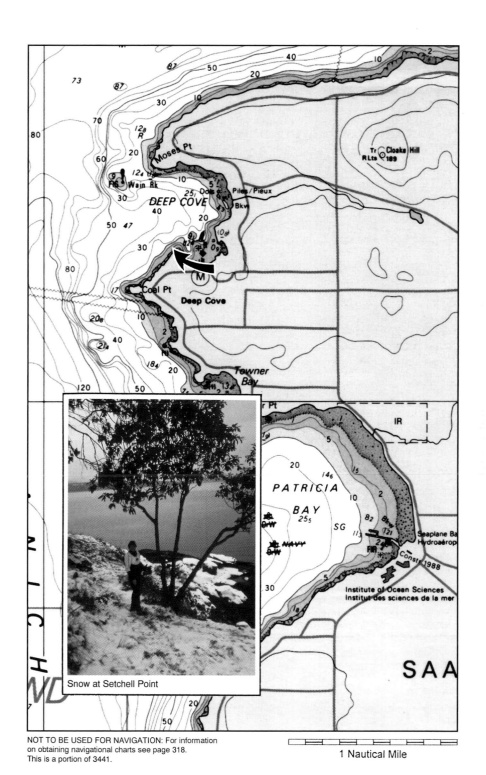

Snow at Setchell Point

NOT TO BE USED FOR NAVIGATION: For information
on obtaining navigational charts see page 318.
This is a portion of 3441.

1 Nautical Mile

83

TOZIER ROCK
Kayak Dive or Boat Dive

Skill: All divers

Why go: Wolf-eels lurch from their dens when divers bring urchins to the den where they live at Tozier Rock – "Miss Piggy" lives here. Octopuses too. You can easily go deep, yet ledges cascade down from the marker. There are places to stop all the way to the ridge at 70 to 80 feet (21 to 24 meters). White and orange plumose anemones tilt from the rocks. Lingcod and quillback rockfish swim in and out of the bottom kelp. And, if you find them, those octopuses, those friendly wolf-eels are here.
Look for lead fishing weights to salvage.

Bottom and Depths: Rocky bottom is 25 to 35 feet (8 to 11 meters) deep on the inlet side of the marker and cascades gently to the ridge at 70 to 80 feet (21 to 24 meters). From there, the bottom drops away into the dark fjord. Flat sandy bottom 20 to 30 feet (6 to 9 meters) on the west side of the marker.

Hazards: Small boats and broken fishing line. Red jellyfish, in the fall. Poor visibility, in summer. Possible danger to kayak-divers by overexertion after the dive. Listen for boats and ascend at the marker well out of the way of boats. Carry a knife. If you have seen any red jellyfish, check for stinging tentacles before removing masks and gloves. Kayak-divers who have dived deep should rest before paddling back; the risk of bends may be increased by overexertion after diving.

Telephones: • Marina at Mill Bay, outside restrooms. • Brentwood Bay, top of ferry landing. • Tsartlip campground office south of store at Brentwood Bay.

Facilities: None at Tozier Rock. Air fills and charters in Victoria, Sidney and Deep Cove; boat rentals in Deep Cove and Mill Bay; launching at Mill Bay; launching year-round at Tsartlip campground in Brentwood Bay, and camping in summer. Dive-kayak rentals in Nanaimo.

Access: Tozier Rock is near Mill Bay ferry landing on the west side of Saanich Inlet. It is 2½ nautical miles (4½ kilometers) southeast of Mill Bay, 3 nautical miles (6 kilometers) northwest of Brentwood Bay, 5 nautical miles (9 kilometers) southwest of Deep Cove.
Charters out of Victoria, Sidney or Deep Cove – even inflatable charters; boat rentals at Mill Bay and Deep Cove; launching at Mill Bay and Brentwood Bay. Kayak-divers could paddle close to shore from Mill Bay for 2½ nautical miles (4½ kilometers) to the dive, anchor near the marker, gear up in shallow water and dive. Beaches to land on all the way, but do not go above high tide line as the property is privately owned. On a calm day, kayak-divers could paddle from Brentwood Bay across the open water of Saanich Inlet to Tozier. But beware of southeast wind, especially in winter. If poor visibility on the surface, do not dismiss the dive – quite often the water clears when you get to 30 feet (9 meters) deep.
Anchor south of the marker in 30 to 40 feet (9 to 12 meters). Do not tie onto the marker. It is a federal offense to tamper with any aid to navigation. Dive southeast of the marker over rocks covered with bottom kelp to the ridge at a depth of 70 to 80 feet (21 to 24 meters). A single chimney sponge reaches out and up from the ledge wall at 65 to 75 feet (20 to 23 meters). One den is above it, another below it.

Comments: If diving on Saturday evening in July or August, watch for fireworks behind Brentwood Bay at Butchart Gardens.

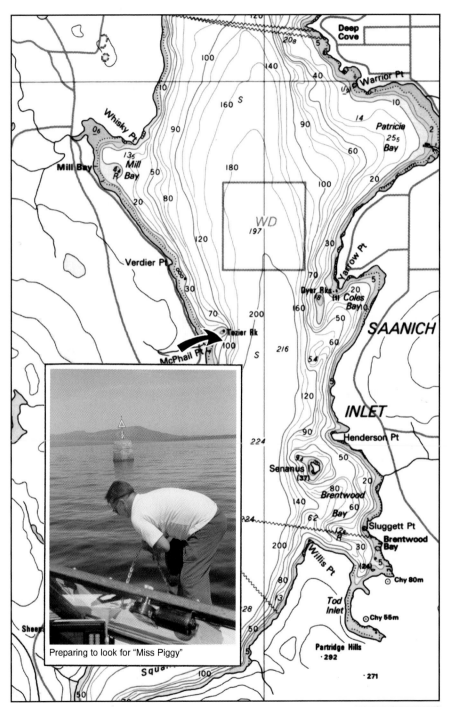

Preparing to look for "Miss Piggy"

NOT TO BE USED FOR NAVIGATION: For information
on obtaining navigational charts see page 318.
This is a portion of L/C-3462.

1 Nautical Mile

85

HENDERSON POINT
Shore Dive

Tide Table: Fulford Harbour

Skill: All divers and snorkelers

Why go: Henderson Point is popular with all divers, day and night, because of easy access, few hazards and a variety of underwater life. Excellent for new divers.
Nudibranchs, big and little, decorator crabs, painted greenlings, kelp greenlings, seaperch, lots of little rockfish and moon jellyfish, you can expect to see them all. We saw one boulder splashed with masses of delicate zoanthids. Look for octopuses, rock scallops and dogfish. They are harder to find, but also present.

Bottom and Depths: Smooth rocks on the shore give way to small rocks scattered with bottom kelp and an occasional boulder. The slope is gentle to smooth sand at 50 to 60 feet (15 to 18 meters) right in front of Henderson Point. To the right, a shallow reef. South of the point, deep chasms of rock.

Hazards: Small boats and poor visibility, in summer. Red jellyfish, in the fall. Listen for boats and ascend along the bottom all the way to shore, well out of the way of them. If you have seen any red jellyfish, you and your buddy should check one another for stinging tentacles before removing your masks and gloves.

Telephone: Prairie Inn, 3 miles (5 kilometers) back at junction of Mount Newton Cross Road and East Saanich Road.

Facilities: None. Limited parking space and the site is very close to private homes. Make a toilet stop before you go; be quiet, when there; and clean up before you leave. In summer, camping at Tsartlip campground at Brentwood Bay, and at McDonald Provincial Park. Dive-kayak rentals in Nanaimo and Vancouver.

Access: Henderson Point is on Saanich Inlet at the north end of Brentwood Bay. It is 10 minutes off Patricia Bay Highway (Highway 17).
From Highway 17 and Mount Newton Cross Road junction, go west 3½ miles (5½ kilometers) on Mount Newton Cross Road. Cross East Saanich Road, then West Saanich Road. Continue west on Senanus Drive another ½ mile (¾ kilometer) to the end of the road. A gravel turnaround gives room for four or five cars to park. If too many divers, come back another day. If not overcrowded, walk 50 paces through the woods to the easy rocky entry.

To get to Mount Newton Cross Road and Highway 17
• From the Parliament Buildings in Victoria – and from the Port Angeles ferry which lands in front of the Parliament Buildings, it takes 35 minutes to Henderson Point. Head north on Blanshard Street (Highway 17) toward Swartz Bay ferry terminal; go 8 miles (13 kilometers) to Mount Newton Cross Road.
• From Swartz Bay and from Sidney ferry terminals to Henderson Point takes 15 minutes. Head south on Highway 17 and follow signs toward Brentwood Bay to Mount Newton Cross Road.
• From Duncan heading south on Highway 1: past Helmcken Road, turn left following signs to "Ferries, Sidney, 17 North and University of Victoria". From this turnoff, 30 minutes to Henderson Point. Go to Highway 17 and then north to Mount Newton Cross Road.
• From Mill Bay ferry at Brentwood Bay, it takes 10 minutes to reach Henderson Point. From the ferry landing, go to West Saanich Road and turn left. Go north on West Saanich Road to Senanus Drive/Mount Newton Cross Road.

Comments: The rocks at Henderson Point make a good picnic spot in the afternoon sun. But be sure to pack out all you took in.

Zoanthids at Henderson Point

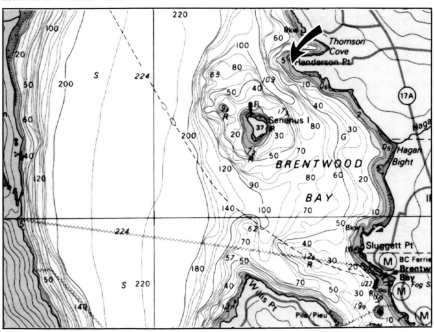

NOT TO BE USED FOR NAVIGATION: For information
on obtaining navigational charts see page 318.
This is a portion of 3441.

1 Nautical Mile

TOD INLET
Kayak Dive and Boat Dive

Tide Table: Fulford Harbour

Skill: All divers

Why go: Tod Inlet is well-protected from almost all winds and so close to Brentwood Bay that I cannot imagine why anything remains. But it does.

In Tod Inlet there is supposed to be a sunken barge – if you can find it. Bottles from an old Chinese settlement could make exotic "finds" for your collection. Plus the ever-present beauty of marine life. We saw red rock crabs and good-sized lingcod, too. I delighted in the sensation of sailing through space, pushing light and airy planets with a flick of my finger as I made my way through thousands of opalescent moon jelly-fish. In summer, Tod Inlet is an ideal place to camp and kayak-dive as you can paddle from your campsite to the dive in twenty minutes; another day, paddle from your campsite to Butchart Gardens at the head of Tod Inlet for sightseeing on land. Yet another day, paddle north up the coast to dive, or south.

Bottom and Depths: Rocky bottom drops gradually to a depth of 30 to 40 feet (9 to 12 meters), then falls away fairly quickly to 80 feet (24 meters) or so. Very silty.

Hazards: Small boats and poor visibility. Red jellyfish, in the fall. Listen for boats and stay close to the bottom all the way to shore, well out of the way of those boats. If you have seen any red jellyfish, check one another for stinging tentacles before removing masks and gloves.

Telephone: • Brentwood Bay, top of ferry landing. • Tsartlip campground office south of store at Brentwood Bay.

Facilities: None at Tod Inlet. Air fills and charters in Victoria, Sidney and Deep Cove; boat rentals in Mill Bay and Deep Cove. Launching year-round, and camping in sum-mer at Tsartlip campground in Brentwood Bay. Camping year-round at Goldstream.

Access: Tod Inlet is on the east side of Saanich Inlet. It is a long, thin finger reaching into Saanich Peninsula at the south end of Brentwood Bay. Brentwood Bay is 15 minutes off Patricia Bay Highway (Highway 17).

Launch at Brentwood Bay or charter out of Deep Cove or Victoria and go to Tod Inlet. From Brentwood Bay, go by dive-kayak or by larger boat: head south and go for 1¾ nautical miles (3 kilometers) to Tod Inlet. Anchor or land at the point past Daphne Islet that is near Butchart Gardens and descend.

To get to Brentwood Bay

• From the Parliament Buildings in Victoria or coming off the ferry from Seattle or Port Angeles, 35 minutes to Brentwood Bay. Head north on Highway 17 towards Swartz Bay. Go to Royal Oak Drive which is Highway 17A. Head west to West Saanich Road and turn right, following a small sign toward the Mill Bay ferry. Go past the Astro-physical Observatory and continue to Brentwood. Turn left to the ferry landing.
• From Swartz Bay or Sidney ferry terminals to Brentwood Bay takes 25 minutes. Head south on Highway 17, and follow signs toward Mill Bay ferry. Turn right into McTavish Road and head west to West Saanich Road. Turn left. Go on West Saanich Road to Brentwood and turn right to the ferry landing.
• From Duncan heading south, leave Highway 1 at the Colwood exit, following signs toward "Ferries, Sidney, 17 North and University of Victoria". From the Colwood exit, 25 minutes to Brentwood Bay. Once on Highway 17, head north for 3 minutes. Then at Royal Oak Drive, follow signs to Highway 17A which is West Saanich Road. Go to

Brentwood and follow signs to the ferry landing.

Comments: After your dive, visit Butchart Gardens overlooking the inlet. A footpath goes from the water to the gardens.

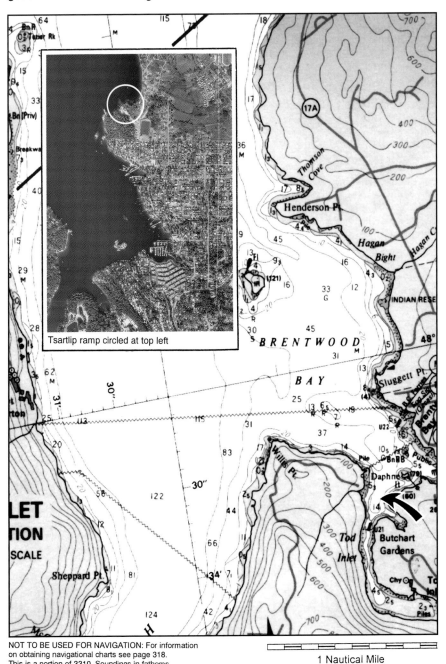

Tsartlip ramp circled at top left

NOT TO BE USED FOR NAVIGATION: For information
on obtaining navigational charts see page 318.
This is a portion of 3310. Soundings in fathoms.

1 Nautical Mile

WILLIS POINT
Shore Dive

Skill: All divers

Why go: Willis Point must be what off-the-wall is. You can fly out over the dark fjord into space, dive deep, then on the way up stop at a perfectly placed ledge with lettuce kelp and shimmering blue kelp. We saw orange plumose anemones and white ones, as well as wispy tube-dwelling anemones; nudibranch eggs, alabaster and dorid nudibranchs and a pale pink giant nudibranch – it was 1 foot (⅓ meter) long. We saw red slipper cucumbers and burrowing cucumbers. Blackeye gobies, quillback rockfish, blennies, silvery perch; sunflower stars, a big white sea star, a blood star. Red rock crabs, shrimp, rock scallops and large chimney sponges.

Willis Point is a protected inlet wall dive, the place-to-go when the wind is blowing outside. And no currents to consider.

Bottom and Depths: The wall starts past the rocky ledge covered with bottom kelp at 15 feet (5 meters). It drops to a ledge at 80 feet (24 meters) or so; then to a depth of 100 to 110 feet (30 to 34 meters). Overhangs scattered throughout.

Hazards: Boats and poor visibility, in summer; red jellyfish, in the fall. Listen for boats and ascend close to the wall all the way to the surface. If you have seen any red jellyfish, check for stinging tentacles before removing masks and gloves.

Telephones: • West Saanich Road, at gas station 1 mile (1½ kilometers) *south* of Wallace Drive. • Brentwood Shopping Centre, at West Saanich Road and southeast corner of Keating Cross Road; 2 miles (3½ kilometers) *north* of Wallace Drive.

Facilities: None at Willis Point. Camping near Trans-Canada Highway 1 at the head of the inlet at Goldstream, and across the inlet at Bamberton Provincial Park.

Access: Willis Point is south of Brentwood Bay on the east side of Saanich Inlet. It is 12 minutes off West Saanich Road (Highway 17A).

At Wallace Drive and West Saanich Road, go west on Wallace and almost immediately turn left into Willis Point Road. You will see signs to Mount Work Regional Park. Go along this curving road through the woods for 5 miles (8 kilometers) to Mark Lane. Turn right. From there, ⅓ mile (½ kilometer) more to the dive. The road is twisting and narrow. Go down a steep hill. When coming close to a curve to the right and near the end of the homes, look for a gravel road on your left-hand side. It is an unmarked fire access road to the sea. You could back down it to drop gear, but park at the roadside in Mark Lane. Swim straight out and down to the ledges and wall.

To get to Wallace Drive and West Saanich Road
• From the Empress Hotel in Victoria – and from the Port Angeles ferry which lands at the Inner Harbour in front of the Empress, it takes 40 minutes to the dive. Head north on Blanshard Street toward Swartz Bay ferry terminal. Go on Highway 17 to Royal Oak Drive. Head west on Royal Oak to West Saanich Road (Highway 17A); turn right, and follow a small sign toward the Mill Bay ferry. Go past the Astrophysical Observatory and continue 1½ miles (2½ kilometers) to Wallace Drive.
• From Swartz Bay and from Sidney ferry terminals to the dive takes 40 minutes. Head south on Highway 17. Follow signs toward the Mill Bay ferry. Turn right into McTavish Road and go to West Saanich Road. Turn left. Go along West Saanich Road past the shops of Brentwood Bay and past turnoffs to Butchart Gardens: from Keating Cross Road, go 2 miles (3½ kilometers) to Wallace Drive.

• From Duncan heading south on Highway 1: when just past Helmcken Road, follow signs to "Ferries, Sidney, 17 North and University of Victoria" – from this turnoff, 30 minutes to the dive. Go to Highway 17 and head north to Royal Oak Drive (Highway 17A) which goes to West Saanich Road. Turn right and go to Wallace Drive.
• From Mill Bay ferry at Brentwood Bay, it takes 20 minutes to reach Willis Point. From the ferry, turn right onto West Saanich Road and go to Wallace Drive.

Comments: Take a light for looking into crevices.

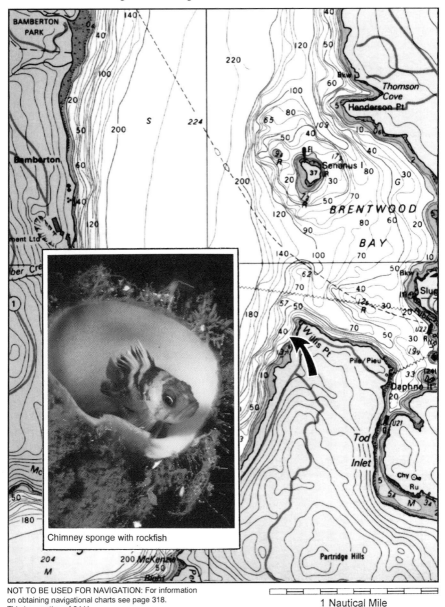

Chimney sponge with rockfish

NOT TO BE USED FOR NAVIGATION: For information on obtaining navigational charts see page 318. This is a portion of 3441.

1 Nautical Mile

THE WHITE LADY
Boat Dive

Tide Table: Fulford Harbour

Skill: All divers

Why go: To see the "Valley of White Sponges". . . where cloud sponges are "so large a diver can jump into them". This extravagant tale helps lure one to The White Lady. Because the magical valley has thus far eluded me, I have to go back. I'm not sure if the whole thing is a dream or not, but it's a nice one. I suspect the divers who took me there were concerned about diver damage to the sponges – a legitimate concern – and did not want me to find the valley. Or else it is too deep for the limits I write about, which is 125 feet (38 meters). If *you* find the valley, *don't* jump into the sponges!

And there's much, much more to see at this wonderful seamount. We saw chimney sponges, tiger rockfish, lingcod, moon jellyfish, sea pens, seals, small nudibranchs and hermit crabs on the seamount. Deer on the beach.

Bottom and Depths: Rocky seamount covered with bottom kelp undulates in the shallows around the marker in a deceptive manner to a depth of 30 to 40 feet (9 to 12 meters), then drops sharply on all sides. The shallows around the marker offer good diving for beginners. Intermediate and expert divers may want to drop deeper to explore for The Valley.

Hazards: Small boats, broken fishing line, and poor visibility. Red jellyfish, in the fall. Listen for boats; if you hear one, stay down until it passes. Even when using your compass, surfacing by the marker is difficult because the bottom immediately around the marker undulates in a deceptive manner. Carry a knife. If you have seen any red jellyfish, check for stinging tentacles before removing masks and gloves.

Telephones: • Goldstream Boathouse at head of Saanich Inlet. • Brentwood Bay, top of ferry landing. • Tsartlip campground office south of store at Brentwood Bay.

Facilities: Small rocky crescent beach near the marker on Repulse Rock is pleasant for a picnic in the wilds. Air fills and charters in Victoria, Sidney and Deep Cove. Boat rentals in Deep Cove and Mill Bay. Launching in Victoria at head of Saanich Inlet, and camping year-round nearby at Goldstream Park. Launching year-round and camping in summer at Tsartlip campground in Brentwood Bay.

Access: The White Lady is three-fourths of the way down the east side of Saanich Inlet. It is 3 nautical miles (6 kilometers) north of the head of Saanich Inlet and 5 nautical miles (9 kilometers) south of Brentwood Bay.

Charter, rent a boat or launch in Victoria, Deep Cove, Brentwood Bay or Sidney. Then go by boat north from the head of Saanich Inlet in Victoria for 3 nautical miles (6 kilometers) to Repulse Rock or The White Lady, which is marked with the usual triangular "white lady" marker, 50 yards (45 meters) offshore from Elbow Point. Or go south by boat from Brentwood Bay, Deep Cove or Sidney to Elbow Point.

Anchor, do not tie onto marker. It is a federal offense to make fast to a marker or tamper with any aid to navigation. Or land on the small rocky beach, and swim out and go down. One diver told me the Valley of White Sponges starts at 90 to 100 feet (27 to 30 meters) below the southeast corner of the marker. Another said at 105 to 115 feet (32 to 35 meters) north of the marker. I have searched on the north side and did not find it. Look under a ledge on the south/southeast side and you might find the Hidden Valley of White Sponges.

Comments: If you find The Valley please lead me to it!

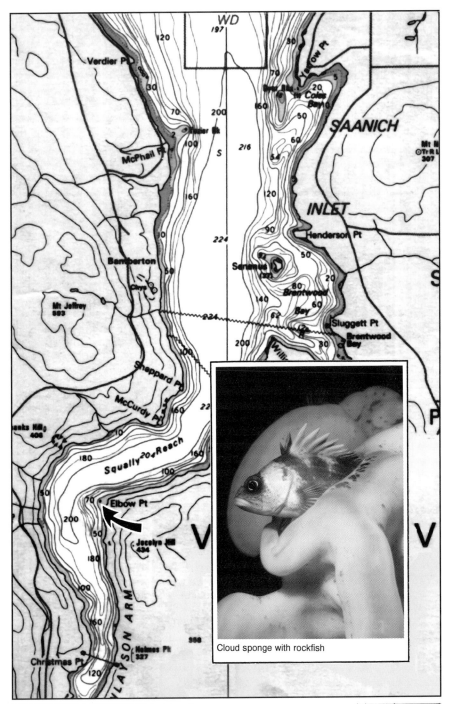

Cloud sponge with rockfish

NOT TO BE USED FOR NAVIGATION: For information
on obtaining navigational charts see page 318.
This is a portion of L/C-3462.

1 Nautical Mile

93

CHRISTMAS POINT
Kayak Dive or Boat Dive

Skill: All divers

Why go: Christmas Point is bright, it's dark, it's spooky. Interesting shallow and deep. Sea stars decorate the rocks near shore: they look like purple and red ornaments on a Christmas tree. Moon jellyfish pulse in the open water like transparent baubles.

As we started paddling our dive-kayaks up the inlet, one seal was following us. When we landed at the point to gear up, an audience of thirty harbor seals came close to watch, flip their tails, splash and play. We felt on stage for the amusement of the seals staring at us. But when we went down they slipped away. I saw only one seal under water, my buddy saw two.

A few kelp greenlings were in the shallows, but very few fish – probably frightened away by the seals. At the edge of the drop-off, we peered into dark nothingness; then we went shallower to find blackeye gobies, large prawns hiding in the kelp, an orange crab with white dots, piles of empty clam shells and crab shells in the rocks, but no octopus. The octopus was probably prowling about – it was night. Shallower still, schools of tiny fish that looked like gold fish were darting between plumose anemones on wooden wreckage. Though the herd of seals "made" this dive for me, there is much more to see and imagine at this site.

On the surface, without anything else, it was spooky paddling back in total darkness. Then my buddy told me about the Cadborosaurus, the legendary – or maybe not so legendary – gentle dragon-like creatures that most people refer to as "Caddy" and that some biologists now believe to be real. The cryptozoologists say that Saanich Inlet is the major breeding ground of these serpentine sea-dwellers that are said to be as long as 60 feet (18 meters). The Caddies have thin coils on their long necks, and heads like a horse or camel. They are shy deep-water animals that come up to feed on ducks at night. Numerous Caddy sightings from Oregon to Alaska have been reported during the past century – many in the Victoria region, with two reported sightings at Saanich Inlet in 1993.

Bottom and Depths: Broken rock covered with brown bottom kelp and iridescent blue kelp drops to a ledge at 35 to 45 feet (11 to 14 meters); another ledge at 75 to 85 feet (23 to 26 meters), depending on tide height. Then plunges. The depth on the chart is 400 feet (120 meters).

Hazards: Small boats, poor visibility; red jellyfish, in the fall. Possible danger to kayak-divers by overexertion after the dive. Listen for boats, and ascend close to the contours of the bottom all the way to the surface. If you have seen red jellyfish, check one another for stinging tentacles before removing masks and gloves. Kayak-divers who have dived deep should rest before paddling back. The risk of bends may increase with strenuous exercise after diving.

Telephones: • Goldstream Boathouse by office, at head of Saanich Inlet. • Brentwood Bay, top of ferry landing. • Tsartlip campground office.

Facilities: None at Christmas Point.

Access: Christmas Point is on the west side of Finlayson Arm just over 1 nautical mile (2 kilometers) from the head of Saanich Inlet.

Charter, rent a boat or launch your own boat or dive-kayak at the ramp at the head of Saanich Inlet. Go north just over 1 nautical mile (2 kilometers) to the giant checkerboard marker on the left-hand side of the inlet. It is beneath the power line.

Or go south by boat for 8 to 12 nautical miles (24 to 36 kilometers) from Brentwood Bay, Deep Cove or Mill Bay to Christmas Point.

If going by dive-kayak, easiest to paddle on an ebbing tide, dive at slack and paddle back with the flood.

Comments: After-dive library research revealed that the point is named after Emily Christmas and not because of its bright stars.

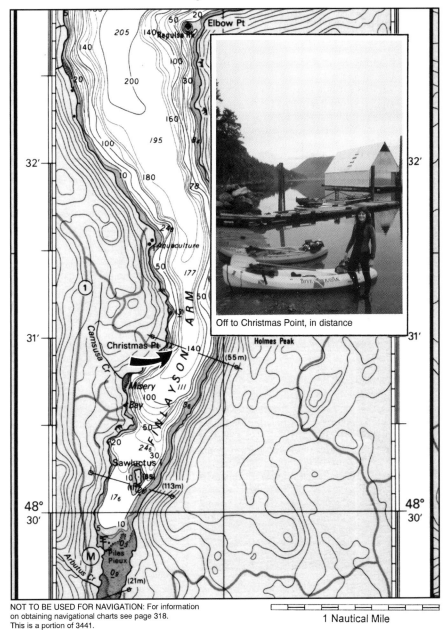

Off to Christmas Point, in distance

1 Nautical Mile

MISERY BAY
Kayak Dive or Boat Dive

Skill: All divers

Why go: Monstrous chimney sponges reach out from the fjord-like free-fall wall at Misery Bay. You can so easily go deep. Yet there are ledges at 50 to 60 feet (15 to 18 meters), if that's where you want to stop. Large lingcod were once plentiful, but they're harder to find these days. Rockfish hang near the wall, and look for gorgeous silver nudibranchs, octopuses, wolf-eels and those monstrous chimney sponges.

This bay is popular with line fishermen, too. And therefore a fine place for divers to salvage lead fishing weights.

Bottom and Depths: Dark, jagged, rocky bottom is 25 to 35 feet (8 to 11 meters) deep near shore and falls to a broad rocky ledge at 50 to 60 feet (15 to 18 meters). From here the bottom drops away into the dark fjord. Light silt over all.

Hazards: Small boats and broken fishing line. Red jellyfish, in the fall. Possible danger to kayak-divers by overexertion after the dive. Listen for boats and ascend close to the wall all the way to the surface, well out of the way of those boats. Carry a knife. If you have seen any red jellyfish, you and your buddy should check one another for stinging tentacles before removing your masks and gloves. Kayak-divers who have dived deep should rest before paddling back. The risk of bends may increase with strenuous exercise after diving.

Telephones: • Goldstream Boathouse at head of Saanich Inlet. • Brentwood Bay, top of ferry landing. • Tsartlip campground office south of store at Brentwood Bay.

Facilities: None at Misery Bay. Air fills and charters in Victoria, Sidney and Deep Cove. Launching in Victoria at head of Saanich Inlet, and camping year-round nearby at Goldstream Park. Launching year-round and camping, in summer, at Tsartlip campground in Brentwood Bay.

Access: Misery Bay is on the west side of Finlayson Arm. It is 1 nautical mile (2 kilometers) north of the head of Saanich Inlet, 8 to 12 nautical miles (24 to 36 kilometers) south of Brentwood Bay.

Charter, rent a boat or launch your own boat or dive-kayak at the ramp at the head of Saanich Inlet. Go north 1 nautical mile (2 kilometers) toward the giant checkerboard marker on the left-hand side of the inlet at Christmas Point. Or go south by boat for 8 to 12 nautical miles (24 to 36 kilometers) from Brentwood Bay, Deep Cove or Mill Bay to Misery Bay, a well-defined bay just north of Sawluctus Island on the west side of Saanich Inlet. Anchor in the shallows at the southern point of the bay near a small private dock and dive south around the point.

If going by dive-kayak, easiest to paddle on an ebbing tide, dive at slack and paddle back with the flood.

Comments: A dark dive in the afternoon. Dive Misery Bay in the morning, and take a light.

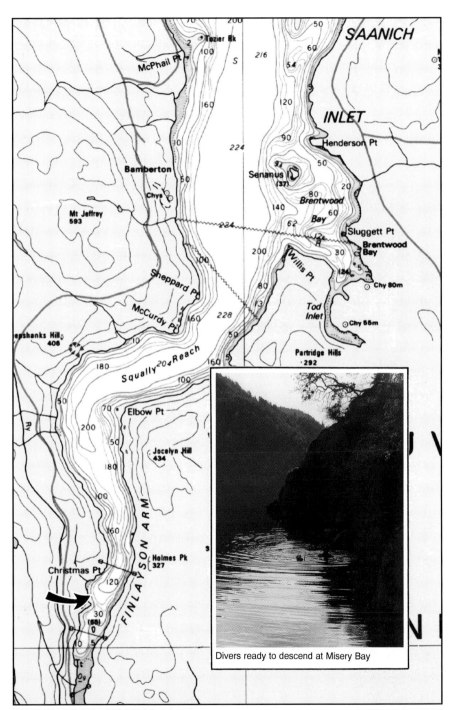

Divers ready to descend at Misery Bay

SAANICH

Tozier Bk

McPhail Pt

Bamberton

Mt Jeffrey
593

Chys

INLET

Henderson Pt

Senanus I
(37)

Brentwood
Bay

Sluggett Pt

Brentwood
Bay

Chy 80m

Sheppard Pt

McCurdy Pt

epshanks Hill
406

Squally Reach

Tod
Inlet

Chy 55m

Partridge Hills
·292

Elbow Pt

Ry

Jocelyn Hill
434

FINLAYSON ARM

Holmes Pk
327

Christmas Pt

NOT TO BE USED FOR NAVIGATION: For information
on obtaining navigational charts see page 318.
This is a portion of L/C-3462.

1 Nautical Mile

Lime Kiln Lighthouse on San Juan Island

At West Beach, Orcas Island

Photographer readies equipment in San Juans

CHAPTER 2
San Juan Islands
including San Juan, Orcas and Lopez

San Juan Islands as seen from space

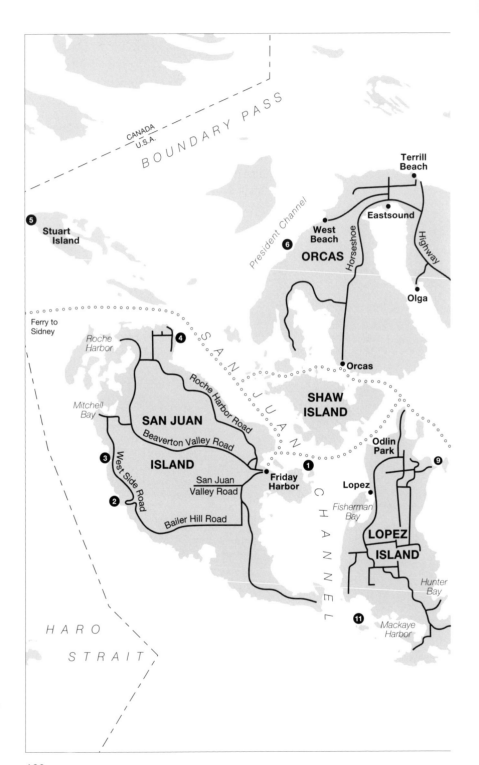

CANADA
U.S.A.

B O U N D A R Y   P A S S

⑤ Stuart Island

President Channel

Terrill Beach

West Beach

Eastsound

Horseshoe

⑥ ORCAS

Highway

Olga

Ferry to Sidney

S A N   J U A N

Roche Harbor

④

Orcas

Mitchell Bay

Roche Harbor Road

SHAW ISLAND

SAN JUAN

Beaverton Valley Road

Odlin Park

⑨

③

West Side Road

ISLAND

San Juan Valley Road

Friday Harbor

①

Lopez

Fisherman Bay

②

Bailer Hill Road

LOPEZ ISLAND

Hunter Bay

C H A N N E L

⑪

Mackaye Harbor

H A R O

S T R A I T

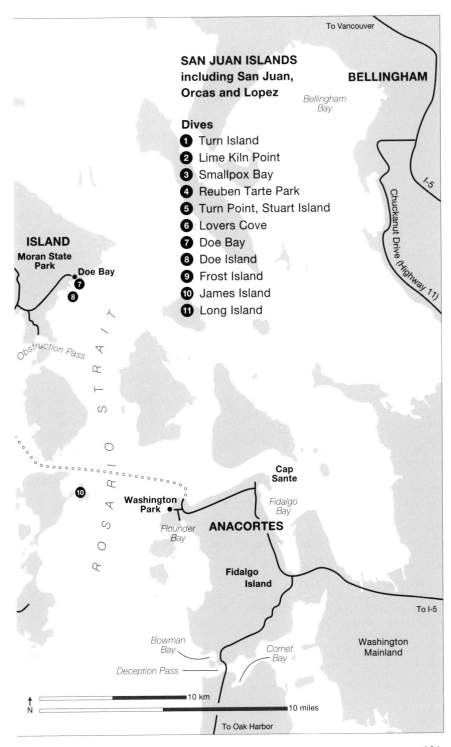

SAN JUAN ISLANDS
including San Juan,
Orcas and Lopez

Dives

1 Turn Island
2 Lime Kiln Point
3 Smallpox Bay
4 Reuben Tarte Park
5 Turn Point, Stuart Island
6 Lovers Cove
7 Doe Bay
8 Doe Island
9 Frost Island
10 James Island
11 Long Island

To Vancouver

BELLINGHAM

Bellingham Bay

I-5

Chuckanut Drive (Highway 11)

ISLAND
Moran State Park
Doe Bay
7
8

Obstruction Pass

R O S A R I O   S T R A I T

10

Washington Park

Flounder Bay

Cap Sante

Fidalgo Bay

ANACORTES

Fidalgo Island

To I-5

Washington Mainland

Bowman Bay

Cornet Bay

Deception Pass

10 km

N

10 miles

To Oak Harbor

SERVICE INFORMATION *
San Juan Islands
including San Juan, Orcas and Lopez

Charts: United States of America NOAA National Ocean Service
* 18421 Strait of Juan de Fuca to Strait of Georgia
* 18423 Bellingham to Everett including San Juan Islands (small-craft folio)
* 18429 Rosario Strait, Southern Part
* 18430 Rosario Strait, Northern Part
* 18432 Boundary Pass
* 18433 Haro Strait, Middle Bank to Stuart Island
* 18434 San Juan Channel

Tide and Current Tables
United States of America NOAA National Ocean Service
Tide Tables, West Coast of North and South America and *Tidal Current Tables, Pacific Coast of North America and Asia North*
or
Canadian Hydrographic Service
Tide and Current Table, Volume 5 and Canadian Hydrographic Service *Current Atlas: Juan de Fuca Strait to Strait of Georgia* (use with *Murray's Tables* or *Washburne's Tables*)

Diving Emergency Telephone Numbers
Dial 911: Say "I have a scuba diving emergency".

Virginia Mason Hospital: To reach the hyperbaric unit, dial (206) 624-1144, ask for Emergency Room, then say "I have a scuba diving emergency".

If medical personnel are unfamiliar with scuba diving emergencies, ask them to telephone DAN (Divers Alert Network): (919) 684-8111, then say "I have a scuba diving emergency".

More Telephone Numbers
Continuous Marine Broadcast (CMB) recorded, 24 hours. Depending on where you are, listen for weather in the Strait of Georgia, Haro Strait or Juan de Fuca Strait, telephone
* Victoria (604) 474-7998
* Vancouver (604) 270-7411
Red Tide Hotline 1-800-562-5632
Sportfishing Information Lines (206) 976-3200 or (206) 427-9500

• Dive Shops and Air Stations
Orcas Island
West Beach Resort
Enchanted Forest Road, end of road
Located at west side of Orcas
Island – not in town
Route 1, Box 510
Eastsound WA 98245
(206) 376-2240
(Air station: air fills at waterfront and roadside; also dive-kayak rentals and boat rentals.)

Lopez Island
Lopez Diving Service
Shark Reef Road, where the anchor is
PO Box 340
Lopez WA 98261
(206) 468-2054
(Air station: telephone to arrange for air fills.)

• Dive Shop and Air Station
San Juan Island
Emerald Seas Aquatics
180 First Street
PO Box 476
Friday Harbor WA 98250
(206) 378-2772; fax (206) 378-5549
(Dive shop; also charters and dive-kayak rentals.)

• Boat Rentals at San Juan Islands
Orcas Island
West Beach Resort
Enchanted Forest Road, end of road
West side of Orcas Island – not in town
(206) 376-2240
(Boat rentals, dive-kayak rentals and launching on President Channel: concrete ramp good at high tides only for large boats, all tides for small boats. Also air fills, hot showers and restrooms. Telephone at head of dock, another on shower house.)

San Juan Island
Emerald Seas Aquatics
180 First Street
PO Box 476
Friday Harbor WA 98250
(206) 378-2772; fax (206) 378-5549
(Dive-kayak rentals and instruction.)

San Juan Boat Rentals & Tours
Port of Friday Harbor main dock
PO Box 2281
Friday Harbor WA 98250
(206) 378-3499
(Boat rentals; dive charters in winter.)

Ken's Diving & Towing
Friday Harbor Marina
PO Box 857
Friday Harbor WA 98250
(206) 378-5808
(Air station: telephone to arrange for air fills.)

• Boat Charters for San Juan Islands
Out of San Juan Island
Blackfish
San Juan Boat Rentals & Tours
Port of Friday Harbor main dock
PO Box 2281
Friday Harbor WA 98250
(206) 378-3499
(Day charters in winter; boat rentals year-round.)

Emerald Diver
Emerald Seas Aquatics
180 First Street
PO Box 476
Friday Harbor WA 98250
(206) 378-2772; fax (206) 378-5549
(Day charters year-round; wheelchair divers welcome. Also dive-kayak rentals and instruction.)

Jersey Girl
Mainstay Charter and Diving
180 First Street
PO Box 476
Friday Harbor WA 98250
(206) 378-2772; fax (206) 378-5549
(Day charters in San Juans.)

• Launching at Orcas Island
West Beach Resort
Enchanted Forest Road, end of road
West side of Orcas Island – not in town
(206) 376-2240
(Launching on President Channel: concrete ramp good at high tides only for large boats, all tides for small boats. Also air fills, boat rentals, dive-kayak rentals and hot showers and restrooms. Telephone at head of dock, another on shower house.)

Bartwood Lodge
Route 1, Box 1040
Eastsound WA 98245
(206) 376-2242
(Launching at Terrill Beach, north shore of Orcas. Concrete ramp, good at all except extreme low tides. No toilets; telephone outside bar and grill.)

From Orcas ferry landing, 15 minutes to Terrill Beach. Follow signs to the center of the village of Eastsound. turn left onto North Beach Road, and follow it for 1 mile (1¾ kilometers) to Andersen Road. Turn right. Go ¾ mile (1¼ kilometers) and turn left to Terrill Beach.

Obstruction Pass Public Ramp
Orcas Island, southeast side
(Launching at Obstruction Pass. Concrete and sand ramp, good at all tides. Toilet; telephone just west of ramp, outside resort.)
From Orcas ferry landing, 35 minutes to Obstruction Pass. Follow signs through the village of Eastsound. Go past the head of the sound to a "T" junction and turn right. Follow signs toward Olga and Mount Constitution. Go through Moran State Park. After crossing a one-lane bridge and leaving the park, go 1½ miles (2½ kilometers) to a café at Olga. Turn left. Continue ½ mile (¾ kilometer) and turn right onto a side road. Go 2 miles (3 kilometers) more to Obstruction Pass public ramp. It is next to Lieber Haven Marina Resort.

• Launching at Lopez Island

Odlin County Park Public Ramp
North end, Lopez Island
RR 2, Box 3216
Lopez WA 98261
(206) 468-2496
(Launching for a fee at Upright Channel, north end of Lopez. Concrete and sand ramp, good at medium and high tides.)
From the ferry landing, go 1¼ miles (2 kilometers). Turn right. Camping, pit toilets and telephone at entrance to park; another telephone back at ferry landing.

Islands Marine Center (IMC) Ramp
Fisherman Bay, west side Lopez
PO Box 88
Lopez WA 98261
(206) 468-3377; fax (206) 468-2283
(Launching at Fisherman Bay: concrete ramp, good at high tides of 6 feet [2 meters] and greater, for small boats. Hot showers and restrooms. Free telephone at dock).

Hunter Bay Public Ramp
End of Islandale Road
Lopez Island, southeast side
(Launching at Hunter Bay, east side Lopez: concrete ramp, good at all except extreme low tides. Pit toilets and telephone 2 miles [3½ kilometers] away – go west and south to junction of Mud Bay Road and Mackaye Harbor Road to find the telephone.)
Located at southeast Lopez, 11 miles (18 kilometers) from the ferry. From the ferry, go to a "T" junction. Take the left fork and go south for 7 miles (11 kilometers) on Center Road. At another "T", go left into Islandale and to the end of it.

Mackaye Harbor Public Ramp
Lopez Island, southwest end
(Launching at Mackaye Harbor, southwest side Lopez: steep grooved concrete ramp, good at all except extreme low tides. Pit toilets and telephone ⅓ mile [½ kilometer] away at junction of Mud Bay Road and Mackaye Harbor Road.)
Located at south Lopez, 11 miles (18 kilometers) from the ferry. From the ferry, go to a "T" junction. Take the left fork and go south for 7 miles (11 kilometers) on Center Road. At a "T", go left. Past Islandale Road, continue ½ mile (1 kilometer) on Mud Bay Road. Turn right off Mud Bay Road and right, again, following signs to Mackaye Harbor.

- **Launching at San Juan Island**
San Juan County Park Public Ramp
380 West Side Road North
Friday Harbor WA 98250
(206) 378-2992
(Launching at Smallpox Bay for Haro Strait: deeply grooved concrete and sand ramp, good at all tides for small boats. At low tides, not for large boats. Also camping – reservations advisable in summer; flush toilets and telephone.)
   Located on west side of the island, see directions to Smallpox Bay, page 114.

Snug Harbor Marina Resort
2371 Mitchell Bay Road
Friday Harbor WA 98250
(206) 378-4762
(Launching at Mitchell Bay for Haro Strait: concrete ramp, good at high tides. Also boat rentals, divers' accommodations and dive packages including cabin, campsite or your RV. Hot showers, restrooms and telephone. Air fills for resort guests only.)

Roche Harbor Resort
PO Box 4001
Roche Harbor WA 98250
(206) 378-2155
(Launching at Roche Harbor for Haro Strait: concrete ramp, good at high tides, small boats only. Hot showers and restrooms at marina. Telephones at gas dock and hotel.)

Services on Mainland for San Juan Islands
- **Boat Charters to San Juan Islands**
Out of Anacortes
Sea Wolf
Discovery Charters
PO Box 636
Anacortes WA 98221-0636
(206) 293-4248
(Weekend liveaboard charters to San Juans. Also 5- and 7-day liveaboard trips to San Juans and Gulf Islands.)

Caldo
Caldo Charters
PO Box 1090
Milton WA 98354
(206) 941-3115
(Spring and summer, to San Juans.)

Kingfisher
Kingfisher Scuba Adventures
PO Box 779
Kingston WA 98346
(206) 598-3569
(Custom charters to the San Juans. Pick up at your location.)

Narcosis
Newport Aero Marine
12510 SE 63rd Street
Bellevue WA 98006
(206) 747-7931
(Year-round to San Juans.)

Starfire
Starfire Charters
849 NE 130th Street
Seattle WA 98125
(206) 364-9858
(Day charters and also occasional live-aboard charters to San Juans.)

Genie Aye
Down Time Ltd.
14404 SE 128th Street
Renton WA 98059
(206) 277-9069
(Day and occasional hotel-dive-package charters in the San Juans.)

Vertigo
Pacific Rim Diving, Inc.
13217 SE 54th Place
Bellevue WA 98006
(206) 643-6584; fax (206) 643-9730
(Custom charters. Accommodate wheelchair divers with prior notice.)

Out of Bellingham
Washington Diver I
Washington Divers
903 North State Street
Bellingham WA 98225
(206) 676-8029; fax (206) 647-5028
(Day charters year-round.)

- **Boat Rentals at Whidbey Island and Bellingham**

Whidbey Island Dive Center
9050-D 900th Avenue W
Oak Harbor WA 98277
(206) 675-1112
(Dive-kayak rental; also air fills.)

Adventures Down Under
701 East Holly Street
Bellingham WA 98225
(206) 676-4177
(Dive-kayak rentals; also air fills.)

Washington Divers
903 North State Street
Bellingham WA 98225
(206) 676-8029; fax (206) 647-5028
(Dive-kayak rentals; also charters, dive guiding and air fills.)

The Great Adventure
201 East Chestnut Street
Bellingham WA 98225
(206) 671-4615
(Dive-kayak rentals.)

- **Launching for Rosario Strait at Whidbey Island, Anacortes and Bellingham**

Cornet Bay Public Ramp
Deception Pass State Park
Whidbey Island, north end
(Concrete ramp: good at all except extreme low tides. Restrooms and hot showers. Telephone at top of privately owned dock at Cornet Bay. It is opposite Canyon Road and ⅓ mile [½ kilometer] west of the public ramp.)
    From Highway 20, when 1½ miles (2½ kilometers) *south* of Deception Pass Bridge, go east on Cornet Bay Road for 1⅓ miles (2¼ kilometers) to Cornet Bay Ramp.

Bowman Bay Public Ramp
Deception Pass State Park
Fidalgo Island, south end
(Concrete ramp for a fee: good only at high tides. Lots of parking space; picnic tables. Telephone and restrooms at CCC Interpretive Center.)
    Off Highway 20: immediately *north* of Deception Pass Bridge and south of Pass Lake, turn west. Follow signs to Bowman Bay.

Washington Park Ramp
Fidalgo Island, north end
Anacortes WA
(Launching at Fidalgo Head, near Anacortes ferry terminal: steep concrete ramp, good at all tides for small boats – can be difficult for larger boats; coin-operated gate to it. Restrooms and coin-operated hot showers. Telephone in front of park superintendent's home beside curve of drive out.)
    Washington Park is 4 miles (6 kilometers) west of Anacortes off Highway 20. Follow signs through Anacortes toward San Juan ferry. From Commercial Avenue and 12th, go 3 miles (5 kilometers) toward the ferry. You will see a sign to a marina: just past it, bear left – do not go straight to the ferry which is ½ mile (1 kilometer). Bear left through the stop sign and go on Sunset Avenue for ¾ mile (1¼ kilometers) to Washington Park Ramp at the end of the road.

Cap Sante Marine
Cap Sante Boat Haven
Next to Harbor Office
PO Box 607
Anacortes WA 98221
(206) 293-3145; 1-800-422-5794
(Sling launch at Fidalgo Bay in city of Anacortes. Restrooms and hot showers; telephones beside marina office.)

Skyline Marina
2011 Skyline Way
Anacortes WA 98221
(206) 293-5134; fax (206) 293-9458
(Sling launch at Flounder Bay, south of Fidalgo Head near Anacortes ferry terminal. Restrooms and hot showers; telephones beside marina office.)

Wildcat Cove Public Ramp
Larrabee State Park
Foot of Cove Road, off Chuckanut Drive
Bellingham WA
(Tarmac ramp; good at medium and high tides. Pit toilets, a picnic table and lots of parking space. Telephone at campground, south on Chuckanut Drive.)
   Located 15 to 25 minutes off I-5 (Interstate Highway 5) between Bellingham and Mount Vernon at Wildcat Cove, south of Bellingham Bay.
• Heading south from Bellingham, take Exit 250 and follow signs to Chuckanut Drive (Highway 11) and Larrabee State Park. The road becomes narrow and curves alongside the water to the park. You will see signs to the launching ramp at Cove Road. From Bellingham, 15 minutes to Wildcat Cove.
• Heading north, past Mount Vernon and Burlington take Exit 231 to Chuckanut Drive (Highway 11) and head north – takes 25 minutes to the launch point. When 10 minutes past Bow-Edison Road and shortly past the two Larrabee campground entrances, you will reach Cove Road. Turn left to Wildcat Cove.

Fairhaven Public Ramp
Harris Avenue, immediately east of 355 Harris (across from 6th Street)
Bellingham Bay, south end
Bellingham WA
(Concrete ramp, good at all except extreme low tides. Limited parking space. Restrooms; and telephone outside restroom.)
   In Bellingham just east of Alaska ferry dock. From I-5 (Interstate Highway 5), take Exit 250 and follow signs to the Alaska ferry. The ramp is 2 miles (3 kilometers) off the highway. Go on Old Fairhaven Parkway to 12th Street. Turn right, then left onto Harris Avenue. The ramp is at the south end of the harbor.

Squalicum Harbor Ramp
Foot of Thomas J. Glenn Drive
Bellingham Bay, north end
Bellingham WA
(Launching for a fee: concrete ramps, good at all tides. Large parking space; freshwater taps in parking area to wash gear. Restrooms and telephones at north end of Harbor Center. Top of the ramp, turn left and walk 80 yards (75 meters) through Harbor Center to the facilities.)
   In Bellingham, 5 to 10 minutes off I-5 (Interstate Highway 5), at north end of Bellingham Bay. Turn off Roeder Avenue at Thomas J. Glenn Drive, and turn right at Boat Launch Parking sign to the ramps.
• Heading south on I-5, take Exit 256. Turn right at Meridian Street and go to traffic light at Squalicum Way. Turn right and follow the Squalicum Harbor signs toward the water; the road curves left into Roeder Avenue. Go on Roeder for just over ½ mile (1 kilometer) passing various harbor facilities. Go to the south end of Squalicum Harbor and turn right into Thomas J. Glenn Drive.
• Heading north on I-5, take Exit 253 to Lakeway Drive and go back under I-5. Go along Lakeway following Squalicum Harbor signs: follow Holly Street through the city center to F Street, turn right on Roeder Avenue, then left at Thomas J. Glenn Drive.

• For More Information on Launching Ramps
Dream a little – dream a lot! Explore for new sites on your own. Additional boat launching ramps and public beaches where you can land and dive from are listed in the following publications:

Henning's Guide to Boat Ramps, Elevators, Slings edited by Henning Helstrom, no date. Helstrom Publications, 3121 SE 167th Avenue, Portland, Oregon 97236, (503) 761-3139. (Scope: Washington and Oregon. Includes photographs of ramps described.)

Morgan's Guide: Boat Launches & Ramps on Puget Sound edited by Bill Hanson, 1991. Sound Publishing, PO Box 7192, Tacoma WA 98407, (206) 565-6568. (Scope: Puget Sound and the San Juan Islands. Well organized user-friendly information, useful for boaters with large craft and with dive-kayaks; well indexed.)

Puget Sound Public Shellfish Sites booklet compiled by Washington Department of Fisheries, 1111 Washington Street SE, PO Box 43136, Olympia WA 98504-3136, (206) 902-2250. Obtain free copy from some dive stores or from Washington Department of Fisheries or from Department of Natural Resources, DNR Photo and Map Sales, 1111 Washington Street SE, PO Box 47031, Olympia WA 98504-7031, (206) 902-1234. (Scope: from southern Puget Sound through San Juans.)

Washington Atlas & Gazetteer, DeLorme Mapping, PO Box 298, Freeport, Maine 04032, (207) 865-4171; toll-free in USA, 1-800-227-1656. (Scope: launching ramps throughout Washington.)

Washington Public Shore Guide: Marine Waters book by James W. Scott and Melly A. Reuling, University of Washington Press, PO Box 50096, Seattle WA 98145-5096, (206) 543-8870. (Scope: throughout Washington State.)

• More Dive Facilities
Discover Scuba
PO Box 33512
Seattle WA 98133
(206) 362-3863
(Guiding services throughout San Juan Islands; specialize in Whidbey Island dive packages including accommodations.)

• Ferry Information
Washington State Ferries
Colman Dock/Pier 52
801 Alaskan Way
Seattle WA 98104-1487
(206) 464-6400: recorded schedules with touch-tone menu choices.
Anacortes: (206) 293-8166
Sidney, British Columbia: (604) 381-1551
Toll-free in Washington State: 1-800-843-3779
(Ferries between Anacortes WA and Sidney BC.)

• Tourist Information

Orcas Island
Chamber of Commerce
PO Box 252
Eastsound WA 98245
(206) 376-2273

Lopez Island
Chamber of Commerce
PO Box 102
Lopez WA 98261
(206) 468-3800

San Juan Island
Chamber of Commerce
PO Box 98, 125 Spring Street
Friday Harbor WA 98250
(206) 378-5240

San Juan County Park Board
PO Box 86
Lopez WA 98261
(206) 468-2131

• Tourist Information for all San Juan Islands

San Juan Islands Visitor
Information Service
PO Box 65
Lopez WA 98261
(206) 468-3663

Washington State Tourism
101 General Administration Building
PO Box 42500
Olympia WA 98504-2500
1-800-544-1800: Toll-free throughout
Canada and the USA, including
Hawaii and Alaska, for *Travel Kit
(Lodging and Travel Guide* and
seasonal *Field Guide)* only.
(206) 586-2088 or (206) 586-2102 for
travel counselling. Parking is very difficult – it is easier to telephone or write.

Washington State Parks
Public Information
7150 Cleanwater Lane
PO Box 42650
Olympia WA 98504-2650
(206) 753-2027, message-taking ma-
chine and respond by mail. To reach a
person on the telephone, contact each
park.
*(Information on camping and launching
ramps.)*

How to Go – Go to the San Juan Islands via Washington State Ferry from Anacortes, Washington, or from Sidney, British Columbia, on Vancouver Island. Ask
about reservations; at the time of writing, only available to and from Sidney.

From the mainland
• Anacortes is accessed off I-5 (Interstate Highway 5): take Exit 230 and head west
on Highway 20 for 30 minutes through Anacortes to the San Juan ferry. Heading
north from Seattle, go 1¾ hours to the turnoff to Anacortes. Heading south from
Vancouver, go 1½ hours to the turnoff. From Bellingham, 30 minutes.

From Vancouver Island
• Sidney is on Saanich Peninsula: It is 13 miles (21 kilometers) north of Victoria and
4 miles (6 kilometers) south of Swartz Bay; then 1 mile (1½ kilometers) east of
Highway 17 at the end of Beacon Avenue. Follow the signs to Sidney. From Highway
17, it takes 5 minutes to the ferry.

*All of this service information is subject to change.

TURN ISLAND
Kayak Dive or Boat Dive

Tide Table: Port Townsend
Add 35 minutes to high slack
Add 56 minutes to low slack

Skill: Intermediate and expert divers

Why go: Rich marine life and an easy first kayak dive are two good reasons to go to Turn Island. Plus camping on Turn Island – it is a state park. The paddle is short and you can land and gear up on the beach. You could turn it into a week of paddling, camping and diving.

Christmas anemones, orange cup corals, flaming red slipper cucumbers and white plumose anemones are on the wall, between the rocks, in crevices. The color! Orange cucumbers and white ones, yellow staghorn bryozoans, gray sponges with knobs, and pink encrusting sponge covers the rocks. Red urchins, purple ones too. Black, copper and quillback rockfish. Lingcod. Swimming scallops. Blood stars. White anemones. Swimming back through the bull kelp and tall brown stalks of kelp, we saw schools of juvenile rockfish. Kelp greenlings. Kelp crabs. Snorkeling we saw moon jellyfish, lots of them, pulsing through the shallows.

My husband and I started the dive with another couple and when we met later on the beach learned that they were now one. He had proposed under water. She nodded yes and pulled off her neoprene mitt. He slid the diamond on her finger. A second surprise for the bride-to-be was that champagne and a dozen red roses were waiting on the sunny beach, delivered by inflatable. There were toasts for soon-to-be marrieds and old marrieds – very appropriate because my husband and I were celebrating our 35th wedding anniversary. We will all remember this day, this dive.

Bottom and Depths: Cobble and sandy beach give way to gravel and rocky bottom with bull kelp at 23 to 33 feet (7 to 10 meters). Around the point, ledges drop in gentle stairsteps. Rock walls indented with crevices, cracks and overhangs spill from ledge to ledge. We reached 70 feet (21 meters) before heading back. It goes deeper. You could also enjoy an entire dive in the shallows or snorkeling.

Hazards: Current, bull kelp and transparent fishing line as well as fishing lures. Dive on slack. Carry a knife.

Telephone: Friday Harbor ferry landing.

Facilities: Visitors may land, moor their boats, picnic, camp, build campfires, hike and dive from the beaches on Turn Island. Air fills, charters, boat rentals, dive-kayak rentals, hot showers at the Port of Friday Harbor.

Access: Turn Island is in San Juan Channel near Friday Harbor, San Juan Island. It is less than ½ nautical mile (1 kilometer) offshore from a public beach on San Juan Island where you can hand-launch a kayak and paddle to Turn Island. It takes 10 minutes. Or you could launch your own boat or charter.

At Turn Island, go north past the mooring buoys at the state park to the northern end of the island. Go to a tiny beach that is around the corner and close to San Juan Channel. Land, gear up and dive from the small beach or dive from your boat. Swim a short way out to the bull kelp and go down. Dive around the point on the right.

• Charters out of Friday Harbor, Anacortes and Bellingham. Or you could rent a boat at Friday Harbor or launch your own boat at Lopez and go to Turn Island. From Friday Harbor, 4 nautical miles (7 kilometers); from Lopez, 6 nautical miles (11 kilometers) to Turn Island.

• Kayak-divers: you reach San Juan Island via the Anacortes-San Juan Islands-

Sidney ferry route. From Anacortes to Friday Harbor on San Juan takes 1½ to 2 hours, depending on island stops. From Sidney to Friday Harbor, 1½ hours.

From Friday Harbor ferry landing to the public beach on San Juan Island, drive 2½ miles (4 kilometers). Head uphill on Spring Street to First Street. Turn left. Go past the ferry line-up; First Street becomes Harrison Street then Turn Point Road; continue straight along this main route. Past Sutherland Road, you will see the water and the main road curves to the right. Go straight and park beside the beach marked "public access". Wild blackberries beside it. From this log-strewn beach on San Juan Island, paddle to the left-hand side of Turn Island. Bring your own dive-kayak or rent one at Friday Harbor; if renting, telephone to arrange it. Wheelchair divers who paddle dive-kayaks and who can cross a small stretch of sand with some logs could dive at Turn Island.

Comments: After kayak-diving at Turn Island, you might want to paddle south to Reef Point, Danger Rock or Pear Point. Slightly longer paddles, but publicly owned beaches to gear up on. Looks interesting on the chart.

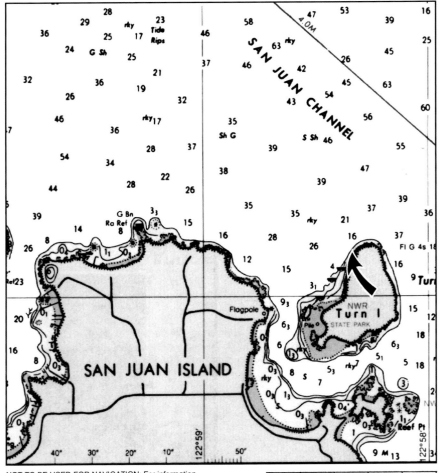

NOT TO BE USED FOR NAVIGATION: For information on obtaining navigational charts see page 318. This is a portion of 18423. Soundings are in fathoms.

½ Nautical Mile

LIME KILN POINT
Shore Dive

Skill: Expert divers

Tide Table: Port Townsend
Subtract 11 minutes from high slack
Subtract 2 minutes from low slack

Why go: Bright dive in the afternoon – the white shells reflect the sunlight. Abalones, gum boot chitons, lined chitons cling to the rocks. Mauve coralline algae feather the bottom from the bright white shallows to the olive-green world beneath the kelp.

Deeper, we see a glass tunicate like a miniature crystal vase. Pink hydrocorals and yellow staghorn bryozoans on the rocks. Giant red and purple urchins, rock scallops, dahlia anemones, white plumose anemones, feather stars, giant barnacles. We swim over a smooth roll of rock down to a ledge. Swimming scallops clap up around us from 30 feet (9 meters) and deeper. A few scallops are still present at 100 feet (30 meters). We see a lingcod, quillback rockfish, kelp greenlings. A giant octopus jets away.

The current is picking up: we crawl along holding onto rocks, cannot afford to let go, are glad when we reach bull kelp – it is something strong to hold onto. We have been lured deep, must stop on the way up. Lots to see in the shallows too: alabaster nudibranchs, sculpins. a Christmas anemone at 10 feet (3 meters). Brilliant red knobby sponge is on the rocks behind big fat leaves of brown bottom kelp.

Acorn barnacles – a giant's bed-of-nails – on the flat rocks near shore as we coast with the current to the lighthouse.

Bottom and Depths: Rocky bottom with brown bottom kelp slopes to a forest of bull kelp at 20 to 30 feet (6 to 9 meters). From there, rock rolls gently but quickly in a series of smooth ledges, folds and smooth walls to a depth of 110 to 120 feet (34 to 37 meters), depending on tide height. Scattered boulders.

Hazards: Current up to 4 knots (7½ kilometers/hour) in Haro Strait; bull kelp, in summer; and a long walk to the water. Dive on slack. Current at Lime Kiln runs parallel to shore and never stops, it just turns around. Carry a knife for kelp. After a deep dive, take it easy heading back to the parking lot; the possibility of bends may be increased by strenuous exercise after diving.

Telephone: San Juan County Park, outside office; 5 minutes north of Lime Kiln.

Facilities: Picnic tables and toilets at Lime Kiln State Park. Air fills at Friday Harbor. Camping at San Juan Park.

Access: Lime Kiln Point is on Haro Strait, southwest side of San Juan Island. San Juan is reached via the Anacortes-San Juan Islands-Sidney ferry route. From Anacortes to Friday Harbor on San Juan takes 1½ to 2 hours, depending on island stops. From Sidney to Friday Harbor, 1½ hours. Then drive 20 minutes to Lime Kiln.

At Lime Kiln Point State Park, follow signs to one of three entry points: for the easiest and safest entry, follow signs toward the lighthouse and when you see the lighthouse, turn north. Continue walking on a well graduated path and go 100 paces past the lighthouse to the abandoned dock in the bay just north of the lighthouse.

For the shortest walk to the site: follow signs from the parking lot to the whale-watching site; go 240 paces and then climb down the rocks to the water. Or, follow signs to the lighthouse, walking along a service road and trail. Go 250 paces to a picnic table – a magnificent spreading arbutus tree is beside it. You could enter at one of the rocky crevices past the arbutus tree and near the lighthouse. Surge from wind and passing freighters sometimes makes entry impossible at Lime Kiln. Dive on a calm day. Safer to dive on the turn to ebb; watch the current direction and work your way north of the lighthouse for half the dive. On the way back, if you accidentally surface you have a short way in which to swim across the current to the cove south of the lighthouse before being swept into Juan de Fuca. If you hit the current right, you can coast home.

To get to Lime Kiln State Park
• From Friday Harbor ferry landing, go 9 miles (14½ kilometers) to Lime Kiln Park: Drive uphill and out of town on Spring Street which runs into San Juan Valley Road. From the ferry, nearly 2 miles (3 kilometers) to Douglas Road. Turn left. At Bailer Hill Road, turn right. Bailer Hill Road runs into West Side Road and you follow it to Lime Kiln.
• Starting from San Juan Park, go 2½ miles (4 kilometers) south on West Side Road to Lime Kiln.

Comments: Lime Kiln Lighthouse was built around 1880. It became a whale research station in 1983, the first whale-watching park in the country in 1984. Killer whales swim past from June to September; the whale-watching lecturer who goes to the site every Sunday in summer says he sees them more than 50% of the times he is there. Divers sometimes meet whales under water at Lime Kiln.

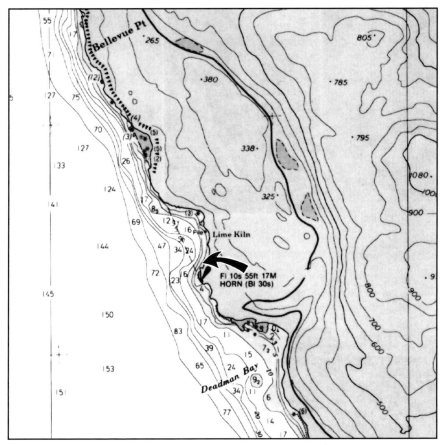

NOT TO BE USED FOR NAVIGATION: For information on obtaining navigational charts see page 318. This is a portion of 18433. Soundings are in fathoms.

½ Nautical Mile

113

SMALLPOX BAY
Shore Dive

Skill: All divers and snorkelers

Why go: Gorgeous seascape – fish and shellfish – plus clean, clear water. Since divers have flocked to Smallpox Bay at San Juan Park for years, I can't imagine how this is all still here, unspoilt and wild. But it is. And all so accessible. You can walk from your tent to the water.

New divers and snorkelers can enjoy easy diving in the bay with its shallow sandy bottom rimmed with rock. Even the tidepools hold lots of life. Small pastel green and pink anemones burgeon like flowers. Tufts of orange cucumbers soften the bright white rocks. Blue starfish, little green urchins, gum boot chitons, kelp greenlings, and giant red urchins decorate the rocky shallows.

Beyond the bay and south around the point you swim into bull kelp and rocky bottom falling away quickly into big-boulder country and rocky overhangs. Shrimp, big black rockfish, lingcod, white plumose anemones, bright yellow encrusting sponge, abalones, and swimming scallops are some of the animals you'll see. Look for octopuses, too. Good diving from a kayak or boat all along the southern shore. Try other sites but not nearby Low Island. People must not come closer to it than 200 yards (180 meters) because it is a San Juan Islands National Wildlife Refuge. This restriction is to protect the young birds, bald eagles and seal pups.

Bottom and Depths: In the bay the shallow sandy bottom is scattered with eelgrass. Rock rims the bay. Beyond the southern point of the bay where the bull kelp begins, the rocky bottom is 10 to 20 feet (3 to 6 meters) deep. From here it falls away fairly quickly in ledges and folds to a depth of 40 to 50 feet (12 to 15 meters) to big boulders, small caves and overhangs. Then into very deep water.

Hazards: Current. Bull kelp, in summer. Beyond the bay, dive on slack. Carry a knife for kelp.

Telephone: San Juan County Park, outside office.

Facilities: Campsites, flush toilets, picnic tables and launching ramp at San Juan County Park; in summer, reservations advisable. Air fills and charters at Friday Harbor; hot showers at the Port of Friday Harbor and at Roche Harbor Marina. At Snug Harbor Resort at Mitchell Bay, dive packages including cabin, campsite or your RV – but air fills for resort guests only.

Access: Smallpox Bay is on the west side of San Juan Island at San Juan County Park. San Juan is the westernmost island stop on the Anacortes-San Juan Islands-Sidney ferry route. From Anacortes to Friday Harbor at San Juan takes 1½ to 2 hours, depending on island stops. From Sidney to Friday Harbor, 1½ hours.

From Friday Harbor ferry landing, go 10 miles (16 kilometers) to the dive. Drive up the hill on Spring Street to Second Street. Turn right. Head out of town on Second which becomes Guard Street, later Beaverton Valley Road. At the Friday Harbor junction of Guard and Tucker, do not turn right to Roche Harbor but continue straight, following signs toward Mitchell Bay. From this junction, go 10 kilometers (6½ miles) along Guard and Beaverton Valley roads to Mitchell Bay Road. Turn left and go along Mitchell Bay Road for 1¼ miles (2 kilometers). When you see signs pointing straight ahead to Snug Harbor, turn left. Go 1¾ miles (3 kilometers) on West Side Road to San Juan County Park. For diving in the bay or beyond the southern point, enter over sandy beach in front of the campground office. Wheelchair access might be possible at the ridged concrete ramp with lots of sand on it – not officially, but it could work. Need able-bodied help to get over about 6 feet (2 meters) of sand.

Comments: When smallpox was rampant, many North American Indians who lived in the San Juans jumped into this bay, believing the saltwater plunge would cure them: thus the bay got its name.

Open-water certification dive at Smallpox Bay

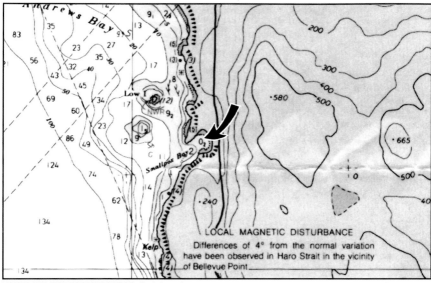

NOT TO BE USED FOR NAVIGATION: For information on obtaining navigational charts see page 318. This is a portion of 18433. Soundings are in fathoms.

½ Nautical Mile

REUBEN TARTE PARK
Shore

Skill: Intermediate and expert divers and snorkelers

Why go: A beautiful reef! The sort of reef you usually have to struggle over lots of water to reach. But here – when the road is open – it's within a few steps from the rocky beach.
The cove has the clean-swept look of a spot with current and much of the life that goes with it. Bright orange burrowing cucumbers, giant barnacles all over the bottom, rock scallops, a scattering of swimming scallops, rockfish, big sea cucumbers, lingcod, trumpet sponges and strange orange and white encrusting sponges. When diving here I held a red Irish lord. I saw a scarlet blenny with vertical stripes. Spider crabs, hermit crabs, and kelp greenlings flashing through the bull kelp. Lots of blue and yellow striped seaperch shimmering in the shallows. Chitons, limpets, bright blue sea stars and giant red urchins stuck to the rocks. It's a good place for available light photography.

Bottom and Depths: White rocky wall with overhangs and crevices drops to a depth of 25 to 35 feet (8 to 11 meters), then undulates slowly to a depth of 50 to 60 feet (15 to 18 meters) and levels off. Big white boulders are scattered around. Bottom kelp and bull kelp are attached to the bright white rocks. Take a light for looking into holes.

Hazards: Current and bull kelp. Dive on the slack. Carry a knife.

Telephones: • Roche Harbor, 6 miles (9½ kilometers) away. Go via Rouleau and Roche Harbor Roads, turn right and go to the end. • Friday Harbor ferry landing, 11 miles (17½ kilometers) away.

Facilities: Parking for four or five cars at Reuben Tarte. Accommodations nearby at Roche Harbor. Your choice – vintage hotel, cottages, or modern condominiums. Or camping at San Juan County Park – reservations advisable in summer.

Access: Reuben Tarte Park is on San Juan Channel at the southeast end of Spieden Channel. It is on the northeast side of San Juan Island. San Juan is reached via the Anacortes-San Juan Islands-Sidney ferry route. From Anacortes west to Friday Harbor at San Juan takes 1½ to 2 hours, depending on island stops. From Sidney to Friday Harbor, 1½ hours.
From Friday Harbor, go 11 miles (17½ kilometers) to Reuben Tarte County Park at the northeast corner of the island. The drive takes 20 minutes. From the ferry landing, head uphill on Spring Street to Second Street. Turn right. Go to Tucker Avenue and turn right following signs toward Roche Harbor and Lonesome Cove. Drive 7 miles (12 kilometers) along Roche Harbor Road, then turn right into Rouleau Road. Go along it to Limestone Point Road and turn right. At San Juan Drive, turn right again. Go ⅓ mile (½ kilometer) to the Reuben Tarte parking area.
From time to time the road from the parking lot to the beach is closed. Then you must walk 300 paces down the steep hill to the water – an extremely difficult hike with dive gear. I do not recommend this dive unless the road is open. But when the road is open this is a shore dive with very easy access. Then you can turn left down the steep hill, drop your gear and return up the hill to park. Once down the hill again, walk a few steps across the beach to the water. Dive around the point on your right.
The situation might change; at the time of writing the road is open for day-time loading and unloading only. Parking is permitted at the bottom of the hill for handicapped persons. If you are at San Juan Island, it is a dive worth checking out.

Comments: Homes are all around, but it's a nice wild-feeling beach for a picnic. Let's keep our welcome – pack out what you pack in.

Hermit crab in Oregon triton shell

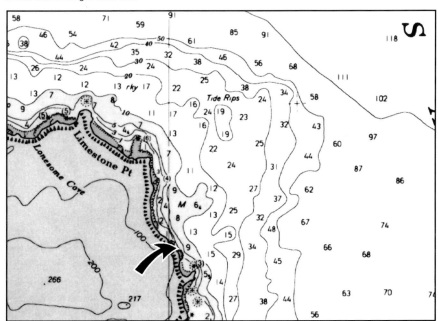

NOT TO BE USED FOR NAVIGATION: For information on obtaining navigational charts see page 318. This is a portion of 18434. Soundings are in fathoms.

½ Nautical Mile

TURN POINT, STUART ISLAND
Boat Dive

Tide Table: Port Townsend
Add 24 minutes to high slack
Add 47 minutes to low slack

Skill: Intermediate and expert divers

Why go: A wall is a wall is a wall: the wall south of Turn Point plunges. Sheers off. It is the blackest, most bottomless wall I have dived. White plumose anemones brighten the black rock as far as we can see. A large undercut cave is the other special thing about this dive. Four of us go in and shine our lights. The roof and walls are brilliant with encrusting sponges, red and orange.

Giant barnacles. A blood star. A beige-and-blue striped sun star. A couple of lingcod. We see one rockfish, yellow staghorn bryozoans like miniature tropical coral. Chitons. Metallic blue kelp. Orange fish in crevices that look like tropical squirrel fish. White dahlia anemones, a Christmas anemone, snakelock anemones. Purple tube worms. Decorator crabs. Painted greenlings. Shrimp. Sea cucumbers. "Dusty" looking cloud sponges. Orange cup corals in 15 feet (5 meters). Brown kelp. Mauve coralline algae in the shallows. Green and purple urchins. We see all of this. And it is all good – it is wonderful!

But the dark wall and the white plumose never-never land is what I will never ever forget.

Bottom and Depths: The sheer dark wall plunges – the chart puts it at 900 feet (270 meters). The cave is undercut into the wall for 25 feet (7 meters). Its floor is at 75 to 85 feet (23 to 26 meters), depending on tide height. Its ceiling is 10 feet (3 meters) high. Bull kelp marks the shallows close beside the wall.

Hazards: Current, big ships and bull kelp. Dive on high slack, on the turn to ebb. Maximum ebb current at Turn Point is almost 3 knots (6 kilometers/hour). If a smaller ebb – up to 2 knots (3¾ kilometers/hour) – you could dive with a "live" boat almost throughout the ebb. But do not dive on the turn to flood. To calculate current, use the speed ratio for "Turn Point, Boundary Pass": multiply 0.6 times the maximum ebb current predicted for Admiralty Inlet (off Bush Point).

If diving from an anchored boat or if a medium or large tidal range, dive on high slack at the start of the ebb. Again, do not dive on the turn to flood. Always stay south of the point, then you will not be swept into the shipping lanes where enormous ships pass. I heard one. Those on the surface told us two Japanese freighters and one Seaspan tug hauling railway cars passed while we were down. If caught in the rip current off the point, you could be pulled out into the shipping lanes. Carry a knife for kelp.

Telephone: Friday Harbor ferry landing.

Facilities: None at Turn Point.

Access: Turn Point is at the northwest tip of Stuart Island on Haro Strait – almost at the United States/Canada border. Stuart Island is 2½ nautical miles (4½ kilometers) north of the top of San Juan Island. Far out.

Charter or launch at Anacortes, Bellingham or San Juan Island and go to the northwest tip of Stuart Island. From Roche Harbor, Mitchell Bay, Smallpox Bay or Friday Harbor at San Juan Island the distance to Turn Point is from 6 to 14 nautical miles (11 to 26 kilometers). Fog in spring or fall could make it impossible to reach this site, but a boat can find protection from most winds at Turn Point unless there is a strong wind from the south. With all except the slightest tidal exchanges dive with a "live" boat. With a very low tidal exchange you could anchor an inflatable or other small boat in the bight just south of the wall. Plan to dive on the ebb and stay south of the point.

The wall dive is south of Turn Point Lighthouse and north of the small bight. The wall you see on the surface is a hint of what is below water – but only a hint. At the site: roll off the boat, swim to the wall and then go down. If you do not swim to the wall, you might never find bottom!

To find the cave: dive deep at the start, then gradually work your way up while drifting slowly south. You should find the dark hole at 75 to 85 feet (23 to 26 meters).

Comments: The massive conglomerate wall at Turn Point is a formation of the Upper Cretaceous age – about 65 to 85 million years old. It has sandstone lenses which weather into caverns. The rocks are folded and could contain fossils.

Beside Prevost Harbor, inviting publicly owned land all around adjacent Satellite Island – might be more superb diving.

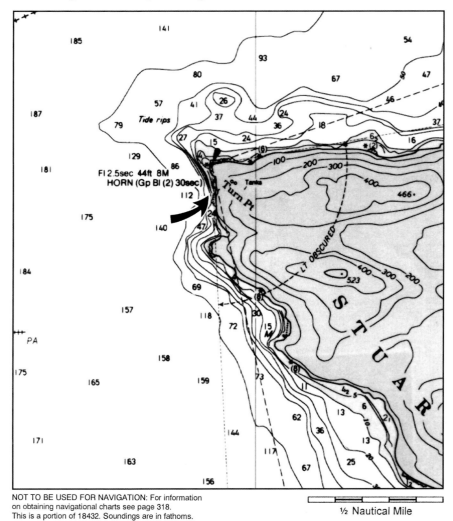

NOT TO BE USED FOR NAVIGATION: For information
on obtaining navigational charts see page 318.
This is a portion of 18432. Soundings are in fathoms.

½ Nautical Mile

LOVERS COVE
Kayak Dive or Boat Dive

Tide Table: Port Townsend
Add 50 minutes

Skill: Intermediate and expert divers and snorkelers

Why go: Lovers Cove offers a sheltered anchorage and can be reached by dive-kayak or small boat. Pile perch and striped seaperch light the shallows. But everything edible is gone.

Lovers Cove was once the most beautiful spot I had ever seen. Shallow reef and drop-off – all at one site, and the moment you put your face in the water you saw abalones and rock scallops. At Lovers – fifteen years ago – we were surrounded with swimming scallops clapping up around us like castanets. We saw a large lingcod and another, then another. Sinuous fingers of bright pink snakelock anemones flowed from the wall. We pushed them away to touch a basket star. It opened its lacy arms like some unearthly flower. You can dive as deep or as shallow as you wish at this site. Still beauty at Lovers Cove, but not like it was.

The total stripping of all edible marine life that occurred at Lovers Cove is scandalous and unnecessary – probably at the hands of recreational divers. So much protected easy-to-dive water is in President Channel, so much to see and explore. My guess is that if you choose almost any place along the way to Lovers, anchor and dive, except for fish, you will find the dive that used to be at Lovers. The fish stocks are depleted throughout the San Juans – Lovers Cove should be a warning about that too. If recreational divers, hook-and-line fishermen, and commercial fishermen keep taking and taking, the edible marine life *will finally* all go away.

But if you are camping in a remote site, look around. You *will* find swimming scallops, rock scallops and abalones. And when you find them, take only what you will eat that day. Study the charts, spread out, find your own sites.

Bottom and Depths: Rocky reef from 5 to 15 feet (1½ to 5 meters) deep slopes off quickly to bull kelp in 20 to 30 feet (6 to 9 meters). North of the reef, a rock wall sheers off to unlimited dark depths.

Hazards: Current, bull kelp and broken fishing line. Dive on the slack. Even then the current never stops completely. It simply changes direction. On larger tidal exchanges, a pickup boat is advisable. You will encounter less current on a high slack. Carry a knife and ascend with a reserve of air; if caught in kelp or transparent fishing line you can cut your way free. Kayak-divers who dive deep should rest before paddling back. The possibility of bends may be increased by overexertion after diving.

Telephones: • West Beach Resort, west end of store. • Orcas Island ferry landing.

Facilities: The rock at Lovers is a lovely place to picnic when it is low tide. Dive-kayak rentals, boat rentals, launching, air fills, hot showers, camping, cabins and trailer hookups nearby at West Beach Resort.

Access: Lovers Cove is in President Channel close to the west shore of Orcas Island 2 nautical miles (4 kilometers) south of West Beach.
• Charter out of Friday Harbor or Anacortes. Launch at Terrill Beach on Orcas; at Mitchell Bay or Roche Harbor on San Juan; rent a boat, or launch your own boat or dive-kayak at West Beach on Orcas Island and go to Lovers. We launched at West Beach then headed southwest for 2 nautical miles (4 kilometers) close along the west shore of Orcas Island, which is usually protected from the wind, winter and summer. We went past one point to a small cove where some old pilings project from

the water. Beyond the next point, in another small cove, a rock just barely sticks out of the water. At high tide, only the very top of the rock shows. Half submerged on the channel side is "Lovers" painted on the rock. Anchor near that rock and go down.

• Kayak-divers can go by car ferry to Orcas Island. Orcas is midway on the Anacortes-San Juan Islands-Sidney ferry route. From Anacortes to Orcas takes 1 to 1½ hours, depending on island stops. From Sidney to Orcas takes 2¾ hours: first sail to Friday Harbor at San Juan Island and transfer to an Orcas-bound ferry.

From Orcas ferry landing to West Beach is 9 miles (14 kilometers). It takes 20 minutes. Follow signs north toward Eastsound; at a right-hand turn to Eastsound, keep going straight. Turn left at the next road which is Enchanted Forest Road and follow signs toward West Beach. When nearly at the end of the road and you see the water, go straight to a public access point at the road end or turn right into the resort.

Easier to kayak to the site when diving on low slack. If you get the tide right, you will get a free ride to Lovers and back. But do it on a smaller exchange.

Comments: Lovers Cove is just one of the many possible dives in President Channel. Explore – you will find countless more "turn-on" dives along these shores.

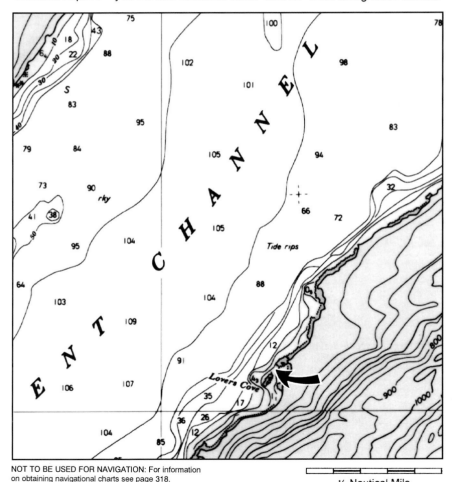

NOT TO BE USED FOR NAVIGATION: For information on obtaining navigational charts see page 318. This is a portion of 18432. Soundings are in fathoms.

½ Nautical Mile

DOE BAY
Shore Dive

Skill: All divers

Why go: Super-easy entry, hot showers after the dive, stacks of marine life.
Kelp greenlings and white-spotted greenlings flash past. Behind curtains of brown bottom kelp we see blackeye gobies. Dungeness crabs. A blood star. Purple sea stars plastered in heaps on the rocks. Two giant sunflower stars that I measure with my arm. They are 3 feet (1 meter) across. Pale blue. We see acorn barnacles on shallow rocks. Clown nudibranchs, alabaster nudibranchs, periwinkles. Around some boulders, the classic signs of octopus: a mess of shells and crab parts scattered on the sand. I look in the nearest hole between the rocks straight at a string of big suckers – 2 inches (5 centimeters) in diameter. This giant's den is in only 20 to 30 feet (6 to 9 meters) of water. Near it, beneath a ledge, we see a tiny grunt sculpin with precise markings like a tropical fish.
We see decorator crabs, gum boot chitons, giant purple urchins. Purple encrusting sponge. A few "dusty" looking sponges that look like they were hurled there after cleaning the car. Brilliant red knobby encrusting sponge beneath an overhang. A few frilly white plumose anemones. A mass of leafy hornmouth whelks filling a slot. A large quillback rockfish, a fat sea cucumber, a rock scallop.
Moon jellyfish as we snorkel across the bay. A large white anemone in shallow water. And a "first" for me: two sea butterflies. They are swimming along upright, waving semicircular pink wings together. Each butterfly is ¼ inch (½ centimeter) across. The movement the butterflies make is like a slow-motion clapping of hands to propel themselves forward through the open water.

Bottom and Depths: Eelgrass in the bay. Rock walls at both sides of the bay. On the left-hand side, the rock wall at the first point bottoms out at 10 to 20 feet (3 to 6 meters). Along the wall, periodic rock outcroppings ledge down to silty sand. At the second point on the left-hand side, rocks and boulders are scattered down to a 10-foot (3-meter) high ledge bottoming out to mud at 38 to 48 feet (12 to 15 meters). Brown bottom kelp covers the rocks. Some sand between. Very thick silt over all.

Hazards: Silt, shallow depth, some current and small boats – many ocean kayaks and sailboats come and go silently in the bay. Do not bob up unexpectedly in the bay; stay near the wall. Try not to stir up silt; weight yourself so you can stay down and yet stay off the bottom. Dive near slack. When ascending, stay close to the rocks and wall all the way to the surface, well out of the way of boats.

Telephone: Doebay Resort.

Facilities: Parking and hot showers for a small day-use fee; also camping, hot showers and café at the resort. Camping with picnic tables, fire rings and hot showers 15 minutes away at Moran State Park; reservations in summer. Air fills and dive-kayak rentals across the island at West Beach.

Access: Doe Bay is next to Rosario Strait on the east shore of Orcas Island. Orcas is midway on the Anacortes-San Juan Islands-Sidney ferry route. From Anacortes to Orcas takes 1 to 1½ hours, depending on island stops. From Sidney to Orcas takes 2¾ hours: first sail to Friday Harbor at San Juan Island and transfer to an Orcas-bound ferry.
From Orcas ferry landing, 35 minutes to Doe Bay. Follow signs to Eastsound. After 8 miles (13 kilometers) turn right. Go through the village of Eastsound, pass the head

of the sound and go to a "T" junction. Turn right. Follow signs toward Olga, Doe Bay and Mount Constitution. Stay on the main arterial road: pass beneath a giant archway into Moran State Park. Pass the left-hand turnoff to Mount Constitution. After crossing a one-lane bridge and leaving the park, curve left, head down a hill and you will see the water. Olga is straight ahead. Turn left into Lawrence Point Road. Follow signs to Doe Bay.

From the beach at Doebay Resort swim across the small bay with buildings facing onto it. It takes about 10 minutes to reach the second point on the left-hand side. Wheelchair access to beach possible with able-bodied help – not a launching ramp, but a steep path. Then a few feet of sand to cross.

Comments: Wildlife on land, too – we saw many deer.

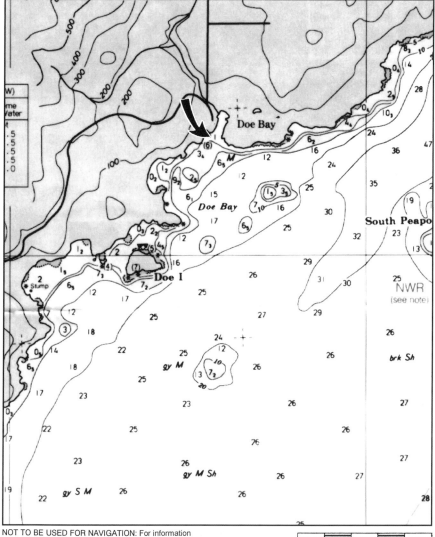

NOT TO BE USED FOR NAVIGATION: For information on obtaining navigational charts see page 318. This is a portion of 18430. Soundings are in fathoms.

½ Nautical Mile

DOE ISLAND
Kayak Dive or Boat Dive

Tide Table: Port Townsend
Add 25 minutes

Skill: Intermediate and expert divers and snorkelers

Why go: Swimming scallops, rock scallops and yellow staghorn bryozoans – lots of them. And it's an easy first kayak dive: a short paddle and you can gear up on the beach. With hot showers after the dive.

The moment I put my face in the water periwinkles tumbled about rolling all over the rocks. We saw hermit crabs. Purple sea stars. A tiny decorator crab with tufts of kelp streaming. Schools of seaperch, schools of young black rockfish and kelp green-lings. Giant purple urchins at the base of the kelp. Under a ledge, glass tunicates, orange sea peaches, a gum boot chiton. Leafy hornmouth whelks. Bright red knobby sponge. Deeper, quillback rockfish. A couple of medium-sized lingcod, a red Irish lord. Orange cup corals on the rocks. Giant barnacles. A small sea lemon. Two gunnels dart past us – I never get to look at them as long as I want to. Some white plumose anemones. Shrimp all over the place.

Swimming scallops are thick from 50 to 70 feet (15 to 21 meters). We cannot put a hand down without touching one. Their bright eyes around the edges of their shells are shining. Some clap up around us.

Bottom and Depths: Rocky bottom with bottom kelp rolls gently down. White sand between the rocks. Light silt over all. Go as deep or as shallow as you want to – all good diving. Bull kelp at 20 to 30 feet (6 to 9 meters), depending on tide height.

Hazards: Current, small boats, bull kelp and fishing line. Dive on slack. The current never stops, it just turns around. Stay close to the bottom throughout the dive; use rocks and bull kelp to pull yourself along. This marine park invites small boats: do not surface unexpectedly beneath one. Ascend in the bull kelp out of the way of boats. Carry a knife for kelp and fishing line.

Telephone: Doebay Resort.

Facilities: Picnic tables, toilets, and fire rings; rustic camping amongst the Douglas firs on Doe Island. Dive-kayak rentals and air fills across the island at West Beach, at San Juan Island and Oak Harbor.

Access: Doe Island is ½ nautical mile (1 kilometer) offshore from Doe Bay on the east side of Orcas Island. It is at the edge of Rosario Strait.
• Charter out of Anacortes, Bellingham or San Juan Island and go to Doe Island State Park. Or launch your own boat at Obstruction Pass Public Ramp and go northeast around Deer Point to Doe Island. Anchor on the outside of the island – the Rosario Strait side – and head down.
• Kayak-divers: go by ferry to Orcas Island (see Doe Bay page 122) and launch at Doe Bay. Paddle for 15 minutes to Doe Island. The entire island is a marine park; you can land wherever you wish. Two beaches. We landed at a crescent of beach on the northeast side of the island to gear up, swam to the point, dived down through the bull kelp and south around the outside of the island. In summer, the bull kelp is thick. It is a good place to go down and up, most likely to be out of the way of boats.

Wheelchair access at Doe Bay for divers who paddle dive-kayaks. Go down a steep but usable ramp; then cross a few feet (meters) of beach to the water.

Comments: Doe Island is only one of countless kayak and boat access sites in the San Juans. The ocean is rich. Unexplored – explore it!

From Doe Bay, off to Doe Island

NOT TO BE USED FOR NAVIGATION: For information
on obtaining navigational charts see page 318.
This is a portion of 18423. Soundings are in fathoms.

1 Nautical Mile

125

FROST ISLAND
Shore Dive or Kayak Dive

Tide Table: Seattle
Add 30 minutes

Skill: All divers who are fit for a long hike and a long swim. All kayak-divers.

Why go: San Juan Island dives with shore access are difficult to find, but this site at Lopez is useful in several different ways:
• The marine life is good at Frost Island. We saw millions of spider crabs in the kelp. Giant red urchins and small green ones. Lots of little rockfish in crevices of the wall. Blennies, a cabezon and pipefish. Rock scallops. Some giant barnacles. Sea squirts, shrimp and sea cucumbers. Crabs in the sand. It's an all-around dive.
• Excellent for kayak-divers – especially those who want to try gearing up and diving from their kayak for the first time.
• Camping facilities at Spencer Spit, when you can get in, are varied and pleasant. After diving, you can enjoy a different type of wildlife viewing: great blue herons, kingfishers, otters and rabbits are often at the saltwater marsh lagoon. And in season, try clamming.
• Spencer Spit is a good take-off point for divers with an inflatable or other small boat. Go to nearby islands, explore and dive. If the campground mooring buoys are not all taken, you can moor your boat at Spencer Spit. We went to James Island from here. Many more islands are within easy reach with publicly owned beaches where you can land and dive.

Bottom and Depths: Rock wall drops in crevices, small caves and overhangs to flat sand at 60 to 70 feet (18 to 21 meters). Very silty. Some bull kelp by the wall in 20 to 30 feet (6 to 9 meters). Lots of flat sand back around the spit – crab country.

Hazards: Some current. Poor visibility; best in September and October. Lots of small boats. Long hike with gear, long swim. Dive on the slack. Weight yourself carefully to stay off the bottom and try not to kick up silt. Listen for boats and ascend close to the wall all the way to the surface, well out of the way of boats. Pace yourself, especially if you have done a couple of dives; rest periodically when walking up the spit. The possibility of bends may be increased by overexertion after diving. You might take off your tank, inflate your buoyancy compensator, walk in the water and tow it to shore.

Telephone: Behind Ranger Station, left-hand side of road as you head out of park.

Facilities: None at Frost Island. On Lopez you will find picnic tables, camping and wheelchair accessible flush toilets at Spencer Spit State Park; camping, launching and wheelchair accessible pit toilets at Odlin County Park. Air fills at Shark Reef Road – telephone to arrange it. Dive-kayak rentals at Orcas and San Juan islands, Oak Harbor and Bellingham.

Access: Frost Island is at the west end of Thatcher Pass close to Lopez Island. Lopez is the first stop on the Anacortes-San Juan Islands-Sidney ferry route. From Anacortes to Lopez takes 40 minutes. From Sidney to Lopez, nearly 4 hours: sail to Friday Harbor and transfer to a Lopez-bound ferry.
From Lopez ferry landing to Spencer Spit State Park is 4½ miles (7 kilometers). Drive 2 miles (3½ kilometers) to a "T" junction. Turn left and follow signs to the park; drive down the gravel road and trail beside the ranger's office to drop gear. You will see a sign: "Loading by Permission". Do not drive onto the spit; it is fragile and vehicles are not permitted. If you drive onto the spit, your vehicle could be ticketed or towed away. Leave your car in the day-parking area, top of the hill. Back at the beach, it's a long carry to the end of the spit – it is ¼ mile (½ kilometer). The swim is

long, too, over gently sloping sand – 100 to 150 yards (90 to 137 meters) from the spit to Frost Island, depending on tide height. Good diving in the kelp and along the rock wall on the northwest side of Frost Island. Wheelchair parking at the beach for divers with kayaks.

Kayak-divers can paddle from where you drop gear to Frost Island in 2 to 3 minutes. The island is publicly owned but there are few or no landing spots. You will probably want to anchor or tie up to the kelp and dive from your kayak – easy when you learn to do it. Spencer Spit is a good place to try (see Kayak-Diving on page 30). If difficulty gearing up on your kayak, you could swim it to the shallows and put on gear.

Comments: Take an underwater light for the dive. After diving, in season, try clamming.

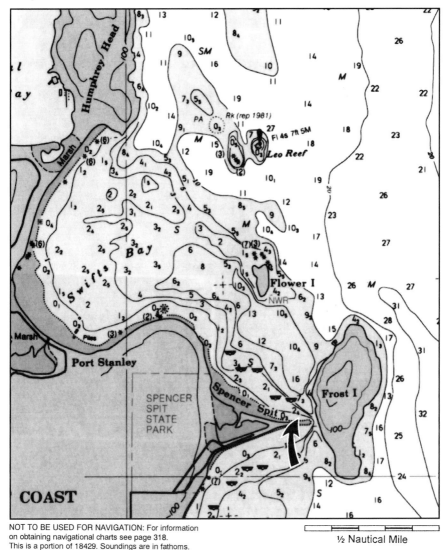

NOT TO BE USED FOR NAVIGATION: For information
on obtaining navigational charts see page 318.
This is a portion of 18429. Soundings are in fathoms.

½ Nautical Mile

JAMES ISLAND
Boat Dive

Skill: All divers

Why go: Get away from it all by camping and diving at James Island where there's something for everyone.

New divers will find big rocks covered with anemones in the bay right in front of the campsite. More adventuresome intermediates can look for abalones and octopuses in the rocky cliffs south of the campsite. Expert divers will find good drop-off diving just north of the campsite. An extraordinary area with some strange invertebrates. Quite barren down to 30 feet (9 meters). Below 30 feet (9 meters) we saw masses of small white cucumbers and flaming red slipper cucumbers with their tentacles withdrawn. The wall looked like a strawberry cake.

Cloud sponges – most unusual for this area – start at 50 feet (15 meters). Millions of amphipods that looked like jumping "ants" – my description – or "mosquitoes" – my buddy's. Giant barnacles, lots of swimming scallops and large rock scallops. A blood star and bryozoans. Dahlia anemones are on the wall – small but beautiful. Practically no fish, but fascinating invertebrate life.

Bottom and Depths: Big rocks in the silty bay. North of the bay, bull kelp at the edge. The bottom slopes fairly quickly from 25 to 75 feet (8 to 23 meters), then drops off.

Hazards: Current, boats and bull kelp. Dive on the slack. Be particularly careful of rip currents at the northwest corner of the island. Listen for boats, and ascend along the bottom all the way up to shore, well out of the way of those boats. Carry a knife for kelp.

Telephones: • Lopez ferry landing. • Washington Park, Anacortes, in front of park superintendent's home up hill from ramp. • Anacortes ferry terminal.

Facilities: James Island State Park provides picnic tables, campsites, pit toilets, dock, mooring buoys and hiking trails. No drinking water.

Access: James Island is in Rosario Strait ½ nautical mile (1 kilometer) east of Decatur Island and 5 nautical miles (9 kilometers) west of Anacortes.

Charter, rent a boat or launch at Anacortes, Bellingham or Lopez Island and go by boat to James Island. A great many launching ramps are in Anacortes: at Washington Park, Flounder Bay and Fidalgo Bay. Also launching ramps in Bellingham. We launched our inflatable at Spencer Spit State Park on the northeast end of Lopez. At James Island, dive from shore in the bay in front of the campsite on the west side of the island facing Decatur Island. You will find easy entry over the sand. When diving the points north and south of the bay, anchor in the kelp and dive from your boat.

Comments: Both divers and non-divers will enjoy the site for a day or a weekend.

Blood star with bryozoans and ring-top snails

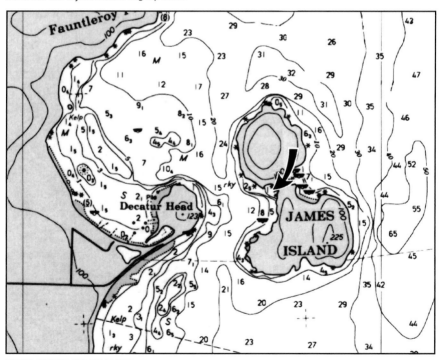

½ Nautical Mile

129

LONG ISLAND
Boat Dive

Skill: Intermediate and expert divers and snorkelers

Why go: Long Island has a couple of good drop-offs as well as shallow diving. And it's protected from the southeast wind.

The bright white wall covered with abalones rolls in rounded mounds down the cliff. The rock wall looks melted and poured. Chitons cling to it. Small white plumose anemones cluster under the overhangs. You can easily snorkel and see abalones here. I saw some as shallow as 5 feet (1½ meters).

The dark wall drops off from clean-swept, kelp-covered white rocks dotted with lacy bright orange tentacles of burrowing cucumbers. It falls from 30 feet (9 meters) down to nowhere. You plummet over the edge. Huge white plumose anemones blanket the wall in froth, cascade down the cliff. The free-fall of white is broken only by a few narrow ledges where giant barnacles cling in the cracks. Some barnacles are so encrusted with sponge that you can't see them – only their pink feeding fans. Crimson slipper cucumbers, also called creeping pedal cucumbers, splash the wall with red. A few small rockfish swim out over the bottomless black. There are very few fish and the abalones have been over-harvested, but if you like drop-offs, this is a good one. Strawberry anemones on the west side of Long Island.

Bottom and Depths: Rocky bottom with bull kelp at 25 to 35 feet (8 to 11 meters), drops off to a depth of 90 to 100 feet (27 to 30 meters), depending on tide height.

Hazards: Boats, lots of current, and bull kelp. Listen for boats and ascend close to the wall all the way to the surface, well out of the way of those boats. Dive on the slack as there is a great deal of current. The current correction is "Cattle Point" on San Juan Channel. Carry a knife for kelp.

Telephones: • Mackaye Harbor Road and Mud Bay Road; from Mackaye Ramp, go up the road ⅓ mile (½ kilometer) to the telephone on the other side of the firehall beside Mud Bay Road. • Fisherman Bay dock.

Facilities: None at Long Island. On Lopez: Air fills – telephone to arrange it. Camping at Spencer Spit State Park and Odlin County Park; accommodations at Fisherman Bay. Launching at Mackaye Harbor, Fisherman Bay, Hunter Bay and Odlin County Park.

Access: Long Island is next to Middle Channel, south of San Juan Channel. It is just offshore southwest of Lopez Island.

Charter out of Friday Harbor, Anacortes or Bellingham. Or take your own boat and launch at Mackaye Harbor and go west 2½ nautical miles (4½ kilometers) to Long Island, or launch at Fisherman Bay, Odlin County Park or Hunter Bay and go to Long Island. Approaching Long Island, be careful not to come close to Mummy Rocks, a San Juan Islands National Wildlife Refuge.

To protect the young sea birds and seals, visitors must stay 200 yards (180 meters) offshore at the wildlife refuge. Anchor in the small bay on the north side of Long Island, leave a boat tender on board and dive from your boat. East to the white wall. West to the dark drop-off.

Comments: Long Island is privately owned; please respect it and stay off the dock.

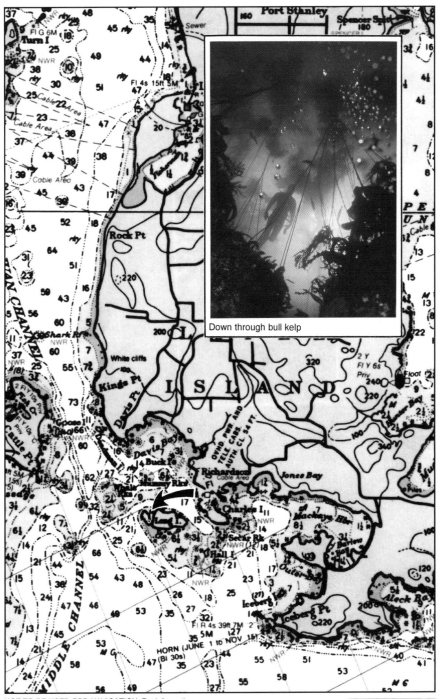

Down through bull kelp

1 Nautical Mile

Beddis Beach on Saltspring Island

Shore access to Tilly Point Caves, Pender Island

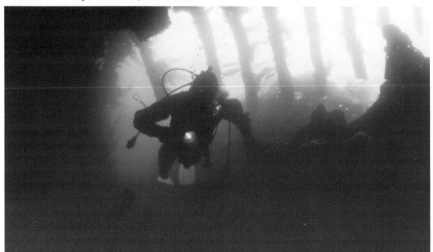

Wreck of *Point Grey* in Porlier Pass

Photographing plumose-topped rock, dotted with orange cup corals

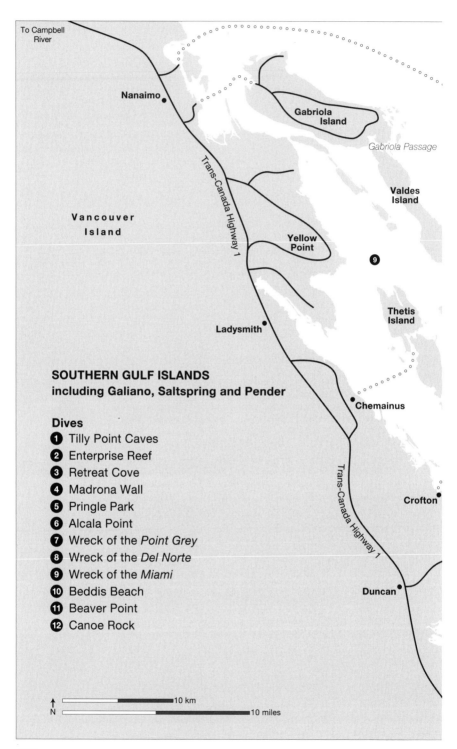

To Campbell
River

Nanaimo •

Gabriola
Island

Gabriola Passage

Valdes
Island

Vancouver
Island

Trans-Canada Highway 1

Yellow
Point

❾

Thetis
Island

Ladysmith •

SOUTHERN GULF ISLANDS
including Galiano, Saltspring and Pender

Chemainus •

Dives
❶ Tilly Point Caves
❷ Enterprise Reef
❸ Retreat Cove
❹ Madrona Wall
❺ Pringle Park
❻ Alcala Point
❼ Wreck of the *Point Grey*
❽ Wreck of the *Del Norte*
❾ Wreck of the *Miami*
❿ Beddis Beach
⓫ Beaver Point
⓬ Canoe Rock

Crofton •

Trans-Canada Highway 1

Duncan •

↑
N

▮▮▮ 10 km

▮▮▮ 10 miles

STRAIT

OF

GEORGIA

To Vancouver

Highway 99

Fraser River
Delta

To I-5,
Bellingham
and Seattle

Tunnel

Tsawwassen

Highway 17

Porlier Pass

North
Galiano

Galiano
Island

Vesuvius

Montague
Harbour

Sturdies
Bay

Active Pass

Long
Harbour

Ganges

Ganges
Harbour

Mayne

Village Island
Bay

Saltspring
Island

Pender
Island

Saturna
Island

Otter
Bay

Port
Browning

Thieves
Bay

Fulford
Harbour

Bedwell
Harbour

To Victoria

Swartz
Bay

To Victoria

SERVICE INFORMATION *
Southern Gulf Islands
including Galiano, Saltspring and Pender
Charts: Canadian Hydrographic Service
- 3310 Gulf Islands–Victoria Harbour to Nanaimo Harbour
- 3441 Haro Strait, Boundary Pass and Satellite Channel
- 3442 North Pender Island to Thetis Island
- 3443 Thetis Island to Nanaimo
- L/C-3462 Juan de Fuca Strait to Strait of Georgia
- L/C-3463 Strait of Georgia, Southern Portion
- 3473 Active Pass, Porlier Pass and Montague Harbour
- 3477 Plans–Gulf Islands
- 3478 Plans–Saltspring Island

Tide and Current Tables: Canadian Hydrographic Service *Tide and Current Table, Volume 5* and Canadian Hydrographic Service *Current Atlas: Juan de Fuca Strait to Strait of Georgia* (use with *Murray's Tables* or *Washburne's Tables*)

Diving Emergency Telephone Numbers
Dial 911: Say "I have a scuba diving emergency".

Vancouver General Hospital: Dial (604) 875-4111 and say "I have a scuba diving emergency. I want the hyperbaric physician on call".

If medical personnel are unfamiliar with scuba diving emergencies, ask them to telephone DAN (Divers Alert Network): (919) 684-8111, then say "I have a scuba diving emergency".

Other Useful Numbers
Continuous Marine Broadcast (CMB) recorded, 24 hours; listen for weather in Howe Sound or Haro Strait, telephone
- Vancouver: (604) 270-7411
- Victoria: (604) 474-7998

Shellfish Infoline, recorded: (604) 666-3169
Sportfishing Information Line, recorded: 1-800-663-9333

• Air Stations
Galiano Island
Galiano Island Diving Service
RR 1
Galiano Island BC V0N 1P0
(604) 539-3109
(Telephone to arrange for air fills – at waterfront and roadside. Guiding services for shore dives; also charters.)

Pender Island
Cooper's Landing Inc.
5743 Canal Road
Pender Island BC V0N 2M0
(604) 629-6133; fax (604) 629-3649
(Telephone to arrange for waterfront and roadside air fills. Also divers' lodge, drying room for gear and charters.)

Saltspring Island
Salt Spring Scuba
132 Upper Ganges Road
RR 3, Driftwood C-7
Ganges BC V0S 1E0
(604) 537-1160
(Telephone to arrange for air fills – at waterfront and roadside; also charters out of Ganges.)

Scuba World (Sports Trader)
Located at Ganges Village Market Mall
#4, 370 Lower Ganges Road
RR 3, S-3, G-6
Ganges BC V0S 1E0
(604) 537-5588 – fax and telephone.

• Boat Charters, Boat Rentals and Launching
Galiano Island

Galiano Island Diving Service
RR 1
Galiano Island BC V0N 1P0
(604) 539-3109
(Charters from North Galiano government float beside Spanish Hills Store; wheelchair divers welcome on dive boat. Also guiding services for shore dives.)

Madrona Lodge
RR 2
Galiano, BC V0N 1P0
(604) 539-2926
(Rowboats for resort guests only, and bring your own motor. The resort has cabins for individuals or groups, and can accommodate up to 30 people. Also a drying room for gear.)

Montague Provincial Park
RR 1, foot of Montague Park Road, south end of island
Galiano Island BC V0N 1P0
(604) 539-2115
(Concrete launching ramp, good at high tides. Telephone in center of park at park headquarters. From the ramp, go ⅙ mile [⅓ kilometer] straight up the road; turn right and right again to the telephone. Pit toilets.)
   From the ferry landing, follow signs along Montague Road for 4 miles (7 kilometers) to Montague Park Road: you will see the water; bear right up Montague Park Road and go to the end of it.

• Charters out of Pender Island
Daytripper
Cooper's Landing Inc.
5743 Canal Road
Pender Island BC V0N 2M0
(604) 629-6133; fax (604) 629-3649
(Charters out of Shark Cove, Port Browning [Browning Harbour], to east and west sides of the island. Also dive packages with accommodation in divers' lodge.)

• Charters out of Saltspring Island
Alec Peere
Road to the Islands Sailing Charters
RR 4, Fort Street, C-8
Ganges BC V0S 1E0
(604) 537-5647
(Charters out of Ganges Harbour.)

Great White
Salt Spring Scuba
132 Upper Ganges Road
RR 3, Driftwood C-7
Ganges BC V0S 1E0
(604) 537-1160
(Charters out of Ganges Harbour.)

• Launching Ramps at Pender Island
Port Browning (Browning Harbour) Public Ramp
Foot of Hamilton Road, North Pender
(Launching for east and west sides of island. Concrete ramp, good at all tides. Also café, hot showers and telephone nearby at Browning Harbour Marina.)
   From Otter Bay, follow signs toward South Pender. Immediately past the Driftwood Centre, turn left down Hamilton Road.

Mortimer Spit Public Ramp
Foot of Mortimer Spit Road, South Pender
(Hand-launching of small boats only. Easy access to east and west sides of island. No toilet, no telephone.)
   From Otter Bay, follow signs toward South Pender. Immediately across the bridge between the islands, turn left to the spit – you can see it from the bridge.

Otter Bay Marina
RR 1, 2311 McKinnon Road
Pender Island BC V0N 2M0
(604) 629-3579
(Launching year-round for west side of island only. Concrete ramp, good at medium to high tides. Also boat rentals. Restrooms with flush toilets and hot showers. Telephone beside ramp.)
   Located at Otter Bay: immediately off ferry, turn right.

Thieves Bay Public Ramp
Foot of Anchor Way, North Pender
(Launching for west side of island only. Concrete ramp, good at high tides. Also pit toilet, picnic tables, and telephone.)
   From Otter Bay, follow signs toward South Pender. Past Driftwood Centre, then Prior Park, turn right down Aldridge Road and almost immediately right again down Schooner Way. Curve around to Anchor Way and go to the water.

• Launching Ramps at Mayne Island
Village Bay Public Ramp
Foot of Callaghan Crescent, west side of island
(Concrete ramp, good at high tides. No toilet; telephone at ferry landing.)
   Immediately off ferry, turn right. Go down Dalton Road and right onto Mariners Way then right into Callaghan Crescent to the water.

David Cove Public Ramp
End of Petrus Crescent, east side of island
(Tarmac ramp, good only at high tides. No toilet, no telephone.)
   From ferry go via Village Bay Road to Fernhill Road to Campbell Bay Road to Porter Road to Petrus Crescent.

Piggott Road Public Ramp
End of Piggott Road, southwest side of island
(Hand-launch, small boats only, down steep grass bank. No toilet, no telephone.)
   From ferry, go via Village Bay Road to Fernhill Road to Horton Bay Road to Gallagher Bay Road to Piggott.

• Launching Ramps at Saltspring Island
Ganges Public Ramp
Ganges Commercial Harbour, east side of Saltspring Island
Centennial Park
Ganges BC
(Launching for Trincomali Channel; concrete ramp, good at all except extreme low tides. Telephones and flush toilets beside wharf manager's office.)
   At Centennial Park off Fulford-Ganges Road in Ganges.

Saltspring Marina Ramp
Head of Ganges Harbour, east side of Saltspring Island
120 Upper Ganges Road
Ganges BC V0S 1E0
(604) 537-5810
(Launching for Trincomali Channel: concrete ramp, good at all tides. Also hot showers and many fireplaces to warm up in front of at Moby's Marine Pub. Restrooms; telephones inside at Moby's Marine Pub and across the road at Harbour House Hotel.)
   At Moby's Marine Pub in Ganges.

Long Harbour Public Ramp
Long Harbour, east side of Saltspring Island
(Launching for Trincomali Channel at high tides. No toilet, no telephone.)
Off Long Harbour Road on Quebec Drive. Go to a "T"; turn right to Ontario Place, then left downhill to the water.

Hudson Point Public Ramp
Off North Beach Road, northeast side of Saltspring Island
(Launching for Trincomali Channel: steep concrete and gravel ramp. Good for hand-launching of small boats. No toilet, no telephone.)
From Ganges, head north via Robinson Road. Then Walker Hook Road. Just past Fernwood Road and the government wharf, you will find room for one car to park beside the ramp. Heading south, look for it 1 mile (1¾ kilometers) past Castillou Way.

Drummond Park Public Ramp
Head of Fulford Harbour, south end of Saltspring Island
Off Isabella Point Road
(Launching for Satellite Channel: gravel and sand ramp; good for hand-launching of small boats. No toilet; no telephone.)
Located immediately south of Fulford-Ganges Road and Isabella Road junction.

• Launching Ramps at Vancouver Island for Gulf Islands
Rotary Public Ramp
Foot of Ludlow Road
Ladysmith BC
(Launching for Gulf Islands: concrete ramp, good at all tides. Toilet and telephone on wharf.)
At traffic light north end of Ladysmith, turn toward sea on Ludlow Road. After crossing second set of railway tracks immediately turn right, still on Ludlow Road, and go to the end of it.

Rotary Public Ramp
Foot of Maple Street,
Off Chemainus Road
Chemainus BC
(Launching for Gulf Islands: concrete ramp, good at all tides. Restrooms at park. Telephone ⅓ mile [½ kilometer] away at ferry terminal foot of Oak Street at Esplanade Street. From ramp, go to Oak Street. Turn left and to the ferry.)
Located 5 minutes off Highway 1 between Duncan and Ladysmith: Follow signs to Chemainus taking Henry Road to Chemainus Road and turn left. Go ¾ mile (1¼ kilometers) to Cedar Street. Turn right and go to Oak Street; turn right again and go to Maple Street. Then almost immediately turn left and go to the water.

• Charters from Vancouver to the Gulf Islands
Adrenalin Diver
Adrenalin Sports
1512 Duranleau Street,
Granville Island
Vancouver BC V6H 3S4
(604) 682-2881
(One-day and weekend boat charters with land-based accommodation out of Vancouver: to Gulf Islands, Victoria, Nanaimo, Campbell River and Port Hardy. Bus charters to Vancouver Island.)

Arasheena
Arasheena Yacht Charters
3656 Blenheim Street
Vancouver BC V6L 2Y2
(604) 736-0938
(Charters out of Vancouver to Gulf Islands.)

Compass Rose
Cooper Boating Center
1620 Duranleau Street,
Granville Island
Vancouver, BC V6H 3S4
(604) 687-4110; fax (604) 687-3267
(Liveaboard sail/dive charters to Gulf Islands. Sail out of Vancouver or fly, bus or drive to meet your charter.)

Komokwa
Cross Current Divers
14-2773 Barnet Highway
Located 2 stoplights west of Coquitlam Centre
Coquitlam BC V3B 1C2
(604) 944-2780; fax (604) 944-2782
(Charters in winter out of Port Moody to Gulf Islands.)

Deep Cove Diver and *Baba*
Deep Cove Dive Shop
4342 Gallant Avenue
North Vancouver BC V7G 1K8
(604) 929-3116; cellular (604) 880-6340
(Charters out of Deep Cove, North Vancouver to Gulf Islands, Port Hardy and Campbell River. Wheelchair divers welcome.)

Lady Goodiver
Lady Goodiver Charters
#381, PO Box 9060
Surrey BC V3T 5P8
(604) 220-7187
(Liveaboard custom charters out of Vancouver – or pick up anywhere, to Gulf Islands; also Port Hardy.)

• **More Services for Gulf Islands:** see service information for Victoria and Nanaimo chapters on pages 51 and 175.
   Note also that all Gabriola Island dives and service information are included in the Nanaimo chapter because land access to Gabriola is by way of Nanaimo.

• **Ferry Information**
British Columbia Ferry Corporation
1112 Fort Street
Victoria BC V8V 4V2
In Saltspring Island: 537-9921
In other Gulf Islands: 629-3215
Toll-free in BC: 1-800-663-7600
Telephoning from outside British Columbia: (604) 386-3431.
Reservations required for vehicles between mainland and Gulf Islands.
(Ferries between Tsawwassen [south of Vancouver], Swartz Bay [north of Victoria], Galiano, Mayne, Pender and Saltspring Islands, and from Crofton [Vancouver Island] to Vesuvius Bay [Saltspring Island]. Ferries between Nanaimo [Vancouver Island] and Gabriola Island, also Chemainus [Vancouver Island] and Thetis Island.)

• **Tourist Information**
Discover British Columbia
1117 Wharf Street
Victoria BC V8W 2Z2
1-800-663-6000: Toll-free throughout Canada and the USA, including Hawaii and parts of Alaska.

Galiano Island Travel Infocentre
PO Box 73
Galiano Island BC V0N 1P0
(604) 539-2233
(Year-round. Booth in July and August only.)

Salt Spring Island Travel Infocentre
121 Lower Ganges Road
PO Box 111,
Ganges BC V0S 1E0
(604) 537-5252; fax (604) 537-4276
(Year-round.)

How to Go – To reach Galiano, Mayne, Pender or Saltspring islands via British Columbia ferry:

• From Vancouver Island, go by ferry from Swartz Bay which is at the northern tip of the Saanich Peninsula: 20 miles (30 kilometers) north of Victoria. Sail to Galiano, Mayne or Pender – no choice of harbour. To Saltspring, sail from Swartz Bay to Fulford Harbour; or sail from Crofton (south of Nanaimo) to Vesuvius Bay on Saltspring.

• From the mainland, go by ferry from Tsawwassen: 20 miles (30 kilometers) south of Vancouver to any one of the Gulf Islands. Sailing to Saltspring from the mainland, you go to Long Harbour. Reservations are required for cars between the mainland and the Gulf Islands.

However, sailing to and fro to Saltspring, you can sail from Tsawwassen to Swartz Bay and connect to Fulford Harbour at Saltspring and to the other Gulf Islands without a reservation and at the Tsawwassen/Swartz Bay fare – ask for a through-fare ticket at Tsawwassen. Likewise, you can sail from Fulford Harbour at Saltspring to Swartz Bay and connect to Tsawwassen at the Swartz Bay/Tsawwassen fare.

Divers with Boats: Most comprehensive and least expensive "water road map" I have heard of is the Canadian Hydrographic Service Chart 3310: Gulf Islands, Victoria Harbour to Nanaimo Harbour. It is a collection of four charts covering all of the southern Gulf Islands. These small-craft charts are suitable for navigation as well as for diving.

*All of this service information is subject to change.

TILLY POINT CAVES
Shore Dive

Tide Table: Fulford Harbour

Skill: Intermediate and expert divers; all divers with guide. Snorkelers in bay.

Why go: Pure magic. It's what you dream diving in a cave should be. You can go in one end and out the other. The oval cave entry is framed with feathery white plumose anemones. Inside, blackness is shot with shafts of sunlight through holes in the rock above. An orange dahlia anemone hangs upside down from the ceiling. We swim through darkness to the end of the room, and then toward the light through a narrow slot between rock walls framed with more white plumose anemones – we're out of the cave. We glance back at it, and see a Puget Sound king crab shimmering – its purple and orange florescent colors glow beneath a rocky ledge. Looking out, we see large orange sea pens arching from the white sand at the base of the island.

The rock wall is bright. It's dark. It's windowed. Large white plumose anemones fill every slot, every seam in the rock. A lingcod swims past, framed by a window of rock. On the surface, we see a harbor seal. The terrain is so picturesque I'll never completely believe it. I know I will have to return again and again to confirm for myself that I did not imagine this scene, to assure myself the Tilly Point Caves exist.

Bottom and Depths: The cave entry is at a depth of 5 to 15 feet (1½ to 5 meters). The main room is 10 feet (3 meters) wide by 30 feet (9 meters) long, and 10 feet (3 meters) high. The exit slot slopes down from the back of the cave to the right-hand side through a narrow channel of rock to the sand at a depth of 40 to 50 feet (12 to 15 meters). Above and below water, the island is a heap of tumbled boulders with small rocks embedded in them. Intricate sandstone and conglomerate. Small undercut caves and slots are all along the outside wall, which bottoms out to bright white sand at 60 to 70 feet (18 to 21 meters).

The bay between the island and the shore has a bottom of white shells scattered with pastel dahlia anemones from zero to 25 feet (8 meters) deep.

Hazards: Current on the outside of the rock, the cave itself, and bull kelp. Dive on slack. Weight yourself to be neutrally buoyant at a depth of 5 feet (1½ meters), so you will not stir up silt. Carry a knife; if caught in kelp you can cut your way free.

Telephone: Bedwell Harbour Hotel & Marina, on the dock; go back along Gowlland Point Road for 1¼ miles (2 kilometers) to Bedwell Harbour Road.

Facilities: Great beach for a picnic at Tilly Point Caves. Air fills, charters and divers' lodge at Shark Cove; telephone to arrange for services. Campsites with pit toilets and fire rings at Prior Centennial Provincial Park, which is surrounded by tall trees. Charters also out of Sidney to Tilly Point Caves.

Access: Tilly Point Caves are in Boundary Pass off the southern tip of South Pender Island. The caves are most easily dived at a high slack tide. Go by way of British Columbia ferry from Tsawwassen or Swartz Bay to Otter Bay at Pender Island. From the ferry landing, it is 11 miles (18 kilometers) to the dive. Takes 35 minutes.

At Pender Island, follow signs toward South Pender, then Bedwell Harbour. When you reach the right-hand turnoff to Bedwell Harbour, do not go in. Continue on the main road for 1 mile (2 kilometers) more to Craddock Drive. Turn right, and go to the end of it. Room for four or five cars to park. From the end of Craddock Drive, walk down 50 shallow stairs to the log-strewn beach. You will see a rock that is an island at high tide. You can walk to it at low tide.

To find the largest cave – the one you can swim through – snorkel out to the right-hand, westernmost side of the rocky island to an indentation on the outside of the rock. The entry is below it. Head down. Look from 5 to 10 feet (3 to 11 meters) deep for the oval entrance framed with white plumose anemones. Enter. Swim slowly straight through the cave. Enjoy everything on your first passage through before the silt is stirred up. At the end of the cave, turn right and go down a narrow slot. You emerge at the base of the wall. Continue exploring around the outside of the island toward its eastern tip. From there, it is a pleasant snorkel to shore.

Weight yourself carefully so you can enter the large cave without touching the anemones – divers following you will appreciate it. Plan to be neutrally buoyant at a depth of 5 feet (1½ meters).

Comments: The caves are honored as an underwater reserve – do not take any marine life. The bay is lovely too; no other snorkeling spot is so exciting!

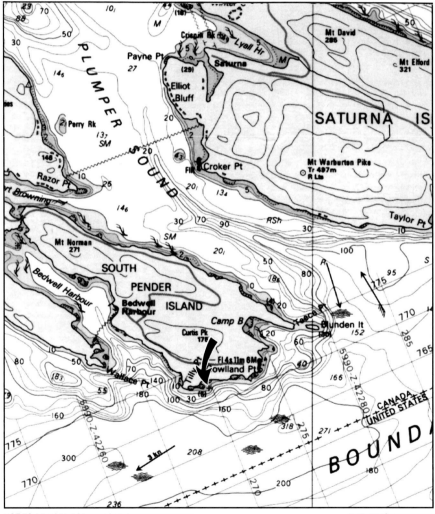

NOT TO BE USED FOR NAVIGATION: For information
on obtaining navigational charts see page 318.
This is a portion of L/C-3462.

1 Nautical Mile

ENTERPRISE REEF
Boat Dive

Skill: Expert divers

Why Go: Enterprise Reef combines rich reef life with one of the best drop-offs in the Gulf Islands. Add the swift currents that flow through Active Pass, and you have the ingredients for one of the most exciting dives around.
You'll probably see Puget Sound king crabs, rock scallops, abalones, large lingcod, rockfish, basket stars and cabezons. Beautiful sea lemons in the kelp. We saw masses of giant red urchins and small green urchins. Work your way around the shallow ledges that look like molten rock flowing southward to go to the drop-off at the southern end of the reef. The wall is a waterfall of white plumose anemones cascading down the sheer side. White fluffy anemones soften the undercut caves and grottoes sheering down to a depth of 90 to 100 feet (27 to 30 meters). Swimming scallops rain up around you all down the wall.
Divers have been chased from the water at Enterprise Reef by a pod of killer whales.

Bottom and Depths: On the north side of the marker, smooth rock ledges fall in folds at 20 to 30 feet (6 to 9 meters) deep. Thick bull kelp. Directly south of the marker the rock wall drops off to a depth of 90 to 100 feet (27 to 30 meters).

Hazards: Swift currents, boats and bull kelp. Currents up to 7 knots (13 kilometers/hour) sometimes flow through Active Pass. Dive on slack on a small tidal exchange. Listen for boats and ascend close to the rocks all the way to the surface. Carry a knife for kelp.

Telephones: • Village Bay ferry landing, Mayne Island. • Montague Harbour ferry landing, Galiano Island.

Facilities: None at Enterprise Reef. Charters out of Saltspring, Galiano and Gabriola islands. Camping and launching at Montague Harbour Marine Park on Galiano Island.

Access: Enterprise Reef is 1 nautical mile (2 kilometers) south of the western entry to Active Pass, the way between Galiano and Mayne islands. Active Pass is one of the busiest and most dangerous passes in the Gulf Islands because it is the main shipping and British Columbia ferry route between Vancouver and Victoria.
Enterprise Reef can be reached by charter from Saltspring or Galiano islands; Sidney, Victoria or Vancouver. Or launch at Mayne Island and go 1 nautical mile (2 kilometers) west – or at Montague Harbour on Galiano Island and go 4 nautical miles (7 kilometers) southeast to the marker at Enterprise Reef. Anchor in the bull kelp in the shallows on the side of the reef that is sheltered from the current, and go down. On ebb tides, anchor on the south side; on flood tides, anchor on the north side of the reef. Do not tie onto the marker. It is a federal offense to make fast to a marker or tamper with any aid to navigation.

Comments: Though Active Pass has both very swift currents and heavy boat traffic, these were not the reasons for its name. It was named after the American survey ship *Active.*

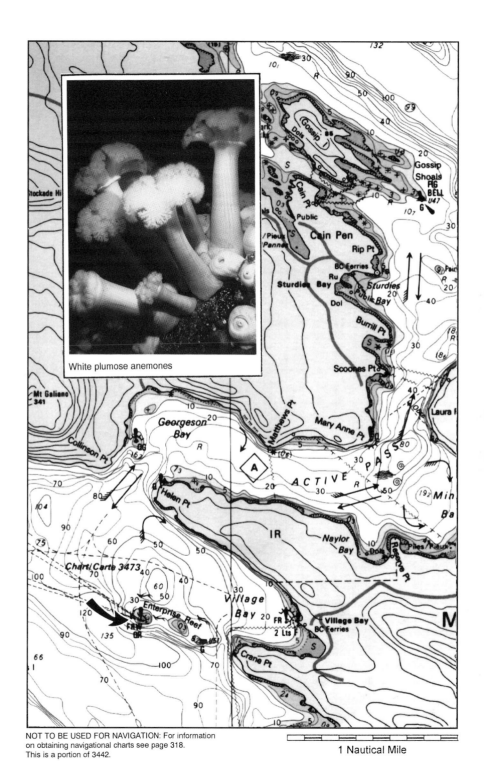

White plumose anemones

1 Nautical Mile

RETREAT COVE
Shore Dive

Skill: All divers and snorkelers

Why go: "There's so much detail – it's like, where do you start?" my buddy said about Galiano diving as we snorkeled across to the shallow wall at Retreat Cove. Lots of invertebrates here. And it's easy to dive.
Alabaster nudibranchs. Sea lemons. A white nudibranch with maroon tips laying eggs like a string of pearls – we saw all of these sights at Retreat Cove. We also saw nudibranch eggs like a coiled ribbon. Sea stars all over the rocks: leather stars, blood stars, brittle stars, vermilion stars and blue ones. Red rock crabs, deep-purple-colored kelp crabs waving their claws as if attacking. Millions of little creatures like underwater grasshoppers. Rock scallops. Chitons, one that looked like a turquoise gemstone. White plumose anemones beneath the overhangs.

Bottom and Depths: A shallow rock wall with overhangs. Boulders are scattered down it. Bull kelp in summer. The wall starts at 4 to 13 feet (1 to 4 meters), bottoms out to sand at 25 to 35 feet (8 to 11 meters). The white sand reflects the light, giving a bright sunny feeling.

Hazards: Bull kelp in summer. Carry a knife; if caught in the kelp you can cut your way free.

Telephones: • Sturdies Bay ferry landing, 7 miles (11 kilometers) away. • Madrona Lodge, outside. It is on the east side of Porlier Pass Road, 3½ miles (5¾ kilometers) north of the Retreat Cove turnoff.

Facilities: None at Retreat Cove. Air fills, cabins, boat rentals and charters nearby on Galiano Island. Camping, picnic tables, pit toilets, mooring buoys and concrete launching ramp, southwest end of the island at Montague Harbour Marine Park.

Access: Retreat Cove is on Trincomali Channel halfway up the west side of Galiano Island.
From Sturdies Bay ferry landing, follow signs to North Galiano. From the ferry, it is 9½ miles (15 kilometers) to Retreat Cove. At a "Y" in the road past the pub, turn right and go north on Porlier Pass Road for 8 miles (12½ kilometers) to a road with a Retreat Cove sign. Turn left down it. Go ½ mile (¾ kilometer) to the wharf. Room for one or two cars to park. Drop off the wharf and snorkel straight across to Retreat Island – took us 5 minutes. Dive north around the island.

Comments: No public toilets on Galiano except at the ferry terminal. Use the facilities at the ferry landing or at Montague Park.

Vermilion star

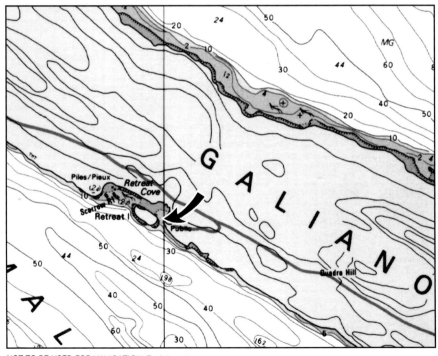

NOT TO BE USED FOR NAVIGATION: For information
on obtaining navigational charts see page 318.
This is a portion of 3442.

1 Nautical Mile

MADRONA WALL
Shore Dive

Skill: All divers

Why go: Over the wall with two kicks of your fins from shore. A superb wall for divers who are comfortable to enter where the drop-off is sheer to 60 feet (18 meters).
Immediately over the wall at 25 feet (8 meters) we saw a large and intricate basket star clinging to the smooth stark rock. We turned left. Frothy bowers of feather stars were clustered on rocks on the bottom, on the wall and beneath the rocky overhang. Brittle stars ran across the bright white sand. We saw giant purple urchins, a tiny grunt sculpin, a decorator crab, a juvenile Puget Sound king crab, a pale pink dahlia anemone on a ledge. Tube worms that look like caramelized popcorn balls encrusting the wall and leafy hornmouth whelks creeping between them. Swimming scallops, rock scallops, a lingcod; an alabaster nudibranch and sea lemons. We saw two sets of nudibranch eggs draped around two rocks like multiple strings of pearls.
Clusters of white plumose anemones were on the rubbly rocky part of the wall. My buddy enjoyed seeing leather stars and slime stars.

Bottom and Depths: The wall bottoms out to a broad sandy ledge at 50 to 60 feet (15 to 18 meters), depending on tide height. The clean rock wall is sheer at the entry point, and stretches both to the right and left. At some places it is undercut. At other points the wall turns into heaps of rock and rubble with lots of nooks and crannies for marine life. Beyond the broad ledge, it sheers off to great depths – drops to a depth of 200 to 230 feet (60 to 70 meters) on the chart. Can be slightly cloudy from silt.

Hazards: Boats and some current. Listen for boats and do not ascend through the open water. Hug the wall all the way to the surface. When you enter, notice the current direction and dive upcurrent at the start. When half your air is gone, you can turn and cruise back at a shallower depth along the wall.

Telephone: Top of the grass launching ramp, immediately across Porlier Pass Road at Madrona Lodge. The telephone is outside.

Facilities: Cabins and rowboats for resort guests at the entry point – bring your own motor. Also air fills at the entry point, but telephone to arrange; guiding services and charters nearby on Galiano Island. No restroom facilities are available for day divers on Galiano. Again, stop at the ferry landing before you head out to dive.

Access: Madrona Wall is on Trincomali Channel three-fourths of the way up the west side of Galiano Island.
From Sturdies Bay ferry landing, follow signs to North Galiano. From the ferry, it is 13 miles (21 kilometers) to Madrona. At a "Y" in the road past the pub, turn right and go north on Porlier Pass Road for 11 miles (18 kilometers) to Madrona – a dive flag is flying on top of one of the lodge buildings on the right-hand side and a dive flag is painted on the building housing the compressor on the left-hand side. Beside it, a grassy launching ramp slopes steeply from the road to the water. About 50 paces. It can be slippery when wet. The entry is across privately owned property. At the time of writing, the owners welcome all divers – day divers as well as resort guests – to walk down the ramp and have a dive. Over the wall, turn right or left depending on current direction.

Comments: Madrona Wall is ideal for night dives, especially if staying at the resort.

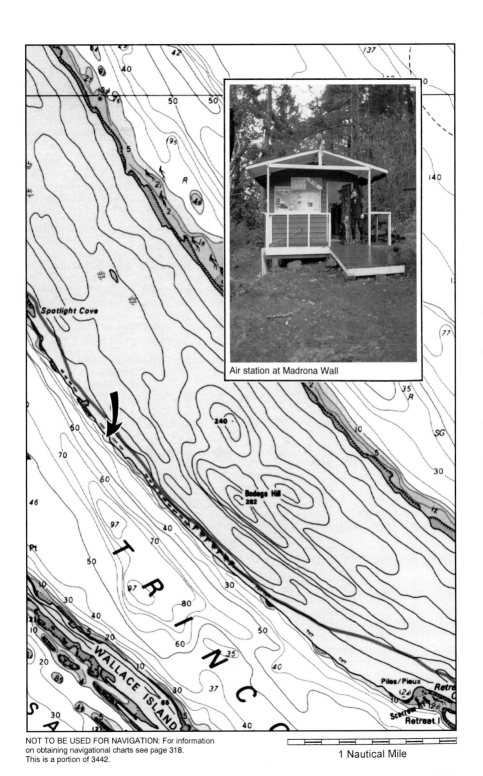

Air station at Madrona Wall

1 Nautical Mile

PRINGLE PARK
Shore Dive

Current Table: Porlier Pass

Skill: All divers

Why go: Incredible variety at this near-to-current but not-in-it site near Porlier Pass. Florescent purple and florescent orange quiver before me. My buddy holds a Puget Sound king crab – it is 1 foot (⅓ meter) across. The exotic giant seems specially designed for this era of hot colors.

We see white plumose anemones beneath a ledge. A blood star. A sunflower star splayed across a rock, nearly 3 feet (1 meter) wide. Purple plume worms decorate a cable down a valley in the rocks. We shine our lights into holes and caverns between tumbled boulders at the base of the wall. See a dark opening. I go in, look up, see an orange-and-red striped tiger rockfish high in the corner.

My buddy signals again. He's holding two barnacled Puget Sound king crabs. They are smaller, their shells the size of a hand with fingers outstretched. We cruise on past two large lingcod, a feather star, gray tennis ball sponges, a sea peach, orange cup corals. See a giant silver nudibranch on the sand, then a giant red one; an alabaster nudibranch and a sea lemon. Beneath a ledge, the delicate curlicues of a basket star in 25 feet (8 meters) of water. A couple of swimming scallops clap up in front of us.

Bottom and Depths: A rock wall slopes to a depth of 20 to 30 feet (6 to 9 meters). Becomes deeper around the corner, 50 to 60 feet (15 to 18 meters), depending on tide height. You could go still deeper to 90 feet (27 meters), but most life is shallower beside the wall. Boulders and rocks are heaped at the base of it. Caverns indent it, some large enough to enter. Sand stretches from the base. Bull kelp in summer.

Hazards: Boat traffic in and out of North Galiano government wharf at Spanish Hills, especially in summer. Some current. Dive near slack and work into the current for the first half of your dive. Listen for boats and hug the wall as you ascend.

Telephone: North Galiano, across from Spanish Hills store and government float.

Facilities: None at Pringle Park. No public flush toilets on the island except at the Sturdies Bay ferry terminal; you could stop there to wash hands and put in contact lenses, as I do, before diving. You will find pit toilets and camping at Montague Provincial Park and at Dionisio Point Provincial Park across the island at Coon Bay. Air fills on the way to Pringle Park – but telephone to arrange it. Guiding services, charters and launching at Galiano.

Access: Pringle Park is on Trincomali Channel near the northwest tip of Galiano Island; it is 1 nautical mile (2 kilometers) south of Alcala Point.

From Sturdies Bay ferry landing on Galiano, follow signs to North Galiano. From the ferry, it is 15 miles (24 kilometers) to the government wharf and float beside Spanish Hills store. Go to a "Y" in the road past the pub, turn right and head north on Porlier Pass Road for 14 miles (22 kilometers) to Spanish Hills store. Immediately past it you will see a sign at Pringle Park. Room for one or two cars to park beside the road. If no more space, drop gear and go back towards Spanish Hills store to park. A gently inclined path leads to the water; dive to the right around the point.

Might be wheelchair accessible if logs were cleared from Pringle Park entry point but there always seems to be a heap of them.

Comments: Fireplace in the pub at Galiano – great after a winter dive.

Juvenile Puget Sound king crab

NOT TO BE USED FOR NAVIGATION: For information
on obtaining navigational charts see page 318.
This is a portion of 3442.

1 Nautical Mile

151

ALCALA POINT
Kayak Dive or Boat Dive

Skill: Intermediate and expert divers. All divers with guide.

Why go: Clusters of white plumose anemones tumble over the rocky cliffs and over-hangs like marvelous big underwater bouquets. But the wolf-eels are the most popular feature of this dive – two mated pairs live at Alcala.

They are almost tame since they have been visited so often by divers who hand-feed them with urchin roe. Do not be surprised if the wolf-eels find you before you find them. And do not be frightened. Immediately off Alacala Point, in summer, you're into bull kelp which streams like olive-colored flags in the current and hides rockfish, urchins and lingcod. We saw trumpet sponges, orange cup corals, yellow hydrocoral and small rock scallops on the walls, swimming scallops and giant barnacles the size of baseballs. Sea pens, kelp greenlings, sea stars, octopuses, tiger rockfish, schools of pile perch, cucumbers and lots of sea lemons. I thought I saw a blue-eyed red brotula slip between the slits of the rocks.

The variety is almost unbelievable, but the wolf-eels are the scene-stealers. The last time I dived Alcala, two wolf-eels were guarding their young. The male did not come out of the den but seemed to swell himself out to fill the opening; he flapped and rippled his rubbery lips in a most comical manner – probably to frighten us away.

Bottom and Depths: Rock ledges and overhangs drop to a broad ledge at 60 to 70 feet (18 to 21 meters). Between boulders, there are small pockets of sand. Thick patches of bull kelp, in summer. Particularly beautiful ledges just to the north.

Hazards: Current, boats and bull kelp. If inexperienced with the site, dive precisely on slack. Local divers sometimes dive it when the current is ebbing because often a back eddy forms at Alcala. But don't count on it; try this only with guiding service. Listen for boats, and ascend up the wall all the way to shore. Carry a knife for kelp.

Telephone: North Galiano, across from Spanish Hills store and government float.

Facilities: None at Alcala. Air fills, charters and guiding services are available at Galiano. Cabins and the government float nearby. Air fills and charters also at Gabriola and Saltspring islands.

Access: Alcala Point is at the extreme northwest corner of Galiano Island on Trin-comali Channel – it is almost in Porlier Pass.

Charter or paddle a dive-kayak from the government wharf and float at Spanish Hills store in North Galiano. You can back your vehicle onto the wharf to drop gear, making it a short carry to the float. From the float, head north close around the shore-line. Past an oak tree at the point, you come to rocky shore. Boat divers usually anchor just inshore from the bull kelp off the point.

If paddling a dive-kayak, allow plenty of time to arrive for slack. Plan on taking 20 minutes for the paddle. You could land on the rocks just around the point. It is easier at high tide, as there is an abrupt ledge at low tide. At low tides you could anchor but then it becomes more of an advanced kayak dive.

Comments: Charters also from other islands in the Gulf, as well as from Spanish Hills at Galiano. Divers come from far and wide to dive Alcala.

At Spanish Hills, North Galiano

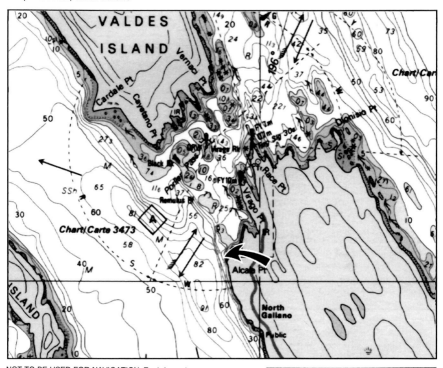

1 Nautical Mile

Skill: Intermediate and expert divers. All divers with guide.

Why go: The *Point Grey* is the most intact genuine wreck in the protected waters of British Columbia that I've dived. Although it is upside down, this 105-foot (32-meter) steel-screw steamer tug is photogenic. It is also shallow and easy to find. Visibility is usually good because Fraser River runoff does not reach it. With a guide, diving this wreck is within the capabilities of new divers. And as a wreck that has been singled out and marked with an interpretive plaque, it is of interest to all divers.

The tugboat *Point Grey* was built in 1911 in North Vancouver. In 1949 it was hauling a barge west to Victoria, entered Porlier Pass in dense fog and crashed into Virago Rock. The barge the *Point Grey* was towing hit the tugboat and the tug became stuck on the rock. It sat precariously on Virago Rock until the winter of 1963 when a storm knocked it off and it rolled upside down. In 1993 its 6-foot (2-meter) high propeller is still nearly intact – two of the three blades are attached to the propeller shaft. They are in shallow water and can be photographed from top to bottom. The third propeller blade and rudder are nearby on the ocean floor.

White plumose anemones cover the drive shaft. More fluffy white plumose anemones are on the ceiling which is really the floor. Dive it soon. In 1992 the *Point Grey* suffered new damage. The bow forward of the boiler broke off and turned right side up. You can still swim through the engine room of this tough steel tug, but it has started collapsing. All wrecks are alive, in a state of change, subject to assault by natural forces and passing vessels and this one is in a vulnerable location.

Bottom and Depths: Virago Rock breaks the surface at the marker. Around it, a thicket of bull kelp. South of Virago, corduroy-like creases in the rock line the bottom running nearly north and south. The *Point Grey* lies in one of these mini-valleys. The wreck rests at 30 to 40 feet (9 to 12 meters), depending on tide height. Beyond the wreck the ridges slope gradually down – we followed one to 90 feet (27 meters).

Hazards: Very strong current and boats: currents up to 9 knots (17 kilometers/hour) sometimes flow through Porlier. Dive on the slack on a small tidal exchange. Leave an experienced pickup person in the boat in case you are swept away by the current. Hug the bottom all the way to the surface well out of the way of boats.

Telephone: North Galiano, across from government wharf and Spanish Hills store.

Facilities: None at the wreck. Air fills, charters, launching, camping and cabins nearby at Galiano Island. Air fills and charters at Gabriola and Saltspring islands.

Access: The *Point Grey* is in the center of Porlier Pass on the south/southeast side of Virago Rock.

Charter out of Galiano, Gabriola or Saltspring islands; Nanaimo, Victoria or Vancouver; or launch at Ladysmith, Chemainus or Galiano. Virago is 10 nautical miles (19 kilometers) north of Montague Harbour on Galiano. Go to Virago Rock in Porlier Pass. Drop anchor and leave a boat tender on board in the event the current picks up before expected. Or dive from a "live" boat. Do not tie up to the marker. It is a federal offense to make fast to a marker or tamper with any aid to navigation. When you roll off the boat, be careful you don't bump your head. It is shallow. Swim to the marker, line up on a 150-degree compass bearing between the marker on Virago Rock and Alcala Point on Galiano Island and swim underwater to it. Or simply eyeball it before heading down at Virago and swim 50 feet (15 meters) from the marker south/southeast to the wreck.

The *Point Grey* lies on the *west* side of a shallow, narrow underwater valley. The propeller is apparent at the rear of the wreck near the marker. You could miss the *Point Grey* altogether if you go over an underwater ridge that is *east* of the marker – I did on my first dive at Virago! If you do not find the wreck right away, come up and start again.

Comments: The *Point Grey* is marked with a Plexiglas plaque on a concrete slab, placed near the stern of the vessel by the Underwater Archaeological Society of British Columbia.

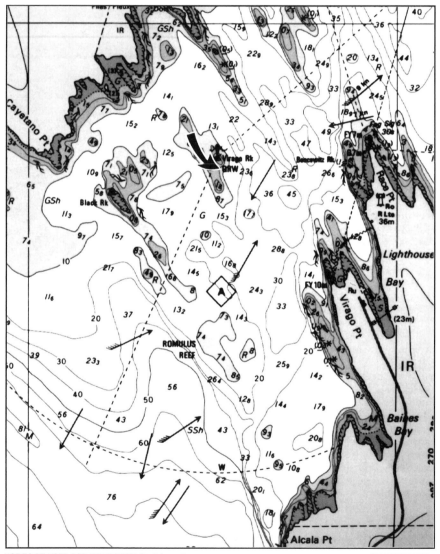

200 Yards

WRECK OF THE DEL NORTE
Boat Dive

Skill: Expert divers

Why go: A sturdy steamer on the northern British Columbia run, the *Del Norte* was launched in San Francisco in 1865. It was afloat for less than four years, and went down after hitting Canoe Islet at the northeast entrance to Porlier Pass.

The sunken sidewheeler lay undiscovered, an untouched wreck, until 1971. Even then its location was not generally known. On the first sport diving expedition on this 200-foot (61-meter) vessel in early 1975, one diver came up with an ornate brass deck lamp. Others swam through the boilers. Many artifacts were removed and members of the Underwater Archaeological Society of British Columbia (UASBC) became concerned. In the late 1970s they placed a plaque on the wreck with a brief history of the steamer and proposed heritage status for it. The two paddlewheels of this old ship are a reminder of an era that has passed, and the oscillating steam engines on the *Del Norte* are rare in North America. These features made it an important wreck to save. A heavy-duty mooring buoy was placed to give boaters a place to tie up so they won't drop their anchors and further damage the boilers and paddlewheels. The buoy has occasionally broken free, but when in place it is easy to find this formerly difficult-to-find wreck.

Even without a wreck, Canoe Islet is an exciting dive. I'll never forget drifting down through a curtain of silvery fish into a rocky field of basket stars. We saw feather stars, orange cup corals and lingcod. Schools of black rockfish parted as we swam off to look for the wreck.

Bottom and Depths: Rock, rubble, sand and shell bottom. There is almost no hull but the paddlewheels, boilers and engine works are relatively intact, with boilers and engine works sitting in their original location in the center of the wreck. The plaque placed by the UASBC lies at the foot of the *Del Norte* engine works. Big boulders are scattered around and you will see lumps of coal. These too are part of the wreck so just look, don't take. Remains of the wreck run from 40 to 90 feet (12 to 27 meters).

Hazards: Very strong current and visibility. Dive on slack on a small tidal exchange, not more than 2 feet (⅔ meter) per hour. The current is most dangerous on an ebbing tide. Plan to dive on a high slack. Leave a pickup person in the boat in case you are swept away by that current. Best visibility in winter when no Fraser River runoff.

Telephone: North Galiano, across from government wharf and Spanish Hills store.

Facilities: None at Canoe Islet. Air fills, charters, launching, camping and cabins nearby at Galiano Island and at Gabriola.

Access: Canoe Islet is ½ nautical mile (1 kilometer) north of Vernaci Point on the Strait of Georgia side of Valdes Island. It is north of the eastern entrance to Porlier Pass. Galiano Island is on the south side of the pass. Porlier is the middle one of the three major passages between the Gulf Islands. Gabriola Passage lies to the north and Active Pass to the south.

Charter out of Galiano, Gabriola or Saltspring islands, Nanaimo, Victoria or Vancouver. Or launch at Ladysmith, Chemainus or Galiano. Look for the orange buoy south of Canoe Islet that marks the wreck. Tie up to the buoy so you do not damage the wreck by dropping anchor and go down the buoy anchor line. From the bottom of the anchor line at 80 to 90 feet (24 to 27 meters), depending on tide height, follow the guide line up the slope to see pieces of the wreck. If the buoy is not in place, search for the *Del Norte* 200 yards (185 meters) south/southeast of Canoe Islet. No landings allowed at Canoe Islet as it is a provincial ecological reserve, a protected sea bird colony.

Comments: A staggeringly beautiful dive. Add the excitement of a heritage wreck, and you have a winner!

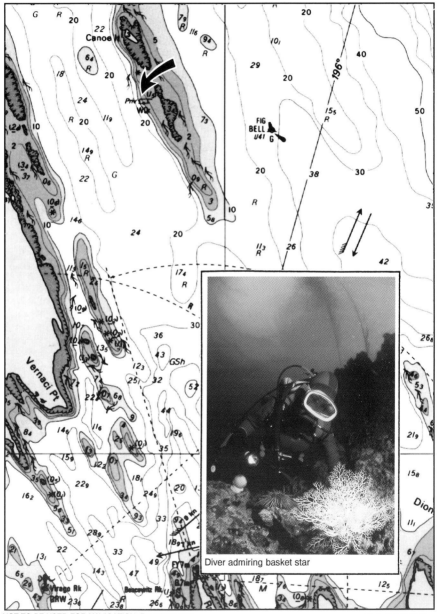

Diver admiring basket star

200 yards

WRECK OF THE MIAMI
Kayak Dive or Boat Dive

Skill: All divers

Why go: The *Miami* is a good safe wreck to dive – it is the skeleton of a ship. It's shallow, easy to find, and easy to dive.

The *Miami* was a 320-foot (100-meter) steel freighter that carried coal. On January 25, 1900, it grounded on White Rocks, now named Miami Islet, and went down. Sport divers have been exploring the *Miami* since 1956. In addition to the fun of swimming around and over a skeleton ship, you might see coal and you'll see lots of marine life living around the wreck. Rockfish hide under the shadow of the hull. Lingcod use the wreck for shelter in spawning season. Millions of small white plumose anemones dot the dark rounded ribs. Look for lion nudibranchs in winter. We saw giant barnacles, sea peaches and painted greenlings. Giant nudibranchs between the broadleaf bottom kelp. Millions of feathery, tube-dwelling anemones and clams in the silty sand around the *Miami*.

Bottom and Depths: The reef is silt-covered smooth rock and slopes gently down to a depth of 50 to 60 feet (15 to 18 meters). On summer low tides a large portion of the *Miami* used to project above water. The main hull rested on the bottom at 25 to 35 feet (8 to 11 meters). The ship broke its back over the ledge. Some of it slipped down the western slope and some parts were in 50 to 60 feet (15 to 18 meters) of water. Now the hull is almost totally disintegrated, and because of tidal effect it is very widely spread across the reef. It changes all the time, which means you might still see coal.

Hazards: Current, wind, poor visibility and the wreck itself. Dive on the slack. Visibility can be poor in summer because of plankton growth, and at any time of year if too many divers stir up the silt. A still, sunny day in winter is the best time to dive. Be careful of sharp metal projections from the wreck.

Telephones: • Ladysmith government wharf. • North Galiano, across road from government wharf and Spanish Hills store.

Facilities: None at Miami Islet. Charters out of Gabriola, Galiano and Saltspring islands; Sidney, Victoria, Nanaimo and Vancouver.

Access: The *Miami* rests on a reef north of Miami Islet in Trincomali Channel, 1 nautical mile (2 kilometers) northwest of Pilkey Point on Thetis Island. Wind from any direction can make for difficulties in going to the *Miami* which is in an extremely exposed position.

Charter out of Gabriola, Galiano or Saltspring islands; Nanaimo, Sidney, Victoria or Vancouver and go to the red buoy that marks the reef. Launch at Ladysmith or Chemainus on Vancouver Island or at Gabriola or Galiano island and go to the reef.

We launched an inflatable at Yellow Point on Vancouver Island and headed east for 1½ nautical miles (3 kilometers) to the reef. On a calm day, you could paddle a dive-kayak to it. From Ladysmith and Chemainus, 7 nautical miles (13 kilometers) to the red buoy. Do not tie up to the marker. It is a federal offense to make fast to a marker or tamper with any aid to navigation. Do not search for the wreck with side-scan sonar as the hull has disintegrated too much to find it with that. Be careful not to hit the wreck. It dries at 11-foot (3-meter) tides. On a low tide you may spot it from your boat. If not, line up on a direct line between the red marker, Miami Islet and Pilkey Point. Anchor on that line near the bull kelp 100 feet (30 meters) south of the red marker and go down. To find the wreckage, swim south under water along the west side of the reef.

Comments: This reef collects wrecks. The *Robert Kerr*, a wooden vessel converted to collier which went down in 1911, lies in slightly deeper water on the reef farther southeast of the *Miami*. More difficult to find than the *Miami*, but if you're on a large boat and have lots of air you may want to look for it, as well. Take a light!

From Miami Marker, looking south toward Pilkey Point on Thetis Island

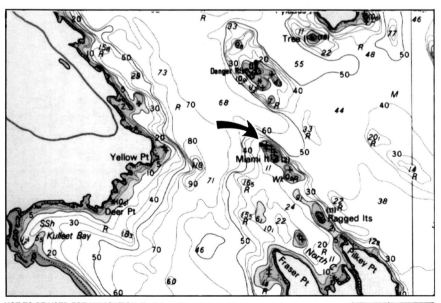

NOT TO BE USED FOR NAVIGATION: For information on obtaining navigational charts see page 318. This is a portion of L/C-3463.

1 Nautical Mile

Skill: All divers and snorkelers

Why go: Low-key easy dive, easy entry, lots to see. White shell beach with a back-drop of the snowy peaks of Mount Baker rising behind the Gulf Islands. Great for a picnic, building sand castles and soaking up summer sun after the dive.

Prickly purple urchins cluster on the rocks in the shallows. Deeper, a purple aura glows around each one – I see "double purple". Then we reach the cool green place. Frothy white plumose anemones hang like a veil beneath an overhang. Kelp green-lings flash past. Oval-shaped chitons are flat on the rocks. They look like black-and-green striped buttons. We see rockfish, painted greenlings, giant barnacles. Red sunflower stars tumble in the current, stick to my arm, stick to the wall. A burrowing cucumber pokes lacy orange fingers between the rocks. Orange cup corals are sprin-kled like confetti. A sea pen rises from the sand like an orange quill pen. A dogfish shark cruises up from the dark depths to meet us. We are at 50 feet (15 meters).

Shallower, I look under a ledge. Crabs scurry. Swimming back across the bay under water we see red rock crabs galore. The egg case of a moon snail. Several gunnels dart through the eelgrass. Hairy siphons of horse clams suck into the silty sand as we swim over. Bright green lettuce kelp is scattered between like torn tissue.

On the beach, one diver told of trying to tease an octopus out by dangling a crab before it, and more tentacles reached out. Two octopuses in the hole. We met a nine-year old who was skin diving in his wet suit and weight belt for the first time.

Bottom and Depths: Gently sloping sand at base of wall at the point. Tumbled boul-ders. Sandy ledges at 30 feet (9 meters), 50 feet (15 meters) and on down. In the bay, silty sand and eelgrass.

Hazards: Current. Dive near slack, especially with large tides and on ebbing tides.

Telephone: Beside Fulford-Ganges Road, immediately after turning right off Beddis Road toward Ganges: the telephone is outside the motel on the right-hand side.

Facilities: Lovely for picnics at Beddis Beach. Air fills, charters and launching at Ganges. Camping with picnic tables, pit toilets and fire rings at Mouat Provincial Park in Ganges and at Ruckle Provincial Park near Fulford Harbour.

Access: Beddis Beach is on Captain Passage at the southeast side of Saltspring Island. It is off Ganges-Fulford Road, 5 miles (8 kilometers) out of Ganges. From Ganges to Beddis Beach takes 10 to 15 minutes; 30 minutes from Long Harbour; 25 minutes from Vesuvius; 20 minutes from Fulford Harbour to the dive.

On Beddis Road just past Lionel Road, you come to a small "Beddis Beach Public Access" sign – Beddis Road curves right uphill. Follow the sign: go left down the dirt track filled with potholes, two minutes to the sea. The end of the road opens out, giving room for six or seven cars to park. From there, fifteen paces to the beach. You could swim to the left and head down at the point. Or walk to the left for 150 yards (140 meters) to the far end of the beach, and dive around the rocky point.

Wheelchair accessible with a 6- to 30-foot (2- to 9-meter) patch of sand to cross – less at high tide, and then kayak or swim 150 yards (140 meters) to the point on the left-hand side.

To get to "Beddis Beach Public Access" past Lionel Road
• From Ganges, follow signs toward Fulford Harbour. Go along Fulford-Ganges

Road. Just past the RCMP station, Beddis Road veers to the left. Go on Beddis for 4 miles (6½ kilometers) to the "Beddis Beach Public Access" sign past Lionel Road.
• From Fulford Harbour, drive up the hill. Turn right into Beaver Point Road; follow the yellow line designating it as the main road. From Fulford-Ganges Road, go 1½ miles (2½ kilometers) to Stewart Road. Turn left. Go 2 miles (3½ kilometers) along Stewart to Cusheon Lake Road. Turn right. Go to Beddis Road and turn right again. Drive along Beddis for 1 mile (1¾ kilometers) to the small dirt track marked with the "Beddis Beach Public Access" sign. It is just past Lionel Road.
• From Long Harbour or Vesuvius follow signs to Ganges. Then follow signs toward Fulford Harbour. Take Fulford-Ganges Road to Beddis Road. Go 4 miles (6½ kilometers) on Beddis to the small "Beddis Beach Public Access" sign.

Comments: The whole family will love Beddis Beach. Full sun as well as dappled shade beneath coppery arbutus trees and huge evergreens twisting out over the sand; deer beside the road.

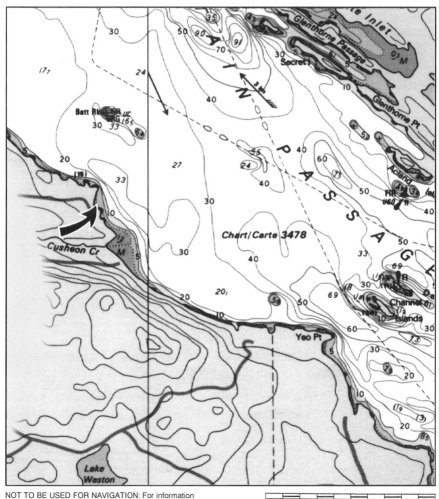

NOT TO BE USED FOR NAVIGATION: For information on obtaining navigational charts see page 318. This is a portion of 3442.

1 Nautical Mile

BEAVER POINT

Boat Dive or Kayak Dive
Shore Dive (with long walk)

Skill: Intermediate and expert divers at point. All divers in bay.

Why go: I think of castles and caves when I think of Beaver Point. Rocky wall encrusted in castle-like staghorn bryozoans falls in caves, grottoes and overhangs. Some caves are large enough to enter. Hiding places for all kinds of life are scattered along this current-swept, crusty wall. We saw fluffy white plumose anemones under the overhangs. Millions of little crabs poking out of cracks between the staghorn. White encrusting sponge and dahlia anemones add further to this scenic site. Huge sea stars, rockfish, octopuses, lingcod and giant barnacles. We even saw a prawn and a gorgeous sea pen living in a pocket of sand. Sponges down deeper.

Current-free diving at any time of day for all divers in the shallow cove on the left of the point. Also look for bottles. Steamship service to Beaver Point began in 1889. Rum runners used to park in the cove and a 60-year-old bottle was found here in 1990. A small reef is on the outer edge of the cove near the opposite shore.

But unique to Beaver Point – and why I love it the most – are the overhangs, castles and caves.

Bottom and Depths: Rock walls, ledges and overhangs drop to broken rock at 30 to 40 feet (9 to 12 meters). Some bull kelp. The drop-off is progressively deeper at the base of the wall as you move around toward the point.

Hazards: Current and bull kelp. Dive on the slack. Carry a knife.

Telephone: Ruckle Provincial Park, beside entrance.

Facilities: Ruckle Provincial Park is a spacious, wild park with broad, slightly-wooded grassy slopes rolling down to the water. Being largely undeveloped is part of its charm. Walk-in camping, drinking water and pit toilets at Ruckle Park. Air fills and charters at Ganges. Launching at Ganges and Drummond Park near Fulford Harbour.

Access: Beaver Point juts into Captain Passage from Ruckle Park on Saltspring Island. It is 6 miles (10 kilometers) from the ferry landing at Fulford, 18 miles (29 kilometers) from Vesuvius Bay, 19 miles (30 kilometers) from Long Harbour to the dive.

Go to Beaver Point Road, then drive 6 miles (10 kilometers) along it to the picnicking area at Ruckle Park. The walk from parking lot to water is a long one, from ⅓ to ½ mile (½ to ¾ kilometer). But it is a well graduated tarmac path – take a wheelbarrow. The path goes almost to the water. Dive in the cove or swim or kayak around to your right towards Beaver Point.

To get to Beaver Point Road
• From Ganges, follow signs to Fulford Harbour. Go on Fulford-Ganges Road for 7 miles (12 kilometers) toward Fulford. Just before you head downhill toward the ferry landing, turn left into Beaver Point Road.
• From Fulford Harbour, head uphill for ½ mile (1 kilometer) and turn right into Beaver Point Road.
• From Long Harbour or Vesuvius Bay follow signs to Ganges; from Ganges follow signs toward Fulford Harbour. Just before Fulford, turn left into Beaver Point Road.

Comments: Locally the area is honored as an underwater reserve.

Near Beaver Point

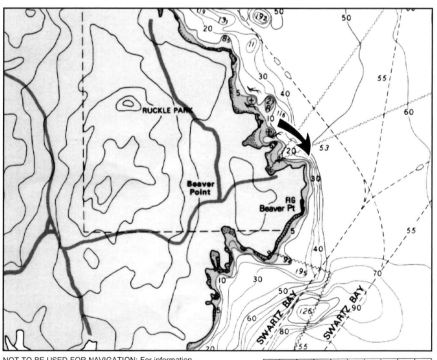

NOT TO BE USED FOR NAVIGATION: For information
on obtaining navigational charts see page 318.
This is a portion of 3441.

1 Nautical Mile

CANOE ROCK
Boat Dive

Skill: Intermediate and expert divers and snorkelers

Why go: All those fish! All that color! And clean, clean water through which to see it all. Canoe Rock is one of those places where the current never stops. It merely changes direction. And there's a fantastic amount of brilliantly colored life in only 25 to 40 feet (8 to 12 meters) of water.
"Carrot tops!" describes the bright orange cucumbers between the chinks of the rocks. Big bright white boulders tumbled over one another are splattered with purple algae. We saw rock scallops, abalones, giant barnacles, great red urchins, masses of soft white plumose anemones and small orange sea peaches. Cracks and crevices between the rocks are filled with fish. So many huge tiger rockfish I could not count them. Large lingcod, cabezons, kelp greenlings and schools of huge black rockfish. Wolf-eels under the ledges.

Bottom and Depths: Boulders, broken and stratified rock with ledges and tables, hollows and crevices and small broken rock lying on top undulates from the marker to 40 feet (12 meters). Some bull kelp. No silt. A clean-swept bottom.

Hazards: Current and bull kelp. Dive on the slack on a small tidal exchange. A pickup boat is advisable. Carry a knife for kelp.

Telephones: • Thieves Bay, Pender Island. • Ganges Commercial Harbour near head of Ganges Harbour, Saltspring Island; it is beside the wharf manager's office.

Facilities: None at Canoe Rock. Air fills, camping, accommodations, boat rentals, charters and launching at Pender and Saltspring islands and Sidney on Saanich Peninsula.

Access: Marked by a light, Canoe Rock is in Moresby Passage 300 yards (275 meters) west of Reynard Point on Moresby Island. It is 2½ nautical miles (4½ kilometers) southwest of Thieves Bay at Pender Island. Launching at Thieves Bay, which is south of Mouat Point on North Pender. Also launching at Drummond Park on Saltspring Island and at Sidney on Vancouver Island. Charter, rent or launch and go to Canoe Rock. Anchor on the inside of the light towards Reynard Point and dive between the rocks and the point.

Comments: An exceptional dive for those who like shallow reefs. A great second dive after diving the *G.B. Church.*

Tiger rockfish

1 Nautical Mile

Mauve anemones at Dodd Narrows

Loading trailerable boat at Public Market

Rolling off *Neptune's Apprentice*

CHAPTER 4
Nanaimo, Hornby Island, and south to Sansum Narrows including Gabriola Island

Steller sea lions

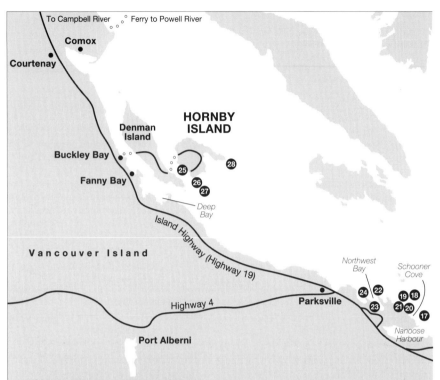

NANAIMO, HORNBY ISLAND, AND SOUTH TO SANSUM NARROWS
including Gabriola Island

Dives

1. Burial Islet
2. Octopus Point
3. Maple Bay Reef
4. Evening Cove
5. Coffin Island
6. Round Island
7. Dodd Narrows
8. Gabriola Passage
9. Drumbeg Park
10. Thrasher Rock
11. Carlos Island
12. Orlebar Point
13. Snake Island
14. Jesse Island
15. Keel Cove
16. Sunrise Beach
17. Sea Lions
18. Yeo Islands
19. Amelia Island
20. Seducer's Beach
21. Dolphin Beach
22. Cottam Point
23. Wall Beach
24. Madrona Point
25. Maude Reef
26. Heron Rocks
27. Norris Rocks
28. Sixgill Sharks

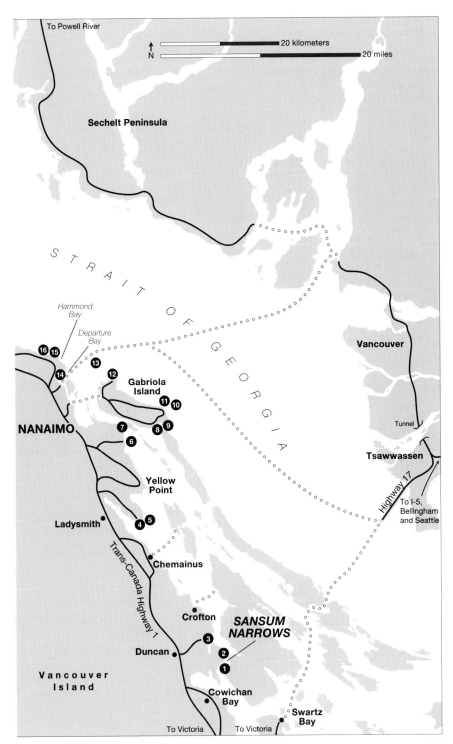

To Powell River

20 kilometers
20 miles
N

Sechelt Peninsula

S T R A I T   O F   G E O R G I A

Hammond
Bay

Departure
Bay

Vancouver

Tunnel

Tsawwassen

Highway 17

To I-5,
Bellingham
and Seattle

16 **15**

13

14

12

Gabriola
Island

11 **10**

NANAIMO

7

8 **9**

6

Yellow
Point

Ladysmith

4 **5**

Trans-Canada Highway 1

Chemainus

Crofton

*SANSUM
NARROWS*

3

2

Duncan

1

Vancouver
Island

Cowichan
Bay

To Victoria   To Victoria

Swartz
Bay

SERVICE INFORMATION *
Nanaimo, Hornby Island, and south to Sansum Narrows including Gabriola Island

Charts: Canadian Hydrographic Service
- 3310 Gulf Islands–Victoria Harbour to Nanaimo Harbour
- 3442 North Pender Island to Thetis Island
- 3457 Nanaimo Harbour and Departure Bay
- 3458 Approaches to Nanaimo Harbour
- 3459 Approaches to Nanoose Harbour
- L/C-3462 Juan de Fuca Strait to Strait of Georgia
- L/C-3463 Strait of Georgia, Southern Portion
- 3475 Plans–Stuart Channel
- 3478 Plans–Saltspring Island
- L/C-3512 Strait of Georgia, Central Portion
- L/C-3513 Strait of Georgia, Northern Portion
- 3527 Baynes Sound

Tide and Current Tables: Canadian Hydrographic Service *Tide and Current Table, Volume 5* and Canadian Hydrographic Service *Current Atlas: Juan de Fuca Strait to Strait of Georgia* (use with *Murray's Tables* or *Washburne's Tables*)

Diving Emergency Telephone Numbers
Dial 911: Say "I have a scuba diving emergency".

Vancouver General Hospital: Dial (604) 875-4111 and say "I have a scuba diving emergency. I want the hyperbaric physician on call".

If medical personnel are unfamiliar with scuba diving emergencies, ask them to telephone DAN (Divers Alert Network): (919) 684-8111, then say "I have a scuba diving emergency".

Other Useful Numbers
Continuous Marine Broadcast (CMB) recorded, 24 hours; listen for weather in the Strait of Georgia, telephone
- Comox: (604) 339-0748
- Vancouver: (604) 270-7411
- Victoria: (604) 474-7998

Shellfish Infoline, recorded: (604) 666-3169
Sportfishing Information Line, recorded: 1-800-663-9333

• Dive Shops at Nanaimo

Island Divers Supply
#5-1400 Wingrove Street, at
  Departure Bay Road
Nanaimo BC V9S 3L7
604) 751-2277; fax (604) 751-2692
(Waterfront and roadside air fills for boaters at beach; also guiding.)

Sundown Diving
1840 Stewart Avenue, at
  the Public Market
Nanaimo BC V9S 4E6
(604) 753-1880; fax (604) 753-6445;
pager (604) 755-8232
(Waterfront and roadside air fills.)

Seafun Divers
300 Terminal Avenue
Nanaimo BC V9R 5C8
(604) 754-4813; fax (604) 754-5383

• Charters at Nanaimo

Jessie Anne II
Big Island Charters
PO Box 584
Nanaimo BC V9R 5J9
(604) 754-5396
(Charters out of Departure Bay.)

Neptune's Apprentice
Sundown Diving
1840 Stewart Avenue, at
   the Public Market
Nanaimo BC V9S 4E6
(604) 753-1880; fax (604) 753-6445;
pager (604) 755-8232
*(Charters out of several destinations as
the boat is trailerable.)*

Scamper II
Scamper II Charters
1204 College Drive
Nanaimo BC V9R 6A4
(604) 754-9996
(Charters out of Nanaimo Boat Basin.)

• Boat Rentals at Nanaimo

North Island Water Sports
2755 Departure Bay Road
Nanaimo BC V9S 3W9
(604) 758-2488
*(Dive-kayak rentals; kayak launching im-
mediately across Departure Bay Road.
Wheelchair access to beach, then go
down four or five steps.)*

Western Wildcat Tours, at
   the Public Market
PO Box 1162
Nanaimo BC V9R 6E7
(604) 753-3234 – fax and telephone.
*(Inflatable rentals, May through Sep-
tember.)*

• Launching at Nanaimo

Brechin Civic Ramps
Foot of Brechin Road, at the Public Market, Nanaimo, BC
*(Launching at Departure Bay: concrete ramp, good at all tides. Picnic tables at ramp.
Handicapped parking stalls. Restrooms in parking lot; telephone at water side of
Public Market.)*
   From the ferry terminal at Departure Bay, immediately turn left at the traffic light
and right toward the Public Market, then left to the ramp.

• Dive Shop, Charters and Launching at Gabriola Island

Gabriola Reefs Dive Shop
Page's Resort & Marina, off
   Coast Road at Silva Bay
RR 2, S-30, C-9
Gabriola Island BC V0R 1X0
(604) 247-8443
*(Waterfront and roadside air fills all day;
telephone to arrange for after-hours air
fills. Also charters.)*

Moloda
Gabriola Reefs Dive Shop
Page's Resort & Marina
RR 2, S-30, C-9
Gabriola Island BC V0R 1X0
(604) 247-8443
(Charters out of Silva Bay.)

Coastal Diver
High Test Dive Charters
RR 2, S-27, C-30
Gabriola Island BC V0R 1X0
(604) 247-9753; cellular (604) 755-5024
*(Custom liveaboard, day and inflatable
charters out of Degnen and Silva Bay.)*

Degnen Bay Public Ramp
Foot of Gray Road, near Gabriola Pass
*(Launching at high tides. No toilet, no
telephone. Nearest telephone at Degnen Bay government wharf.)*
   From South Road and Degnen Bay
Road, head west ⅓ mile (½ kilometer)
to Cooper Road; turn left and left again
into Gray Road and go to the end of it.

• Dive Shops and Air Stations north of Nanaimo

T.D. Sports
Ocean View Plaza
2885 Cliffe Avenue
Courtenay BC V9N 2L8
(604) 338-1633; (604) 338-1307: After hours, summer only.
(Also guiding for shore dives.)

Diver's Den
216 Fifth Street
Courtenay BC V9N 1J6
(604) 338-2111

Hornby Island Diving
Ford Cove
Hornby Island BC V0R 1Z0
(604) 335-2807
(Resort air station: waterfront and road-side air fills; also charters and dive packages for groups.)

Octopus Adventures Inc.
4924 Argyle Street
Port Alberni BC V9Y 1V7
(604) 723-3057

• Charters and Boat Rentals for Hornby Island

Hornby Island Diving
Ford Cove
Hornby Island BC V0R 1Z0
(604) 335-2807
(Day charters for groups. Also divers' bunkhouse accommodations. Wheelchair diving groups welcome.)

My Joan
Sail Pacific Yacht Charters
PO Box 1555
Comox BC V9N 8A2
(604) 339-7850 or 336-2150
(Liveaboard sail/dive charters out of Comox marina to Denman, Hornby and Mitlenatch. Also day charters.)

Comox Valley Kayaks
1595 Comox Road
Courtenay BC V9N 3P7
(604) 334-2628; fax (604) 334-0328
(Dive-kayak rentals; sometimes double dive-kayaks available.)

Sunseeker
Diver's Den
216 Fifth Street
Courtenay BC V9N 1J6
(604) 338-2111
(Charters out of Fanny Bay to Denman and Hornby islands. Also inflatable charters.)

• Launching for Hornby Island

Hornby Public Ramp
Ford Cove
Hornby Island BC
(Hand-launching, small boats only. No toilets; telephone at grocery store.)

From Hornby Island ferry landing, head up the hill to your left. Go 5 miles (8 kilometers) along the main road to the Co-op Store. Turn right and go 3 miles (4¾ kilometers) on Central Road to Ford Cove.

Denman Public Ramp
Gravelly Bay
Denman Island, east side
Beside ferry landing
(Launching only: steep concrete ramp, good at all tides – best at low tides. No toilets; telephone at ferry landing.)

Deep Bay Ramp
Ship & Shore Marine
RR 1, S-160, C-69
Bowser BC V0R 1G0
(604) 757-8750
(Launching only: concrete ramp, good at all tides. Restrooms and hot showers; telephone at store.)

Off Island Highway (Highway 19) between Bowser and Fanny Bay: look for Gainsburg Road when almost 2½ miles (4 kilometers) north of Bowser and 5 miles (8 kilometers) south of Fanny Bay. Follow signs for 1½ miles (2¼ kilometers) to Deep Bay; go down Gainsburg Road for 1⅓ miles (2 kilometers) to Burne Road and turn left on Chrome Point Road to the water. The ramp is located next to the government wharf.

Pacific Village Motel Resort Ramp
8256 South Island Highway
RR 1, S-29, C-9
Fanny Bay BC V0R 1W0
(604) 335-2333
(Launching only: concrete ramp, good at all except extreme low tides. At high tides, good for wheelchair divers. Restrooms and hot showers; telephones at restrooms and Highway 19.)

• Charters, Boat Rentals and Launching at Schooner Cove, Northwest Bay and Nanoose Harbour

Schooner Cove Resort Hotel & Marina
3521 Dolphin Drive
RR 2, Box 12
Nanoose Bay, BC V0R 2R0
(604) 468-7691; fax (604) 468-5744
Charter reservations, toll-free in BC: 1-800-663-7060.
(Charters out of Schooner Cove. Also boat rentals and launching: concrete ramp, good at all tides 2 feet [½ meter] and greater. Restrooms; telephone outside marina office.)

Beachcomber Marina
1600 Brynmarl Road, off
   Northwest Bay Road
RR 1, Box 21, Beachcomber
Nanoose Bay BC V0R 2R0
(604) 468-7222
(Charters out of Northwest Bay – wheelchair divers welcome. Also boat rentals and launching. No public toilets or telephone.)

Snaw-naw-as Marina Ramp
209 Mallard Way
Lantzville BC V0R 2H0
(604) 390-2616; fax (604) 390-3365; pager (604) 977-9334
(Launching at Nanoose Harbour: concrete ramp, good at all tides. Wheelchair accessible marina float. Restrooms. Telephones at top of ramp and outside campground office. In summer, coin-operated hot showers at campground.)
   Located ⅓ mile (½ kilometer) off Island Highway (Highway 19). Take the northern turnoff to Lantzville; it is 4 miles (6 kilometers) north of Woodgrove Centre at Hammond Bay Road, the same distance south of Northwest Bay Road.

• Dive Shop, Charters, Boat Rentals and Launching south of Nanaimo

Pacific Coast Diving Services
Located at 6683 Beaumont Avenue,
   near government dock at Maple Bay
RR 1, Duncan BC V9L 1M3
(604) 746-4188
(Waterfront and roadside air fills; also charters.)

Sally-Anne
Pacific Coast Diving Services
6683 Beaumont Avenue, Maple Bay
RR 1, Duncan BC V9L 1M3
(604) 746-4188
(Charters out of Maple Bay. Wheelchair divers welcome.)

Maple Bay Public Ramp
Beaumont Avenue, north of government dock and float
Maple Bay BC
(Launching at all tides: concrete ramp. Toilets at park south of pub, open in summer only. Telephone at grocery store.)
   Located 10 minutes from Duncan: turn east off Highway 1 at Trunk Road following

signs to Maple Bay. Trunk Road becomes Tzouhalem Road which then becomes Maple Bay Road and goes to the government dock at Maple Bay. The launching ramp is just north of it.

Genoa Bay Marina
5100 Genoa Bay Road, RR 1
Duncan BC V9L 1M3
(604) 746-7621
(Launching only: concrete ramp, good at all tides. Restrooms; telephone outside marina office.)

Hecate Park Public Ramp
1800 Block Cowichan Bay Road
Cowichan Bay BC
(Launching only: concrete ramp, good for all boats at 4-foot [1¼-meter] tides and greater. Large parking area. Toilet and a picnic table; telephones nearly ½ mile [¾ kilometer] south in middle of Cowichan Bay at post office; another telephone at head of Cowichan Bay, top of government dock and at hotel lobby, available 24 hours.)
    Located south of Duncan on Cowichan Bay Road: From Trans-Canada Highway (Highway 1) go on Cowichan Bay Road. It is 3 miles (5 kilometers) from either north or south end to the public ramp. Heading north, look for the ramp ½ mile (1 kilometer) past the hotel. Heading south, you reach the ramp before the marinas and hotel.

Pier 66
1745 Cowichan Bay Road
Cowichan Bay BC V0R 1N0
(604) 748-8444
(Boat rentals; restrooms; telephone two doors northwest at post office, more telephones at top of dock and at hotel, head of Cowichan Bay.)

Anchor Marina and Charters
1721 Cowichan Bay Road
Cowichan Bay BC V0R 1N0
(604) 746-5424
(Boat rentals and water taxi. Restrooms; telephone 175 yards [160 meters] northwest at post office, more telephones at top of dock and at hotel, at head of Cowichan Bay.)

Rotary Public Ramp
Foot of Ludlow Road
Ladysmith BC
(Launching for Gulf Islands: concrete ramp, good at all tides. Toilet and telephone on wharf.)
    At traffic light north end of Ladysmith, turn toward sea on Ludlow Road. After crossing second set of railway tracks immediately turn right, and still on Ludlow Road, go to the end of it.

Rotary Public Ramp
Foot of Maple Street, off Chemainus Road
Chemainus BC
(Launching for Gulf Islands: concrete ramp, good at all tides. Restrooms at park. Telephone ⅓ mile [½ kilometer] away at ferry terminal foot of Oak Street at Esplanade Street. From ramp, go to Oak Street. Turn left and to the ferry.)
    Located 5 minutes off Highway 1 between Duncan and Ladysmith: Follow signs to Chemainus, taking Henry Road to Chemainus Road and turn left. Go ¾ mile (1¼

kilometers) to Cedar Street. Turn right and go to Oak Street; turn right again and go to Maple Street. Then almost immediately turn left and go to the water.

• Liveaboard Charters out of Nanaimo Region

Clavella Adventures
Magna Yachting Limited
PO Box 866, Station A
Nanaimo BC V9R 5N2
(604) 753-3751 (office); fax (604) 755-4014; (604) 949-4014 (vessel).
(Out of Nanaimo to Gulf Islands, October to March; will pick up groups in Gulf Islands and Sidney. Out of Port Hardy, March to October.)

Sea Venturer
Exta-Sea Charters
PO Box 1058
Nanaimo BC V9R 5Z2
(604) 756-0544; fax (604) 758-4897
(Out of Nanaimo to Gulf Islands, November through March; out of Port Hardy, August through October; out of west coast Vancouver Island April through July.)

Blue Fjord
Blue Fjord Charters
PO Box 1450
Ladysmith BC V0R 2E0
(604) 245-8987
(Out of Ladysmith – out of anywhere.)

• **More Services for Nanaimo Region:** see service information for Gulf Islands on page 139. Note also that all Gulf Islands dives and service information except for Gabriola Island are included in the Gulf Islands chapter. Gabriola Island information is included in the Nanaimo chapter because of land access to Gabriola via Nanaimo.

• Ferry Information
to Gabriola Island and Mainland

British Columbia Ferry Corporation
Departure Bay (Nanaimo) Terminal
Nanaimo BC
(604) 753-6626: Recorded schedules available 24 hours.
Toll-free in BC: 1-800-663-7600: "live".
Telephoning from outside British Columbia, (604) 386-3431 – also "live".
(Ferries from Departure Bay to Horseshoe Bay [West Vancouver]; and from Departure Bay to Tsawwassen [south of Vancouver].)

British Columbia Ferry Corporation
Nanaimo Harbour Terminal
Located across from Harbour Park Mall
  in downtown Nanaimo
Toll-free in BC: 1-800-663-7600. Or (604) 753-9344.
(Ferries from downtown Nanaimo to Gabriola Island.)

British Columbia Ferry Corporation
Little River Terminal
Comox BC
Toll-free in BC: 1-800-663-7600. Or (604) 339-3310.
(Ferries between Comox and Powell River.)

Ferry Information
to Denman and Hornby islands

British Columbia Ferry Corporation
Denman Island Terminals
Denman Island BC
Toll-free in BC: 1-800-663-7600. Or
(604) 335-2744 (East Terminal) and
(604) 335-0151 (West Terminal).
(Ferries between Buckley Bay on Van-couver Island, and Denman and Hornby islands.)

British Columbia Ferry Corporation
Hornby Island Terminal
Shingle Spit
Hornby Island BC
Toll-free in BC: 1-800-663-7600. Or
(604) 335-2733.
(Ferries between Denman and Hornby islands.)

British Columbia Ferry Corporation
Buckley Bay Terminal
Toll-free in BC: 1-800-663-7600. Or
(604) 335-0323.
(Ferries between Comox and Powell River.)

• Tourist Information

Discover British Columbia
1117 Wharf Street
Victoria BC V8W 2Z2
1-800-663-6000: Toll-free throughout
Canada and the USA, including Hawaii
and parts of Alaska.

Duncan Travel infocentre
381 Trans-Canada Highway 1
Duncan BC V9L 3R5
(604) 746-4436; fax (604) 746-8222

Comox Valley Travel Infocentre
2040 Cliffe Avenue
Courtenay BC V9N 2L3
(604) 334-3234; fax (604) 334-4908

Nanaimo Travel Infocentre
266 Bryden Street
Nanaimo BC V9S 1A8
(604) 754-8474; fax (604) 754-6468
Toll-free in BC: 1-800-663-7337

Gabriola Island Travel Infocentre
Folklife Village Mall, 575 North Road
PO Box 249
Gabriola Island BC V0R 1X0
(604) 247-9332
(Summer only.)

Denman/Hornby Tourist Services
Denman Island BC V0R 1T0
(604) 335-2293; fax (604) 335-1665

How to go – Nanaimo is a major "gateway" to a vast diving area on Vancouver Island by way of British Columbia ferries. A great many car ferries bring visitors from the mainland of British Columbia to Departure Bay (Nanaimo) on Vancouver Island. Sailings from Horseshoe Bay (West Vancouver) to Departure Bay take 1 hour and 35 minutes. While sailings from Tsawwassen (south of Vancouver) to Departure Bay take 2 hours.

From Nanaimo you can drive north to Campbell River in 2½ hours and south to downtown Victoria in 2 hours. More good diving a 20-minute ferry ride away from downtown Nanaimo at Gabriola Island.

*All of this service information is subject to change.

BURIAL ISLET
Boat Dive

Current Table: Active Pass
Subtract 35 minutes, turn to flood
Add 25 minutes, turn to ebb

Skill: Expert divers. Intermediate divers with guide.

Why go: Life upon life encrusts this pyramid of rock beneath the sea. On the surface, it's a barren islet with a marker on top like a feather in its rounded skullcap. A whirlwind of currents are around it; but almost always a quiet side somewhere behind the islet.

Makes for a rich dive. We saw a Puget Sound king crab, yellow staghorn bryozoans, kelp crabs, lots of quillback rockfish, a buffalo sculpin. Christmas anemones. Plump white anemones. Large orange plumose anemones. Swimming scallops. Alabaster nudibranchs. A sea lemon. Giant barnacles. Purple urchins. Painted greenlings, kelp greenlings, a black rockfish, lingcod, a red Irish lord and lots of pretty little white plumose anemones. Orange cup corals and rock scallops with orange "lips" dot the rocks. We saw three harbor seals on the surface. Look for wolf-eels.

Bottom and Depths: The rock pinnacle called Burial Islet is exposed at all tides. It drops away gradually in stairstep ledges, a pyramid beneath the sea. You can choose your depth. Bull kelp at 20 to 30 feet (6 to 9 meters) and a bright shell bottom scattered with boulders and rocks on the southwest side. Ledges down to a depth of 80 to 90 feet (24 to 27 meters).

Hazards: Current, boats and transparent fishing line. Bull kelp, in summer; jellyfish, in the fall. Dive on slack; plan your dive date and time carefully. Listen for boats; when ascending, hug the islet all the way to the surface. Carry a knife for fishing line and kelp. If you see any jellyfish, you and your buddy should check one another before removing masks and gloves. At Burial Islet I was stung by a jellyfish for the first time ever. I swam into an almost transparent tentacle that grazed my upper lip and the stinging sensation lasted nearly twenty-four hours.

Telephone: Maple Bay Store.

Facilities: None at Burial Islet. Air fills, charters and launching at Maple Bay and Sidney on Vancouver Island. Also charters out of Saltspring Island. Launching at Genoa Bay and Cowichan Bay on Vancouver Island.

Access: Burial Islet is on the east side of Sansum Narrows close to Saltspring Island and near Maple Bay on Vancouver Island.

Charter, rent a boat or launch your own boat at Vancouver Island and go to the barren islet with a only a marker on it. Anchoring, beware of shallow big rocks at the southwest corner. Almost always an eddy this side too. Anchor so you are not pushed onto the islet by the eddying current. • From Maple Bay, head east and south through Sansum Narrow. It is 4 nautical miles (7 kilometers) to Burial Islet. • From Genoa Bay or Cowichan Bay, go 3 nautical miles (6 kilometers). • From Sidney, cross Satellite Channel and go north of Moses Point to Burial Islet.

Plan dive date and time as follows: The current is different at Sansum Narrows; choose to dive on a day with a big exchange as slack is more predictable then. Probably because wind has a greater effect on current on days when a small exchange follows slack.
1. Look at the Tide Table for Fulford Harbour to see what kind of exchange is happening. Pick a big one. It is best on low slack, but high slack will do.
2. Look at the Current Table for Active Pass with corrections for Sansum Narrows.

a. If diving at low slack, note the time of the turn to flood and add 25 minutes to it.

b. If diving at high slack, note the time of the turn to ebb and subtract 35 minutes from it.

3. In summer, also correct for daylight saving time (add 1 hour).

4. Be ready to dive 30 minutes before the corrected time of the turn. Then, at Burial, if you still hit it wrong, look for the side of the islet with the back eddy where you can "hide" from the current.

Comments: Once you've dived Burial, more to explore in Sansum Narrows – why not try Octopus Point, Sansum Point, Musgrave Rock or Separation Point?

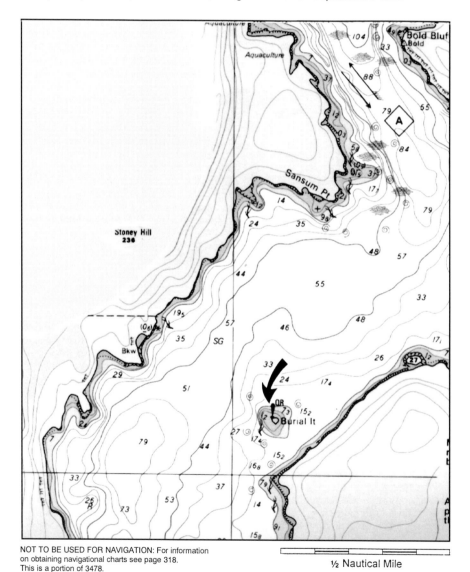

NOT TO BE USED FOR NAVIGATION: For information on obtaining navigational charts see page 318. This is a portion of 3478.

½ Nautical Mile

OCTOPUS POINT
Kayak Dive or Boat Dive

Current Table: Active Pass
Subtract 35 minutes, turn to flood
Add 25 minutes, turn to ebb

Skill: Expert divers. Intermediate divers with guide.

Why go: Octopus Point drops straight down. It is such a clean sweep that my buddy and I didn't try to anchor on the bottom. We anchored around a tree. Rolling over the side of our inflatable we fell straight into the abyss.

Castles and turrets of staghorn bryozoans encrust the palisades in pale lemon yellow. Dream-like underwater skyscraper castles look like something from a picture book. Huge lingcod swim out from the bottomless dark and slowly swim back. Large black rockfish cruise past in schools. Tiger rockfish hang close to the wall. So many animals live on the wall you can hardly see the rock. Gigantic rock scallops stud the straight-up-and-down wall like almonds down the side of a richly decorated almond cake. Giant barnacles, pink tube worms, small crabs peeping from empty barnacle shells, mustard-yellow trumpet sponges and large orange peel nudibranches cling to the sheer bluff. Tiny orange cup corals and white encrusting sponges dot the rocks. Red-and-pink dahlia anemones, fluffy white plumose anemones, and pink-beige sea lilies feather from the wall.

A magnificent drop-off.

Bottom and Depths: Sheer rock wall falls cleanly away to 165 then 330 feet (50 then 100 meters) according to the chart. Some bull kelp on the very narrow broken rock ledge immediately next to the shore.

Hazards: Current, bull kelp and depth. Dive on the slack. Carry a knife. Kayak-divers who dive deep should rest before paddling back to avoid overexertion which may increase risk of bends.

Telephone: Maple Bay Store.

Facilities: None at Octopus Point. Air fills, charters, launching at Maple Bay. Also charters out of Sidney and Saltspring Island. Dive-kayak rentals in Departure Bay.

Access: Octopus Point is on the west side of Sansum Narrows between Vancouver Island and Saltspring Island. It is 1½ nautical miles (3 kilometers) southeast of Maple Bay and 5 nautical miles (9 kilometers) northeast of Genoa Bay and Cowichan Bay ramps on Vancouver Island.

Go by boat to the second small point south of Octopus Point. You could paddle a dive-kayak to it from Maple Bay. Some bull kelp on the very narrow ledge by the drop-off, but not enough room for a boat to anchor and swing. We went by inflatable boat, threw our anchor around a tree and went down.

• Charter, rent or launch at Maple Bay; launch at Genoa Bay or Cowichan Bay; or charter out of Saltspring Island or Sidney.

• Kayak-divers: launch at Maple Bay near Duncan. From Maple Bay, cross 1 nautical mile (1¾ kilometers) of open water to Paddy Mile Stone and then stay close to shore the rest of the way to Octopus Point. Allow 20 to 30 minutes to paddle. Wheelchair divers who paddle dive-kayaks will find easy access at this ramp.

Plan dive date and time carefully. The current is different in Sansum Narrows: choose to dive on a day with a big exchange the same as at Burial Islet. See directions for calculating current in Sansum Narrows on pages 178 and 179.

Comments: Best in late morning when sun lights the water.

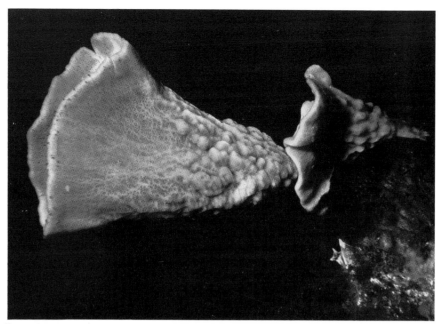

Trumpet sponges

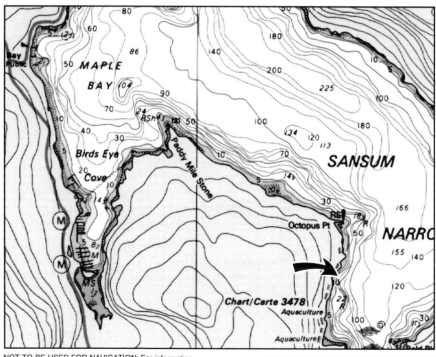

NOT TO BE USED FOR NAVIGATION: For information
on obtaining navigational charts see page 318.
This is a portion of 3442.

1 Nautical Mile

MAPLE BAY REEF   **Tide Table:** Fulford Harbour
UNDERWATER SANCTUARY
Shore Dive

Skill: All divers

Why go: An underwater sanctuary, Maple Bay Reef offers a very pleasant afternoon of sightseeing and photography. One of the beauties of Maple Bay Reef is that it is shallow, and therefore usually bright enough for available light photography. And there are fish, octopuses and a variety of invertebrates along the three arms of the reef.

When diving here we saw masses of nudibranchs. My buddy was kept very busy taking pictures. We saw some giant silver nudibranchs – gray with white tips. Several spotted nudibranchs and a sea lemon sitting on the edge of broadleaf kelp. Large orange plumose anemones, small white anemones, shrimp all over the place. And tube-snouts moving along jerkily through the shallows. Seaperch hovering around the reef. Some little golden fish that I haven't seen before. Rockfish hide in the crevices of the wall at the end of the left arm of the reef. Lingcod, too.

A satisfying dive.

Bottom and Depths: At about 100 feet (30 meters) beyond the dock, the reef starts. It has three arms and is trident shaped. The right arm points toward Paddy Mile Stone. The middle arm is a rocky backbone pointing directly out into Maple Bay. The left arm juts toward Arbutus Point and ends as a rock wall dropping from 20 to 30 feet (6 to 9 meters) – depending on tide height, to a depth of 50 to 60 feet (15 to 18 meters). Bottom kelp all over the reef which is 20 to 30 feet (6 to 9 meters) deep on top and drops a short way on either side.

To find the reef set your compass towards Paddy Mile Stone, the point on your right, jump off the dock and swim out 100 feet (30 meters) under water.

Hazards: Small boats and poor visibility in summer. Red jellyfish, in the fall. Many, many small boats coming and going. When ascending, listen for boats; if you hear one, stay down until it passes. Or better yet, use a compass and navigate all the way back to shore under water. If you and your buddy have seen any red jellyfish, check one another for stinging tentacles before removing your masks and gloves.

Telephone: Maple Bay Store.

Facilities: Air fills, charters and launching in Maple Bay. Toilets at park before pub. Government dock and small store.

Access: Maple Bay is near Duncan on Vancouver Island. The dive is 10 minutes off Trans-Canada Highway 1.

Heading north or south on Highway 1, go to Duncan. Turn east at Trunk Road, following signs to Maple Bay. Trunk Road becomes Tzouhalem Road which then conveniently becomes Maple Bay Road and goes to the government dock at Maple Bay. Room for ten or fifteen cars to park.

Comments: Maple Bay is popular for night dives. By municipal by-law the bay is a marine sanctuary. As a consequence, spearfishing and specimen collecting are prohibited.

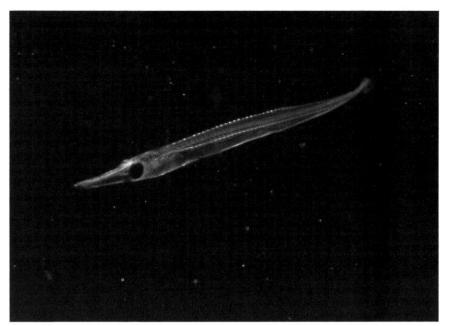

Tube-snout

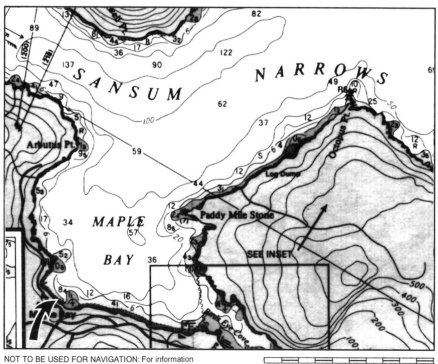

1 Nautical Mile

EVENING COVE
Shore Dive

Skill: All divers and snorkelers

Why go: Acres of sightseeing along this rocky reef reaching a long, thin finger out into Evening Cove.
  Hordes of rockfish live around the rocks. Anemones, sea stars, sea peaches, little nudibranchs, and sculpins. Octopuses on the reef if you can find them. Once on a night dive I found one too easily. I was poking along the rocks and saw one small white tentacle coiling and uncoiling. I suddenly realized I was almost lying on the mantle of a very large, very red octopus. It must have been 25 pounds (11 kilograms), at least, and in only 15 feet (5 meters) of water. The octopus was just as startled as I was. The shy creature tried to escape under a small ledge much too narrow to shelter it. I backed off and moved on.
  Hermit crabs, flounders, pipefish and tube-dwelling anemones live on the sand on either side of the reef. Box crabs in the middle of the cove. A variety of life, easy access and lack of current add up to Evening Cove being a good dive anytime – day or night.

Bottom and Depths: A shallow ridge of rocks reaches out into Evening Cove. Some bottom kelp on the rocks. Sand scattered with small rocks on either side at 15 to 35 feet (5 to 11 meters). A very definite reef and shallow for a very long way out, finally going to 50 feet (15 meters) deep. Then a break, but farther out the reef comes up to 30 feet (9 meters) again.

Hazards: Poor visibility, small boats, red jellyfish in the fall. Listen for boats, use a compass and navigate back to shore under water. If you have seen red jellyfish, check for stinging tentacles before removing masks and gloves.

Telephones: • Kumalockasun campground, down Tideview Road. • Trans-Canada Highway 1, at gas station south of Brenton-Page Road.

Facilities: None at Evening Cove. Camping and hot showers nearby at Kumalock-asun campground, and also at Stuzuminus (Ivy Green) Park on the east side of Highway 1. You come to it just after turning south onto the highway toward Lady-smith.

Access: Evening Cove is near Ladysmith on Vancouver Island. It is reached off Trans-Canada Highway 1 between Nanaimo and Ladysmith. Ten minutes off the highway to the dive.
  From Highway 1, turn into Brenton-Page Road. When you come to the first "V", bear right following Brenton-Page Road. At the second one, do not go right to Mañana Lodge. Continue straight on Shell Beach Road and go to the end of it; pass Tideview Road on the left. You will see the water. Turn right into Elliott Way and drive to the water's edge. Eight or ten cars can park. To find the reef, face the cove. Look for a small rocky point jutting into the water between Coffin Point and Sharpe Point. The reef goes out from the small point on your right, 75 yards (70 meters) west of the road end. Follow the finger of rocks straight out into the cove.

To get to Brenton-Page Road
• From Nanaimo, go south on Highway 1 for 15 minutes. When 1⅓ miles (2 kilometers) south of the Nanaimo airport and just past the Cedar Road traffic light, you will see a sign to Mañana Lodge at Brenton-Page Road.

• From Ladysmith, head north on Highway 1; when 3½ miles (5¾ kilometers) past the traffic light – 5 minutes past Ladysmith, look for a sign to Mañana Lodge at Brenton-Page Road.

Comments: Evening Cove is beautiful above water, too, especially in spring when the old orchard is in bloom. Walking on the southwest corner of the beach, be careful not to damage the shellfish reserve, where the public can collect oysters.

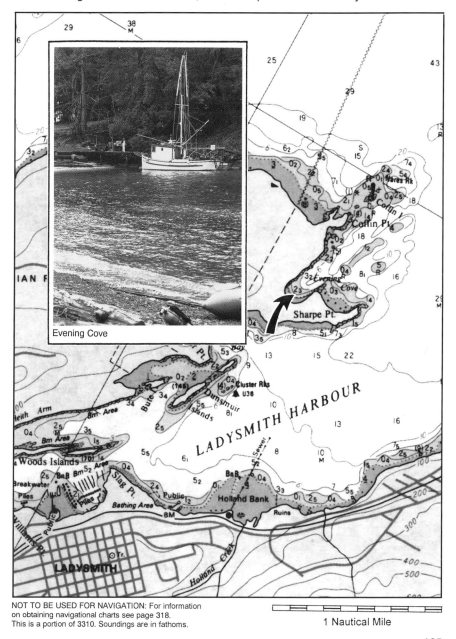

Evening Cove

NOT TO BE USED FOR NAVIGATION: For information
on obtaining navigational charts see page 318.
This is a portion of 3310. Soundings are in fathoms.

1 Nautical Mile

COFFIN ISLAND
Kayak Dive or Boat Dive

Tide Table: Point Atkinson

Skill: Intermediate and expert divers and snorkelers

Why go: Coffin Island is an extravaganza ranging from minute sea pens to giant nudibranchs to thousand-pound sea lions.
Wine-red giant nudibranchs tipped with mauve, and others that glitter like tinseled bows on a Christmas parcel, seem flung across the sea floor. We saw tiny alabaster nudibranchs, giant red urchins, sea squirts, large elegant orange plumose anemones, sea stars and lots of small white anemones. Feather stars on the smooth rock rolling away down deep. Burrowing anemones, minute sea pens and giant sea pens in the sand.
By mistake I put my hand on a large cabezon. We noticed rockfish in the crevices and a couple of large lingcod lying on their chins. A huge pair of playful sea lions made many passes near us, but never touched us. I couldn't decide whether to be frightened or delighted. I could not take my eyes off their eyes. Exciting to have them with us throughout the dive! You're more likely to meet them in winter.

Bottom and Depths: A large area of 25- to 35-foot (7- to 11-meter) rocky bottom scattered with boulders and broadleaf bottom kelp is all around Coffin Island. Some white sand, eelgrass and bull kelp. About 300 yards (275 meters) north of the island, smooth stark, dark rock rolls from 50 to 60 feet (15 to 18 meters) to a depth of 80 to 90 feet (24 to 27 meters).

Hazards: Current, and broken fishing line. Boats, poor visibility and bull kelp in summer. Red jellyfish, in the fall. Wind in winter. Dive on the slack. Carry a knife. Use a compass and listen for boats, ascending with a reserve of air; if you hear a boat you can stay down until it passes. If you have seen any red jellyfish, you and your buddy should check one another for stinging tentacles before removing your masks and gloves. Coffin Island is exposed to winds from all directions.

Telephone: Island Highway, at Ivy Green gas station south of Brenton-Page Road.

Facilities: Gravel launching ramp, camping and showers nearby at Kumalockasun campground. Launching at all tides at Ladysmith. Camping and hot showers at Ivy Green (Stuzuminus) Park.

Access: Coffin Island is 300 yards (275 meters) east of Coffin Point in Stuart Channel, 1½ nautical miles (2¾ kilometers) south of the 49th Parallel which runs through Ladysmith.
Because Coffin Island is a ½-mile (¾-kilometer) swim from the closest access point at the road end at Evening Cove, use a boat. Either launch a dive-kayak over the log-strewn beach at Evening Cove or the gravel ramp at Kumalockasun and paddle to Coffin Island; launch a boat at Ladysmith or take a charter. Anchor north of Coffin Island and go down.
Wheelchair divers who paddle dive-kayaks could probably launch at Kumalock-asun.

Comments: Winter is the best time to dive Coffin Island.

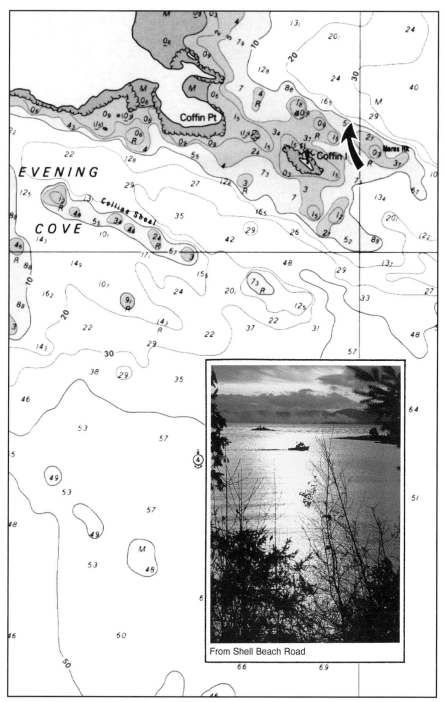

EVENING

COVE

Coffin Pt

Coffin I

Collins Shoal

From Shell Beach Road

200 Yards

ROUND ISLAND
Kayak Dive or Boat Dive

Skill: Expert divers

Why go: Rockfish, lingcod, octopuses, anemones and nudibranchs abound on the current-swept ledges north of Round Island.
When here we saw an enormous variety of dahlia anemones. We saw leather stars and sea pens. First one lingcod appeared, then another. During one dive we saw six lingcod. Many species of rockfish – including tiger rockfish – were on the ledges.
Then we saw an octopus sitting out in the open on a rock. I stroked it. Its mantle reddened and it wriggled under my touch. It became nervous and slowly jetted 5 feet (1½ meters) away where it stopped and waited for us to catch up. We approached slowly, and stroked it again. It writhed, seeming to enjoy every minute of our attention, reddened more and then speckled. That octopus never tired of our company, but we were nearly out of air! As we moved towards shore we passed rock scallops, delicate orange nudibranchs with white tips and large sea lemons.
Sea lions and killer whales are also seen at Round Island.

Bottom and Depths: Rocky shore gives way to white sand, then kelp attached to small rocks in 20 to 30 feet (6 to 9 meters) of water, depending on tide height. Northward the bottom slopes gradually to 50 feet (15 meters) where rocky ledges stair-step to 60 feet (18 meters) and more.

Hazards: Strong current and bull kelp. Dive on high slack. The current is more acute on a falling tide than on a rising tide. Carry a knife for kelp.

Telephones: • Grocery store at Cedar Road and Yellow Point Road. • Degnen Bay government wharf, Gabriola Island, 4 nautical miles (7 kilometers) away. • Brechin Civic Ramp, at water side of the Public Market, 8 nautical miles (15 kilometers) from Round Island.

Facilities: None on Round Island. Charters, boat and dive-kayak rentals in Nanaimo.

Access: Round Island is 1⅓ nautical miles (2½ kilometers) south of Dodd Narrows in Stuart Channel, only 300 yards (275 meters) across the water from Vancouver Island.
If you think you can swim it, don't. Currents are treacherous. Charter in Nanaimo or launch your own boat at Brechin Civic Ramp in Nanaimo and go 8 nautical miles (15 kilometers) south through Dodd Narrows to Round Island. Or launch your boat or dive-kayak at the foot of Barnes-Murdock Road and go by boat 300 yards (275 meters) east to Round Island. Anchor or land in the small horseshoe-shaped cove at the northwest tip. Follow a compass heading due north through the kelp, then dive.
Barnes-Murdock Road Ramp is convenient but only usable by most boats at high tides; dive-kayaks could be launched at any tide. To go there from Nanaimo drive south on Island Highway. Take Cedar turnoff and go east. After 1¾ miles (2¾ kilometers), just after crossing a bridge, turn right following signs to Cedar Road and Yellow Point Road. Go ½ mile (¾ kilometer) to a grocery store. Turn left and go to Holden-Corso Road. Continue along Holden-Corso for 1⅓ miles (2 kilometers) then along Barnes Road for 1⅓ miles (2 kilometers). At Murdock Road angle right and go ½ mile (1 kilometer). Launch and cross 300 yards (275 meters) to Round Island.

Comments: Pleasant place for a picnic.

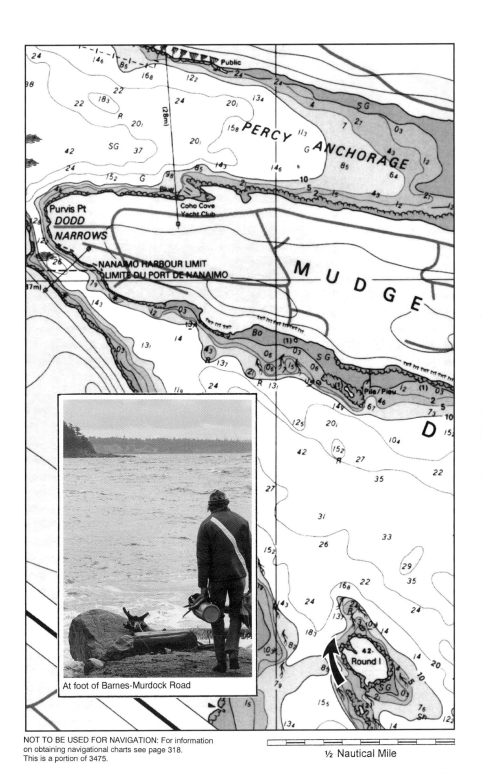

Public

168
122
24
24
24
24
146
85
24

38
22
22
183
24
20₁
134
4
SG
7
27
03
22
20₁
158
PERCY
113
G
ANCHORAGE
43
42
SG
37
20₁
G
85
64
12
24
152
G
98
85
143
146
10
2
5
5
15
43
27
Bkw
12

Purvis Pt
Coho Cove
DODD
Yacht Club

NARROWS

26
NANAIMO HARBOUR LIMIT
LIMITE DU PORT DE NANAIMO
M   U   D   G   E

37m)
79
143
03
12
14
Bo
(1) 0
131
14
06
03
SG
06
D
152
R
24
031
21
06
05
075
(1) 0
Pile/Pieu
12
(1) 01
2
5
146
67
73
10
110
24
147
125
20₁
104
D
152
42
152
R
27
35
22
35

27

31

152
26
33

29
35

168
22
35
143
24
24
183
137
8₉
4 2.
Round I
14
20
10 3
85
14
10
5
79
SG
01
2
155
76
Sh
122
15
134
14

At foot of Barnes-Murdock Road

NOT TO BE USED FOR NAVIGATION: For information
on obtaining navigational charts see page 318.
This is a portion of 3475.

½ Nautical Mile

DODD NARROWS
Boat Dive

Current Table: Dodd Narrows

Skill: Expert divers and snorkelers

Why go: For a magic carpet ride – in reverse. Visit an inside-out world. Mauve aggregate anemones smother the rocks and you – not the carpet – are moving.
Ride the current up and down and over the gentle indentations in the smooth, smooth rocks near the surface. Heaps of purple sea stars border the tidal stream like big fat flowers. Most life is from the surface down to 60 feet (18 meters). We saw lingcod, large cabezons, a buffalo sculpin, kelp greenlings, schools of striped seaperch. Rock scallops, giant barnacles, swimming scallops, yellow staghorn bryozoans.
Encrusting sponges coat the rocks and millions of small white plumose anemones light up the depths, spill into side-canyons, scatter over the rocks and rocky walls at the edge of the river of sand on the floor of Dodd Narrows.
The deeper you go, the smaller the anemones and the less current there is. At the start of our dive we went deep, then hauled ourselves up the rocks and side-canyons for the magic carpet ride. Before the dive, we cruised past California sea lions at Harmac. After the dive, saw three black orcas, or killer whales, easily slip upstream against the ebbing current in Dodd Narrows.

Bottom and Depths: At the northern entry to Dodd Narrows, smooth rock ledges cascade down to sand bottom at 85 to 95 feet (25 to 29 meters) depending on tide height. Boulders at the base. South through the narrows, it shallows to a depth of 60 to 70 feet (18 to 21 meters). Narrow canyons cut the sides at intervals, provide shelter from the current. Bull kelp, in summer, in the eddies where you start and stop, at a depth of 25 to 35 feet (8 to 11 meters).

Hazards: Current, boats and broken fishing line. Bull kelp in summer. Carry a knife. Dive on slack with a "live" boat. Dive with a low exchange, and know it will still be a drift. Joan Point is like a nozzle: currents shoot through up to 8 knots (15 kilometers/hour) on the ebb, 9 knots (17 kilometers/hour) on the flood. Throughout the dive find "hiding places" from the current in canyons and behind rocks. Use handholds and stay close to the bottom. Hang on! – to rocks on the bottom, to bull kelp in the shallows, to anything you can find to slow your drift. If you fly to the surface, it's an out-of-control roller-coaster ride and you are exposed to boats in the Narrows.
Safer in winter or weekdays in summer because of fewer small boats. When you surface look for tugboats hauling log booms, fish farms and other freight. Fish-farm pens may have nets trailing.

Telephones: • Brechin Civic Ramp, at water side of the Public Market, 6 nautical miles (11 kilometers) from Dodd. • Degnen Bay government wharf, Gabriola Island, 5 nautical miles (10 kilometers) away.

Facilities: None. Air fills, charters, boat rentals and launching at Gabriola Island, Nanaimo, Departure Bay and Ladysmith.

Access: Dodd Narrows is near Nanaimo on Vancouver Island. It is 11 nautical miles (20 kilometers) northwest of Ladysmith and the 49th Parallel; 6 nautical miles (11 kilometers) southeast of Departure Bay and even closer to Gabriola Island. You can charter at Degnen Bay on Gabriola and be at the dive in 15 minutes.
Charter or launch at Gabriola Island, Nanaimo, Departure Bay or Ladysmith and go 5 to 11 nautical miles (9 to 20 kilometers) to Dodd Narrows. If diving at the end of

flood, you will find a sheltered place to enter in the kelp north of the marker at Joan Point; an exit eddy north of the power line. Dodd Narrows is 250 feet (75 meters) wide at its narrowest point south of Joan Point; it continues at that width for 600 feet (180 meters). Before diving, check out approaching boats. An entire fish farm – ⅓ mile (½ kilometer) long – was towed through just before we were to begin our dive. We had to wait 15 minutes. No choice, our dive became more of a drift. You can dive on the ebb or flood.

Comments: A charter operator says of Dodd Narrows: "A great drift at slack water".

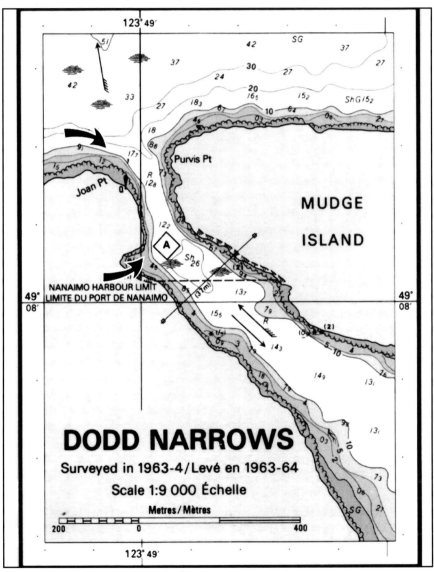

220 Yards

GABRIOLA PASSAGE
Boat Dive

Skill: Expert divers and snorkelers

Why go: Shallow and packed with life, as only a spot with current can be, Gabriola Pass holds excitement for everyone – photographers, junk collectors and sightseers.
Gabriola Passage is where I made my first dive in a current-swept passage. I couldn't believe that the current never entirely stopped. But in retrospect, the place is not an alarming one for a first big-current experience. Two small points stick out into Gabriola Passage, giving you someplace to swim for in case the current becomes unmanageable.
What's there? To say what isn't in Gabriola Passage is easier. We saw so much that I couldn't pick out anything at first. There were lots of kelp greenlings, some rock scallops. Orange burrowing cucumbers poked up between giant red and small green urchins. Huge lingcod, tiger rockfish, cabezons, yelloweye rockfish and octopuses share the shallow ledges tiering down into the pass. An old anchor, too.
The shallows are also incredibly rich. Large flower-like plumose anemones flourish in 5 feet (1½ meters) of water. Giant sea lemons, bright blue sea stars and little red rock crabs crowd the rocky shores. Even gorgeous sea pens in small pockets of sand. Marvelous snorkeling.

Bottom and Depths: Rocky ledges tier down to a depth of 30 to 40 feet (9 to 12 meters) deep. There are caves just east starting at Joseph Point, where giant octopuses and lingcod live. One hole is 120 to 130 feet (37 to 40 meters) deep. Boulders and bull kelp. Some silt with the constant movement of current. The best visibility you can expect is 50 to 60 feet (15 to 18 meters) in winter.

Hazards: Very swift current, boats and bull kelp. Dive precisely on the slack on a small tidal exchange: currents up to 9 knots (17 kilometers/hour) sometimes run through Gabriola. Be prepared to pull out of the dive if the current starts picking up. Currents do not always run when predicted. A pickup boat is required. Other boat traffic also uses the slack. Throughout your dive, listen for boats and ascend along the bottom all the way to shore well out of the way of those boats. Use a compass and watch the current to find your direction. When you surface, look for tugboats hauling log booms. Carry a knife for kelp.

Telephone: Degnen Bay, top of government wharf.

Facilities: None at Valdes Island. Air fills, charters and launching, camping and accommodations nearby at Gabriola Island and Nanaimo. Inflatable charters out of Degnen Bay at Gabriola.

Access: Gabriola Passage is the northernmost of the three major passages between the Gulf Islands. Gabriola Island is on the north side and Valdes Island on the south side of Gabriola Passage. The other two major passes are Porlier and Active.
Charter out of Degnen Bay or Silva Bay at Gabriola; or out of Nanaimo, Vancouver or Victoria, and go to Gabriola Passage. Or launch at Degnen Bay on Gabriola Island and go ¾ nautical mile (1⅓ kilometers) to the south side of the passage. Have a pickup boat follow you. A must.

Comments: A very special dive.

Kelp greenling eating urchin

Silva Bay

Tugboat (14 m)

RVYC

52

Sear Island

DRUMBEG PARK

Degnen Bay

Josef Pt

GABRIOLA

PASSAGE

33

Cordero Pt

Wakes Cove

Dibuxante Pt

Kendrick I

RVYC

½ Nautical Mile

Skill: Intermediate and expert divers and snorkelers. All divers with guide.

Why go: At Drumbeg Park you can walk into the water from shore near the infamous Gabriola Passage.

Drumbeg Park waters are not nearly so treacherous as at the passage itself, but much of the same current-fed life lives here. Swimming out along the rock-rimmed shore at your left you'll see giant urchins, sea peaches, grunt sculpins, rockfish, giant barnacles and burrowing cucumbers along the wall. If you stop to watch, sometimes you will see one finger of a burrowing cucumber bend from its extended position to its mouth to lick, then move out again to find more food. But the feeding devices of barnacles are not so much fingers as toes. One diver described giant barnacles feeding: "They kick the water with their feet, then lick their toes".

When we were diving at Drumbeg Park a young dogfish came up, observed us with curiosity, and then moved on. Strange sponges are on the sand.

Bottom and Depths: Rock-rimmed bay drops 25 to 35 feet (8 to 11 meters), depending on tide height, to current-swept sandy bottom.

Hazards: Current and boats. Dive near slack, on the ebb only. Do not dive on the flood tide. Listen for boats and ascend close to the wall. A great deal of boat traffic heading into Silva Bay passes between Drumbeg and Rogers Reef. Do not dive Rogers Reef from shore – it looks like a reasonable thing to do, but because of the current and boat traffic is too far to swim. Take a charter.

Telephones: • By road: go to Gabriola Reefs Dive Shop and Page's Resort & Marina, foot of Coast Road, Silva Bay. • By water: go 1½ nautical miles (3 kilometers) southwest to government wharf, Degnen Bay.

Facilities: Grassy park, beach and pit toilets. Parking for five or six cars. Air fills, camping, accommodations, charters, and launching nearby on Gabriola Island; also in Nanaimo.

Access: Drumbeg Park is east of Gabriola Passage at the southeast corner of Gabriola Island. It is a 20-minute ferry ride from Nanaimo to Gabriola. Then a 20-minute drive. From the ferry landing, go 9 miles (14 kilometers) to the dive.

Take the British Columbia ferry from the small ferry terminal at Nanaimo Harbour near Harbour Mall in downtown Nanaimo. Once at Gabriola, drive along South Road (or North Road) for 9 miles (14 kilometers). Turn toward the sea into Coast Road. Go 100 yards (90 meters) and turn right into Stalker Road. Continue ½ mile (1 kilometer) to a dirt road marked "Public Access" on a small concrete marker on the ground. Turn left to Drumbeg Park. Walk a few steps to the water and dive along the left side of the bay toward the lights at Rogers Reef and Breakwater Island. But do not dive or swim to the reef – stay close alongside the rock wall on the left-hand side of the bay.

Comments: Pleasant for a day of swimming, diving and picnicking on the beach.

Shore divers and boat divers at Drumbeg Park

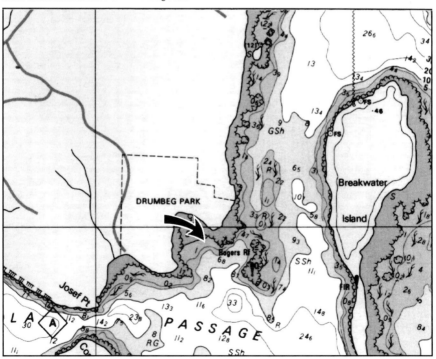

NOT TO BE USED FOR NAVIGATION: For information
on obtaining navigational charts see page 318.
This is a portion of 3475.

½ Nautical Mile

THRASHER ROCK
Boat Dive

Current Table: Gabriola Pass

Skill: Expert divers

Why go: Thrasher Rock must be one of the wildest, most complicated current hot spots in the Strait of Georgia.
The current is not only swift, but also capricious. When diving here I felt as though an eggbeater was working in the water. Current came from all directions. The result: some of the biggest of fish. We saw a lingcod so big that instead of admitting our presence we became as invisible as possible. We were glad when it seemed not to notice us. This is wolf-eel country, too. We saw rockfish all over the place, kelp greenlings, large seaperch, tiger rockfish and giant urchins. Plumose anemones, orange cup corals, coal and scattered bits of wreckage.
Thrasher Rock is named after the wooden sailing ship *Thrasher* stranded on the rock while under tow on the evening of July 14, 1880. The ship was carrying 2,600 tons (2,400 tonnes) of coal loaded at Nanaimo, the old coaling center. A hundred years later, divers still see bits of the wreckage north/northeast of the marker at Thrasher Rock in 30 feet (9 meters) of water and, near it, chunks of coal. You really dive the rock but you might see a few timbers, an anchor chain and the capstan.

Bottom and Depths: Thrasher Rock is a large round rock with some boulders and crevices. At the marker the depth is 10 feet (3 meters). The reef extends 200 to 300 feet (60 to 90 meters) on either side. Dense bottom kelp covers the rocks. Around the rock it is 20 to 30 feet (6 to 9 meters) deep. North of the rock is a 50- to 60-foot (15- to 18-meter) ledge.

Hazards: Current. Dive on the predicted slack, but use your common sense. Pull out of the dive if the current is picking up. Current is often unpredictable at Thrasher.

Telephones: • Silva Bay, beside Gabriola Reefs Dive Shop and Page's Resort & Marina. • Silva Bay Resort, beside pub.

Facilities: None at Thrasher Rock. Air fills, camping, accommodations, charters, and launching at Gabriola Island.

Access: Thrasher Rock, indicated by a concrete marker at the northeast tip of Gabriola Reefs in the Strait of Georgia, is just over 2 nautical miles (3¾ kilometers) offshore east of Silva Bay at Gabriola Island which is just east of Nanaimo. Check the wind when you plan to dive here. Winter is usually stormy. Spring is a good time to dive at Thrasher.
Charter out of Silva Bay or Degnen Bay at Gabriola, out of Nanaimo, Vancouver or Victoria, or launch at Degnen Bay and proceed to Thrasher Rock. Anchor and dive. Do not tie onto marker. It is a federal offense to make fast to a marker or tamper with any aid to navigation. Leave a pickup person in the boat in case you are swept away by current. The remains of the *Thrasher* are north/northeast of the marker in 25 to 35 feet (8 to 11 meters) of water.

Comments: How big can a lingcod be? I looked it up! Lingcod maximum recorded size is 5 feet (1½ meters) long and 100 pounds (45 kilograms).

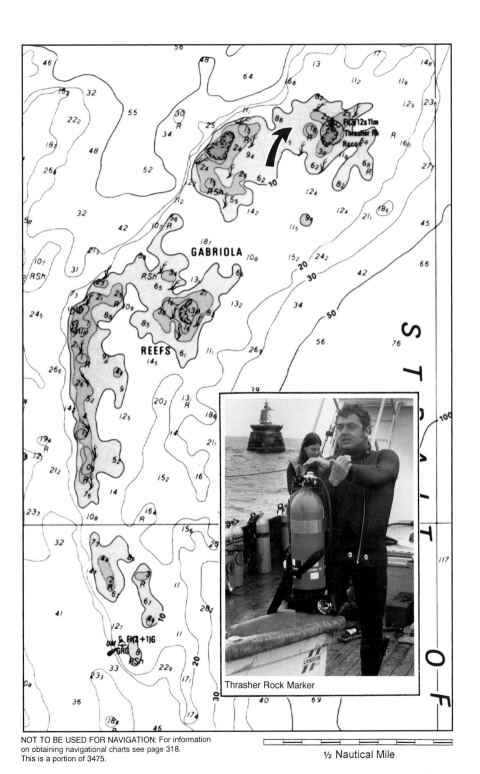

Thrasher Rock Marker

GABRIOLA

REEFS

S T R A I T   O F

NOT TO BE USED FOR NAVIGATION: For information
on obtaining navigational charts see page 318.
This is a portion of 3475.

½ Nautical Mile

CARLOS ISLAND
Boat Dive

Tide Table: Point Atkinson
Add 5 minutes

Skill: Intermediate and expert divers. All divers with guide.

Why go: Grandiose broad slopes sweep down into the land of the sponges and make Carlos Island – one of the Flat Top Islands – popular with divers who like to dive deep.

Often when springtime Fraser River runoff has restricted visibility in many other locations, waters are still clear around the Flat Tops. When diving here we had a free-wheeling feeling as we dropped from one beautiful ledge to the next – each one seeming broader and wider and more open than the one before. Stairsteps in tiers of sandstone fall to clean rocky ledges covered with sand, then sweep down again. A tremendous sense of space.

Sea pens live in the white, white sand. Rockfish, lingcod and occasional swimming scallops beside the wall. Round orange sponges. And chimney sponges, big and little, lead down to the edge of the dark abyss where dogfish and ratfish cruise along the edge of nothingness at Carlos.

Bottom and Depths: Rocky bottom covered with bottom kelp and bull kelp at 20 to 30 feet (6 to 9 meters) deep, just north of the island. Clean-cut sandstone tiers down, forming ledges which trap pools of sand on the narrow stairsteps. This drop-off plunges to 360 feet (120 meters).

Hazards: Some current but very little on flood tides, bull kelp and depth. Dive near the slack. Carry a knife. Be aware of down-time.

Telephones: • Silva Bay, beside Gabriola Reefs Dive Shop and Page's Resort & Marina. • Silva Bay Resort, beside pub.

Facilities: None at Carlos Island. Air fills, charters, camping and accommodations at Silva Bay on Gabriola. Charters – including inflatable charters – and launching at Degnen Bay on Gabriola Island.

Access: Carlos Island is in the Strait of Georgia in the Flat Top Islands, northeast of Gabriola Island. The dive is less than 1 nautical mile (2 kilometers) north of Silva Bay and 3 nautical miles (5½ kilometers) north of Degnen Bay at Gabriola.

Charter out of Silva Bay or Degnen Bay at Gabriola; charter out of Nanaimo, Vancouver or Victoria. Or launch at Degnen Bay and go to Carlos. Anchor north of the island near the bull kelp and descend.

Comments: Once you've dived Carlos, why not try Gaviola, Saturnina or Acorn Island or do a "drift" through Commodore Passage?

Collecting for Vancouver Aquarium off Carlos Island

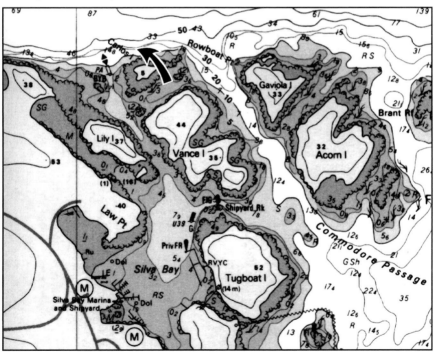

NOT TO BE USED FOR NAVIGATION: For information on obtaining navigational charts see page 318. This is a portion of 3475.

½ Nautical Mile

ORLEBAR POINT
Shore Dive

Skill: Intermediate and expert divers over the wall. All divers in shallows with guide.

Why go: It's a wall. Dark gray. Plunging to nowhere-land right from shore at Orlebar Point on Gabriola Island.

We follow the dark valley to the edge, then fly out over it. Glide past snakelock anemones – they fling their pink fingers into space. The wall is covered with big scarlet dahlia anemones, pink ones, and fabulous white fluffy plumose anemones cascading out of sight. We see tiny hard pink hydrocorals, transparent sea peaches, orange cup corals, yellow staghorn bryozoans like hard coral. Chimney sponges from 15 meters (50 feet) on down and down. Small puffs of white cloud sponges. A grand-daddy lingcod – 3 feet (1 meter) long. A tiger rockfish beneath a ledge. Yelloweye rockfish commonly called red snapper at 120 feet (37 meters). More fish too. Kelp greenlings, black rockfish, lots of quillback rockfish.

Drama shallow and deep. What is in the shallows? Kelp – more different types than you will probably ever see at another site. Iridescent blue kelp, feathery kelp like red shoestring potatoes. Broad-leafed bottom kelp hiding sea stars, striped red, white and brown. Tall brown trees of kelp, standing upright like ferns. Lots of purple urchins in the rocks. Incredible life. In the sand, tube-dwelling anemones and sea pens. In rocky tidepools, clusters of pink and gray anemones. In the surrounding open water, harbor seals. And we saw sea lions.

Bottom and Depths: Rocky and sandy bottom 10 to 20 feet (3 to 6 meters) in the shallows at Orlebar. It's a five-minute swim over these shallows to the sheer wall of sandstone that starts at 45 to 55 feet (13 to 17 meters), plunges to greater than 120 feet (37 meters).

Hazards: Current, bull kelp, wind and depth. Dive near slack. Visibility is best on outgoing tides. Wind from the north can create surf, making swimming through the kelp difficult. Carry a knife; if caught in kelp you can cut your way free. Early morning is best because of less wind and waves. Be aware of how long you are down – it's deep. On your way up, stop and enjoy the shallows.

Telephones: • Surf Lodge, inside front hall and available 24 hours. It is ½ mile (¾ kilometer) back down the road toward the ferry. • Gabriola ferry landing, beside pub.

Facilities: Picnic table near the site. Room for three or four cars to park. Air fills, camping, charters and launching nearby on Gabriola Island; also in Nanaimo.

Access: Orlebar Point juts into Forwood Channel at the northeast corner of Gabriola Island. It is a 20-minute ferry ride from Nanaimo; then a 10-minute drive to Orlebar.

Take the British Columbia ferry from the small ferry terminal at Nanaimo Harbour near Harbour Mall in downtown Nanaimo. At Gabriola, drive up the hill to signs toward Gabriola Sands Provincial Park at Taylor Bay Road. Turn left. Follow Taylor Bay Road until it becomes gravel and goes off to the left. You stay on the main road which is now Berry Point Road. At Norwich Road, turn left. Continue along Berry Point Road, curving around beside the water. From Surf Lodge, go ½ mile (¾ kilo-meter) more to Orlebar Point. Two picnic tables are on the left. Just beyond the picnic tables, pull off facing the lighthouse.

To dive the wall or the shallows, walk down the rocks on the left-hand side and go toward the lighthouse on Entrance Island. Entry is easier at high tides. To reach the wall, follow a compass bearing of 20 degrees; swim beneath the water for five minutes to an underwater valley or trench. Then follow the fold in the rock to the drop-off.

Comments: Going home if it's low tide, turn right on Malaspina Drive to see the intriguing wind- and wave-carved rock walls of Gabriola – often called Malaspina Galleries.

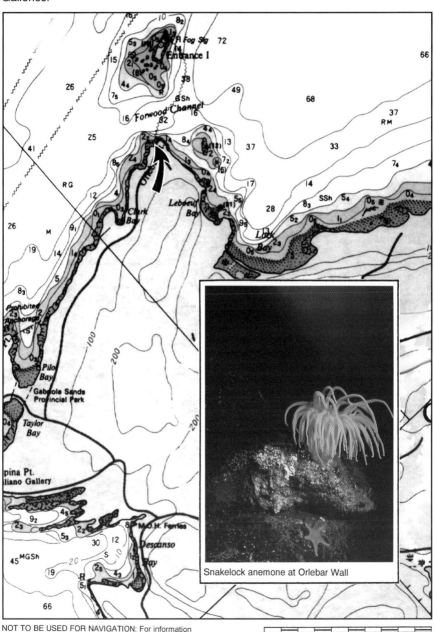

Snakelock anemone at Orlebar Wall

1 Nautical Mile

SNAKE ISLAND
Boat Dive

Skill: Intermediate and expert divers and snorkelers. All divers with guide.

Why go: Good sightseeing shallow and deep; you might meet harbor seals to snorkel with. Deeper, lingcod and rockfish and some yelloweye rockfish, commonly called red snapper, at Snake Island.
    In addition to fish we saw many invertebrates: kelp crabs, sea stars and nudibranchs. Some anemones. Bright orange dead man's finger sponges poke up through the bottom kelp in the shallows. Bull kelp around 30 feet (9 meters), and chimney sponges starting at 80 feet (24 meters). We saw lots of harbor seals which frequent this area. Seals do not migrate – you might see them year-round. And the chance of seeing them is growing: the harbor seal population in the Strait of Georgia has increased from 2,100 in 1973 to 12,500 in 1987 and to 20,000 in 1992.
    A great place to snorkel with harbor seals. The greatest numbers of seals are present during low tides, especially when the low tide occurs in the morning.

Bottom and Depths: Rocky bottom covered with bottom kelp and some bull kelp. Ledges and cliffs fall away fairly quickly all around the island. On the Nanaimo side, caves undercut the island at 140 feet (45 meters). The chart shows a drop to 400 feet (120 meters).

Hazards: Boats, bull kelp and wind. Listen for boats and ascend along the bottom all the way to shore. Carry a knife for kelp.

Telephone: Near Brechin Civic Ramp, water side of the Public Market.

Facilities: None. Air fills in Nanaimo – including waterfront air fills at the Public Market.

Access: Snake Island is near Nanaimo on Vancouver Island. It is 4 nautical miles (7½ kilometers) northeast of Departure Bay between Rainbow Channel and Fairway Channel and just south of the Horseshoe Bay-Departure Bay ferry route. Consider the wind when planning a dive. Snake Island is very exposed to wind from all directions.
    Charter or rent a boat in Nanaimo or Departure Bay. Or launch at Brechin Civic Ramp and go northeast to Snake Island. Anchor in the bull kelp at the northwest corner of the island or in the bay on the north side. If you leave a boat or other gear on the beach, beware of wash from passing ferries.

Comments: Maybe it's myth, but locals say that the northwest corner of each island in the Nanaimo area is where you are most likely to see fish.

Seals at Snake Island

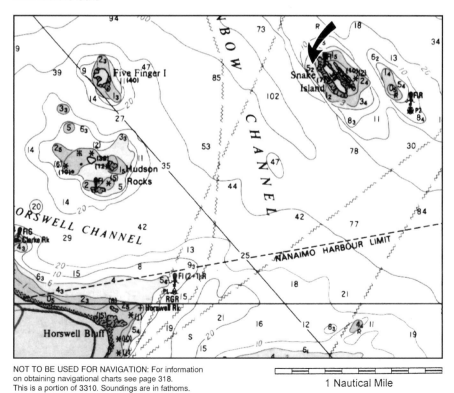

1 Nautical Mile

JESSE ISLAND
Kayak Dive or Boat Dive

Skill: All divers

Why go: Would you believe rock falls and tunnels, walls covered with bright red colonial anemones, and old bottles from the 1800s? All at one site?

Jesse Island is safe and easy to dive day or night. It is close to dive-kayak launching where you do not have to cross ferry traffic and close to a good boat launching ramp. This popular open-water certification site is picturesque and pretty for photographers and sightseers.

Locally honored as a reserve, you would be unpopular if you took any marine life but there is a lot of interesting marine life to see. Sea pens and sea whips are on the sand. My buddy who was taking photographs pointed out something I'd never seen before. A hermit crab had moved into a small shell, then a yellow sponge had covered the shell, dissolving the hermit crab's adopted home. A nudibranch was eating the sponge!

Bottom and Depths: Carved sandstone arches and tunnels are along the north side, even above the surface. Depths at the base of the rock wall range from 30 feet (9 meters) at the northwest corner to about 50 to 60 feet (15 to 18 meters) at the northeast end. Sandy bottom to the base of the wall. Bottles pitched off old Nanaimo coal ships may be found anywhere.

Hazards: Small boats, especially in summer. Departure Bay is heavily populated and salmon fishing is popular just outside the bay. Listen for boats and ascend right up the side of the island.

Telephones: • Departure Bay (north end), at store across Departure Bay Road from beach. • Brechin Civic Ramp, water side of the Public Market.

Facilities: None on privately owned Jesse Island. Newcastle Provincial Marine Park, an island in Nanaimo Harbour, is nearby: Campsites, picnic tables, drinking water and wharfage are at the park year-round. In summer, go to Newcastle from Nanaimo by pedestrian ferry that leaves from Maffeo-Sutton/Swy-a-nana Lagoon Park behind the civic arena. To reach the ferry, go to the foot of Bowen Road which becomes Comox Road as it nears the water. Year-round go by your own boat to the south end of Newcastle and tie up at the dock. Dive-kayak rentals on the waterfront in Departure Bay. Air fills in Nanaimo – including waterfront air fills at the Public Market and in Departure Bay. A superb set-up for camping and diving.

Access: Jesse Island is in Departure Bay just north of Nanaimo on Vancouver Island. Charter or rent a boat in Nanaimo or launch at Brechin Civic Ramp and go just over 1 nautical mile (1¾ kilometers) north to Jesse Island. Kayak-divers could launch at the park at Departure Bay Beach and paddle just under 1 nautical mile (1¾ kilometers) east to Jesse Island. Pull your dive-kayak onto whatever ledge is exposed when you arrive, or anchor in a little bay at the northwest corner and dive along the north side of Jesse Island.

Wheelchair divers who paddle dive-kayaks could launch at Brechin Boat Ramp and paddle to Jesse Island, but watch out for the British Columbia ferries.

Comments: Jesse Island is convenient and easy to dive at night, particularly if you launch at Brechin Civic Ramp. A bright light by the ramp makes sorting gear easy.

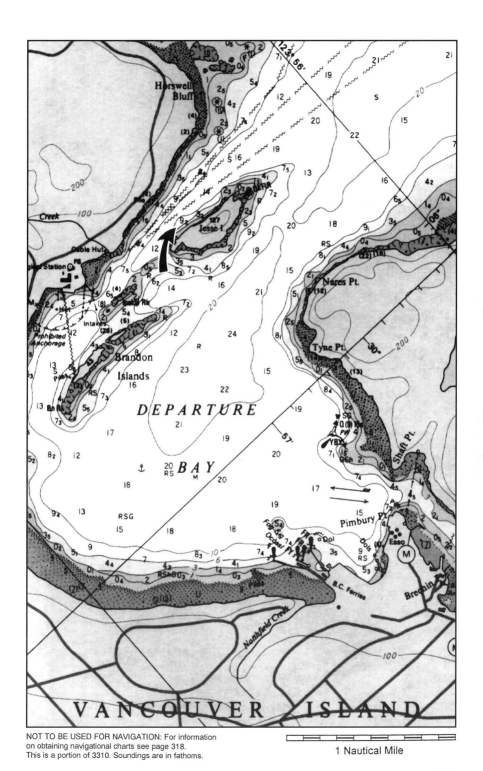

NOT TO BE USED FOR NAVIGATION: For information
on obtaining navigational charts see page 318.
This is a portion of 3310. Soundings are in fathoms.

1 Nautical Mile

KEEL COVE
Shore Dive

Tide Table: Point Atkinson

Skill: All divers and snorkelers

Why go: Two easy-to-find wrecks, a tire reef and several natural boulder reefs. In town. Good diving in winter – it's protected from southeast winds.

A grunt sculpin to greet you at a tiny port window of the *Vance*. You can almost count on it. An octopus beneath the hull and lots of rockfish in it. On the boulder reef we saw two more octopuses. Cabezons, swimming scallops, lots of young lingcod. Kelp crabs, blackeye gobies, red rock crabs, painted greenlings. We saw decorator crabs. Feather stars, sea squirts, chitons, a brittle star. And lots of urchins. Heading back over the luxuriant forest of big-leafed green and brown bottom kelp and through tall brown kelp, we saw orange cucumbers, a school of young tube-snouts, a moon snail egg case. So much on the boulder reef we didn't make it to the tire reef.

The *Vance*, a former trawler and shrimp boat, is 35 feet (11 meters) long. The *Shoddy Error* is another small boat. It sank since I dived Keel Cove and is shallow.

Bottom and Depths: Cobbled beach gives way to sand then rocky bottom smothered in broad-leafed kelp. The bottom slopes gently from shore to boulder reef and wrecks. The *Shoddy Error* is on the eastern end of the boulder reef in 35 to 45 feet (11 to 14 meters); the *Vance* is farther out in 50 to 60 feet (15 to 18 meters). The fixed-rope trail stops at the *Vance*. The tire reef is west of it on the sand.

Hazards: Steep short trail to beach. You could carry gear down in stages.

Telephones: • Departure Bay (north end), beside store across from beach. From McGuffie, go 3 miles (4¾ kilometers) south on Hammond Bay Road to Departure Bay Road. • Hammond Bay Road and Island Highway, southeast corner by gas station. From McGuffie, go north on Hammond Bay Road for 3¼ miles (5 kilometers).

Facilities: Off Hammond Bay Road, a toilet at Pipers [Page] Lagoon Park. Air fills in Nanaimo.

Access: Keel Cove is on Horswell Channel north of Nanaimo. It is reached by way of Hammond Bay Road off Departure Bay Road at its south end and off Island Highway at its north end. From the ferry, 15 minutes to the dive.

From Hammond Bay Road, turn into McGuffie and go to the end of it. Room for one or two cars to park. Walk down a steep trail to the log-strewn beach. A white buoy marks the start of a fixed-rope trail to the wrecks – it might be covered at very high tides. The wrecks are on a compass bearing directly north. First go to the *Shoddy Error* poised on the boulder reef. Next the *Vance*. Bear left off its bow to the tire reef.

To get to Hammond Bay Road
• From the ferry at Departure Bay, follow signs toward Parksville. Immediately after turning onto Island Highway, turn right into Departure Bay Road. Head downhill to the water. At the north end of Departure Bay, turn right into Hammond Bay Road. Go 3 miles (4¾ kilometers) on Hammond Bay Road to McGuffie Road.
• From Nanaimo, go north on Highway 1 which becomes Island Highway (Highway 19). Ten minutes north of the center of the city and just before Northbrook mall, turn right into Departure Bay Road. Head downhill to the water. At the north end of Departure Bay, turn right into Hammond Bay Road. From here, go 3 miles (4¾ kilometers) on Hammond Bay Road to McGuffie Road.
• From Parksville, go south. When 10 minutes past Northwest Bay Road (south end)

look for Hammond Bay Road. Turn left off Island Highway. Go 3¼ miles (5 kilometers) to McGuffie Road. If you reach the pub you have gone too far.

Comments: Day or night, take a light!

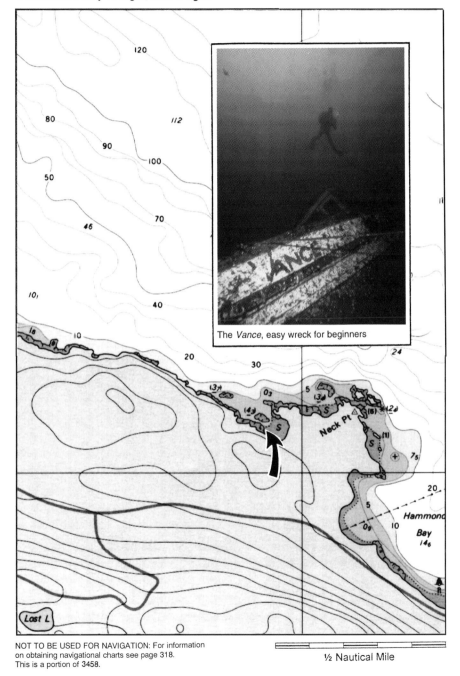

The *Vance*, easy wreck for beginners

½ Nautical Mile

SUNRISE BEACH
Shore Dive

Tide Table: Point Atkinson

Skill: All divers and snorkelers

Why go: Quick and easy. Sunrise Beach is a good place to drop into the water if you're in Nanaimo and have only a couple of hours for a dive.

Entry is exceptionally easy down a car-top boat launching ramp or, at low tide, across a small rocky beach at the end of the ramp. Then swim out and to the left a very short way over shallow rocks covered with bottom kelp to a shallow ledge that parallels the shore. You'll see all the animals that go with this kind of bottom: lots of decorator crabs, nudibranchs, hairy crabs and maybe an octopus. During one quick dive here I saw a dozen small colorful painted greenlings.

An agreeable little dive.

Bottom and Depths: A shallow shelf parallels the shore and drops to a depth of 30 to 40 feet (9 to 12 meters). Bottom kelp on the rocks and some sand between.

Hazards: Wind from the southeast can cause surf which makes entry difficult. Boats at launching ramp. Ascend close to shore.

Telephones: • Hammond Bay Road and Island Highway, southeast corner by gas station. From Entwhistle, 2¼ miles (3½ kilometers). • Departure Bay (north end), beside store. From Entwhistle, go 4 miles (6½ kilometers) south on Hammond Bay Road to Departure Bay Road.

Facilities: Parking space at Sunrise Beach and car-top boat launching. Toilet at Pipers [Page] Lagoon Park off Hammond Bay Road; go south on Hammond Bay Road for 2½ miles (4 kilometers) to Pipers Lagoon turnoff and follow the signs.

Access: Sunrise Beach is on Horswell Channel north of Nanaimo. It is reached by way of Hammond Bay Road off Departure Bay Road at its south end; and off Island Highway (Highway 19) at its north end. From the ferry, 15 minutes to the dive.

From Hammond Bay Road, turn into Entwhistle Drive. Go ⅓ mile (½ kilometer) to Fillinger Crescent. Turn right. Continue a very short way to a parking area on the left-hand side. It is a car-top boat launching ramp marked "Public Access to Beach". You could drive down the ramp to drop gear. Then park. Room for six or seven cars. Wheelchair access down the launching ramp to the rocky beach which is 50 feet (15 meters) wide at low tide.

To get to Hammond Bay Road
• From Nanaimo or coming off the ferry at Departure Bay, go north on Island Highway. Follow signs toward Parksville. At Island Highway before Northbrook mall, immediately turn right and head downhill on Departure Bay Road. The road curves down to the water. At the north end of Departure Bay, turn right into Hammond Bay Road. Curve around past Pipers [Page] Lagoon Park, Charlaine Boat Ramp, a grocery and pub. From Departure Bay, 4 miles (6½ kilometers) to Entwhistle Drive where you turn right.
• From Parksville, go south. When 10 minutes past Northwest Bay Road (south end) turnoff look for Hammond Bay Road. Turn left off Island Highway. Go 2¼ miles (3½ kilometers) to Entwhistle – when reaching a curve to the right on Hammond Bay Road, you turn left in the elbow of that curve to Entwhistle.

Comments: "Nanaimo", an Indian word meaning "meeting of the tribes".

Painted greenling, or convict fish

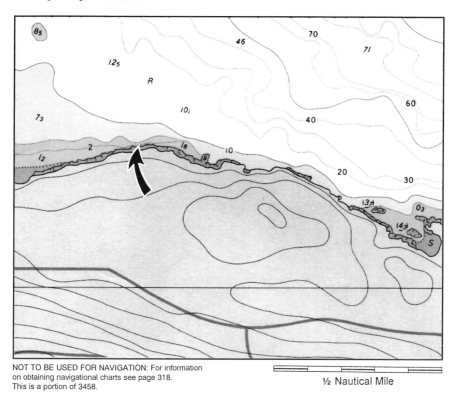

½ Nautical Mile

SEA LIONS
Boat Dive

Skill: Expert divers

Why go: Go to Ada Rock to look at sea lions – so the sea lions can look at you! At peak time, as many as 500 haul out at Ada Rock. Steller, or northern sea lions, are tan colored. California sea lions have darker fur and are smaller – they are the ones that bark.

Big eyes. That's what you see first. And last. The sea lions are curious. They come and go in waves. Dart down, look, and shoot away. Before we reach our seamount destination, six sea lions swim to meet us. At the seamount, twelve sea lions – 18,000 pounds (8 tonnes) of wildlife – flip their tails in front of us! The weight of one adult male Steller might be 1,000 to 2,200 pounds (450 to 1,000 kilograms); average length is 10 feet (3 meters). Female Stellers weigh half as much and are up to 8 feet (2½ meters) long. But you are more likely to meet the big ones as there are mostly bulls at the haulout sites.

The Stellers arrive like a group of friends visiting the zoo, playing and rubbing against one another. One stands on its nose, twirls, and stares at us. A thick-necked one shoots down, arches, blows bubbles, then disappears up and away. Bubbles are the first sign of aggression, I'm told. Probably a bull – perhaps the "leader of the pack". Our leader signals us to leave. We move slowly, stay close to the wall as long as possible. When we reach open water, I look behind me. And, yes, a lone sleek big-eyed sea lion follows. Swoops back and forth behind us, beside us, between us. Gracefully, without menace but with seeming intent, it escorts us out of her "yard".

More marine life is at the site, but it is irrelevant: "Once you see the sea lions," our guide said "you're not looking for anything else".

Bottom and Depths: An underwater seamount which dries at 2-foot (½-meter) tides, bottoms out to sand at 15 to 25 feet (4½ to 8 meters).

Hazards: The sea lions themselves – reports of divers injured by playful sea lions have been confirmed: A broken arm, a separated shoulder, severe bruising. Probably accidents. However...if you still choose to dive with sea lions, how can you do it as safely as possible? Watch them. Keep your back to a wall. Since blowing bubbles might be a sign of aggression, do not look directly at a sea lion and exhale. The sea lions become less cautious the longer divers are present; do not stay down long. They also become less cautious the greater number of encounters they have with divers.

Throughout our dive the sea lions stayed 3 to 6 feet (1 to 2 meters) away. It was as if they were stopped by a glass wall, were shy or cautious or respected our space. Divers should respect their space, too, because of their sheer size, if nothing else. In addition, the Fisheries Act forbids disturbing, molesting or killing marine mammals. You may not touch them nor do anything that interferes with whatever the animals are normally doing.

Telephone: Schooner Cove, outside marina office.

Facilities: None at Ada Rock. Hot showers, hot tub and sauna at Schooner Cove. Air fills at Courtenay and Nanaimo.

Access: Sea lions haul out on Ada Rock, southeast side of Ballenas Channel, from November through March. Ada Rock is the name used by locals; it is one of the Ada Islands on the charts. This rock is white in color and has no shrubs or trees on it. The site is 2 nautical miles (3¾ kilometers) east of Schooner Cove on Vancouver Island. You cannot miss it when sea lions are present. Plan to go December through February or telephone the marina at Schooner Cove at (604) 468-7691 to check if sea lions are at Ada. Timing is important – it is a winter dive.

Charter, rent or launch a boat at Schooner Cove, launch at Nanoose Harbour or charter out of Nanaimo. From Schooner Cove, go 1½ nautical miles (2¾ kilometers) to Ada Rock. From Nanoose Harbour, just over 2 nautical miles (3¾ kilometers). Circle Ada at a distance: do not alarm the sea lions but *do* gain an impression of their size and power.

Then return to the sheltered cove on the southwest side of a small island west of Ada Rock to anchor. A compass would be useful. Snorkel two or three minutes toward an underwater seamount which dries at 2-foot (¾-meter) tides. The seamount is about halfway to Ada Rock. Go part way on the surface; descend and swim under water to it. Wait with your back to the wall. The sea lions will probably come to meet you before you reach it. If not, bang a rock on the bottom.

Comments: Winter thing-to-do: More sea lion haulouts south of Nanaimo at Harmac – mostly California sea lions there. Stellers haul out at Eagle Rock near the south tip of Denman Island, at Scotch Fir Point near Powell River and at Race Rocks.

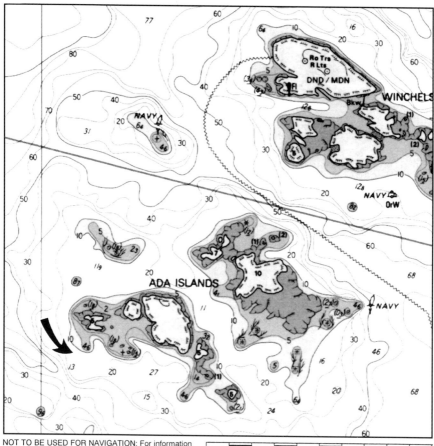

NOT TO BE USED FOR NAVIGATION: For information
on obtaining navigational charts see page 318.
This is a portion of 3459.

½ Nautical Mile

211

YEO ISLANDS   **Tide Table:** Point Atkinson
Kayak Dive or Boat Dive

Skill: All divers

Why go: The Yeo Islands are close offshore. Because several islands make up this group, someplace is almost always sheltered from the wind. And it's beautiful shallow diving on all sides. A very divable site for all.
We reveled in the moon snails and tall, graceful orange sea pens. Clams and rock scallops. Giant red urchins, huge sea lemons hide in the thick kelp. Small perfect-petalled alabaster nudibranchs, too. Enormous gum boot chitons stick to the rocks. My buddy found a small aqua-colored chiton that looked like a turquoise. Diving at the Yeo Islands on a sunny day is like dipping into a bright box of jewels.

Bottom and Depths: White sand bottom scattered with small broken rock provides attachment for lots of bull kelp which is very thick in summer. A huge shallow area, from 25 to 35 feet (8 to 11 meters) deep, lies all around the Yeo Islands.

Hazards: Bull kelp. Carry a knife.

Telephone: Schooner Cove Marina, outside marina office.

Facilities: None at the Yeo Islands. Charters, boat rentals, launching, hot showers at Schooner Cove. Charters, boat rentals and launching at Northwest Bay. Dive-kayak rentals in Nanaimo at Departure Bay.

Access: The Yeo Islands are on the south side of Ballenas Channel, 10 nautical miles (19 kilometers) northwest of Nanaimo. The islands are just 1 nautical mile (2 kilometers) north of Schooner Cove. From Northwest Bay, it is 8 nautical miles (15 kilometers) to the Yeo group.
Charter, rent or launch at Schooner's Cove or Northwest Bay and go to the Yeo Islands. On a calm settled day you could kayak to it from Seducer's Beach (see Seducer's Beach on page 216). From there, it is less than 1 nautical mile (less than 2 kilometers) to the Yeo Islands. Wheelchair divers who paddle dive-kayaks might paddle from Seducer's Beach or Schooner Cove. Anchor or land your dive-kayak or boat and tie up wherever there is shelter. The northwest corner is a good spot.
The marinas at Schooner Cove and Northwest Bay are reached from Northwest Bay Road off Island Highway (Highway 19) between Nanaimo and Parksville. From the highway, 10 or 15 minutes to the marinas.
• From Nanaimo, go north on Highway 19 – 30 minutes to Northwest Bay Road (south end). It is at a traffic light past Lantzville. Follow signs toward Schooner Cove. If heading to Schooner Cove, go 1¾ mile (3 kilometers) to Stewart Road, turn right and continue following signs to Schooner. If heading to Northwest Bay, continue for ⅕ mile (⅓ kilometer) past Stewart to Claudet Road and turn right to the marina.
• From Parksville, go south on Highway 19; immediately past Rathtrevor Provincial Park turnoff, follow signs toward Craig's and Beachcomber Marina. Bear left onto Northwest Bay Road (north end). Go 3½ miles (5¾ kilometers) to Claudet Road; turn left following signs to Northwest Bay. Or continue ⅕ mile (⅓ kilometer) to Stewart Road and turn left to Schooner Cove.

Comments: Sea pens look like bright orange feathers in daylight and in the beam of your flashlight. If you switch off your light and ripple their fronds in the dark, they shimmer neon green.

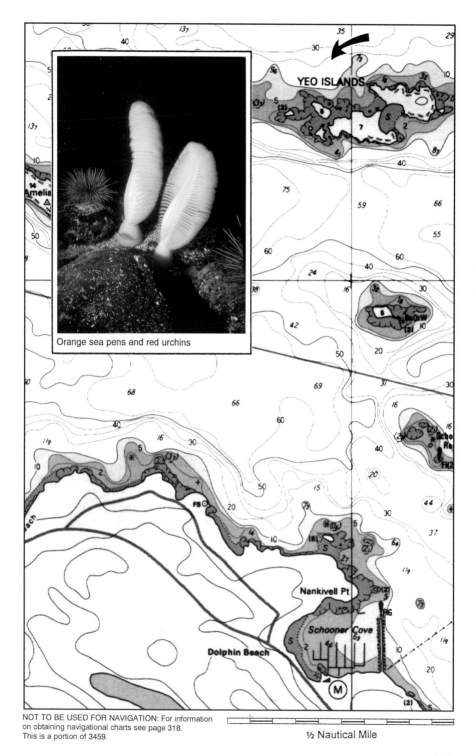

YEO ISLANDS

Orange sea pens and red urchins

Nankivell Pt

Schooner Cove

Dolphin Beach

Ⓜ

½ Nautical Mile

AMELIA ISLAND
Kayak Dive or Boat Dive

Tide Table: Point Atkinson

Skill: All divers

Why go: Gorgeous shallow and deep – Amelia Island is a beautiful dive. My favorite kind of place.

I love to go over an immediate cliff, like this, that drops off to infinity. Or seems to. Below you it's dark and black and there is no bottom. Big chimney sponges – some hiding decorator crabs inside – sweep down the wall. Small swimming scallops look infinitesimal against the dark abyss. Yellow cloud sponges and bright orange sponges that appear to have come from the bathtub are scattered down the wall. A dogfish swims out of the dark and circles. You see a yelloweye rockfish.

It's time to go up, but not too fast. There's a lot to see on the way. Stop at the shallow shelf at 10 feet (3 meters). Glimmering white nudibranch eggs, like a perfect coil of apple peel, hang from the rocks. Painted greenlings, kelp greenlings, decorator crabs, abalones and rock scallops hide in the kelp. Bull kelp, bright green lettuce kelp, red kelp and blue-purply kelp that's almost transparent. An extravaganza of kelp. A heap of Christmas tissue paper.

Bottom and Depths: Rocky shores go to a shallow shelf at 10 to 20 feet (3 to 6 meters), depending on tide height, where there is bull kelp and other kinds of bottom kelp. From here the drop is right off to 165 feet (50 meters).

Hazards: Current, depth and bull kelp. Dive near the slack. Carry a knife. Kayak-divers who dive deep should rest before paddling back to avoid overexertion which may increase risk of bends.

Telephone: Schooner Cove, outside marina office.

Facilities: None at uninhabited Amelia Island. Charters, boat rentals and launching at Schooner Cove and at Northwest Bay. Also hot showers, hot tub and sauna at Schooner Cove; nominal fee for drop-ins. Air fills at Courtenay and Nanaimo. Dive-kayak rentals in Nanaimo at Departure Bay.

Access: Amelia Island is on the south side of Ballenas Channel. It is 1½ nautical miles (2¾ kilometers) northwest of Schooner Cove where you will find charters, boat rentals, a launching ramp. It is 4 nautical miles (7½ kilometers) from Northwest Bay where you will find boat rentals and launching.

Charters available out of Nanaimo. Or you could kayak to it from Seducer's Beach or Dolphin Beach (see Seducer's Beach on page 216, Dolphin Beach on page 218). From those points it is less than 1 nautical mile (just over 1 kilometer) to Amelia. Wheelchair divers who paddle dive-kayaks could paddle from Seducer's Beach. The drop-off is in the middle of the south side of Amelia Island.

The marinas at Schooner Cove and Northwest Bay are reached from Northwest Bay Road off Island Highway (Highway 19) between Nanaimo and Parksville. From Island Highway, 10 or 15 minutes to the marinas.

• From Nanaimo, go north on Highway 19 – 30 minutes to Northwest Bay Road (south end). It is at a traffic light past Lantzville. Follow signs toward Schooner Cove. If heading to Schooner Cove, go 1¾ mile (3 kilometers) to Stewart Road, turn right and continue following signs to Schooner. If heading to Northwest Bay, continue for ⅕ mile (⅓ kilometer) past Stewart to Claudet Road and turn right to the marina.

• From Parksville, go south on Highway 19. Immediately past Rathtrevor Provincial Park turnoff, follow signs toward Craig's and Beachcomber Marina. Bear left onto

Northwest Bay Road (north end). Go 3½ miles (5¾ kilometers) to Claudet Road; turn left following signs to Northwest Bay. Or continue ⅕ mile (⅓ kilometer) to Stewart Road and turn left to Schooner Cove.

Comments: Amelia Island is only one of the beautiful dives in the Ada, Winchelsea and Ballenas islands area so famed for sponges.

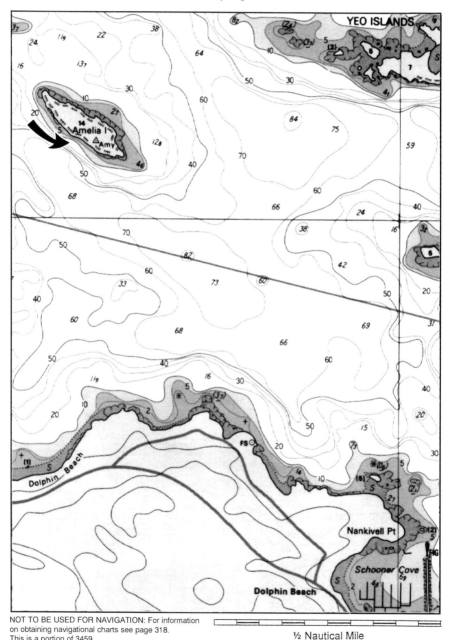

½ Nautical Mile

SEDUCER'S BEACH
Shore Dive

Skill: All divers and snorkelers

Why go: Easy access, sandy and rocky bottom, marine life shallow and deep; also a "first" for me on this dive. The whole dive feels different. Exotic.

Pink hydrocorals and yellow staghorn bryozoans like hard tropical corals, an extravaganza of giant silver nudibranchs – probably a hundred of them and half a dozen with eggs. We saw leather stars, purple sea stars. Deeper, feather stars. Orange cucumbers. One swimming scallop. Lingcod, a cabezon, and a quillback rockfish. Lots of round orange sponges the size of tennis balls with tiny knobs all over them – I call them "puff balls". Then down to the chimney sponges.

Many perch swim about in the sandy shallows. We also enjoyed seeing schools of young tube-snouts, kelp greenlings and black rockfish. Wispy tube-dwelling anemones. Egg cases of moon snails. Blackeye gobies. Swarms of mysids, or opossum shrimp, like millions of tiny ghosts. They are transparent – if the sun is shining you can see their shadow before you see them. The "first" for me this dive was seeing a clinging jellyfish. We found it beneath a leaf of kelp as we poked around at the end of our dive. This jellyfish has adhesive pads on its tentacle tips, and is the only jellyfish that can attach itself to kelp without self-destructing. It is transparent except for the pink cross on its bell.

Bottom and Depths: Sandy bottom with eelgrass soon gives way to rocky bottom 30 to 40 feet (9 to 12 meters) deep. The top of the wall begins at 50 to 60 feet (15 to 18 meters) and bottoms out to sand at a depth of 110 to 120 feet (34 to 37 meters), depending on tide height. Green and brown bottom kelp, with some bull kelp in summer. Staying shallow is easy. But the bottom drops off quickly to sponge-land, so it is also easy to go as deep as you want to – your choice.

Hazards: Wind in winter, might be some current but it will not carry you away. Dive near slack.

Telephone: Schooner Cove Marina, ½ mile (1 kilometer) east, outside marina office.

Facilities: Unspoilt beach for a picnic. Hot tubs, hot showers and sauna nearby at Schooner Cove – all the comforts you wish you had at home after the dive.

Access: Seducer's Beach, also known as Tyee Beach or Tyee Cove, is on Ballenas Channel. It is reached by way of Northwest Bay Road off Island Highway (Highway 19) between Nanaimo and Parksville. From Island Highway, 20 minutes to the dive. From Northwest Bay Road, turn into Stewart Road. Go to Dolphin Drive. Turn right. Go 1½ miles (2⅓ kilometers) on Dolphin to Blueback Drive. Turn left. Go for ½ mile (1 kilometer) to Tyee Crescent. Turn left. Go 100 feet (30 meters) and park at the roadside. Left of the fire hydrant is a trail between the thimbleberries to a cobbled beach. Wheelchair access is possible on the flat trail. You might want to take a machete to cut back the thimbleberries.

To get to Stewart Road
• From Nanaimo, go north on Highway 19 – 30 minutes to Northwest Bay Road (south end). It is at a traffic light past Lantzville. Follow signs toward Schooner Cove on Northwest Bay Road. Go 1¾ miles (3 kilometers) to Stewart Road.
• From Parksville, go south on Highway 19; immediately past Rathtrevor Park turnoff, follow signs toward Craig's and Beachcomber Marina. Bear left onto Northwest Bay

Road (north end). Go 3¾ miles (6 kilometers) to Stewart Road.

Comments: Seducer's Beach is great for beginners, and for all divers who want a quick dive close to town.

Seducer's Beach

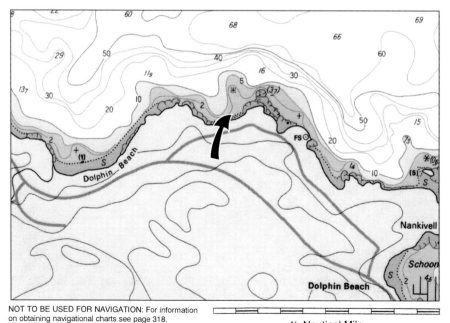

NOT TO BE USED FOR NAVIGATION: For information on obtaining navigational charts see page 318. This is a portion of 3459.

½ Nautical Mile

DOLPHIN BEACH
Shore Dive

Skill: All divers and snorkelers

Why go: Sponge-land is right at hand. I know of no other dive from shore where sponges are so easily accessible as at Dolphin Beach.

Dolphin Beach is good for the deep diver. Good for shallow divers and snorkelers too. We saw seaperch and rockfish swimming in the bull kelp and hiding in crevices. White-petalled alabaster nudibranchs and an assortment of others. Moon snails in the eelgrass. Deeper were ratfish, some lingcod and round orange sponges clinging to the wall. Big chimney sponges start at 80 feet (24 meters).

Because this site has been popular for years, food fish have been nearly hunted out in the shallows. But over the wall you might still find some lingcod to photograph.

Bottom and Depths: Rocky beach gives way to eelgrass and sand in the shallows, then tall brown kelp, rocks and bull kelp. Some deep cracks in the rocks. Swim past two valleys to reach the main wall. Beyond the kelp, steeply sloping sand falls away quickly to 80 feet (24 meters) where a stark rock wall drops off to a depth of 110 to 120 feet (34 to 37 meters) in "The Basement".

Hazards: Bull kelp, especially in summer, and wind in winter. Carry a knife. If wind makes entry difficult, you can always dive at Seducer's Beach.

Telephone: Schooner Cove Marina, ½ mile (1 kilometer) east, outside marina office.

Facilities: None at Dolphin Beach.

Access: Dolphin Beach is on Ballenas Channel near Parksville on Vancouver Island. It is reached via Northwest Bay Road off Island Highway (Highway 19) between Nanaimo and Parksville. From Island Highway, 20 minutes to the dive.

From Northwest Bay Road, turn into Stewart Road. Go to Dolphin Drive to Blueback Drive – Stewart to Blueback is 2½ miles (4 kilometers). Bear left onto Blueback: go down the hill ⅓ mile (½ kilometer). You go into a dip, the road comes near the water. Houses are close by on either side. This is Dolphin Beach. Park by the road, walk a couple of steps through the brush to the rocky beach. Swim straight out and down. You will pass a couple of underwater valleys before you reach the main wall.

To get to Northwest Bay Road and Stewart Road
• From Nanaimo, go north on Island Highway; 30 minutes to Northwest Bay Road (south end). It is at a traffic light past Lantzville and before a gas station. Follow signs toward Schooner Cove on Northwest Bay Road. Go 1¾ miles (3 kilometers) to Stewart Road.
• From Parksville, go south on Island Highway; immediately past Rathtrevor Provincial Park turnoff, follow signs toward Craig's and Beachcomber Marina. Go off the highway; bear left onto Northwest Bay Road (north end). Go 3¾ miles (6 kilometers) to Stewart Road.

Comments: The rocky beach is good for winter campfires. Despite the surrounding homes Dolphin Beach feels wild and secluded. If wanting to build a fire from April 15th through October 15th, either telephone the Nanoose Volunteer Fire Department, PO Box 47, Nanoose Bay BC V0R 2R0, (604) 468-7141 or telephone BC Forest Service, 4227 Sixth Avenue, Port Alberni BC V9Y 4N1, (604) 724-9205 and ask if beach fires permitted. When you leave, be sure to put out the fire.

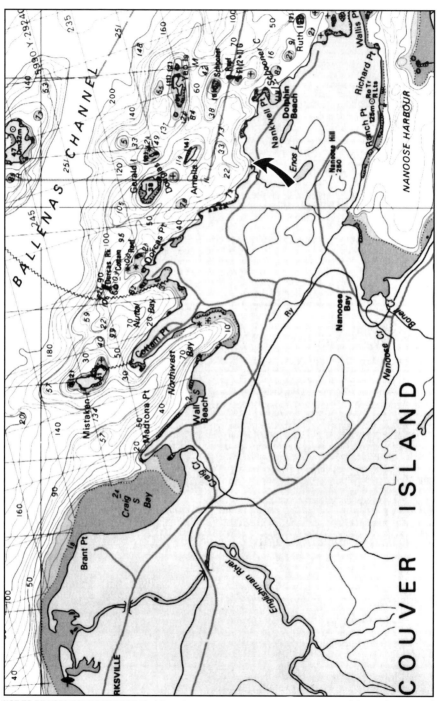

1 Nautical Mile

219

COTTAM POINT
Shore Dive

Tide Table: Point Atkinson

Skill: All divers and snorkelers

Why go: Beautiful for sightseeing and photography. Plus the remains of a couple of small wrecks.
Diving here is like jumping into an aquarium. Cottam Point teems with life. Millions of little rockfish, nudibranchs, sea stars, kelp greenlings and red rock crabs. Painted greenlings. Large white fluffy anemones. Huge boulders, covered with so many small orange fuzzy anemones that you can't see any rock at all, stand immovable between olive-colored bull kelp banners flying in the current. If you look, you may see an octopus or a wolf-eel. Sea lions, in winter.
And the wrecks: *Seadog*, a 25-foot (7-meter) plywood-hulled cabin cruiser, sank in 1985. The head and kitchen sink are still intact. It is home to lots of lingcod and rockfish. The *Bachelor*, a 30-foot (9-meter) oak-hulled cabin cruiser, sank in 1989. Lots of lingcod on it too. Abalones are returning, and rock scallops. But just look, don't take. Cottam Point is a sanctuary. A diver's flag sign is beside the steps to the water. Written on it: "Observe but do not touch".

Bottom and Depths: Smooth rocks roll gently down into the water where brown kelp stands tall, lettuce kelp and bull kelp grow luxuriantly over the ledges and reef. Scattered boulders and some sand between. *Bachelor* rests on silty sand, *Seadog* on the reef – both at a depth of 50 to 60 feet (15 to 18 meters), depending on tide height.

Hazards: Small boats, current, and wind. In summer, bull kelp. Very heavy boat traffic close to shore. Listen for boats, use a compass and ascend along the bottom all the way to shore. Current up to 2 knots (3¾ kilometers/hour) and more. When large tidal exchanges, dive near slack. Carry a knife. Do not dive if wind from the northwest makes entry difficult.

Telephones: • Northwest Bay Road (north end) and Island Highway, tourism office. • Northwest Bay Road (south end) and Island Highway, at gas station. • Beachcomber Marina, inside.

Facilities: None. Parking space is limited. Air fills at Courtenay and Nanaimo.

Access: Cottam Point is at Northwest Bay near Parksville on Vancouver Island. It is reached by way of Northwest Bay Road off Island Highway (Highway 19) between Nanaimo and Parksville. The dive is 10 to 15 minutes off Island Highway.
From Northwest Bay Road, turn onto Claudet Road; after 1 mile (1¾ kilometer) you turn left, and Dorcas Point Road goes off to the right. Keep going 1¼ miles (2 kilometers) more to Sea Dog Road. Turn left to the water. Follow the path beside the cable to ten concrete steps built between the roots of a tree and down to the rocks. Homes are on both sides. In front of the steps, Cottam Point. The reef goes straight out from the point toward Mistaken Island. *Seadog* lies at the northeast tip of the reef. Look to the left of the steps for a diver's flag and the wreck symbol painted on the rocks along with a 280- to 300-degree compass bearing. Follow it out to the *Bachelor*. An easy entry over smooth rocks.

To get to Northwest Bay Road
• From Nanaimo, go north on Island Highway – 30 minutes to Northwest Bay Road (south end). It is at a traffic light past Lantzville. Follow signs toward Schooner Cove. Go on Northwest Bay Road, 2 miles (3¼ kilometers) to Claudet Road.

• From Parksville, go south on Island Highway; immediately past Rathtrevor Park turnoff, follow signs toward Craig's and Beachcomber Marina. Bear left onto Northwest Bay Road (north end). Go 3½ miles (5¾ kilometers) to Claudet Road.

Comments: Good visibility year-round, ranging to 100 feet (30 meters) in winter.

Quillback rockfish

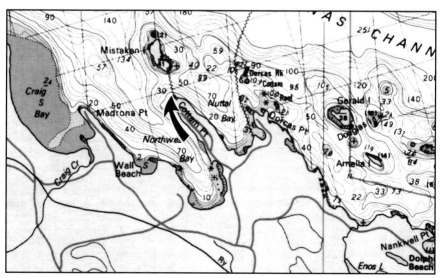

NOT TO BE USED FOR NAVIGATION: For information
on obtaining navigational charts see page 318.
This is a portion of L/C-3512.

1 Nautical Mile

WALL BEACH
Shore Dive

Skill: Intermediate and expert divers. All divers with guide.

Why go: Octopuses and wolf-eels are the big lure for most at Wall Beach. But I loved the fish life, the sea stars, the staghorn bryozoans. We saw lots of seaperch, a big fat kelp greenling, lingcod – probably fifty of them. Rockfish galore: two tiger rockfish, quillback rockfish, black rockfish. We were lucky and saw a juvenile yelloweye rock-fish, commonly called red snapper. And two ratfish. We saw a painted star, purple stars, striped sun stars, sunflower stars. In the shallows, the egg case of a moon snail, tiny sea pens, sea peaches, and a yellow longish creature with vertical ribs that looked like a sea cucumber without its outer knobby rough skin. I'm still looking in the books for that one.

Bottom and Depths: Smooth rock on shore rolls gently down to eelgrass on silty sand bottom. Farther out, lettuce kelp and brown bottom kelp; brown stalks of kelp stand tall. Ten minutes out from shore, a ledge drops 10 to 15 feet (3 to 4½ meters). Depth ranges from 50 to 60 feet (15 to 18 meters). Boulders scattered along it; sand between. Smooth sand bottom slopes gently off beyond the ledge.

Hazards: Current, long swim, small boats and wind. Dive near the slack. Listen for boats, use a compass and ascend along the bottom all the way to shore well out of the way of boats. Do not dive at Wall Beach if wind from the southeast – makes entry difficult.

Telephones: • Northwest Bay Road (north end) and Island Highway, beside tourism office. • Northwest Bay Road (south end) and Island Highway, at gas station.

Facilities: None. Parking space is limited. Air fills at Courtenay and Nanaimo.

Access: The Wall Beach dive is at Northwest Bay near Parksville on Vancouver Island. It is reached by way of Northwest Bay Road off Island Highway (Highway 19) between Nanaimo and Parksville. The dive is 10 minutes off Island Highway.
From Northwest Bay Road, turn onto Wall Beach Road. Go ½ mile (1 kilometer) – almost to the water. Turn right onto Seahaven; it becomes a dirt road. Go for ½ mile (¾ kilometer) along Seahaven Road to the end of it. A gate is on your left. Next to it, room for five or six cars to park. Straight ahead, a short trail to the sloping smooth rocks to the water. Swim straight out on the surface for five minutes or until you lose the bottom, then continue under water following a compass heading straight out.
Wheelchair accessible for groups with a great deal of able-bodied support to help get over the smooth rock that forms the beach. Expect barnacles at low tide.

To get to Northwest Bay Road
• From Nanaimo, go north on Highway 19 – 30 minutes to Northwest Bay Road (south end). It is at a traffic light past Lantzville and before a gas station. Follow signs toward Schooner Cove. Take Northwest Bay Road, but keep going past Stewart and Claudet to Wall Beach Road. From Northwest Bay Road, 3¾ miles (6 kilometers).
• From Parksville, south on Highway 19; immediately past Rathtrevor Park turnoff, follow signs toward Craig's and Beachcomber Marina. Bear left off the highway onto Northwest Bay Road (north end); 1¾ miles (3 kilometers) to Wall Beach Road.

Comments: Great at night – one diver saw three octopuses, another diver saw eight wolf-eels on one night dive here. The wolf-eels hang out around the boulders.

Spearfishing is discouraged by local divers as this is a highly accessible dive and could easily be destroyed.

Logging the dive at Wall Beach

½ Nautical Mile

MADRONA POINT
Shore Dive

Skill: All divers and snorkelers

Why go: An octopus every five minutes – that's what I saw here! And they are shallow. There are wolf-eels, too, out deeper. But you have to look hard for both.

Madrona Point, commonly called Arbutus Point, is rimmed with beautiful rocky ledges and overhangs making all kinds of places for octopuses to hide. Crabs – a ready meal for octopuses – scurry over the sand which comes up to the rock wall rimming the point. You will see a good mixture of anemones, sea stars, some nudibranchs and rockfish as well. In winter, perhaps sea lions.

A vast plain of ghostly white sea whips stretches north in deep water offshore from the rocky overhangs to the ledge which drops into wolf-eel country and sponge-land.

Bottom and Depths: Rock wall filled with nooks and crannies where octopuses hide. It drops to flat sandy bottom at 25 to 35 feet (8 to 11 meters). This slopes gradually out for a long way. The sea whips are on muddy bottom at 80 to 90 feet (24 to 27 meters). Set your compass and head north across the plain of sea whips. After 100 yards (90 meters) you will come to a ledge that drops off to deeper water where the wolf-eels live.

Hazards: Boats. Listen for boats; if you hear a boat, stay down until it passes.

Telephones: • Northwest Bay Road (north end) and Island Highway, beside tourism office. • Northwest Bay Road (south end) and Island Highway, at gas station.

Facilities: None. Air fills at Courtenay and Nanaimo.

Access: Madrona Point is at Northwest Bay near Parksville on Vancouver Island. It is reached by way of Northwest Bay Road off Island Highway (Highway 19) between Nanaimo and Parksville. The dive is 10 to 15 minutes off Island Highway.

From Northwest Bay Road, turn onto Arbutus Drive. Go to Madrona Drive, turn left and go ½ mile (1 kilometer) more to the end of the road. Room for one or two cars to park. Walk down a short, flat path between tall trees to the layered rock ledges of Madrona Point. Enter and swim around the rocky shore to look for an octopus or snorkel north and go down to look for wolf-eels.

Wheelchair accessible – no ramp, but it is a flat path and possible for those able to get a few feet (meters) over the rocks.

To get to Northwest Bay Road
• From Nanaimo, go north on Island Highway – 30 minutes to Northwest Bay Road (south end). It is at a traffic light past Lantzville and before a gas station. Follow signs toward Schooner Cove, taking Northwest Bay Road. Keep going past Stewart Road, Claudet Drive and Wall Beach Road. From the turnoff, 4 miles (6¾ kilometers) to Arbutus Drive.
• From Parksville, go south on Island Highway. Immediately past Rathtrevor Provincial Park turnoff, follow signs toward Craig's and Beachcomber Marina. Go off the highway; bear left onto Northwest Bay Road (north end). Go 1⅓ miles (2¼ kilometers) to Arbutus Drive.

Comments: Beautiful rock ledges for a picnic.

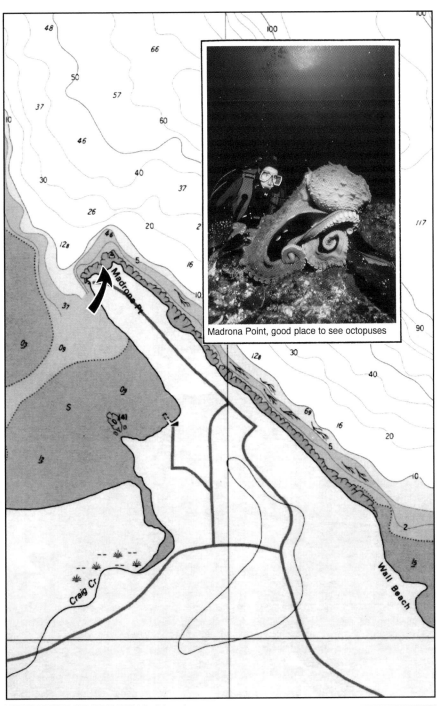

Madrona Point, good place to see octopuses

48
66
100
100
50
57
37
60
10
46
40
30
37
26
20
2
117
12₈
46
5
37
16
10
09
09
90
09
12₈
30
S
(4)
69
40
13
16
20
5
10
2
Craig Cr
Wall Beach
15

½ Nautical Mile

MAUDE REEF

Kayak Dive or Boat Dive

Skill: Intermediate and expert divers

Why go: An underwater garden opens before you on the channel side of Maude Reef.

When diving here I had the sensation of everything being pretty, pretty! And the fish! There seem to be big fish everywhere. Lingcod and large cabezons. Rockfish and kelp greenlings all over the place. Schools of black rockfish. Dogfish mixed in with the rest. And we even saw a little grunt sculpin. Forests of sea pens tilt out of pools of sand between the rocks. We saw sea peaches. Giant red urchins. Decorator crabs. And a couple of swimming scallops. A jungle of bull kelp, white cucumbers and orange ones, and lettuce kelp so fine it's like nylon stockings.

Flounders and eelgrass flourish in the sand between the reef and Hornby Island.

Bottom and Depths: Rocky reef bottoming out to sand at 30 to 40 feet (9 to 12 meters) parallels the shore of Hornby. The reef dries at 14-foot (4-meter) tides.

Hazards: Current, boats and bull kelp. Dive on the slack. Listen for boats and ascend close to the reef and marker all the way to the surface. Carry a knife for kelp.

Telephone: Ford Cove, grocery store.

Facilities: Air fills, charters and accommodation for diving groups at Ford Cove on Hornby Island – wheelchair divers welcome. Also private campgrounds at Hornby.

Access: Maude Reef is ½ nautical mile (1 kilometer) northwest of Ford Cove at the southwest end of Hornby Island. It is between Denman and Hornby Islands in Lambert Channel, and has a marker on it.

Charter at Hornby, Denman or Vancouver Island. Or launch your own boat or dive-kayak at Ford Cove on Hornby, and go north ½ nautical mile (1 kilometer) to the marker on Maude Reef. Do not tie onto the marker. It is a federal offense to make fast to a marker or tamper with any aid to navigation. Wheelchair divers who paddle dive-kayaks might board their dive-kayaks from the government float at Ford Cove.

If you have a larger boat, launch at the ramp at Gravelly Bay next to the ferry landing on the east side of Denman Island and go 1½ nautical miles (2¾ kilometers) northeast across the water to Maude Reef. Or launch or rent a boat on Vancouver Island at Deep Bay or Fanny Bay and go 3 to 6 nautical miles (5½ to 11 kilometers) to the southern end of Denman Island and north to Ford Cove and Maude Reef.

To get to Ford Cove on Hornby Island by ferry and car
• Sail from Vancouver Island to Denman, then Hornby Island. Go from Denman Island ferry landing at Buckley Bay. It is midway between Campbell River and Nanaimo off Island Highway – 1 to 1¼ hours from each.

Take the ferry from Buckley Bay to Denman: 10 minutes. Drive 7 miles (11 kilometers) across Denman, following signs to the Hornby Island ferry. Cross to Hornby in 10 minutes. From Hornby Island ferry landing, head up the hill to your left. Go 5 miles (8 kilometers) along the main road to the Co-op Store. Turn right and go 3 miles (4¾ kilometers) on Central Road to Ford Cove.
• Returning to Vancouver Island, beware of the ferry schedule – at the time of writing, the last ferry leaves Hornby at 6 p.m., except on Friday when it leaves at 10 p.m.

Comments: An excellent "mixed bag" at Maude Reef.

Kelp greenling with kelp above

HORNBY
ISLAND

Mt Geoffrey
280

Chart / Carte 3527

NOT TO BE USED FOR NAVIGATION: For information
on obtaining navigational charts see page 318.
This is a portion of L/C-3513.

1 Nautical Mile

227

HERON ROCKS
Kayak Dive or Boat Dive. Shore Dive for those who plan ahead and who are lucky enough to book a campsite at Heron Rocks Camping Cooperative.

Skill: All divers

Why go: Heron Rocks is one of the most magnificent of dives. The fish life is fantastic. And masses of invertebrates, too.
Have you ever, on one dive, seen a pair of wolf-eels, lots of little rockfish, schools of young herring, ten large lingcod, numerous yelloweye rockfish, ratfish, tiger rockfish, pink-and-white giant nudibranchs, red dahlia anemones, orange cup corals, staghorn bryozoans, rock scallops, gum boot chitons, blood stars, rose stars and giant red urchins? That's Heron Rocks at Hornby Island. The bottom is interesting too – even if there were no life. In the shallows, wave-sculptured sandstone drops in shallow ledges. Deeper, beautiful sand-covered corridors through the rocks give an almost lacy feeling to the ocean floor. Deeper still, ledges shelter stacks of life.

Bottom and Depths: Smooth rock shallows scattered with small round rocks graduates to sand at Toby Island. At 15 to 25 feet (5 to 8 meters) deep, eelgrass. Then a steep sand slope to the wall and huge boulders. Ledges and overhangs down to the base of the wall at 65 to 75 feet (20 to 23 meters). Some bottom kelp.

Hazards: Exposed to southeast wind; be prepared to dive another day if wind is high.

Telephone: Ford Cove, grocery store.

Facilities: On Hornby: air fills, charters and accommodations for diving groups at Ford Cove. Cabins and camping are limited on Hornby. In summer, arrange in advance. Air fills and charters at Courtenay and Nanaimo, also charters out of Comox and Fanny Bay. Launching at Deep Bay and Fanny Bay; dive-kayak rentals in Courtenay and Nanaimo – all on Vancouver Island.

Access: The Heron Rocks site is near the south end of Lambert Channel off the southeast side of Norman Point at Hornby Island. Wind from the southeast during winter storms and late afternoon winds from the west during warm weather can make anchoring difficult, so look at the weather before you go.
Anchor in 25 to 35 feet (8 to 10 meters) offshore from the first series of rocks you come to that are awash. Smaller boats and dive-kayaks can be anchored in more protected inside waters of Toby Island or pull up on one of the rocks that is exposed.
Toby Island, immediately southeast of Norman Point, is the shallowest point and at low tides is connected to Hornby Island. It dries at 7-foot (2-meter) tides – approach cautiously as there are shoals running from Norman Point to Norris Rocks. Go down and dive east along the submerged rocks and ledges that follow the shape of the shore from Toby Island along the southeast side of Norman Point. They are shown as Heron Rocks on the chart.
• Charter or launch at Ford Cove on Hornby and go 1½ nautical miles (2¾ kilometers) southeast around Norman Point to Heron Rocks. Launch at Denman Island or launch at Deep Bay or Fanny Bay on Vancouver Island and go to Heron Rocks.
• Kayak-divers: from Hornby Island ferry landing, head up the hill to your left. Drive 5⅓ miles (8½ kilometers) along the main road to the Co-op Store. Turn right and go along Central Road for 3 miles (4¾ kilometers) to Ford Cove. Paddle 1½ nautical miles (2¾ kilometers) southeast around Norman Point to Heron Rocks. If it's a low-tide day, you could land on Toby Island to gear up. If high tide, this dive is for kayak-divers with advanced skills. Anchor your dive-kayak and dive from it. Go on a quiet

day before the wind gets up.

Wheelchair divers who paddle dive-kayaks will find access off the government float at Ford Cove.

• Shore access is not possible unless you are a member of the Heron Rocks Camping Co-operative or a registered guest camper who has booked in advance – absolutely no drop-ins. Visiting divers who are not registered should not even enter the campgrounds to request a site, you will be trespassing. The private cooperative *does* offer camping to non-members on a very limited basis, primarily in June and September. Request a booking well in advance – at least by May.

Write to Heron Rocks Camping Co-operative Association, General Delivery, Hornby Island BC V0R 1Z0. Once booked and when you arrive at Hornby, persons at the cooperative will provide you with directions to access the diving area from their premises. Both camping and diving are worth the advance planning required to visit this beautiful sanctuary.

To get to Hornby Island by ferry and car
• Sail from Denman Island ferry landing at Buckley Bay: it is midway between Campbell River and Nanaimo off Island Highway – 1 to 1¼ hours from each.

Take the ferry from Buckley Bay to Denman: 10 minutes. Drive 7 miles (11 kilometers) across Denman, following signs to the Hornby Island ferry. Cross to Hornby in 10 minutes.

• Returning to Vancouver Island, beware of the ferry schedule – at the time of writing, the last ferry leaves Hornby at 6 p.m., except on Friday when it leaves at 10 p.m.

Comments: For years local divers have honored this site as a reserve. Do not take, touch, or disturb any marine life – just look. In 1992, the waters at Heron Rocks became part of Helliwell Provincial Park.

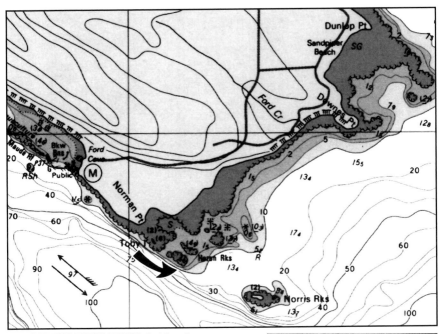

NOT TO BE USED FOR NAVIGATION: For information on obtaining navigational charts see page 318. This is a portion of 3527.

1 Nautical Mile

NORRIS ROCKS
Boat Dive

Skill: Intermediate and expert divers

Why go: Cannonball weights – look for other fishing tackle too. Octopuses, wolf-eels and lingcod are more good reasons to dive at Norris Rocks. On one dive here we saw at least fifty lingcod, the first one in 20 feet (6 meters) of water while we were starting down. Sightseeing is excellent. In addition to the usual pretty white, brown and beige plumose anemones under the overhangs, we saw sea cucumbers, rockfish and kelp greenlings, orange and white sea stars, dahlia anemones, sea pens, orange cup corals, rock scallops and brittle stars.

The dive is most memorable for lingcod, but don't take any. For many years local divers have honored the waters around the southern shore of Hornby as an aquatic reserve. In 1992, the waters around Norris Rocks became part of Helliwell Provincial Park.

Bottom and Depths: Shallow rocky bottom covered with lettuce kelp. Some bull kelp undulates around the rocks down to a depth of 40 to 50 feet (12 to 15 meters). Some big boulders and sand between.

Hazards: Boats, wind, current and transparent fishing line. Listen for boats. Best as a winter dive as boats swarm the reef in summer; but if windy, dive with a boat tender. Dive near slack. Carry a knife. If caught in fishing line you can cut your way free.

Telephone: Ford Cove, grocery store.

Facilities: None at Norris Rocks. Air fills, charters and accommodation for diving groups at Ford Cove on Hornby Island – wheelchair divers welcome. Also private campgrounds at Hornby. Camping at Fillongly Provincial Park at Denman Island with a dig-your-own clam digging beach. Air fills and charters out of Courtenay and Nanaimo on Vancouver Island.

Access: The Norris Rocks site is in the Strait of Georgia ¾ nautical miles (1½ kilometers) southeast of Norman Point at the southern tip of Hornby Island. It is exposed to southeast wind. Charter out of Hornby. Or launch your own boat at Hornby, Denman or Vancouver Island and go to Norris Rocks.

To get to Norris Rocks site
• From Ford Cove at Hornby Island, go 1½ nautical miles (3 kilometers) around the southern tip of Hornby to Norris Rocks.
• From Denman Island, launch at the ramp by the ferry landing at Gravelly Bay on the east side of Denman. Go 2½ nautical miles (4½ kilometers) southeast to Norris Rocks.
• On Vancouver Island, head north on Island Highway: from Nanaimo, 1¼ hours to the Deep Bay turnoff. It is 2½ miles (4 kilometers) north of Bowser; or continue for 5 miles (8 kilometers) more to Fanny Bay where you can launch and go to Norris Rocks.
• On Vancouver Island, heading south, you reach Fanny Bay when 19 miles (30 kilometers) south of Courtenay. Deep Bay turnoff is 5 miles (8 kilometers) south of Fanny Bay. Launch at Fanny Bay or Deep Bay and go to Norris Rocks.

Comments: No spearfishing. No taking of marine life.

Norris Rocks, off snowy shore of Norman Point, Hornby Island

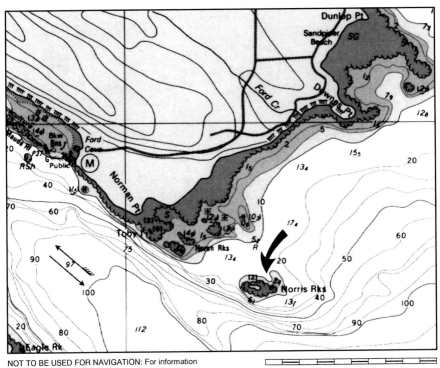

1 Nautical Mile

SIXGILL SHARKS
Boat Dive

Skill: Expert divers. Intermediate divers with guide.

Why go: Dive Flora Islet to see a sixgill shark, to take videos or photos of it, to count its gills or maybe to swim with one of the ghostly giants.
Flora is one of two locations in the world where divers can plan to see sixgills. Not guaranteed – this is wilderness. But some lucky and alert divers see sixgills on their first dive at Flora. My "guesstimate" is that 30% of searching-for-sixgill-shark dives here are successful. I saw one my fourth try. It swam slowly – cruising. It curved seductively along the base of the wall, close to the sandy bottom of a narrow ledge, slipped along sinuously, then suddenly was gone, back to the void it had come from.
The sixgills are pale gray. They normally range in length from 8 to 12 feet (2½ to 3½ meters); one as long as 18 feet (5½ meters) has been reported. They usually move slowly and dreamily but can turn in a flash. In summer, they come up from great depths, perhaps from 800 feet (250 meters) usually to sand-covered shelves at 90 feet (27 meters). They have been seen in water as shallow as 40 feet (12 meters). Little else is known about them. Reports by divers are scattered and casual, yet dozens of divers have photographed sixgills, many photos include diver and sixgill in the same shot. "Mug shots" of the sixgills could become a valuable record, as each shark has distinguishing scars and marks.
Divers first sighted sixgills at Flora in 1977 or 1978. Flora is still the only location in the Strait of Georgia where sixgills are seen often. Another place with frequent sightings is Tyler Rock on the west coast of Vancouver Island. Sporadic sightings have been made in other locations, from Three Tree Point in southern Puget Sound to the Hood Canal and Saanich Inlet.

Bottom and Depths: Broadleaf kelp covers the rocky bottom at 30 to 40 feet (9 to 12 meters) where you go off the boat; then the bottom rolls away in a series of rocky ledges. A rock wall sheers off from 80 to 90 feet (24 to 27 meters) to a narrow sandy ledge at 120 to 130 feet (37 to 40 meters). From there, the bottom drops to nowhere. At the end of the dive is an easy safety stop in 15 feet (4 meters) beside Flora with lots to see – orange cup corals behind the bottom kelp at 10 feet (3 meters).

Hazards: Depth, current, boats; the sharks themselves, and *your desire to stay with them*. If you see sharks at the end of your dive, be careful of narcosis. It is tempting to stay too long – even to follow the sharks down when they head deep. Plan for a safety stop. Dive on slack. Ascending, listen for boats and go up the anchor line. Or follow the contour of the bottom all the way to Flora and then swim to your boat. The sharks may swim close; the temptation to touch them is great. No reports of attacks, but you could be hit by a tail, and the sixgills are meat eaters. They have very large mouths with exceedingly sharp teeth. In spite of their sluggish appearance they can react with startling speed when annoyed. It is safer not to touch.

Telephone: Ford Cove, grocery store.

Facilities: Air fills, charters and accommodations for diving groups at Ford Cove on Hornby. Cabins and camping on Hornby are limited. In summer, arrange in advance. Air fills and charters also in Courtenay on Vancouver Island.

Access: Flora Islet is off the southeastern tip of Hornby Island, near the north end of the Strait of Georgia. The site is exposed to southeast wind. Pick a calm, sunny day. For calmer water, dive early in the morning. Sixgills have been seen only from mid-

April through late October – it is a summer dive. Most likely to see them in July and August.

Charter or launch at Ford Cove on Hornby Island. Charter out of Nanaimo, Comox or Fanny Bay or launch at Deep Bay on Vancouver Island to go to Flora. The distance ranges from 11 to 14 nautical miles (20 to 26 kilometers). Anchor in 30 to 40 feet (9 to 12 meters) off the southwestern shore of Flora. Swim a short way straight out and go down over a series of ledges. Divers and sixgills usually meet at a depth of 80 to 90 feet (24 to 27 meters).

One method visitors use to find sixgills is to hit the bottom with a rock or hit their tank to make noise. Sound and light both seem to attract the sharks. Other divers stay shallow and scan the dark void with a powerful light for the flash of a long white tail, then quietly drop to the sixgills. Once you sight sharks, passive behavior – just watching them will usually keep the sharks with you longer.

Comments: This is a sensitive habitat. For years local divers have honored it as a reserve. Do not take, touch, or disturb any marine life – just look. In 1992, the waters around Flora Islet became part of Helliwell Provincial Park.

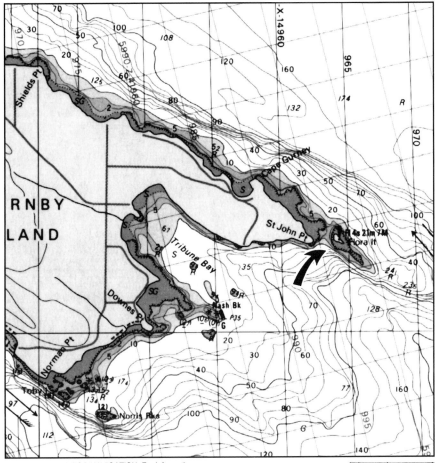

NOT TO BE USED FOR NAVIGATION: For information on obtaining navigational charts see page 318. This is a portion of L/C-3513.

1 Nautical Mile

Snorkeling with salmon

Gearing up

Most Outrageous at slack tide, Seymour Narrows

Friendly seal at Gowlland Harbour

Pink jungle of soft corals, strawberry and brooding anemones at Richmond Reef

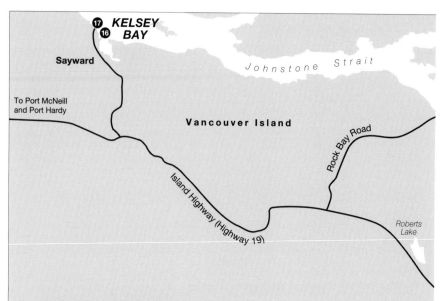

CAMPBELL RIVER TO KELSEY BAY

Dives

1 Mitlenatch Island
2 Big Rock
3 Snorkeling with Salmon
4 Argonaut Wharf
5 Whiskey Point End-of-the-Road
6 Richmond Reef
7 Wa-Wa-Kie Beach
8 Rebecca Spit
9 Viner Point
10 Moulds Bay
11 Steep Island
12 Copper Cliffs
13 Seymour Narrows
14 Chatham Point
15 Rock Bay
16 Ship Breakwater
17 Ferch Point

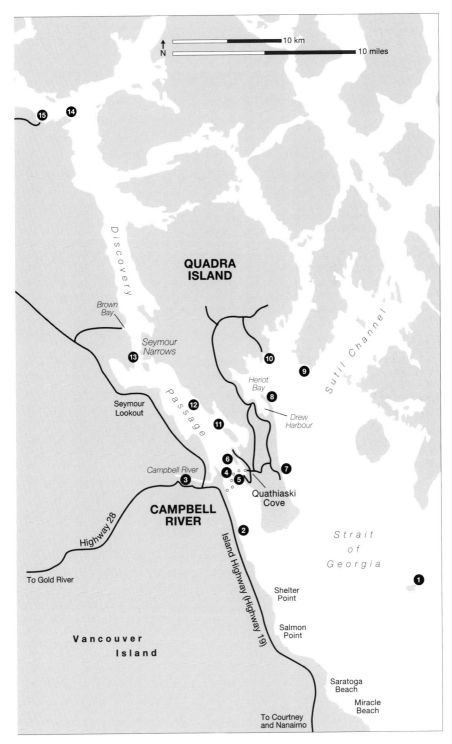

SERVICE INFORMATION *
Campbell River to Kelsey Bay

Charts: Canadian Hydrographic Service
- 3312 Jervis Inlet and Desolation Sound (sailing directions in booklet form)
- L/C-3513 Strait of Georgia, Northern Portion
- 3538 Desolation Sound and Sutil Channel
- 3539 Discovery Passage
- 3540 Approaches to Campbell River
- 3543 Cordero Channel
- 3544 Johnstone Strait, Race Passage and Current Passage

Tide and Current Tables: Canadian Hydrographic Service
Tide and Current Table, Volume 6.

Diving Emergency Telephone Numbers
Dial 911: Say "I have a scuba diving emergency".

Vancouver General Hospital: Dial (604) 875-4111 and say "I have a scuba diving emergency. I want the hyperbaric physician on call".

If medical personnel are unfamiliar with scuba diving emergencies, ask them to telephone DAN (Divers Alert Network): (919) 684-8111, then say "I have a scuba diving emergency".

Other Useful Numbers
Continuous Marine Broadcast (CMB) recorded, 24 hours; listen for weather in the Strait of Georgia or Johnstone Strait, telephone
- Comox: (604) 339-0748

Shellfish Infoline, recorded: (604) 666-3169
Sportfishing Information Line, recorded: 1-800-663-9333

• Dive Shops
Campbell River

Beaver Aquatics
760 North Island Highway
Campbell River BC V9W 2C3
(604) 287-7652; fax (604) 287-8652

Seafun Divers
1761 North Island Highway
Campbell River BC V9W 2E8
(604) 287-3622; fax (604) 286-6267

South of Campbell River

T.D. Sports
2885 Cliffe Avenue, Ocean View Plaza
Courtenay BC V9N 2L8
(604) 338-1633. After hours, summer only: (604) 338-1307.
(Also dive guiding for shore dives.)

Diver's Den
216 Fifth Street
Courtenay BC V9N 1J6
(604) 338-2111

• Charters out of Campbell River

Bonnie Belle
Bonnie Belle Charters
PO Box 331
Campbell River BC V9W 5B6
(604) 287-7775 or 285-3578
(Charters out of Campbell River.)

Christina I
See More Charters
1858 O'Leary Road
Campbell River BC V9W 5Y8
(604) 287-7855
(Charters out of Campbell River. Wheelchair divers welcome.)

Misty Ridge
Misty Ridge Charters
PO Box 326
Campbell River BC V9W 5B1
(604) 286-3697; fax (604) 286-1361
(Charters out of Campbell River.)

Discovery Launch Water Taxi
PO Box 164
Campbell River BC V9W 5A7
(604) 287-7577; fax (604) 923-7700
(Water taxi out of Campbell River.)

Accessible R & R Charters
216 South McCarthy Street
Campbell River BC V9W 2R2
(604) 287-7566; cellular (604) 287-6649; fax (604) 286-1254
(Wheelchair accessible charters out of Campbell River.)

Shoal Searcher and *Champagne Lady*
Pacific Northwest Diving Adventures
122 West Kings Road
North Vancouver, BC V7N 2L8
(604) 983-9454 – fax and telephone.
(Day, weekend, week-long and longer liveaboard charters out of Vancouver. Also a land-based option at Cortes Island. Will pick up in Campbell River. Wheelchair divers welcome.)

Sportfish Centre
975 Shopper's Row, Tyee Plaza
Campbell River BC V9W 2C5
(604) 287-4911; fax (604) 287-7372
(Charters and boat rentals out of Campbell River. Wheelchair divers welcome.)

• Charters out of Quadra Island

Outrageous and *The Most Outrageous*
Abyssal Diving Charters
PO Box 421
Quathiaski Cove BC V0P 1N0
(604) 285-3724
(Charters and dive package that includes charters, hot tub, accommodation and meals. Air fills with charters only.)

• Boat Rentals at Campbell River
River Mouth Boat Rentals
2-1416 Perkins Road
Campbell River BC V9W 4R9
(604) 287-3010
(Boat rentals, May to September, at Campbell River mouth.)

Rub a Dub Dub Boat Rentals
1003 Discovery Crescent
PO Box 212
Campbell River BC V9W 6Y4
(604) 287-4999; fax (604) 287-8767
(Boat rentals year-round at Discovery Marina, downtown Campbell River. Restrooms with hot showers at marina; telephone outside marina office.)

Sportfish Centre
975 Shopper's Row, Tyee Plaza
Campbell River BC V9W 2C5
(604) 287-4911; fax (604) 287-7372
(Boat rentals year-round at Discovery Marina, downtown Campbell River; also charters. Wheelchair divers welcome. Restrooms with hot showers at marina.)

• Boat Rentals and Launching, north of Campbell River
Brown's Bay Marina
15021 Ripple Rock Road, PO Box 743
Campbell River BC V9W 2E3
Launching: (604)286-3135
Boat Rentals: (604)286-0012
(Launching at Brown Bay north of Seymour Narrows: concrete ramp, good at all tides; an RV park is next to the marina. Boat rentals May through October. Restrooms, hot showers and telephones on fuel dock.)
Turn off Island Highway onto Brown's Bay Road when 11 miles (18 kilometers) north of Campbell River – it takes

20 minutes. Or when 15 minutes – 7 miles (12 kilometers) south of Roberts Lake Resort. Follow signs to the marina; go 2 miles (5 kilometers) along this unpaved road. From the highway, 10 minutes to Brown Bay.

Fish and Game Club Ramp
Foot of road, past government wharf
Kelsey Bay BC
Telephone (604) 282-3216, 282-3602, 282-3204 to obtain use of key to ramp for a fee. Mailing address: c/o Stan Clark, 211 Ambleside Drive, Sayward BC V0P 1R0.
(Launching only: concrete ramp, good at all except extreme low tides. No toilet; telephone at dock.)
  Turn off Island Highway (Highway 19) onto Sayward Road when 39 miles (63 kilometers) north of Campbell River – it takes 50 minutes. Or 1½ hours – 80 miles (128 kilometers) south of Port McNeill. Go on Sayward Road to the end of it – 7 miles (12 kilometers). Another launching ramp in Kelsey Bay is described (see Ship Breakwater on page 274).

• **Charters, Boat Rentals and Launching south of Campbell River**

Shelter Bay Resort
3880 South Island Highway
Campbell River BC V9W 2J2
(604) 923-5338
(Launching year-round; boat rentals in summer: this concrete ramp, good at all tides. Restrooms; telephone outside office.)

Salmon Point Resort
2176 Salmon Point Road
Campbell River BC V9W 3S4
(604) 923-6605
(Launching year-round: concrete ramp, good at 4-foot (1-meter) tides and greater. Restrooms; telephone outside office.)

Pacific Playgrounds
9082 Clarkson Road
Saratoga Beach
Campbell River BC V9W 3S4
(604) 337-5600
(Launching year-round: concrete ramp, good at all tides. Boat rentals mid-April to mid-October. Restrooms; telephone outside office.)

My Joan
Sail Pacific Yacht Charters
PO Box 1555
Comox BC V9N 8A2
(604) 339-7850 or 336-2150
(Liveaboard sail/dive charters out of Comox marina to Mitlenatch, Denman, Hornby, Vivian and Texada islands and to Powell River. Also day charters to Hornby.)

Sunseeker
Diver's Den
216 Fifth Street
Courtenay BC V9N 1J6
(604) 338-2111
(Charters out of Fanny Bay to Denman and Hornby islands and to Powell River. Also inflatable charters.)

• **More Dive Facilities:**
Campbell River Snorkel Tours
760-B Island Highway
Campbell River BC V9W 2C3
(604) 286-0030; fax (604) 287-8652
(From mid-June through mid-October, snorkel tours on Campbell River.)

• Launching at Campbell River
Tyee Spit Public Ramp
Campbell River BC
(Launching: concrete ramp, good at all tides but difficult to load and launch when the wind blows. Suitable for wheelchair divers to dive Argonaut Wharf from. No toilets; telephone across road.)

From Tyee Plaza heading north out of town, go on Island Highway for 1 mile (1½ kilometers) to Spit Road; from junction of highways 19 and 28, go on Island Highway toward downtown Campbell River for just over ½ mile (1 kilometer) to Spit Road.

At Spit Road: drive out the spit for 1 mile (1¾ kilometers). You will reach the ramp shortly past Western Mines or Argonaut Wharf.

Lucky Louie Boat Rentals
907 South Island Highway
Campbell River BC
(604) 923-1242
(Launching: concrete ramp, good at all tides. Suitable for wheelchair divers to dive Big Rock from in winter when no boat rentals but may be debris on the ramp. Boat rentals from March to October. No toilets; telephone across highway at Big Rock Store.)

Fresh Water Marina
2705 North Island Highway
Campbell River BC V9W 2H4
(604) 286-0701; fax (604) 286-1343
(Launching year-round: concrete ramp, good at 4-foot [1-meter] tides and greater. A protected launch when the wind blows. Restrooms. Telephone top of ramp at office and on fuel dock.)

• Launching at Quadra Island, West Side
April Point Lodge and Marina
Foot of April Point Road, Quadra Island
PO Box 1,
Campbell River BC V9W 4Z9
(604) 285-2222
(Launching only: steep concrete and gravel ramp, good at all tides. Restrooms; telephone outside marina office.)

Quathiaski Cove Public Ramp
Immediately north of ferry dock
Quathiaski Cove, Quadra Island
(Launching only: concrete ramp, good at all tides. Restrooms and telephone nearby at ferry landing.)

• Launching at Quadra Island, East Side
Heriot Bay Public Ramp
Across bay from ferry dock
Heriot Bay,
Quadra Island BC
(Launching only: concrete, good at all tides. Restrooms, hot showers and telephone at nearby Heriot Bay Inn.)

From Quathiaski Cove on Quadra, drive up the hill. At the shopping center, turn left and follow signs toward the Cortes Island ferry. When you reach Heriot Bay and see the shopping center on your right, turn left off West Road just before the shopping center. Follow the sign toward Granite Bay and go down Cramer Road, then Antler Road. Ramp is off the wharf at the foot of Antler Road.

Rebecca Spit Marine Park Ramp
Rebecca Spit Provincial Park
Quadra Island BC
(Launching at Rebecca Spit side of Drew Harbour. Concrete ramp, good at all tides. Pit toilets in the park. A public telephone, in summer, at campsite immediately outside park.)

From Quathiaski Cove on Quadra, drive up the hill. At the shopping center, turn left and follow signs to Cortes Island Ferry. When you reach Heriot Bay and see the shopping center on your right, do not continue straight to Heriot Bay ferry landing. Turn right and follow signs curving around Drew Harbour to Rebecca Spit Park. At the park, part way out on the spit you will see the launching ramp on your left-hand side for launching in Drew Harbour.

• **More Services for Campbell River Region:** see Service Information for Gulf Islands on page 139 and 140.

• **Ferry Information**
British Columbia Ferry Corporation
Campbell River Terminal
Discovery Crescent
Campbell River BC
Toll-free in BC: 1-800-663-7600. Or (604) 286-1412
Telephoning from outside British Columbia: (604) 386-3431
(Ferries from Campbell River to Quadra Island.)

British Columbia Ferry Corporation
Little River Terminal
Comox BC
Toll-free in BC: 1-800-663-7600. Or (604) 339-3310.
Telephoning from outside British Columbia: (604) 386-3431
(Ferries from Comox on Vancouver Island to Powell River.)

British Columbia Ferry Corporation
Quadra Island Terminal
Quathiaski Cove BC
Toll-free in BC: 1-800-663-7600. Or (604) 285-3233.
Telephoning from outside British Columbia: (604) 386-3431
(Ferries from Quadra Island to Campbell River.)

• **Tourist Information**
Discover British Columbia
1117 Wharf Street
Victoria BC V8W 2Z2
1-800-663-6000: Toll-free throughout Canada and the USA, including Hawaii and parts of Alaska.

Campbell River Tourism
Tyee Plaza, PO Box 482
Campbell River BC V9W 5C1
(604) 286-1616; fax (604) 286-6490
1-800-463-4386: Toll-free throughout North America.

Comox Valley Travel Infocentre
2040 Cliffe Avenue
Courtenay BC V9N 2L3
(604) 334-3234; fax (604) 334-4908

Campbell River Travel Infocentre
Tyee Plaza, PO Box 400
Campbell River BC V9W 5B6
(604) 287-4636; fax (604) 286-6490

How to go – Campbell River is located on the east side of Vancouver Island at the top of the Strait of Georgia. It is beside Discovery Passage.
• From Nanaimo drive north on Island Highway (Highway 19) through Qualicum Beach, Parksville, Fanny Bay, Buckley Bay and Courtenay to Campbell River. It takes 2½ hours.
• From Port Hardy, Port McNeill or Telegraph Cove, head south on Island Highway (Highway 19) to Campbell River. From Port Hardy, it takes 3½ hours. From Port McNeill, almost 3 hours. From Telegraph Cove, more than 3 hours to Campbell River.
• From Powell River, you go by British Columbia ferry to Comox, then drive to Courtenay and continue north on Island Highway 19. The ferry ride takes 1¼ hours; then drive 10 minutes to Courtenay and 45 minutes more to Campbell River.

*All of this service information is subject to change.

MITLENATCH ISLAND
Boat Dive

Tide Table: Point Atkinson
Add 10 minutes

Skill: All divers and snorkelers

Why go: Mitlenatch Island is a showcase for abalones, the best place to see them in the Strait of Georgia.

Abalones have been protected at Mitlenatch since at least 1976. At that time it was illegal to take any within 1,000 feet (300 meters) of the island. Since 1980, abalones have been protected for 1 mile (1½ kilometers) out to sea from Mitlenatch. Consequently, their future is guaranteed. Look on the rocks for a black fuzzy mantle surrounding a mottled shell. A ring of small holes rims one side of the shell. Abalones emit puffs of blue "smoke" from these holes when frightened. They're fascinating animals as they glide over beautiful kelp-covered shallows around Mitlenatch Island.

Big seaperch glisten blue and yellow around the spring-green bottom kelp. We saw schools of black and silver fish. Large red-and-maroon striped painted greenlings guard their territories. Rockfish crowd the crevices. Small orange cup corals, dahlia anemones and huge rock scallops dot the rocks. Big orange sea peaches are bulbous beneath narrow ledges. Furry white anemones fuzz the space under other overhangs. Orange encrusting sponge spreads across the rocks. Abalones glide over any rocks that are left.

A couple of dogfish were cruising around the base of this island where abalone is king.

Bottom and Depths: Rocky reef extends northwest for ½ mile (1 kilometer). The 25- to 35-foot (8- to 10-meter) deep reef covers a large area.

Hazards: Current and boats. Dive on the slack. Listen for boats, use your compass and ascend close to the bottom all the way to shore.

Telephones: • Miracle Beach Resort, Vancouver Island. • Miracle Beach Provincial Park on Vancouver Island, at entrance.

Facilities: Picnic tables and pit toilets. No overnight camping at Mitlenatch. Camping, hot showers, trailer hookups, boat rentals and launching at Shelter Bay, Saratoga Beach and Miracle Beach on Vancouver Island. Air fills in Campbell River and Courtenay. Charters out of Campbell River, Comox and Fanny Bay.

Access: Mitlenatch Island stands alone in the middle of the Strait of Georgia. It is 11 nautical miles (20 kilometers) east of Miracle Beach Provincial Park on Vancouver Island; and 14 nautical miles (26 kilometers) west of Lund on the other side of the strait. Mitlenatch can be reached from Campbell River, Miracle Beach or even from the other side of the Strait of Georgia. But pick a calm day. Wind, current and fog are all potential hazards which might make crossing to Mitlenatch difficult.

Charter out of Campbell River, Comox or Fanny Bay, rent a boat or launch at one of the resorts at Shelter Bay, Salmon Point or Saratoga Beach. Hand-launch an inflatable over the sand at Miracle Beach Resort and go east to the island. Or charter or launch at Lund and go west to Mitlenatch. Anchor in Northwest Bay or Camp Bay. Excellent shallow diving below the "hide" on the north side of the island and all along the reef going north.

Comments: This is a nature park: all waters within 1 mile (1½ kilometers) of Mitlenatch are considered a sensitive habitat and divers honor it as a reserve for all creatures that live there. Do not take, touch or disturb any marine life.

Thousands of sea birds breed at Mitlenatch: glaucous-winged gulls are most numerous, pelagic cormorants are on the high southern bluffs, and pigeon guillemots fly under water. During summer, volunteer wardens are at Mitlenatch. A self-guiding pamphlet is available to direct visitors around the trail system and to the "hide", or bird blind. It is available from BC Parks, Miracle/Strathcona Zones, 1812 Miracle Beach Drive, Black Creek BC V0R 1C0, (604) 337-5121; fax (604) 337-5695.

The "hide"

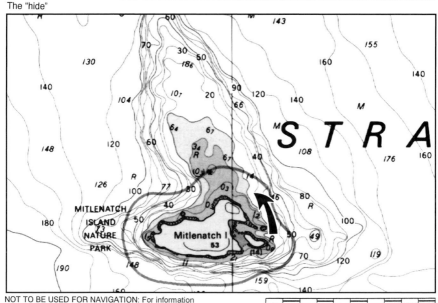

NOT TO BE USED FOR NAVIGATION: For information on obtaining navigational charts see page 318. This is a portion of 3538.

1 Nautical Mile

BIG ROCK
Shore Dive

Skill: Intermediate and expert divers

Why go: A good mix of fish live on the reef in front of Big Rock and because of the back eddies Big Rock is quite a safe place to dive.

Since the bottom is varied the fish are varied, too, but visibility is usually poor. We could see only 5 to 8 feet (1½ to 2½ meters). The water was murky with silt stirred up by the current and back eddies. Through the silt we saw a great variety of fish. Red Irish lords, small lingcod, flounders and rockfish. An octopus, too. Urchins, giant barnacles and pale orange sponges, nourished by the current, cling tight to the rocks. And lots of purply-red geoduck (pronounced gooey-duck) clams poke up through the silt, with a strand of bull kelp attached to each one. I watched, fascinated, as we drifted slowly downcurrent touching first one then another siphon. As we touched them each geoduck retracted into the sand, pulling the kelp down with it.

Bottom and Depths: The reef at Big Rock parallels the shore and is about 20 to 30 feet (6 to 9 meters) deep. Gently sloping sandy bottom scattered with rocks and some boulders forming the reef. Bull kelp attached to the rocks and geoducks.

Hazards: Current, boats and bull kelp in summer. Current is not as vicious at Big Rock as at many other Campbell River sites because of that back eddy. However, plan to dive on or near the slack. Salmon-fishing boats are an important consideration at Big Rock as at most Campbell River sites. Fly a floating dive-flag – important at all sites but especially important at this one, and do not count on the dive flag to protect you. Winter is safer from the standpoint of fewer boats, but all things considered the dive is safer in summer when lots of kelp to hang onto. Listen for boats; use a compass and navigate back to shore under water. Carry a knife for kelp.

Telephones: • Big Rock Store, 906 South Island Highway. • Rotary Beach Park, north of Big Rock. • Big Rock Motel, 1020 South Island Highway.

Facilities: Small green park immediately south of Big Rock with parking space for three or four cars. Large green grassy site with picnic tables, toilets and a great deal of parking at Rotary Park Beach. Boat rentals, launching, and accommodations all along the route. Air fills in Campbell River and Courtenay.

Access: Big Rock is at the southern entry to Discovery Passage in the town of Campbell River beside South Island Highway. Two roadside parks are good entry points. It is best to dive Big Rock in winter from October through March – no kelp to tangle your dive-flag float in, good visibility and fewer boats. Best to dive on the ebb tide because then you can count on the current direction; at flood tide, often a back eddy sets up and the direction of flow is also northward – but you do not know when it will happen.

One entry is in the 900 block south on Island Highway, room for one or two cars at a small green park 330 yards (100 meters) *south* of Big Rock. The second entry point is Rotary Beach Park. It is ½ mile (1 kilometer) *north* of Big Rock. The most interesting part of the reef is in the kelp opposite Big Rock Motel. To dive here, enter the water at the small park south of Big Rock at the end of an incoming tide. Swim out, drift north to the kelp bed and go down. After your dive drift back. Or drift from park to park – you could do this no matter which way the current is flowing. If you have two cars, set up a car shuttle. Or walk it. Total distance between parks is just over ½ mile (1 kilometer).

Wheelchair access is possible in winter at a launching ramp north of Big Rock at a perfect place to enter. The ramp is immediately opposite Big Rock Store. The ramp is not open in winter but the owner, at the time of writing, says it is quite acceptable for wheelchair divers to enter at the ramp when it is closed.

To get to Big Rock
• From Tyee Plaza in Campbell River, go 3 miles (5 kilometers) south on Island Highway to Big Rock.
• From Courtenay head north on Island Highway through Oyster Bay and Willow Point. When 15 minutes past the turnoff to Miracle Beach and 1 mile (1½ kilometers) past Willow Point you will see Big Rock.

Comments: A good quick dive!

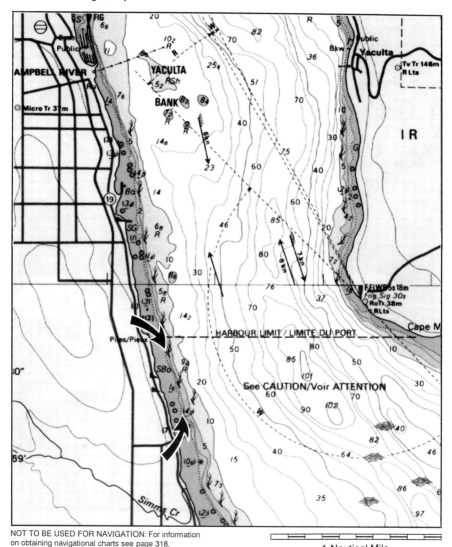

NOT TO BE USED FOR NAVIGATION: For information on obtaining navigational charts see page 318. This is a portion of 3312.

1 Nautical Mile

SNORKELING WITH SALMON
Shore Dive

Tide Table: None; this is in the non-tidal part of the river

Skill: All snorkelers

Why go: To meet salmon nose-to-nose – pinks, chinooks, cohos and maybe sockeyes and chums.

We guessed we saw thousands of pinks. They were mostly 24 inches (60 centimeters) long, slim and silvery gray. My buddy saw two chinooks – they are big. Chinooks sometimes weigh in at 40, 50 and 60 pounds (18, 23 and 27 kilograms) and larger. The chinooks were just starting upstream for the season when we floated the Campbell. They were in the river but waiting for rain to swell the river to make it easier to swim upstream. You see more salmon after rain. Sockeyes are the most colorful, turning brilliant red and green when heading upriver. However, only 200 sockeyes are left to spawn in the Campbell each year. Swimming with salmon in the wilds is a rare treat – only three other times I have seen them. Yet in Campbell River, in season, it is a sure thing.

Prime season to go is from early August through mid-October. First you see the silvery pinks – we were there at the height of their run at the end of August. In late August and early September, expect the giant chinooks – my buddy saw two of them, and maybe you'll see some chums. In October, red and green sockeyes are in the Campbell but the run is small. Throughout the year you might see steelhead – they are not salmon but are sea-run rainbow trout. You can contact Quinsam River Hatchery Salmonid Enhancement Program, PO Box 467, Campbell River BC V9W 5C1 at (604) 287-9564 or fax (604) 286-0261 to check if fish are in the river.

Bottom and Depths: Rocky bottom. Depth ranges from dry rocks to 10 feet (3 meters), averages 3 to 4 feet (1 to 1¼ meters) deep. Most of the time you could stop and stand up if you want to in the quiet shallow parts. But it is easier floating downstream if you look for the deepest channel. Canoeists and kayakers have an advantage: my whitewater kayaking experience was useful to help me "read" this river.

With greater riverflow, expert snorkel river-runners sometimes start at the power plant, ¾ mile (1 kilometer) upstream – I have kayaked from there but do not advise snorkeling it. The upper section has more rapids, while the section described here that begins at the logging bridge, is usually deeper and more suitable for snorkeling.

Hazards: Current, fallen trees, branches and rubbish. The Campbell feels like a gentle roller-coaster ride but could be dangerous. Even in slight current there is potential danger of becoming caught when swimming a river. When you reach rocky shallow parts, which you can spot because of the white water, roll over on your back and float downstream feet first with your feet held high so they will not become caught between rocks. Harder bumping along on your "bum" than going head first, but safer.

Fallen trees or "sweepers" are also potential hazards on rivers. The banks of the Campbell are relatively clean as the river is dam-controlled and there is steady riverflow throughout the year, except for occasional big releases which clean it out. Nevertheless, watch the riverbanks and avoid any tree branches or "sweepers" that hang into the river. And when you reach the highway bridge, watch out for steel bars – remnants of the old highway bridge that stick up midstream beneath the existing bridge. If you keep to the main channel along the right-hand side, you will probably avoid them. The river is tidal from the highway bridge on, and the current slows down.

Telephone: • Near logging bridge: at Elk Falls Provincial Park, Quinsam Campground entry; from logging bridge, go ⅓ mile (½ kilometer) north on Highway 28 and turn left into campground. • Near highway bridge: at gas station on southeast corner of Island Highway and Willow Street; from the river, go south and cross Island Highway to gas station. • Near exit from river: at gas station on southwest corner of Island Highway and Maple Street.

Facilities: Snorkel guides with rental wet suits, snorkels and masks in Campbell River; also rental equipment at dive shops. Hot showers at Discovery Marina.

Access: Spawning salmon are in Campbell River from early August through October. The river flows through the town of Campbell River. Access to the take-out is from Highway 19 (Island Highway) and to the put-in from Highway 28 (Gold River Highway). Allow 40 to 50 minutes to snorkel the river.

Float with a buddy. Look for salmon in pools beneath the logging bridge at the start of the run and at the highway bridge near the end of it. In swift parts, watch for salmon in eddies behind rocks as you fly over them. In quiet parts, stop, stand up and look ahead for deep pools, dark sections of river with little or no white water. Look for pools at the outside of each bend; groups of salmon rest in them. Past the highway bridge, move to river-right and drift toward your take-out at Maple Street.

To get to the take-out and put-in

Distance between put-in and take-out is 1 mile (2 kilometers): use two cars or walk it. If walking, easier to do before you float – takes 15 to 25 minutes. If driving, first go to the take-out and leave one car; then go to the put-in.

• To the take-out: from Tyee Plaza in downtown Campbell River, head north on Highway 19. Go 1 mile (1½ kilometers) to Maple Street – it is just past Spit Road. The Quinsam Hotel is on the corner. Turn right. At the end of Maple, climb down the riprap to the water; look around or leave a marker so you know where to come off the river. Space for one or two cars to park.

• To the put-in: from Maple Street, turn right onto Highway 19. Go ½ mile (¾ kilometer) to Highway 28 junction. Do not turn right on Highway 19 – continue straight: go west ¾ mile (1¼ kilometers) on Highway 28 to the logging bridge. The bridge is on the right-hand side. Park at the roadside and walk down an easy path to the river. Gear up with wet or dry suit, mask, snorkel and fins, but leave your tank and weight belt behind.

Comments: Swimming with salmon: a new twist to the salmon mystique of Campbell River.

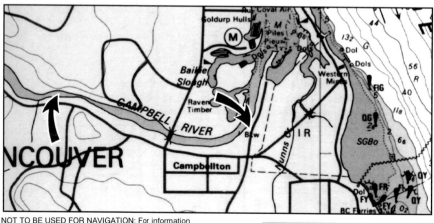

NOT TO BE USED FOR NAVIGATION: For information on obtaining navigational charts see page 318. This is a portion of 3312.

1 Nautical Mile

ARGONAUT WHARF
Shore Dive

Skill: All divers

Why go: Night diving under the wharf at Western Mines – or Argonaut Wharf as it is still called by most – is a favorite of local divers.

When seeing the spot I realized why night diving here is so popular. At night, the resident octopuses come out. I saw four on one night dive. Also fishing lures are more easily seen in the flash of your light at night. These can be profitable salvage. It would be unsafe to dive here by day because of so many small salmon-fishing boats going past, and so many people fishing from the wharf. Day or night, there's lots of marine life. Decorator crabs, red and pink dahlia anemones and white plumose anemones on the pilings. Flounders all over the bottom. Some red Irish lords and a cabezon. And in summer you might see masses of gray cod on the sand beyond the pilings.

Enormous skates used to live here. I've heard of 125-pound (57-kilogram) giant skates with a 7-foot (2-meter) wingspan off Tyee Spit, but haven't seen any. They must have been hunted out. Today all that's left of them is the legend.

Bottom and Depths: The 20- to 30-foot (6- to 9-meter) sandy bottom gradually deepens as you move into the channel. Rocks around the pilings where octopuses hide.

Hazards: Large ships docked for loading, small boats, current, fishermen and broken fishing line. Do not dive when large ships are docked for loading. In summer, stay under the wharf. In winter, use a compass or stay close to the pilings. Listen for boats and ascend up a piling, well out of the way of boats. Dive near slack. Carry a knife.

Telephone: Thunderbird Resort, across road from dive entry point.

Facilities: Sandy beach and a launching ramp with picnic table and a great deal of parking space at Tyee Spit. In summer, you could try for a hot shower at the campground across the road from the dive site entry. Air fills in Campbell River and Courtenay.

Access: Argonaut Wharf is located in Discovery Passage. It is at Tyee Spit in the town of Campbell River off Island Highway (Highway 19). Go out Spit Road for 1 mile (1½ kilometers) onto the sandy spit. Just past the large buildings and wharf on your right is a beach with a very easy entry over the sand. Swim to the wharf and go down.

Wheelchair access at the launching ramp for divers who can kayak – or swim, 220 yards (200 meters) from the ramp back to the entry. Then swim to the wharf.

To get to Spit Road
• Head north on Island Highway through Campbell River: go 1 mile (1½ kilometers) past the ferry and Tyee Plaza. Turn right into Spit Road.
• Head south into Campbell River on Island Highway or Highway 28: drive for ½ mile (1 kilometer) past the traffic light at the junction of Highways 28 and 19. Turn left into Spit Road.

Comments: Argonaut Wharf is a good place to see an octopus – but just look. Or gently stroke. Love 'em and leave 'em so they don't disappear like the giant skates. Octopuses can be killed by rough handling. Local divers honor it as a reserve.

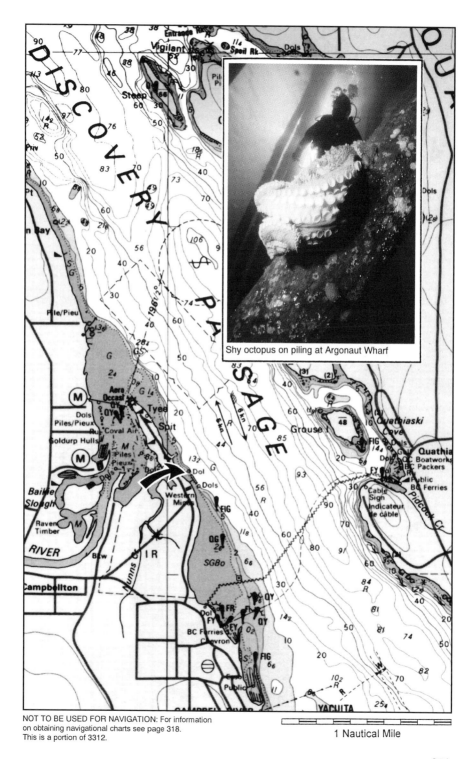

Shy octopus on piling at Argonaut Wharf

NOT TO BE USED FOR NAVIGATION: For information
on obtaining navigational charts see page 318.
This is a portion of 3312.

1 Nautical Mile

251

WHISKEY POINT END-OF-THE-ROAD

Shore Dive

Skill: Expert divers. Intermediate divers with guide.

Why go: The most accessible burst of color and life described in this guidebook is splashed across the bottom at Whiskey Point.

As though created by a painter gone deliriously wild, tiers of rock covered with color cascade in gradual folds from the shores of Quadra Island down into Discovery Passage. Swimming under water close to the side, each rock I put my hand on is yet another color – red, yellow or purple. Strawberry anemones so close together that you can write your name in them. I touched some and they closed. Changed from fuzzy multi-tentacled flowers to small bright red berries in a basket. Purple algae are splashed on the rocks. Bright blue starfish. And sunny yellow encrusting sponge over all the rest.

Masses of life covers the clean-swept rocky bottom. Strange sponges that look like tennis balls. Others like orange bath-sponges. Purple-spotted Puget Sound king crabs. Snakelock anemones. Barnacles the size of baseballs, some abalones and some rock scallops. Fish hide under every ledge. Lingcod, red Irish lords and kelp greenlings so tame they'll eat from your hand.

Bottom and Depths: Clean-swept rocks tier down from 30 to 60 to 90 feet (15 to 18 to 27 meters). A lot of bull kelp.

Hazards: Currents, upcurrents, downcurrents, whirlpools, small boats, the British Columbia ferry and bull kelp. Dive on slack. And, though you can reach this dive by road, the spot is so dangerous that on most days you should have a "live" boat ready in case you are swept away. Strong swimmers can dive here without a pickup boat on slight tidal exchanges. One rule of thumb suggested as safe by a local diver is a change in tide height of 2 feet (⅔ meter) or less: refer to Campbell River tide table for this. Refer to Seymour Narrows current table for slack. Be geared up and ready one hour before slack tide, watching and waiting for the current to slow down.

Best at Whiskey Point on the turn from a flood to an ebbing tide when no back eddies occur, and there is less of a rip. Ascend along the bottom all the way to shore, well out of the way of the many salmon-fishing boats and the British Columbia ferry. Carry a knife for kelp.

Telephones: • Quathiaski Cove ferry landing. • Quathiaski Cove shopping center, up hill from ferry.

Facilities: Room for two or three cars to park at the site. Charters, launching and dive package on west side of Quadra. Hot showers year-round at Whiskey Point Lodge – you'll see it on the right-hand side as you leave the ferry and drive uphill at Quathiaski Cove. Air fills in Campbell River.

Access: Whiskey Point End-of-the-Road dive is on Discovery Passage at Quadra Island. From Campbell River it is a 10-minute ferry ride and 5-minute drive to it.

Take the ferry from downtown Campbell River to Quathiaski Cove on Quadra Island. From the ferry you see Whiskey Point on your right. At Quadra, drive up the hill. Take the first right into Green Road. At Noble Road, turn right again. Continue on it passing Helanton Road. Stay on the pavement and curve around to the right to the end of the road. Two or three cars could park. You are now looking back at Quathiaski Cove. Enter the water and snorkel south towards Whiskey Point. Work your way south under water to a most beautiful wall at 50 feet (15 meters).

Comments: A gorgeous dive. Well worth waiting for the right moment!

Strawberry anemone with tiny club tips, about ten times life-size

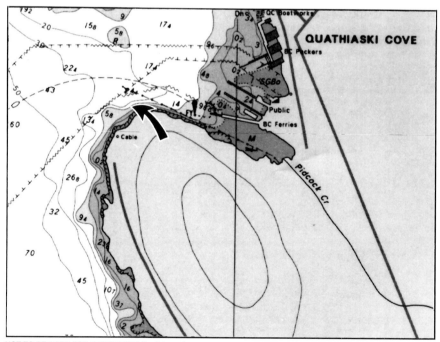

200 Yards

RICHMOND REEF
Shore Dive

Skill: Expert divers with guide

Why go: To visit the eye of a "whirlwind" of currents. A pink jungle at Richmond Reef. Strawberry anemones cover the top of the reef between the kelp. Brooding anemones and soft corals – fuzzy pink ones and bubble-shaped pink ones are heaped side by side. A red Irish lord sits on top of it all, almost invisible because of the color around it. Pale yellow soft corals are massed on the rocks, and lumpy cream-colored miniature cucumbers. Rock greenlings dart between the kelp. Mauve and pink brooding anemones climb the stalks of the kelp. It's a pink jungle – not enough rock bottom to attach to.
    We drop over a ledge. I shine my light into a niche: golden yellow cloud sponges gild its interior, transform it into a mini-cathedral. We see yellow staghorn bryozoans, Christmas anemones, a lingcod, a rock scallop so large it fills a crevice. Abalones glide over the rocks. We see a mustard-colored trumpet sponge, white cloud sponges, gray tennis ball sponges. Swimming scallops cling to the rock walls covered with mauve, pink and yellow encrusting sponges.
    Current curls around the corner of a rock. Blows us away. We climb to the kelp, hold on. Pull along on the kelp to the top of the reef. The current is building. We prowl in the eye of the storm for awhile, but the kelp bends, tears loose – it's time to go. We ascend through a cloud of herring. On the surface, signal the boat that we are okay and wait to be picked up.

Bottom and Depths: Richmond Reef is a rough flattened pyramid with corners and dips, and some places to hide from the current. The top of the reef is rocky with sand between. In summer, kelp is attached to the rocks. On the surface, the kelp is thinly spaced. On the reef, the kelp is thick, giving hand-holds to pull yourself along. The top of the reef is 20 to 30 feet (6 to 9 meters) deep and drops off quickly in rocky ledges to a depth of 170 to 180 feet (52 to 55 meters) into Discovery Passage.

Hazards: Current, boats and kelp. Richmond Reef is one of the most difficult sites for current that I have dived. Dive with a "live" boat – the first time with a charter operator experienced at the site. Dive at the end of an ebbing current with a tidal exchange no greater than 1 foot (⅓ meter) per hour. For height, refer to the tide table for Campbell River. For time to dive, refer to the current table for Seymour Narrows. Ascent is through open water in the boating channel: Listen for boats. Heads up, look up and come up. Carry a knife for kelp.

Telephones: • Quathiaski Cove ferry landing. • Quathiaski Cove shopping center, uphill from ferry.

Facilities: None. Charters, launching and hot showers on west side of Quadra Island. Air fills, boat rentals and showers in Campbell River. At Quadra, dive package which includes charters, air fills, hot tub, accommodation and meals.

Access: Richmond Reef is in Discovery Passage close to the west side of Quadra Island. It is a 5-minute boat ride from Quathiaski Cove at Quadra.
    Charter or launch out of Quathiaski Cove and go north 1 nautical mile (1¾ kilometers) to the second rock wall on Quadra around the corner from the northern entrance to Quathiaski Cove. Arrive early – at least ¾ hour before predicted turn of the current and watch the water. Plumb with a lead line to find the reef which is 300 feet (90 meters) offshore from the center of the rock wall or use a depth sounder. The

top of the reef is 20 to 30 feet (6 to 9 meters) deep. When you find it, measure the exact depth with a heavily weighted line, tie a plastic bottle at that depth and throw it in. Surface current might still be strong when the bottle surfaces, but the water on top of the reef is slowing down – this is the time to dive. Drop anchor on top of the reef – it's bare rock. Immediately roll over the side and descend on the anchor line.

Essential to dive with a "live" boat to pick you up.

Comments: If you like Richmond Reef, you might also want to dive April Point Reef close-by to the north and Row-And-Be-Damned to the south.

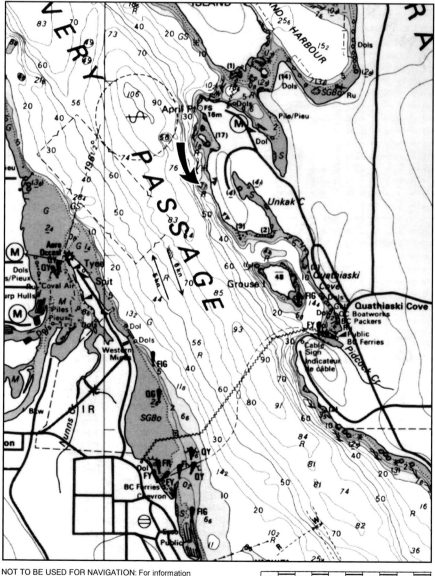

NOT TO BE USED FOR NAVIGATION: For information on obtaining navigational charts see page 318. This is a portion of 3312.

1 Nautical Mile

WA-WA-KIE BEACH
Shore Dive

Skill: All divers

Why go: There's a wide cross-section of life at this relatively current-free site where access is so easy – Wa-Wa-Kie Beach. It's a great place to try deep diving without other complications. Descend from shore through several zones in rapid succession. Rocky bottom with bull kelp from shore to 30 feet (9 meters) gives way to silty sand from 30 to 75 feet (9 to 23 meters). Steep clay undercut with inconspicuous narrow slit ledges slopes off at 75 to 100 feet (23 to 30 meters). This range of substrate provides homes for many different fish and invertebrates.

Lingcod, tiger rockfish and octopuses live down the clay slope. And yelloweye rockfish, commonly called red snapper, down deep. Moving up to the silty sand we saw a giant nudibranch, beige with blue tips, and numerous 1-inch (2½-centimeter) nudibranchs, white with beige tips. But my favorite part of this dive is up in the kelp at 20 to 30 feet (6 to 9 meters). Here, just hang still in the water and let the life come past. The rockfish accepted us as part of their scene and swam right up to our masks. One rockfish yawned at us, its thick yellow lips opening wide. A huge cloud of herring passed around us. I wondered which way was up and which down. We saw dozens of tube-snouts, stroked a red Irish lord, and saw a hermit crab living in an orange sponge which had dissolved the crab's adopted shell home.

Bottom and Depths: Rocky bottom to bull kelp at 20 to 30 feet (6 to 9 meters). Silty from 40 to 75 feet (12 to 23 meters). Narrow slit ledges down to 100 feet (39 meters).

Hazards: Small fishing boats. Listen for boats, use your compass and ascend along the bottom all the way to shore well out of the way of those boats.

Telephones: • Quathiaski Cove ferry landing. • Quathiaski Cove shopping center, up hill from ferry.

Facilities: None at Wa-Wa-Kie Beach. Camping, hot showers, accommodations, and launching at Heriot Bay, east side of Quadra. Camping, in summer, at camp-ground next to Rebecca Spit. Air fills in Campbell River.

Access: Wa-Wa-Kie Beach is on Sutil Channel, east side of Quadra Island. From Campbell River it is a 10-minute ferry ride and a 10-minute drive to Wa-Wa-Kie. Take the ferry from downtown Campbell River to Quathiaski Cove on Quadra Island. Drive up the hill to the shopping center. Turn left into Harper Road, and then right. Continue straight along Heriot Bay Road to Smith Road. Do not turn right to Cape Mudge. Drive along Smith Road to the east side of the island. Go around a sharp hairpin bend to the right, down the steep hill and take the first turn to your left. Three or four cars can park close to the rocky beach. Walk 5 feet (1½ meters) to the beach and climb over large rocks. It is easier to enter at high tide. Swim straight out and down.

Comments: Beautiful wild rocky beach strewn with logs bleached silver by the sun and sea.

Totem at Cape Mudge, Quadra Island

QUADRA ISLAND

Quathiaski Cove

QC Boatworks
BC Packers
Public
BC Ferries

NOT TO BE USED FOR NAVIGATION: For information
on obtaining navigational charts see page 318.
This is a portion of 3312.

1 Nautical Mile

257

REBECCA SPIT
Shore Dive

Skill: All divers

Why go: If you've missed slack or just want a straightforward Quadra Island dive, Rebecca Spit is a good place to go. Access is easy. Swim out over the gently sloping rocky bottom scattered with eelgrass, bottom kelp, tall brown kelp and orange and white burrowing cucumbers. You'll find a single shallow ledge dropping from about 20 to 40 feet (6 to 12 meters).

I was told an octopus lives at the ledge, but I didn't see it. Probably easier to find it at night. However, a lot of other little things are easy to find at Rebecca Spit. We saw many small rockfish, some kelp greenlings, flounders, lots of little hermit crabs, a couple of rock scallops, a spider crab and red rock crabs. Beyond the ledge legions of sea pens sprout from the sharply sloping sand.

Bottom and Depths: Rocky bottom with eelgrass, bottom kelp and tall brown kelp slopes gently to 20 feet (6 meters). Here a rock ledge drops to 40 feet (12 meters). Beyond the ledge, sharply sloping sand.

Hazards: Small boats, especially in summer and fall. This is a popular salmon-fishing site. Use a compass to navigate back to shore, listen for boats and ascend with a reserve of air, keeping close to the bottom all the way up to the beach.

Telephones: • Heriot Bay shopping center, outside. • Beaver's Restaurant, inside. Returning to Heriot Bay, on right-hand side of road, nearly at shopping center. • We-Wai-Kai campground, outside Rebecca Spit Park, summer only.

Facilities: Picnic tables, pit toilets, launching and lots of parking at Rebecca Spit Park. Camping and hot showers at campground close-by in summer. Hot showers year-round at Heriot Bay Inn. Air fills in Campbell River.

Access: Rebecca Spit is at the western edge of Sutil Channel on the east side of Quadra Island in Rebecca Spit Provincial Park. From Campbell River it is a 10-minute ferry ride and a 15-minute drive to Rebecca Spit.

Take the ferry from downtown Campbell River to Quathiaski Cove on Quadra Island. Drive up the hill. At the shopping center, turn left and then right and follow signs to Cortes Island ferry.

When you reach Heriot Bay and see the shopping center on your right, do not continue straight to the Heriot Bay ferry landing. Turn right and follow signs curving around Drew Harbour to Rebecca Spit Park. At the park, drive as far out the spit as you can go. The launching ramp for Drew Harbour is on your left-hand side. Wheelchair divers, who paddle dive-kayaks, could paddle from here around the spit to the rocky beach on the east side of the spit. Other divers, walk a few paces straight from your car to the rocky beach on the east side of the spit. Swim straight out and down to find the ledge.

Comments: Oysters on the beach at Rebecca Spit. Oysters are edible all year. The best ones are found at very low tide in springtime, but always check for deadly "red tide" before collecting them. Warnings are out almost every year at this location. Telephone the Shellfish Infoline, recorded: (604) 666-3169.

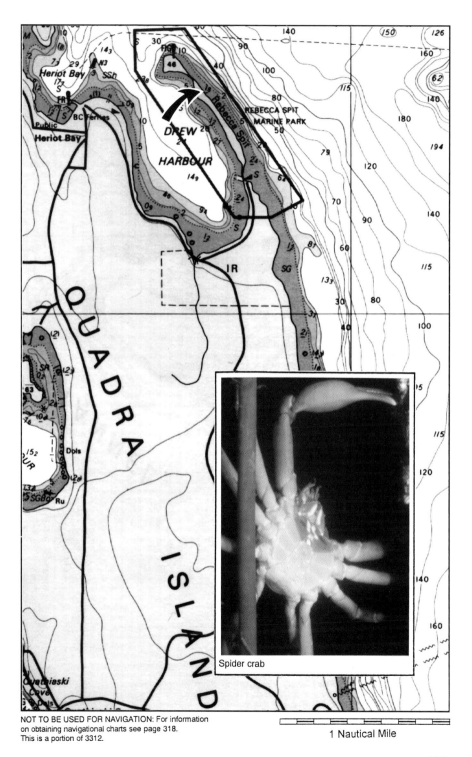

Spider crab

1 Nautical Mile

VINER POINT
Boat Dive

Tide Table: Campbell River

Skill: All divers

Why go: A stark, dark wall lush with red snakelock anemones drops off to nowhere. Really different from other Campbell River area sites. Deeper, there are sponges and juvenile yelloweye rockfish. A ratfish followed us around like a pet. The wall dropped off cleanly and deep and we felt as though we were in a huge room. Up in the shallows we saw large sea peaches, bright orange tube sponges, large dead man's finger sponges, lots and lots of nudibranch eggs and orange solitary cup corals in only 5 feet (1½ meters) of water.

We had gone to Viner Point expecting to see rock scallops and abalones. But we found something else that was good. The drop-off.

Bottom and Depths: Rocky bottom covered with bottom kelp down to 30 to 40 feet (9 to 12 meters). Then a smooth wall sheers off down to deep water over 100 feet (30 meters).

Hazards: In summer, small fishing boats. Viner Point, like many other good dive sites in the Campbell River area, is popular with salmon fishermen. In summer, especially, listen for boats and ascend close to the wall and rocks right up to the surface.

Telephones: • Heriot Bay Inn. • We-Wai-Kai campground, which is outside Rebecca Spit Park, summer only.

Facilities: None at wild and untamed Viner Point. Launching ramps at Drew Harbour and Heriot Bay on the east side of Quadra Island. Picnic tables and pit toilets at Rebecca Spit Park. Camping and hot showers at campground next to park. Trailer hookups, nearby. Accommodations and hot showers at Heriot Bay. Groceries at shopping center across the road.

Access: Viner Point is on Sutil Channel at the southernmost tip of Read Island. It is 2 nautical miles (4 kilometers) east of the Breton Islands, and 5 nautical miles (9 kilometers) northeast of Heriot Bay on Quadra Island. In winter, Viner Point is exposed to southeast winds. Waves can become very big. Choose a calm day.

Charter out of Quathiaski Cove, Quadra Island, or out of Campbell River; or launch at Heriot Bay or Drew Harbour on the east side of Quadra Island and go northeast to Viner Point. A small cove at the southeast tip of Read Island is convenient for anchoring. Dive on the wall north of this cove.

Comments: In late summer and fall, take your fishing rod to catch a salmon on your way home.

Snakelock anemone

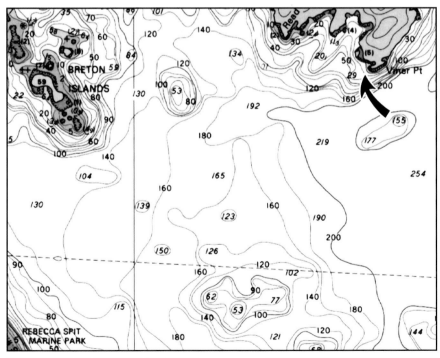

1 Nautical Mile

MOULDS BAY
Shore Dive

Skill: All divers

Why go: Current-free, easy entry, a variety of life: two dives at this one bay with a lovely wild-feeling beach for a picnic between dives.
Christmas anemones are scattered across the dark rock wall. Fat red-and-green bases topped with fleshy tendrils, each one so distinct, so round, so there. We see a dinner-plate-sized sea star with dark blue tips. A kelp greenling. A rock scallop. A moon jellyfish pulsing. Copper colored anemones beneath a ledge. Sea cucumbers draped around a rock. An orange sea peach. Then a transparent one. And a few tiny orange sea pens, their bulbs buried in the sand at the base of the wall. An orange plumose anemone alone on a rock – it is 2½ feet (¾ meter) tall.
We don't have a camera. Wish we did. My buddy click, clicks at me. A sculpin slips into a crack to hide. I shine my light at it. We look down into darkness and cannot see bottom. Look up. Millions of tube-dwelling anemones burgeon from the sand. They look like transparent flowers.
Heading north of the bay, you might see Puget Sound king crabs. Look for the friendly octopus. In summer, a great many lingcod.

Bottom and Depths: Shallow rocky bottom to the edge of the narrow horseshoe-shaped bay, then slopes quickly to 25 feet (7½ meters). You can dive on the left-hand side, as you face out to sea. Tumbled rocks make a rough wall which bottoms out at 60 feet (18 meters). Diving on the right-hand side, you will find a steep, rounded rock wall curving quickly down to a depth of 80 to 90 feet (24 to 27 meters). Maybe deeper. We stopped at 65 feet (20 meters) and could not see bottom.

Hazards: Winter wind from the southeast.

Telephones: • Heriot Bay shopping center. • Heriot Bay Inn. Both telephones are at Heriot Bay which is 11 miles (17 kilometers) away. Return along Valdes Drive, turn left. Go along Hyacinthe Bay Road to West Bay Road. Turn left and go to Quadra Island Market in the shopping center on the right-hand side or to Heriot Bay Inn.

Facilities: Lovely site for a picnic on the rocky beach at Moulds Bay. Hot showers available at Heriot Bay Inn. Camping, in summer, on the east side of Quadra beside Rebecca Spit. Air fills in Campbell River.

Access: Moulds Bay is on the east side of Quadra Island. From Campbell River you are a 10-minute ferry ride and a 30-minute drive away from it; half the drive is on good gravel road.
Take the ferry from downtown Campbell River to Quathiaski Cove on Quadra Island. Drive up the hill to the shopping center. Turn left into Harper Road, then right. When you see signs to Cortes Island Ferry, Heriot Bay, Village Bay Lakes and Granite Bay, follow them and turn left into West Road. When nearly at Heriot Bay, you come to Hyacinthe Bay Road. Go straight. If you miss Hyacinthe, turn left at the next junction just before the Heriot Bay shopping center, which is on the right-hand side. Turn left into Cramer Road following signs toward Village Bay Lakes and Granite Bay: Cramer goes into Hyacinthe.
Go along Hyacinthe Bay Road to Valdes Drive. The road becomes gravel. Keep to your side and drive with your headlights on. Logging trucks could be on the road too. On weekdays, school buses. When you reach a left-hand turnoff to Granite Bay, continue straight: go just over 1 mile (2 kilometers) more to Valdes Drive. Turn right,

go to the end of the road, and drop gear. Park at the roadside. An easy entry over the rocky beach. Easier entry at high tides.

Comments: Wild feeling above and below – my favorite kind of place.

Preparing for dive at Moulds Bay

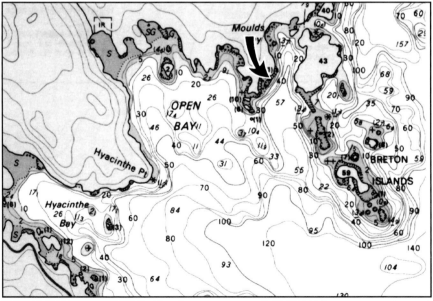

NOT TO BE USED FOR NAVIGATION: For information on obtaining navigational charts see page 318. This is a portion of 3312.

1 Nautical Mile

STEEP ISLAND
Boat Dive

Skill: Expert divers. Intermediate divers with guide.

Why go: Purple bouquets of feather duster tube worms cascade down the sheer rock face at Steep Island: A purple waterfall. Purple jungle. A purple profusion too fantastic to describe. Mixed with strawberry anemones. Trumpet sponges. Wolf-eels. Tennis ball sponges. Puget Sound king crabs. Orange cup corals. Octopuses, rock scallops and swimming scallops. Kelp greenlings, lingcod, tiger rockfish and Big Red, the yelloweye rockfish that comes out to greet divers and that probably weighs 40 to 50 pounds (18 to 23 kilograms) – all can be seen at Steep. But mostly I love Steep for those marvelous giant feather duster bouquets – many of them 3 feet (1 meter) tall. Take a light to see the richness of the purple.

I had *dived* this site before I wrote the first edition of *141 Dives* but did not *write* about it then. I had promised not to. But so many people know of Steep now and Steep is honored as a reserve – as all sites in Discovery Passage are – it's safe, and so I have been released from that promise. Steep is so splendid I want to chronicle it. Single it out. Shout about it. Steep is one of those dives I label as having "Star" quality.

Divers who want to visit the most special places in the world will want to go to Steep.

Bottom and Depths: Plummets to a depth of 120 to 130 feet (37 to 40 meters) at the northwest corner. Ledges off gently into Discovery Passage from the middle to the southern end of the island. Bull kelp in summer.

Hazards: Current, boats and kelp. On all except the lowest tidal exchanges of less than 1 foot (⅓ meter) per hour, dive with a "live" boat; and dive at the end of an ebbing current. For height, refer to the tide table for Campbell River. For time to dive, refer to the turn at Seymour Narrows. Listen for boats and ascend up the side of the island all the way to the surface. Carry a knife.

Telephones: • Quathiaski Cove ferry landing. • Quathiaski Cove shopping center.

Facilities: None at Steep Island. Charters and launching on west side of Quadra and out of Campbell River. Camping and hot showers, in summer, east side of Quadra. Hot showers year-round at Whiskey Point Lodge, Quathiaski Cove. Also on west side of Quadra, dive package which include charters, air, hot tub, accommodation and meals. Air fills and boat rentals in Campbell River.

Access: Steep Island is in Discovery Passage near Campbell River and close to Gowlland Island. It is 3 nautical miles (6 kilometers) north of Quathiaski Cove, Quadra Island.

Charter or launch at Quathiaski Cove or Campbell River. Go to the northern tip of Steep Island. Best at the end of an ebbing tide. Arrive early and watch the water. When the current slows down, about half an hour before the turn, go in and work your way around the wall on the Discovery Passage side of the island. Follow giant purple tube worms feathering down the northwest corner of Steep, then head south. You can gradually work your way up from ledge to ledge throughout the dive.

After the dive you might want to go through Gowlland Harbour; usually seals are around the log booms on the east side of Gowlland Island.

Comments: Big Red is probably at least as old as I am! Yelloweye rockfish have been know to reach the ripe old age of 114 years. Go to look. Go to take memories. Go to take photographs. But no taking of marine life – locals honor it as a reserve.

Looking for seals at Gowlland Harbour

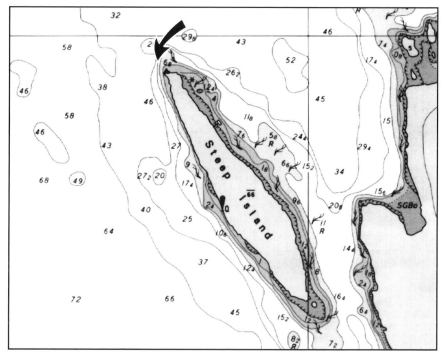

200 Yards

COPPER CLIFFS
Boat Dive

Current Table: Seymour Narrows

Skill: Intermediate and expert divers. All divers with guide.

Why go: Copper Cliffs, an immense rock wall rising over 300 feet (90 meters) straight out of Discovery Passage, is almost too big to be true. Under water everything is equally big. Everything from boulders to cloud sponges to lingcod.
Enormous white plumose anemones cluster on the steep rock wall that falls away before you. Giant feather duster tube worms are also on the wall, their stalks covered with brooding anemones. A school of huge black rockfish swims past. Excellent visibility makes everything seem even more oversized. Giant boulders, dotted with thousands of tiny orange cup corals are scattered on a large ledge below. In only 60 feet (18 meters) of water big clumps of cloud sponges with small skinny brittle stars oozing out of them, billow between mammoth rocks.
During one dive my buddy and I saw fifteen or twenty lingcod, each 3 to 4 feet (1 to 1¼ meters) long, and lots of red-and-black striped tiger rockfish. Peeping under a large boulder covered with strawberry anemones on its north face, we saw a mosshead warbonnet. Even the warbonnet was large for its species, about 4 inches (10 centimeters) long. I looked up while swimming upcurrent and there was a yelloweye rockfish, commonly called red snapper, staring at me. Colorful giants fed by giant currents.
Grandiose!

Bottom and Depths: Clean-cut volcanic rock wall sheers to a ledge with large boulders at 50 to 60 feet (15 to 18 meters). Then drops away again to a depth greater than 100 feet (30 meters).

Hazards: Current and small boats. Dive precisely on the slack at the end of the ebb. Be geared up and ready one hour before the turn, watching and waiting for the current to slow down. Very powerful currents run through here. On large tidal exchanges leave a pickup person in your boat in case you are swept away. This is a popular salmon-fishing area: in summer, small boats come within inches (centimeters) of the wall. Listen for boats and ascend close to the wall all the way to the surface well out of the way of them.

Telephones: • Thunderbird Resort, across from Argonaut Wharf, Spit Road in Campbell River. • Quathiaski Cove ferry landing, Quadra Island.

Facilities: None at Copper Cliffs. Charters, launching and hot showers on west side of Quadra; also on west side of Quadra, dive package which includes charters, air, hot tub, accommodation and meals. Air fills, charters, boat rentals and launching in Campbell River.

Access: Copper Cliffs, usually called Copper Bluffs, is in Discovery Passage on the west side of Quadra Island. It is 4 nautical miles (7 kilometers) north of Campbell River. Charter on the west side of Quadra Island; charter, rent a boat or take a water taxi from Campbell River. Or launch your own boat at Tyee Spit in Campbell River and go north to that immense rock wall. You cannot miss it.

Comments: Eagles in the sky and cormorants on the cliffs.

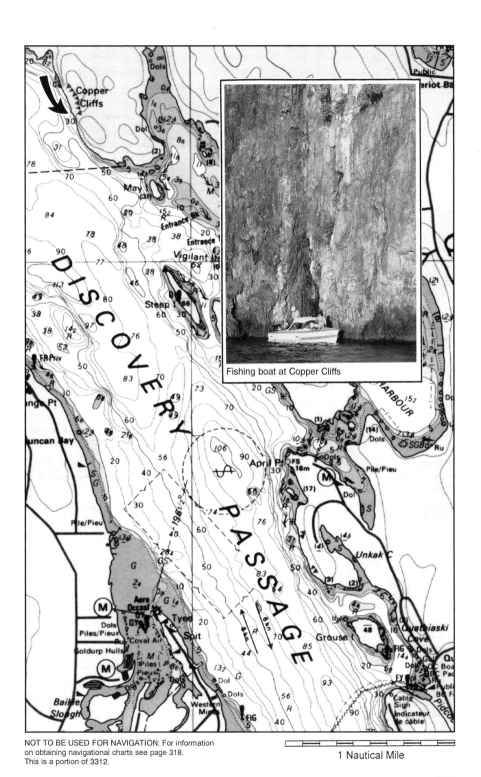

Copper Cliffs

Fishing boat at Copper Cliffs

DISCOVERY PASSAGE

May

Entrance Bk

Vigilant I

Steep

FR Priv

Duncan Bay

Pile/Pieu

Aero

Tyee
Spit

Coval Air

Goldurp Hulls

Piles/Pieux

Baikie
Slough

Western
Mines

April Pt

FS

16m

Dols

Unkak C

Grouse

Quathiaski
Cove

Pile/Pieu

HARBOUR

Cable
Sign
Indicateur
de câble

NOT TO BE USED FOR NAVIGATION: For information
on obtaining navigational charts see page 318.
This is a portion of 3312.

1 Nautical Mile

SEYMOUR NARROWS
Boat Dive

Current Table: Seymour Narrows

Skill: Expert divers. Intermediate divers with guide.

Why go: Anemone-land – unbelievably soft, pale pinky-orange anemones with long transparent filaments streaming into the current are massed and tumble loosely over the rocks. We see large white anemones like giant snowflakes. A few tall white plumose anemones tilting into the current. Christmas anemones with flaming red tops and green-and-red bases – their tops look speckled green-black-and-white until you shine a light on them. Red snakelock anemones too. And mixed in, mauve and pink brooding anemones, the size of small cotton balls. Millions of white "stunted" anemones heaped over all like drifted snow. Little guys – have they stayed tiny so they won't be washed away?

We see yellow staghorn bryozoans attached to the rocks. A trumpet sponge. Encrusting sponge coating the rocks with bright yellow. Orange ball sponges. Chitons. Giant red urchins and small green urchins making craters in the rocks. At one depth, miniature white cucumbers cover the ledge – a strange filter feeder I have not seen often and only at very high current sites. Abalones. Swimming scallops. Big fat rock scallops in the crevices. Kelp greenlings. Lingcod – lots of them. A red Irish lord.

Take a light to fully see the technicolor world of Seymour Narrows.

Bottom and Depths: Rounded ledges start at 20 to 30 feet (6 to 9 meters) and roll gently down into Seymour Narrows deeper than you could go – to 360 feet (110 meters) on the chart. Most life is between 40 and 60 feet (12 and 18 meters). Crevices, nooks and crannies indent the ledges giving places to hide from the current. In summer, the kelp gives a protected place to ascend out of the way of boats.

Hazards: Current, tide rips and whirlpools; ships, tugs, barges, fishing boats and small boats. A tremendous "parking lot" of boats waits for slack at Seymour Narrows, particularly at fishing openings and at Alaska supply season. Dive on slack with a "live" boat. While down, watch current direction and be aware when it changes. Do not bob up mid-channel: Seymour Narrows is the main route for large vessels heading up the Inland Passage to Prince Rupert and Alaska. When ascending, listen for small boats. Hug the side of the passage: go up crevices, hang onto rocks and surface in the kelp out of the way of boats. Carry a knife for kelp.

Seymour Narrows is big, deep and swift – immense volumes of water move through. It is one of the top three fastest-flowing tidal streams in the world, along with Sechelt Rapids and Nakwakto Rapids for speed. The channel is 3½ nautical miles (6½ kilometers) long with a width of ½ nautical mile (1 kilometer). It is powerful – respect that power.

Telephones: • Brown Bay, on fuel dock; Brown Bay is 1½ nautical miles (2¾ kilometers) north of the dive site on the Vancouver Island side of the channel. • Tyee Spit, south of launching ramp at entrance to Thunderbird Resort across road from Argonaut Wharf; Tyee Spit is 7 nautical miles (13 kilometers) south of the dive site on the Vancouver Island side of the channel.

Facilities: None at Seymour Narrows. Charters out of Quathiaski Cove and Campbell River. Launching and RV park at Brown Bay.

Access: Seymour Narrows is near the middle of Discovery Passage. It is 10 nautical miles (19 kilometers) north of the town of Campbell River.

Charter or launch out of Quathiaski Cove on Quadra Island or out of Campbell River and head north to Seymour Narrows. After going beneath the power lines, head north 330 yards (300 meters) – go one-third of the way up the west side of Seymour Narrows to a sheltered cove where the depth is only 20 to 30 feet (6 to 9 meters). In summer, you can find this cove by the kelp.

Plan in advance: current can roar through Seymour Narrows up to 16 knots (30 kilometers/hour) on the flooding tide. Up to 14 knots (26 kilometers/hour) on the ebb. Even with low exchanges, the water stops only momentarily. Go on a day of the month when the current is no greater than 11 knots (20 kilometers/hour) at maximum flood or ebb. Any greater current and the back eddies do not stop.

Be geared up and ready to dive an hour before the predicted turn, waiting for the current to slow down. Watch the water, watch the kelp. When the current has slowed sufficiently to dive, roll off the boat and head down. Try to go with the current for the first half of your dive – try for a free ride. Watch the kelp while diving, too. When the kelp turns, head back for another free ride. Try for it, but the current might pick up without warning. Dive with a "live" boat; your first time, go with a charter operator experienced at Seymour Narrows.

Comments: For years, local divers have honored the entire expanse of Discovery Passage as a reserve.

NOT TO BE USED FOR NAVIGATION: For information on obtaining navigational charts see page 318. This is a portion of 3312.

1 Nautical Mile

CHATHAM POINT
Boat Dive

Skill: Intermediate and expert divers

Why go: Lingcod – large and small – live at this current-swept rounded reef. Giant red urchins and a scattering of swimming scallops. Also you might meet the minke whale that lives near Chatham Point. It is 40 feet (12 meters) long.

Bottom and Depths: The reef between the rocks and lighthouse rounds down quickly to a sandy bottom at 50 to 60 feet (15 to 18 meters). There are two large troughs between the shore and the light. It is much deeper in the channel beyond the light. In summer thick bull kelp grows on the reef.

Hazards: Current, boats and bull kelp. Dive on slack. At this site the current is *always* running in one direction or the other. You must dive on slack when the current at least slows down. Do not rely on the tables alone. Sit by the water and watch for the current to slacken, then go in. Usually there is more time to dive on the low-water slack at this site.
     On large tidal exchanges a pickup boat is necessary in the event you are swept away. In addition, be aware that the large seine boats like to "cut off" this corner. They often run between the light and the shore – there could be a parade of them. Listen for boats. Dive with a compass, stay down throughout the dive and ascend back up the rocks or in the kelp. Then swim to your boat. Current combined with kelp can be a help or it can be extremely hazardous. Carry a knife for kelp.

Telephones: • Chatham Point Light Station. • Roberts Lake Resort on Island Highway: it is almost 6 miles (10 kilometers) south of Rock Bay Road turnoff and takes one hour to reach by road.

Facilities: None at Chatham Point. Charters and water taxi out of Campbell River. Launching at Rock Bay.

Access: Chatham Point is where Discovery Passage turns northwest into Johnstone Strait. It is 2¾ nautical miles (5 kilometers) east of Rock Bay.
     Charter or take a water taxi out of Campbell River, or launch at Rock Bay and go 2¾ nautical miles (5 kilometers) east to Chatham Point (see Rock Bay page 272). We took an inflatable from Rock Bay and landed on the rocks halfway between the shore and the lighthouse marking Beaver Rock. Descend and dive toward Beaver Rock. On big tidal exchanges have a pickup boat follow you.

Comments: Chatham Point is an unspoilt wilderness of big fish and worth every ounce of effort required to dive.

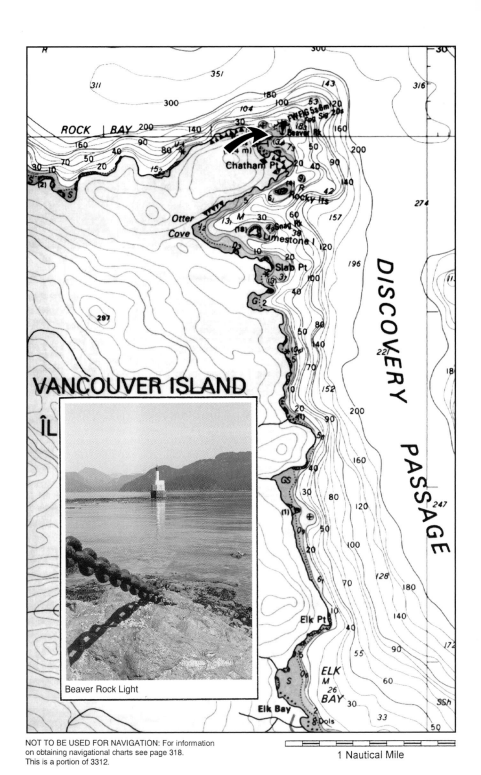

ROCK BAY

VANCOUVER ISLAND

ÎL

Chatham Pt

Otter Cove

Rocky Its

Limestone I

Slab Pt

DISCOVERY PASSAGE

Elk Pt

ELK
BAY

Elk Bay

Beaver Rock Light

1 Nautical Mile

ROCK BAY
Shore Dive

Tide Table: Owen Bay
Subtract 30 minutes

Skill: Intermediate and expert divers. All divers and snorkelers with guide.

Why go: History, shallow diving in the kelp, and deep diving to sponge-land are attractions at this relatively current-free site where you can dive almost any time of day. It is excellent for photography, with water that's usually clear and with a good mixture of marine life. Entry is easy. Plus there's the chance of a valuable bottle or china find. Union steamships called here from the early 1900s until at least 1927.

Back in the late 1800s a large logging community was at Rock Bay. A big hospital was built there in 1905. It burned and another 25-bed one was built in 1911. Though the second hospital was abandoned some years ago when the logging operation closed down, right up until the mid-1950s the hospital plumbing was still connected and you could take a cold shower – the site was made for divers! Then that building burned on Christmas day in 1971. Today not much remains of the once-large community at Rock Bay: only the hospital ruins and old bottles hidden under the sea and the new seasonal population at the RV campground.

When diving here I saw lots of marine life. Kelp greenlings, delicate nudibranchs, a bright red blenny with blue markings, lingcod, a huge octopus sprawled across a rock as though sunning itself, and a cloud sponge so orange it was almost red. One blue swimming scallop clapped right up to my buddy's mask and I almost lost my regulator from laughing.

Bottom and Depths: It's easy to make either a shallow or a deep dive at this site. Rocky bottom scattered with boulders and bull kelp slopes gently to a depth of 30 to 40 feet (9 to 12 meters). Some sand between the boulders. Then a rapid drop to as deep as you want to go.

Hazards: Boats, current and bull kelp. Listen for boats and dive with a compass: at the end of your dive navigate to shore, staying close to the bottom all the way. In the bay, dive on or near slack and be watchful of swirling currents. If you go around the point on the left, you must dive on slack. Watch for downcurrents on ebb tides at the left-hand side of the bay. Carry a knife for kelp. .

Telephone: Roberts Lake Resort on Island Highway: it is almost 6 miles (10 kilometers) south of Rock Bay Road turnoff and takes 1 hour to reach.

Facilities: Camping, toilets, fresh water and a hard gravel launching ramp that is good at all tides, plus parking – all for a fee at privately owned Rock Bay.

Access: Rock Bay is near the east end of Johnstone Strait. It is at the end of Rock Bay Road off Island Highway (Highway 19). The turnoff is between Port McNeill and Campbell River.

Go down Rock Bay Road. Allow 30 to 45 minutes from Island Highway to the dive. There might be logging traffic, too, so drive with your headlights on. On the way you'll see moss-covered remnants of railway trestles from steam-engine-logging days. Go down this pothole-filled road for 11 miles (18 kilometers) to Rock Bay where you can drive to the water's edge. Expect to pay a modest parking fee at privately owned Rock Bay. The launching ramp shelves gently but is gravel and probably not usable by wheelchair divers.

To get to Rock Bay Road
• From Campbell River go north on Island Highway for 30 minutes to the Rock Bay

turnoff. When almost 6 miles (10 kilometers) past Roberts Lake Resort you will see a narrow secondary road to Rock Bay. The sign is small and easy to miss. If you cross Amor de Cosmos Creek you have gone too far. Turn right into Rock Bay Road.
• From Port McNeill go south for 2 hours on Island Highway to the Rock Bay turnoff. When 14 miles (23 kilometers) past the Sayward Road junction and immediately across Amor de Cosmos Creek, turn left down Rock Bay Road.

Comments: This popular open-water certification site is still unspoilt and has much to offer all divers.

Rockfish in kelp

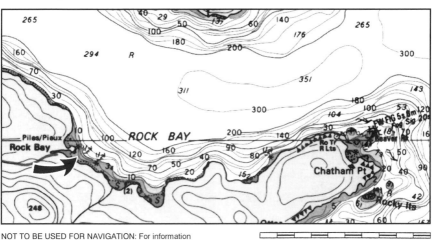

1 Nautical Mile

SHIP BREAKWATER
Shore Dive

Tide Table: Alert Bay
Add 30 minutes

Skill: All divers and snorkelers

Why go: Under the shadow of the breakwater of ships there is an amazing amount of colorful life and the site is so shallow and accessible.

Masses of dahlia anemones cluster on the rocky bottom under the first ship. They look like a delicious heap of pale green and pink bonbons. Other anemones encrust the hull. We saw small golden-dotted shrimp. A pair of slim grass-green gunnels, 18 inches (28 centimeters) long. Then another. And another. Almost completely hidden in the kelp by their color and shape, they looked like diminutive moray eels.

While swimming to the next ship, we saw thousands of small silvery fish flying up out of the smooth white sand like a glittering silver lamé curtain. Heady stuff. So unexpected and beautiful. If lucky you might see giant skates. I missed them. But someone catches an 80- to 90-pound (36- to 41-kilogram) skate each year at the annual Fishing Derby in Kelsey Bay. It is a line-fishing competition for salmon, but sometimes they hook the wrong fish. A fish head or a chicken is used for bait. You often hear stories of giant skates at Kelsey Bay – a snorkeler reported seeing one in 1990. Look for skates.

Bottom and Depths: Smooth sand from 10 to 30 feet (3 to 9 meters) deep. Much of the area dries at very low tides. Small rocks and lettuce kelp under the ships.

Hazards: Boats combined with shallow depths. Difficult to stay down, but most important to. Dive on high tides, wear extra weight, listen for boats. Ascend up the side of the ship breakwater and snorkel back to the ramp.

Telephone: Government dock at Kelsey Bay, at roadside. Go to the end of the road at Kelsey Bay to find it.

Facilities: Great deal of parking area and launching ramp at the end of the dike.

Access: The ship breakwater is in Kelsey Bay at Sayward. Reach it off Island Highway (Highway 19) at a turnoff midway between Port McNeill and Campbell River. From Campbell River go north; from Port McNeill go south: 1 hour from each to Sayward Junction.

At Sayward Junction, turn off Island Highway and go north on Sayward Road for 7 miles (12 kilometers). As you come into Sayward you will see houses on the hillside on your left. A road named Kelsey Way goes off the main road on the left-hand side, then comes back to it. Immediately past the north end of Kelsey Way, you will see a "Kelsey Bay Division" sign and a truck water tower on your right-hand side. Immediately past that, turn right into Kelsey Bay Camp.

From here, only ½ mile (1 kilometer) to the ship breakwater but go carefully. If trucks are hauling, follow them to the gravel dike. Or follow the yellow signs saying "Boats Use Extreme Caution" through the camp toward the huge heaps of logs at the dryland sort area. When you reach the dryland sort, turn right and skirt the area. Past the heliport, stay on the outer periphery of the sort as you drive out the narrow gravel dike. Go to the end of it. Park and pick a ship. We started with the first one on our right. Entry is easy down the launching ramp.

Wheelchair access at the launching ramp with lots of nearby parking space.

Comments: A surprisingly different and pleasant dive. I want to go there again to look for skates.

Gunnel beneath breakwater of ships

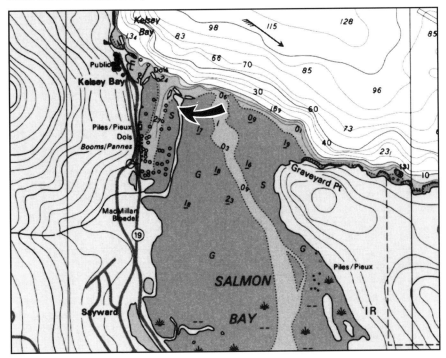

½ Nautical Mile

FERCH POINT
Shore Dive

Skill: Intermediate and expert divers

Why go: It's tame. It's wilderness. It's current swept. And it's quick and easy to dive. The resident harbor seal you might meet at the entry makes this dive feel domesticated. While at the point, it's like wilderness. Small cloud sponges are beneath the ledges at only 25 feet (7½ meters). Large sponges at 40 feet (12 meters). We swam past lampshells clustered beneath the overhangs. Diving here, I enjoyed a "first time" sight: a bright orange slipper cucumber in the open. It was tiny, altogether no greater than the size of my thumb. The main body – that was the part I had not seen before because it is usually buried or anchored – was like a heap of roe. Delicate orange tentacles streamed from it. Also, my buddy held out a juvenile Puget Sound king crab to show me. It was the size of my thumbnail, bright orange, and pointed on top as if it were wearing a peaked cap.

Bottom and Depths: Gently sloping sand to the rock wall.

Hazards: Current and boats. Dive on the slack, and best with a low tidal exchange. The current rips around this corner, and if slack does not occur when you expect it, you might want to call off the dive. The current did not respond as predicted in the tables when we dived there. It was at least an hour later. Listen for boats and ascend close to the shore.

Telephone: Top of government wharf at Kelsey Bay, at the roadside.

Facilities: Launching ramp at the dive entry. Limited roadside parking.

Access: Ferch Point is located in Kelsey Bay at Sayward. Reach it off Island Highway (Highway 19) at a turnoff midway between Port McNeill and Campbell River. From Campbell River go north; from Port McNeill go south: 1 hour from each to Sayward Junction.
At Sayward Junction, turn off Island Highway and go north 12 kilometers (7½ miles) to Kelsey Bay. Continue to the end of the road. You'll see the Fish and Game Club Launching Ramp. It's an easy entry. Swim out from the cove to wilderness water at the point.
Wheelchair access possible, especially in winter, if you arrange to obtain a key to the ramp. Telephone (604) 282-3216, 282-3602, 282-3204 to obtain use of key to the ramp for a fee. Mailing address: c/o Stan Clark, 211 Ambleside Drive, Sayward BC V0P 1R0.

Comments: If you see a seal, as we did, don't expect to see fish on your dive. They chase them away.

Lampshells in Kelsey Bay

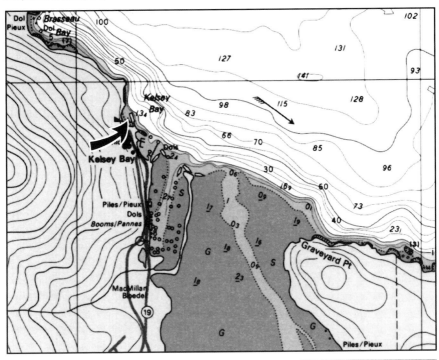

½ Nautical Mile

Haddington Island, with quarry rock lower right

Bear Cove Historic Marker

Wolf-eels at Hunt Rock

278

Boarding *Sun Fun* for day charter

Oceaner, pioneering diving at Port Hardy

Sea Venturer liveaboard, at anchor

Winter day charter, Telegraph Cove   *Clavella* anchored near Turret Rock

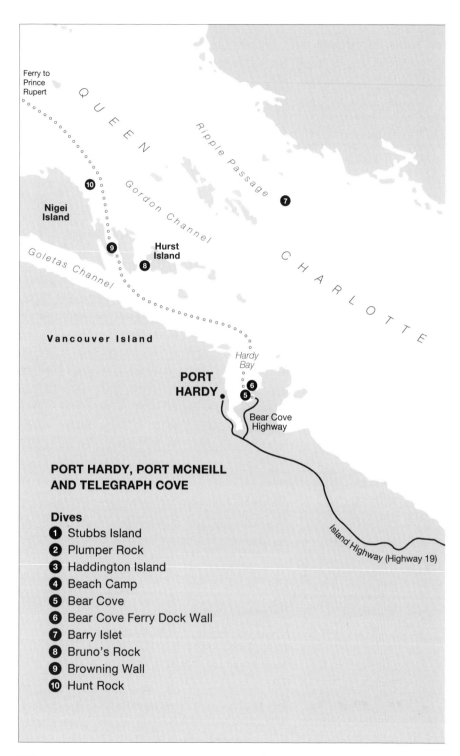

Ferry to
Prince
Rupert

Q U E E N

Ripple Passage

Gordon Channel

**Nigei
Island**

⑩

⑦

⑨

**Hurst
Island**

⑧

C H A R L O T T E

Goletas Channel

Vancouver Island

*Hardy
Bay*

**PORT
HARDY** ●

⑥
⑤

Bear Cove
Highway

**PORT HARDY, PORT MCNEILL
AND TELEGRAPH COVE**

Dives

❶ Stubbs Island
❷ Plumper Rock
❸ Haddington Island
❹ Beach Camp
❺ Bear Cove
❻ Bear Cove Ferry Dock Wall
❼ Barry Islet
❽ Bruno's Rock
❾ Browning Wall
❿ Hunt Rock

Island Highway (Highway 19)

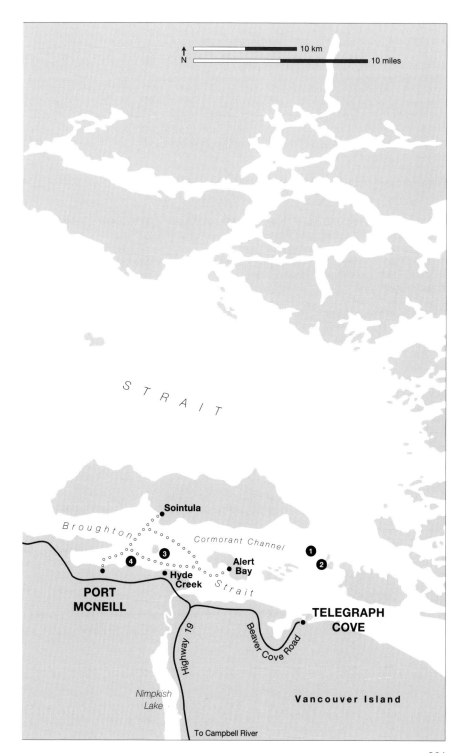

N

10 km

10 miles

S T R A I T

Sointula

Broughton

Cormorant Channel

❶

❷

❸

❹

Alert Bay

Hyde Creek

S t r a i t

PORT McNEILL

Highway 19

Beaver Cove Road

TELEGRAPH COVE

Nimpkish Lake

Vancouver Island

To Campbell River

SERVICE INFORMATION *
Port Hardy, Port McNeill and Telegraph Cove

Charts: Canadian Hydrographic Service
• 3546 Broughton Strait
• 3548 Queen Charlotte Strait, Central Portion
• 3549 Queen Charlotte Strait, Western Portion
• L/C-3605 Quatsino Sound to Queen Charlotte Strait

Tide and Current Tables: Canadian Hydrographic Service
Tide and Current Table, Volume 6.

Diving Emergency Telephone Numbers
Dial 911: Say "I have a scuba diving emergency".

Vancouver General Hospital: Dial (604) 875-4111 and say "I have a scuba diving emergency. I want the hyperbaric physician on call".

If medical personnel are unfamiliar with scuba diving emergencies, ask them to telephone DAN (Divers Alert Network): (919) 684-8111, then say "I have a scuba diving emergency".

Other Useful Numbers
Continuous Marine Broadcast (CMB) recorded, 24 hours; listen for weather in Johnstone Strait or Queen Charlotte Strait, telephone
• Alert Bay: (604) 974-5305
• Comox: (604) 339-0748
Shellfish Infoline, recorded: (604) 666-3169
Sportfishing Information Line, recorded: 1-800-663-9333

• Dive Shops and Air Stations
Port McNeill
Sun Fun Divers
1630 McNeill Road, at Beach Drive
Port McNeill BC V0N 2R0
(604) 956-2243 – fax and telephone.
(Dive shop with roadside and waterfront air fills. Telephone to arrange for waterfront air fills.)

Port Hardy
North Island Diving & Water Sports
Market at Hastings
PO Box 1674
Port Hardy BC V0N 2P0
(604) 949-2664; fax (604) 949-2600
(Dive shop with roadside air fills.)

God's Pocket Resort
Hurst Island, PO Box 471
Port Hardy BC V0N 2P0
(604) 949-9221; also VHF Channel 73.
(Open March to October: waterfront air fills at resort; also dive packages – advance booking required. The resort is 12 nautical miles (22 kilometers) north of Port Hardy.)

• Boat Rentals at Port Hardy
North Island Boat, Canoe and Kayak Rentals
8600 Granville Street
Seagate Wharf
PO Box 291
Port Hardy BC V0N 2P0
(604) 949-7707 – fax and telephone.
(Dive-kayak rentals complete with safety pack that includes marine flares and pump; also boat rentals – open June 1st through September 15th.)

• Day Charters and Dive Resorts

MV *Lukwa* and MV *Gikumi*
Stubbs Island Charters
PO Box 7
Telegraph Cove BC V0N 3J0
(604) 928-3185 or (604) 928-3117; fax
(604) 928-3102
(Day charters out of Telegraph Cove,
February through April; again in October
and November. Dive group packages
include guest house accommodation
with sauna, meals, tanks and air.)

New Look and *Baroness*
Viking West Lodge and Charter
PO Box 113
Port McNeill BC V0N 2R0
(604) 956-3431, cellular (604) 974-
8088; fax (604) 956-4633
(Day charters all year-round out of Port
McNeill with inflatable tender. Also
inflatable charters.)

• Liveaboard Charters

Adrenalin Diver
Adrenalin Sports
1512 Duranleau Street
Granville Island
Vancouver BC V6H 3S4
(604) 682-2881
(One-day and weekend boat charters
with land-based accommodation out of
Granville Island in Vancouver: to Port
Hardy, Gulf Islands, Victoria, Nanaimo,
Campbell River and Powell River. Also
bus charters.)

Blue Fjord
Blue Fjord Charters
PO Box 1450
Ladysmith BC V0R 2E0
(604) 245-8987
(Liveaboard charters out of Port Hardy
– out of anywhere.)

Clavella Adventures
Magna Yachting
PO Box 866, Station A
Nanaimo BC V9R 5N2
(604) 753-3751 (office); fax (604) 755-
4014; (604) 949-4014 (vessel).
(Liveaboard charters out of Port Hardy,
March through October. Out of Nanaimo
to Gulf Islands, October to March.)

Hurst Isle
God's Pocket Resort
Hurst Island, PO Box 471
Port Hardy BC V0N 2P0
(604) 949-9221; also VHF Channel 73.
(Boat diving for guests only: dive pack-
ages with air fills, boat diving, land-based
accommodation and meals – advance
booking required. Hurst Island is 12
nautical miles (22 kilometers) north of
Port Hardy. Guests are picked up in Port
Hardy. Open March to October.)

Sun Fun
Sun Fun Divers
1630 McNeill Road, at Beach Drive
PO Box 1240
Port McNeill BC V0N 2R0
(604) 956-2243 – fax and telephone.
(Day charters year-round out of Port
McNeill; also out of Port Hardy.)

Oceaner
Diver's World
1817 West 4th Avenue
Vancouver BC V6J 1M4
(604) 732-1344; fax (604) 273-0201
(Liveaboard charters out of Port Hardy
in summer; also day charters and live-
aboard charters out of Vancouver year-
round.)

Sea Venturer
Exta-Sea Charters
PO Box 1058
Nanaimo BC V9R 5Z2
(604) 756-0544; fax (604) 758-4897
(Liveaboard charters out of Port Hardy
August through October; out of Nan-
aimo November through March; out of
west coast of Vancouver Island April
through July.)

MV *Skeena*
Blue Horizon Charters
#9, 558 Cardero Street
Vancouver BC V6G 2W6
(604) 681-2849
(Liveaboard charters out of Port Hardy,
August and September; out of Egmont at
Sechelt Peninsula the rest of the year.)

• Launching Ramps

Telegraph Cove Ramp
Telegraph Cove Resort
PO Box 1
Telegraph Cove BC V0N 3J0
(604) 928-3131; fax (604) 928-3105
(Launching for Johnstone Strait: concrete ramp, good at all tides. Hot showers and restrooms at campground, in summer; pit toilet in winter. Telephones at boat ramp.)
 Take the Beaver Cove turnoff from Island Highway (Highway 19) and follow signs to Telegraph Cove. After 6 miles (10 kilometers) you reach a "T" junction; turn left and continue almost 3 miles (5 kilometers) to Telegraph Cove. From Island Highway, it is 9 miles (15 kilometers) and takes 25 minutes to drive over the rough industrial roads to Telegraph Cove.

To get to Beaver Cove and Telegraph Cove turnoff
• Heading north from Campbell River on Island Highway: past Nimpkish Lake, look for the turnoff to Beaver Cove and Telegraph Cove. It is almost 3 hours north of Campbell River. You will see a sign about forestry tours on the right-hand side just past the turnoff.
• Heading south from Port Hardy on Island Highway, the turnoff is 45 minutes south of Port Hardy. When 10 minutes past Port McNeill, look for the turnoff to Beaver Cove and Telegraph Cove.

Port McNeill Public Ramp
Off Beach Road, just west of McNeill Road
Port McNeill BC
(Launching for Broughton Strait and Queen Charlotte Strait: concrete ramp, good at all tides. Parking space available. Restrooms north at ferry dock; telephone at Beach Road and McNeill Road.)

To get to McNeill Road
• Heading north from Campbell River on Island Highway (Highway 19), go 128 miles (206 kilometers) to Port McNeill. It takes 3 hours. Look for the turnoff when 10 minutes past the turnoff to Telegraph Cove.
• Heading south from Port Hardy on Island Highway, go 25 miles (41 kilometers) to Port McNeill. It takes 35 minutes.

Bear Cove Public Ramps
Bear Cove Road
Port Hardy BC
(Launching for Queen Charlotte Strait: steep tarmac ramps, good at all tides. Picnic tables and pit toilets. Wheelchair toilets at ferry ticket office, end of road. Hot showers in summer at campground between Bear Cove and the highway. Telephone outside Petro-Canada building: go ½ mile [1 kilometer] back toward highway, then walk down road between Petro-Canada and Bear Cove Ice Ltd.)
 From Island Highway (Highway 19) south of Port Hardy: go 2¾ miles (4½ kilometers) north on Bear Cove Highway to the launching ramps.

To get to Bear Cove and Prince Rupert ferry turnoff
• From Port Hardy, go on Highway 19 South for 2¾ miles (4½ kilometers) – takes 5 minutes; turn left following signs to Bear Cove.
• From Port McNeill, go on Highway 19 North for 22 miles (36 kilometers). It takes 30 minutes. Turn right following signs to Prince Rupert ferry.

Port Hardy Public Ramp
Next to Quarterdeck RV Park & Marina
6555 Hardy Bay Road
Port Hardy BC
(604) 949-6551; fax (604) 949-7777
(Launching at Hardy Bay for Queen Charlotte Strait: concrete ramp, good at all tides. Public parking extremely limited. Parking available for a fee next to the ramp at Quarterdeck Marina. Restrooms and hot showers; telephone at top of ramp.)

• **More services for Port Hardy region:** see service information for Gulf Islands on page 140.

• **Ferry Information**
British Columbia Ferry Corporation
Bear Cove Terminal
Port Hardy BC
Toll-free in BC: 1-800-663-7600. Or (604) 949-6722.
Telephoning from outside BC: (604) 386-3431.
(Ferries from Port Hardy to Prince Rupert – reservations required.)

• **Tourist Information**

Discover British Columbia
1117 Wharf Street
Victoria BC V8W 2Z2
1-800-663-6000: Toll-free throughout Canada and the USA, including Hawaii and parts of Alaska.

Port Hardy & District Travel Infocentre
7250 Market Street,
PO Box 249
Port Hardy BC V0N 2P0
(604) 949-7622; fax (604) 949-6653

Port McNeill Travel Information Centre
Beach Road, east of McNeill
 Road at ferry dock
PO Box 129
Port McNeill BC V0N 2R0
(604) 956-3131; fax (604) 956-4977
(At ferry dock, summer only. Contact year-round at fax or mailing address.)

How to Go – From Nanaimo it takes 5½ hours to drive to Telegraph Cove or Port McNeill, 6 hours to Port Hardy. Go north on Island Highway (Highway 19) to Campbell River. From Campbell River, continue on Island Highway. Or go by way of Highway 28 to Gold River, gravel roads to Woss, then north on Island Highway.
• From Campbell River to Telegraph Cove takes more than 3 hours. Head north on Island Highway for 2 hours to the Woss turnoff. Past the Woss turnoff, continue on Island Highway for 40 minutes more to Beaver Cove Road where you turn right following signs to Beaver Cove and Telegraph Cove: go 6½ miles (10½ kilometers) to a "T" junction at a gravel industrial road, turn left and go 3 miles (4¾ kilometers) more to Telegraph Cove. Drive with your headlights on as there might be logging traffic. From the highway, it takes 25 minutes.
• From Campbell River to Port McNeill takes almost 3 hours. Head north on Island Highway; past Nimpkish Lake and when 4 miles (7 kilometers) past the Beaver Cove/Telegraph Cove turnoff, turn right and follow signs to Port McNeill.
• From Campbell River to Port Hardy takes 3½ hours. Head north on Island Highway; when 35 minutes past Port McNeill, look for the turnoff to Port Hardy.

*All of this service information is subject to change.

STUBBS ISLAND
Boat Dive

Current Table: Weynton Passage

Skill: Expert divers and snorkelers. Intermediate divers with guide.

Why go: A carpet of hot-pink brooding anemones and small green pin-cushion anemones covers the rock. I love the big mint-green anemones, large clumps of hard pink hydrocoral, pink soft corals and basket stars like dreadlocks of spun ivory.

We saw giant orange peel nudibranches, an angry lingcod, blue rockfish, red Irish lords, China rockfish in crevices. Yellow sponges, red knobby sponges. Rock scallops, abalones, giant barnacles and urchins. Huge plumose anemones down deep. And look for Puget Sound king crabs.

In this whale-watching capital of the world, you might meet killer whales on any dive. When we surfaced, the boat tender told us a whale had passed. We followed it to gain information for scientific records of the movements of the whales. The charter operator photographed its rippled dorsal fin with a spot and later identified it certainly as P-1, a transient whale. The resident pods eat fish, the transients eat seals and similar mammals. You might get in on informal and fascinating whale watching after your dive. In September harbor seals are on the islands; divers sometimes see Dall's porpoises. You can see many of the beauties of the dive snorkeling!

Bottom and Depths: The steep rocky sides of the island are indented with deep crevices. The northwest corner is the shallowest, the southeast and west sides are deepest, bottoming out to sand at 120 feet (37 meters). Most life for scuba divers to see is at 50 to 60 feet (15 to 18 meters). In summer, some thickets of bull kelp.

Hazards: Current, lots of boats, bull kelp and wind. The current floods in through Queen Charlotte Strait and splits at Stubbs Island. It can run up to 6 knots (11 kilometers/hour). It helps to have slack but you can almost always find one face of Stubbs that is protected from current. Listen for boats, and ascend up the side of the island. Carry a knife for kelp. When a southeasterly wind blows, you must have a boat tender. When a westerly wind, it is difficult to dive Stubbs. Try Plumper Rock.

Telephone: Telegraph Cove, top of launching ramp.

Facilities: Charters, diving packages and launching at Telegraph Cove. Charters and launching at Port McNeill and Port Hardy. Air fills at Port McNeill and Port Hardy.

Access: Stubbs Island is at the east end of Cormorant Channel. It is 3½ nautical miles (6½ kilometers) north of Telegraph Cove; 11 nautical miles (20 kilometers) from Port McNeill. To dive the most beautiful southeast corner, plan to dive on slack.

Charter or launch at Telegraph Cove or Port McNeill, or take a liveaboard charter out of Port Hardy and go by boat to Stubbs Island. Anchor at the southeast corner if you can – it is the very best location. The current table for Weynton Passage is accurate for the east point of Stubbs where you *must* dive on slack. Dive the end of the flooding tide, get into a notch and head left.

The rest of the island is incredible too. If unable to dive the southeast corner for whatever reason, try someplace else. With current of 5 knots (9 kilometers/hour) and greater, plan to start your dive 10 or 15 minutes before the turn. With less current, enter 30 minutes before the turn and "work" the back eddies. On ebbing tides, you can dive the north side on the full ebb except when a westerly wind is blowing. From November though February, wind can blow for several days at a time.

Comments: Stubbs Island is locally honored as a marine sanctuary.

After the dive, whale watching

2 kn

121
75
49

14 46
37 34 Stubbs I

95
68
49 37

110

WEYNTON

95
104

112 100 57 99

53
55
38
46
38

24
10₁ 35 64
26
37 18₃

38 70 18 PLUMPER 60
38
(16) 89 (37) 85 ISLANDS 46
40 35 (2)(83) 20₁
(8) (1)
49 55 37 20₁ 174 (12)
A 128 (2) 26 20 (8)
53 3 80
lekduma I 35 Ksuiladas I IR 9 50
22 48 (31) 108
37 (1) 41 52
51 48 80 40 52
62 20₁
48 73 12₅ 15₈ 10₆

PASSAGE

3 (21) 37
48 (21) 27
3 37
(11) 46 (18) (18)
50 Stephenson I 66
101 64 46
66 (8) (49)
(2) (3) 57 (21)
14 16₅ 54
134 35 33
77 51
146
110

3 kn
294

251
364

300
200 238
110 100
157 50 64
42 22 (20)
62 44

Telegraph
Cove Wastell Pt
elegraph McDonald
Cove Hill
24 26 37

130
51
75 62 33 59
55 146 42
113
66
59
6
20
27

102

443

59
183
44 Blinkhorn

NOT TO BE USED FOR NAVIGATION: For information
on obtaining navigational charts see page 318.
This is a portion of 3546.

1 Nautical Mile

PLUMPER ROCK
Boat Dive

Current Table: Weynton Passage
Subtract 30 minutes

Skill: Expert divers. Intermediate divers with guide.

Why go: The marine life is a spectacle – not an inch of rock showing except above water at the colorful underwater seamount called Plumper Rock. And when the wind is blowing elsewhere, you can usually still dive Plumper.

China rockfish – you see them on every dive, but the hard pink hydrocoral and basket stars are still my favorites at this site. Closest thing to wall-to-wall basket stars in the shallows I have seen anyplace: we saw a beautifully sculpted basket star in only 30 feet (9 meters). Also schools of black rockfish, lots of kelp greenlings, lingcod, red Irish lords and tiger rockfish. Yellow sponges and orange cup corals brighten the scene.

We saw tennis ball sponges, rock scallops, giant barnacles and tube worms waving purple thread-like fingers. Masses of small pink dahlia anemones. A valley of huge white plumose anemones lured us down and down. It looks like the tropics. The color! The underwater visibility! Usually you can see 80 to 100 feet (24 to 30 meters) in winter – when we dived Plumper the last day of February, visibility was down to 75 feet (23 meters). Timing is important; the algae bloom usually comes in April.

After diving, look for bald eagles – we counted twenty-four in a glance.

Bottom and Depths: Plumper Rock dries at 13-foot (4-meter) tides. The valley of plumose-covered rock goes down on the northeast side. It bottoms out to sand at 120 to 130 feet (37 to 40 meters). A scattering of bull kelp streams in the current.

Hazards: Current – even downwellings, and boats. You must dive on slack. The current is moving all the time; it just turns around. Listen for boats and hug the rock as you ascend.

Telephone: Telegraph Cove, top of launching ramp.

Facilities: None at Plumper Rock. Launching at Telegraph Cove, Port McNeill and Port Hardy. Air fills in Port McNeill and Port Hardy. Charters year-round out of Port McNeill, and in some winter months out of Telegraph Cove. At Telegraph Cove, dive group packages include guest house accommodation with sauna, meals, tanks and air. In summer, camping with hot showers at Telegraph Cove.

Access: Plumper Rock is on the east side of Weynton Passage in the Plumper Islands. It is in the passage between Ksuiladas Island and the island north of it. Charter or launch at Telegraph Cove and go 2¾ nautical miles (5 kilometers) to Plumper Rock or at Port McNeill and go 12 nautical miles (22 kilometers) to Plumper. Or take a liveaboard charter out of Port Hardy. Best time to start your dive at Plumper is 45 minutes before high slack to get a back eddy around the rock. Arrive at Plumper with gear ready at least an hour before the turn and watch the water and kelp. Best to have a pickup boat. To find the valley, dive toward the northeast.

Comments: The picturesque boardwalk town of Telegraph Cove was founded in the 1920s and is worth a visit for non-divers. Most of the town is on stilts over the water. They say at one time in the late 1970s, nearly every resident of Telegraph Cove was a diver.

China rockfish

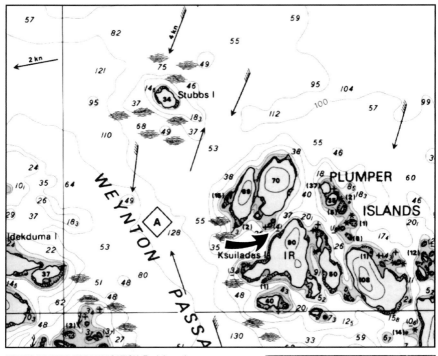

1 Nautical Mile

HADDINGTON ISLAND
Kayak Dive or Boat Dive

Skill: Expert divers. Intermediate divers with guide.

Why go: Lingcod, black rockfish, quillback rockfish, kelp greenlings cruise in droves from superb hidey-holes behind giant, squared-off volcanic-rock blocks tumbled down the steep wall at the rock quarry at Haddington Island.

White plumose anemones are huge too – they light the wall, feather the pearly gray rock blocks with glorious white. Many of the blocks are grooved, a different geometric look for an underwater habitat. Painted greenlings hide beneath dark ledges. Crimson slipper cucumbers, orange cup corals and gum boot chitons are on the wall. Green urchins, giant red and purple urchins are heaped in the valleys. Inviting holes to poke your light into where giant lingcod hide are everywhere behind these blocks. They were left behind after the stone was quarried to build the facade of the Parliament Buildings in Victoria, completed in late 1897; and to build the causeway in front of the Empress Hotel in the early 1900s.

The rock quarry dive possesses the same elegance – no, is the source of elegance of these two provincial landmarks that originated at Haddington Island.

Bottom and Depths: A slim line of kelp rims the shore and its tumble of giant blocks in the narrow belt of shallows. The wall is steep, the tumbled blocks spill down to gravel, sand and shells at 115 to 125 feet (35 to 38 meters) depending on tide height. With 13 feet (4 meters) of tide, we saw the most life from 40 to 60 feet (12 to 18 meters).

Hazards: Current and depth; possible danger to kayak-divers from overexertion after the dive. Divers with pickup boat could dive throughout the flood. With no pickup boat, dive on high slack. Slack is difficult to predict in Broughton Strait as it is affected by wind. Also the current never stops, it just slows down and then turns. Kayak-divers who have dived deep should take a lunch break and take it easy heading home. The risk of bends may be increased by strenuous paddling after the dive.

Telephones: • From Port McNeill Public Ramp, go south one block to Beach Drive and McNeill Road. • At Mine Road and Campbell Way: telephone is on building at northeast corner. From Beach Camp, go 1 mile (1¾ kilometers) up Mine Road to it.

From Hyde Creek, 4 miles (6½ kilometers); go to the highway, turn right and go 2½ miles (4 kilometers) toward Port McNeill, turn right down Campbell Way and go to Mine Road; the telephone is on building at northeast corner.

Facilities: None at Haddington. Air fills, charters and launching in Port McNeill.

Access: Haddington Island is in Broughton Strait. It is 3 nautical miles (5½ kilometers) from the launching ramp in Port McNeill, and almost 1 nautical mile (1½ kilometers) across open water from Hyde Creek where kayak-divers might launch.

Charter or launch your own boat at Port McNeill or launch your dive-kayak at Hyde Creek and go to the middle of the rock quarry heap just below a small wooden wreck at the southeast end of Haddington. Plan to dive at the end of the flood on high slack. The flooding current streams around both sides of the island more-or-less meeting at the rock quarry. It's better visibility with high tide too. While diving, work your way around the wall toward the Vancouver Island side until you get into current, then head back to the lee side of the island. Lots of rocks to hold onto and pull yourself along. Ascend up one of many valleys protected from current.

Fog and wind can make crossing to Haddington extremely hazardous. Wind blows up quickly in Broughton Strait. Fog can come anytime but usually less fog from May through September. Before setting off, all boaters should check weather reports and be sure your craft is properly equipped to get there given the conditions expected.

• Boat divers: launch at Port McNeill Public Ramp and go 3 nautical miles (5½ kilometers) to the rock quarry at the southeastern tip of Haddington Island.

• Kayak-divers: paddle from the foot of the road at Hyde Creek; the turnoff is 1⅓ kilometers west of the bridge over the Nimpkish River. It is midway between Beaver Cove Road and Port McNeill turnoff. From either, go 2½ miles (4 kilometers) to Hyde Creek Road; then go on Hyde Creek Road for 1 mile (1½ kilometers) to the sea. Roadside parking for one or two cars. Walk across a narrow stretch of grass, launch and paddle north for almost 1 nautical mile (1½ kilometers) to the rock quarry at the southeastern end of Haddington Island. If diving on the flood, aim for the *western* end of the island to allow for the current drifting you eastward. Approach close to Haddington and paddle close to shore around to the rock quarry. With perfect conditions – flat water, no fog, no wind, the open-water crossing takes 35 to 45 minutes. At the quarry, always some rocks above water where you can land to gear up. Returning to Hyde Creek, again allow for the current.

Before leaving, tell someone where you are going so they will check on your return. Advisable to take marine flares – this is wilderness. Also obtain a ferry schedule. At the time of writing, the ferry from Alert Bay to Port McNeill crossed the path we took and while we were paddling the ferry passed us. Its wash was minimal but you never know; beware of potential wash from all passing vessels.

Comments: Back in Port McNeill, I was treated to a pleasant after-dive warm-up drink called Beaver Cove Tea.

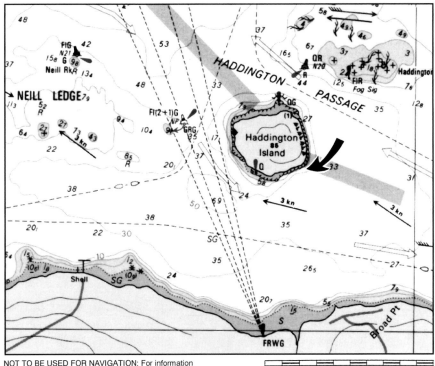

NOT TO BE USED FOR NAVIGATION: For information on obtaining navigational charts see page 318. This is a portion of 3546.

1 Nautical Mile

291

BEACH CAMP
Shore Dive

Skill: All divers

Why go: Super-easy access, no current to consider, and no matter what the weather you can dive at Beach Camp. Plus potential for old bottles – a mixed-bag dive.
    On the sand we saw sculpins, gunnels and crabs – hermit crabs, Dungeness crabs and red rock crabs; a rose star, orange stars with turned up toes, a leather star, sunflower stars and huge sea cucumbers. In the kelp we saw pink nudibranchs, white nudibranchs and coils of nudibranch eggs like an apple peel. In winter look for lion nudibranchs. White plumose anemones and purple plume worms are on the pilings. Kelp greenlings, big flounders, blackeye gobies and ratfish swim about. We found a 2½ foot (¾ meter) wolf-eel living in an old tire. An octopus in residence, I'm told. Beach Camp would be a great night dive.

Bottom and Depths: Silty sand bottom with small green lettuce kelp and large brown bottom kelp slopes gently to dock pilings at 40 to 50 feet (12 to 15 meters).

Hazards: Boats and cables around the dock; red jellyfish in July and August. Listen for boats and ascend up a piling or dive with a compass so you can navigate back to shore under water. Watch for cables and stay with your dive partner. If equipment of one diver becomes caught on a cable the other diver can free him or her. If you have seen jellyfish, check for stinging tentacles before removing mask and gloves.

Telephone: Mine Road and Campbell Way; telephone is on building at northeast corner. From Beach Camp, go 1 mile (1¾ kilometers) up Mine Road to it.

Facilities: Room for twenty cars to park.

Access: Beach Camp is just east of Hoy Bay in Broughton Strait east of Port McNeill; it is 8 minutes off Highway 19. When you see signs to Port McNeill, turn onto Campbell Way, go ½ mile (1 kilometer) and turn right at Mine Road. Go straight on Mine Road past Woodland Drive. When you see large gasoline storage tanks at a "Y" in the road, keep left and go to the water. From Woodland Drive, the last ½ mile (1 kilometer) of road is gravel. A fuel dock is at the end of the road and barges come about once a week and deliver gasoline at the dock. They come on the outside. Logs to sit on to gear up; then walk down a gently sloping seldom-used launching ramp, swim to the pilings and head down. Wheelchair access is possible down the concrete launching ramp at 10-foot (3-meter) tides and greater.
    Beach Camp is privately owned property. If in future it is closed to the public, please respect it. In the meantime, common sense should prevail. Park carefully and leave room for the trucks to turn.

To get to Port McNeill
• Heading north on Highway 19: from Campbell River to Port McNeill takes almost 3 hours. Past Nimpkish Lake and when 4 miles (7 kilometers) past the Beaver Cove Road turnoff to Telegraph Cove, turn right following signs to Port McNeill.
• Heading south on Highway 19: from Port Hardy, 25 minutes to Port McNeill. Turn left, following signs to Port McNeill on Campbell Way.

Comments: After diving you might enjoy a ferry ride to Alert Bay to see the *Spirit Lodge* presentation with its magical Holavision effects and story, and the tallest totem pole in the world.

Beach Camp, Haddington Island beyond

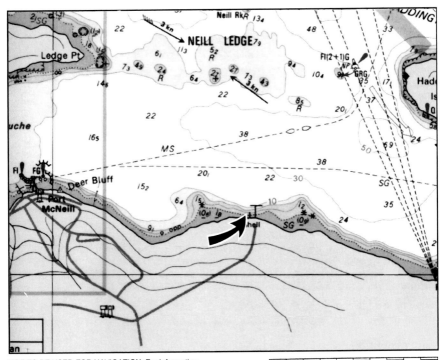

NOT TO BE USED FOR NAVIGATION: For information
on obtaining navigational charts see page 318.
This is a portion of 3546.

1 Nautical Mile

293

BEAR COVE
Shore Dive

Skill: All divers and snorkelers

Why go: Entry is easy, the dive is shallow. A great winter dive when you see minia-ture "ghosts" on every stringy stalk of kelp at Bear Cove.
The ghosts pulse. They bow. They nod their transparent, shapeless heads in the current. Each one measures 3 to 6 inches (7½ to 15 centimeters) high. This was a "first" for me. I'll never forget it. These marine ghosts are called hooded nudibranchs, or lion nudibranchs. We saw other nudibranchs too: lemon yellow ones with white tips and white nudibranchs with blue tips as well as nudibranch eggs.
On the reef, plumose anemones clump on top of the rocks. We saw lots of kelp greenlings and rockfish, a painted greenling in a clam shell, sea peaches, an abalone. Lots of tube worms and huge snakelock anemones. We saw egg cases of moon snails and sea pens on the sand. Local divers say two octopuses are in resi-dence and we saw leavings of crab – probably at the octopus lair. A pleasant easy site year-round for a quick dive or to try out new gear. And you can almost count on seeing lion nudibranchs from January into early March.

Bottom and Depths: Two shallow ledges down to a rocky reef at 30 to 40 feet (9 to 12 meters), depending on tide height. Bottoms out to silty sand. Bull kelp, sparse in winter but still useful to show you where the rocks are.

Hazards: Boats, poor visibility, bull kelp in summer, and red jellyfish in the fall. Listen for boats and ascend in the bull kelp or use a compass and navigate close to the bottom all the way back to shore north of the ramps. Safer in winter when fewer boats. Best visibility when the ferry is not in, especially in winter. Carry a knife for kelp. If you have seen jellyfish, check for stinging tentacles before removing masks and gloves.

Telephones: • Ferry terminal ⅕ mile (⅓ kilometer) north at end of road; telephones are inside the terminal but available most daylight hours. • Outside Petro-Canada building: go nearly ½ mile (⅘ kilometer) back toward Highway 19 and walk down road between Petro-Canada and Bear Cove Ice Ltd. to the telephone.

Facilities: Picnic table, pit toilet and parking space. Air fills in Port Hardy and Port McNeill. Restrooms with wheelchair-accessible flush toilets at ferry terminal, avail-able most daylight hours. In summer, dive-kayak rentals at Port Hardy.

Access: Bear Cove is at the southeast corner of Hardy Bay. It is 5 miles (8 kilome-ters) from Port Hardy on Bear Cove Highway.
From Island Highway (Highway 19), go nearly 2¾ miles (4½ kilometers) along Bear Cove Highway to the launching ramp. Drop gear, park and enter at the launching ramp on the right-hand side. Swim straight out over two short ledges and turn right to the rocky reef. Safer to stay north of the green navigational marker throughout the dive – it marks the boat entry. Wheelchair divers with good brakes could launch at this fairly steep ramp.

To get to Bear Cove and Prince Rupert ferry turnoff
• From Port Hardy, go south on Highway 19 for 2¾ miles (4½ kilometers) – takes 5 minutes; turn left, following signs to Bear Cove.
• From Port McNeill, go north on Highway 19 for 22 miles (36 kilometers). It takes 30 minutes. Turn right, following signs to Prince Rupert ferry.

Comments: Divers with dive-kayaks could launch at Bear Cove and paddle 2 nautical miles (3¾ kilometers) to Daphne Point. Looks inviting.

"Ghosts of the sea"

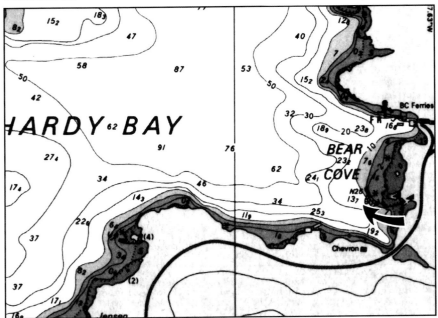

NOT TO BE USED FOR NAVIGATION: For information
on obtaining navigational charts see page 318.
This is a portion of 3548.

200 Yards

BEAR COVE FERRY DOCK WALL
Shore Dive

Tide Table: Alert Bay

Skill: All divers

Why go: Plumose anemones and purple plume worms decorate the cables and pilings holding the ferry dock. Whitish "Spanish moss" drips from the overhangs. Orange and white cucumbers are everywhere. We saw clusters of small orange anemones beneath an overhang, threadlike tube-dwelling anemones, fat dahlia anemones, sea peaches, a giant silver nudibranch, sea cucumbers, clown nudibranchs and a juvenile wolf-eel swimming along the bottom. Schools of pile perch, lots of small rockfish. Enormous sunflower stars, vermilion stars and purple stars are plastered on the wall. A scenic dive.

Bottom and Depths: Rock wall bottoming out to sand at 40 to 50 feet (12 to 15 meters), depending on tide height. Lettuce kelp on rocks in the shallows.

Hazards: Ferry boats year-round; red jellyfish in the fall. Check the ferry schedule at the terminal. I remember when ferries arrived only once a week, but at the time of writing schedules have increased. Because a ferry comes in or goes out every day; this dive might become impossible. When down, listen for boats. If you have seen jellyfish, check one another before removing masks and gloves.

Telephones: • Ferry terminal: telephones are inside terminal but available most daylight hours. • Outside Petro-Canada building: go just over ½ mile (1 kilometer) back toward Highway 19 and walk down road between Petro-Canada and Bear Cove Ice Ltd.

Facilities: Restrooms with wheelchair-accessible flush toilets in terminal during most daylight hours. Lots of parking space. Hot showers in summer at campground between Bear Cove and the highway. Air fills in Port Hardy and Port McNeill.

Access: Bear Cove ferry dock wall is in Bear Cove, southeast side of Hardy Bay. It is 5 miles (8 kilometers) south of Port Hardy at the end of Bear Cove Highway.
From Island Highway (Highway 19): go 3 miles (4¾ kilometers) along Bear Cove Highway to the ferry terminal. Before diving find out when the next ferry is due. If all clear, climb down the rocks at the left of the terminal, snorkel 100 yards (90 meters) out between the ferry "bumpers" and cross to the wall on the right-hand side. Go down and explore.

To get to Bear Cove and Prince Rupert ferry turnoff
• From Port Hardy, go south on Highway 19 for 2¾ miles (4½ kilometers) – takes 5 minutes; turn left, following signs to Bear Cove.
• From Port McNeill, go north on Highway 19 for 22 miles (36 kilometers). It takes 30 minutes. Turn right, following signs to Prince Rupert ferry.

Comments: Bear Cove Prehistoric Site is the oldest known settlement on Vancouver Island, dating from over 8,000 years ago. You can see some items found at this site at Port Hardy Museum.

Bear Cove Ferry Dock

1 Nautical Mile

BARRY ISLET
Boat Dive

Skill: Intermediate and expert divers

Why go: A deep dive with soft corals for the reward – that's what we went for. But our end-of-the-dive safety stop was the clincher for me – it became an underwater dance of the seven veils.

No rock was visible. First we gently pulled one brown or olive-colored frond of kelp aside, then another. Behind each one was another surprise. We saw a large cabezon at 10 feet (3 meters). Kelp greenlings, purple stars, leather stars, purple urchins. Deeper, we saw tall plumose anemones, pink brooding anemones, masses of soft corals, a valley with jillions of flat little white anemones. Deeper still, orange peel nudibranchs, basket stars, giant barnacles covered with encrusting sponge and hydrocorals – blue, deep purple and white. Bright yellow sulfur sponges, orange encrusting sponge, rock scallops, orange cup corals, a red Irish lord. Look for octopuses and wolf-eels hiding beneath the undercuts.

And, yes, it was fabulous much deeper, too, where we saw a 1-foot (⅓-meter) high, bright red bushy gorgonian coral.

Bottom and Depths: Sheer wall with undercuts from 30 to 80 feet (9 to 24 meters). Bottoms out at 110 to 120 feet (34 to 37 meters), depending on tide height, to a broad ledge. Then slopes gently deeper.

Hazards: Current, boats and bull kelp; red jellyfish in the fall. Go early and wait for slack. Listen for boats and ascend up the wall in the bull kelp. Carry a knife for kelp. If you have seen any jellyfish, check masks and gloves before removing them.

Telephone: Cellular telephone or VHF radio on your boat.

Facilities: None.

Access: Barry Islet is in Queen Charlotte Strait at the south end of Ripple Passage. It is a tiny islet east of the well-known Deserters Group.

Charter or launch at Port Hardy and go north 10 nautical miles (19 kilometers) to Barry Islet. Choose where to dive depending on the current: you can always dive one end or the other. Those who know it best say the northeast side of the islet is best. Dive the northeast side on the turn to ebb. On the turn to flood, start at the southwest side and work around the islet – that was good enough for me!

Comments: Barry Islet is a tempting sample to show how magnificent British Columbia diving can be – this dive is worth a return plus much much more. I have met a number of dive shop operators who make their annual holiday a liveaboard charter trip out of Port Hardy.

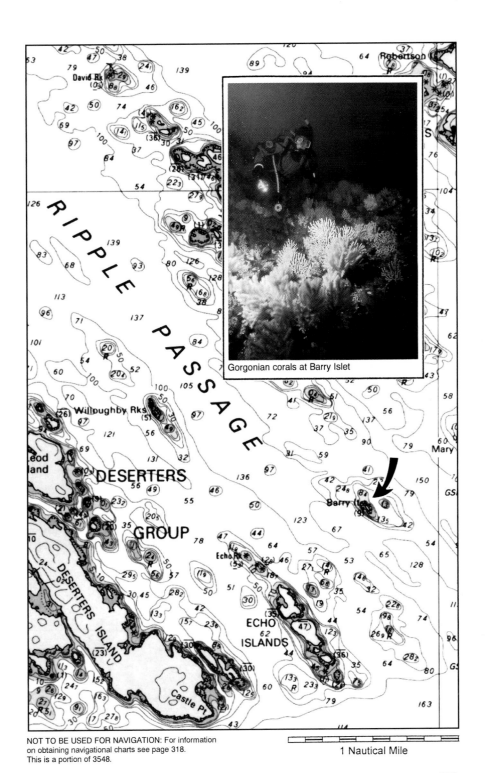

Gorgonian corals at Barry Islet

1 Nautical Mile

BRUNO'S ROCK
Boat Dive

Tide Table: Alert Bay

Skill: All divers

Why go: A low-key shallow dive with two juvenile wolf-eels in residence and at least two resident octopuses to see. In season, a coffee shop and possibly hot showers while your tank is filled after the dive.

On one dive at Bruno's Rock my buddy and I saw flamboyant bouquets of white plumose anemones, giant barnacles, China rockfish, lots of kelp greenlings, a red Irish lord. Mint colored anemones, dahlia anemones, a ratfish in the distance and two harbor seals. We found the two resident octopuses: a little one that slid out and sat in the open with its head peaked up, then slipped into its hole again. It measured 3 feet (1 meter) in diameter. The big one hid: all we could see was its 1-inch (2½-centimeter) siphon and suckers that measured 1½ inches (3¾ centimeters) across.

We saw orange sea peaches, rock scallops, tiny orange cup corals and huge sea stars clinging to the rocks. Orange sea pens rising from the sand around. Egg cases of moon snails on the sand. We swam over big-leafed lettuce kelp hiding sea lemons, abalones, purple and black urchins; through stringy bull kelp, and then long brown seaweed near the surface. On the surface, we saw four river otters and eagles in the sky – only missed out on Bruno, the large male wolf-eel. He has departed but two juvenile female wolf-eels have moved in. Visibility April to mid-May averages 40 to 50 feet (12 to 15 meters). Crystal clear water from September to November through winter.

After diving Bruno's Rock you could go to the Lucan Islands in nearby Browning Passage to camp, the next day dive Browning Wall.

Bottom and Depths: At the deepest point, the rock bottoms out to sand at 45 to 55 feet (12 to 17 meters). Some bull kelp but it is stringy and you can swim through it.

Hazards: Current and red jellyfish, in the fall. Dive near the slack. If you have seen any jellyfish, check for stinging tentacles before removing masks and gloves.

Telephone: Cellular telephone or VHF radio on your boat.

Facilities: At God's Pocket Resort on Hurst Island, from March to October: air fills, hot showers and a great coffee shop for drop-in divers. Dive package includes boat diving, air fills, accommodation and meals with advance reservation at God's Pocket Resort. Boat rentals year-round in Port Hardy.

Access: Bruno's Rock is in Christie Passage, 400 feet (120 meters) offshore from God's Pocket Resort at Hurst Island. It is 12 nautical miles (22 kilometers) north of Port Hardy. You could take your own boat or arrange for boat or helicopter transport from Port Hardy to God's Pocket Resort – but reserve well in advance. Easiest boat access is normally in September and October when it is usually calm, or when the southeast wind blows and knocks down the swell. Fog can come anytime, but usually less fog from May through September when more daylight hours for travelling.

When staying at God's Pocket Resort, you can dive Bruno's Rock as a resort dive from their dock. Or take your own boat from Port Hardy, anchor and dive. Look for the octopuses by starting in a notch on the outside (south side) of the rock and swimming west. We found them within 30 feet (9 meters). It would be a great night dive.

Comments: No spear guns and no taking of marine life from this site or from any of the frequently dived sites in this region. Locals honor them as reserves.

God's Pocket, Hurst Island

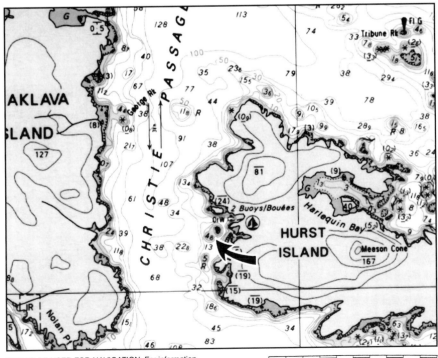

NOT TO BE USED FOR NAVIGATION: For information
on obtaining navigational charts see page 318.
This is a portion of 3549.

1 Nautical Mile

BROWNING WALL
Boat Dive

Skill: Intermediate and expert divers. All divers with guide.

Why go: Pink soft corals and yellow sulfur sponges hide the rock. This sheer drop-off is a living, ever-changing tapestry – yet always recognizable. Once you've been there you know it when you see photographs of Browning Wall.
　The intricate curlicue tangles that are basket stars, yellow-and-black China rockfish, kelp greenlings and sponges galore are more creatures you are sure to see. White encrusting sponge makes everything bright. Fuzzy gray cobalt sponges like jelly are along the wall. Look for octopuses, too. Mint green anemones are in the shallows. Red urchins. Rock scallops – lots of them. We see an orange peel nudibranch. Nudibranch eggs like a string of jewels. Giant barnacles – all are woven into the rich tapestry.
　Drift this pink and yellow wall once and you'll want to do it again. I want to go back to Browning just for the wall, but also for the chance to meet leaping, playful schools of Pacific white-sided dolphins, a relatively frequent but so far unpredictable treat for divers in the Queen Charlotte Strait region. You might also see Dall's porpoises. They do not jump, but they are one of the fastest-swimming mammals in the world. Look for both animals following in the wakes of boats.
　Browning Passage is usually protected – even in a southeast wind, another good reason to dive Browning Wall. Boat passage to Browning is possible when it is difficult to reach many other sites out of Port Hardy.

Bottom and Depths: Sheer drop-off to a ledge at 95 to 105 feet (29 to 32 meters), depending on tide height. The wall feels bottomless, drops to 215 feet (66 meters) on the chart; bottoms out to white sand, I'm told. A great deal of life between 40 and 70 feet (12 and 21 meters) – an excellent drift zone. Some stringy kelp.

Hazards: Boats, depth, current; red jellyfish in the fall. When ascending, listen for boats and stay close to the wall or in the kelp – a great many boats pass immediately alongside. Dive on slack and it will still be a drift. Before you head down, make a dive plan; then stick with your plan. The scene is so beautiful it would be easy to forget to come up. Dive with a "live" boat. If you have seen any red jellyfish, check for stinging tentacles before removing masks and gloves.

Telephone: Cellular telephone or VHF radio on your boat.

Facilities: None at Browning Wall. Primitive camping at the Lucan Islands south end of Browning Passage. Charters, boat rentals, launching and air fills in Port Hardy. Dive package at God's Pocket, and air fills for drop-ins.

Access: Browning Wall is on the west side of Browning Passage at the south end of Nigei Island – it is the only wall that drops off to 215 feet (66 meters) on the chart.
　Charter out of Port Hardy or God's Pocket, or launch your own boat and go to Browning Passage. From Port Hardy go 12 nautical miles (22 kilometers) northwest across Goletas Channel to Browning Passage. From God's Pocket at Hurst Island go 4 nautical miles (7½ kilometers), crossing Christie Passage and going around the southern end of Balaklava Island to Browning Passage. Easiest boat access from Port Hardy to Browning Wall is normally in September and October when it is usually calm. Fog can come anytime, but usually there is less fog from May through September when there are also more daylight hours for travelling. From Port Hardy, go to Browning Passage and dive with a "live" boat. A superb drift.

Drift diving Browning is like jumping into a kaleidoscope and becoming part of the moving scene. It's magical. As one diver on our charter said "You can be a space cadet and it's okay".

Comments: And, again, no taking of marine life permitted along Browning Wall, as at all of the prime sites in the region.

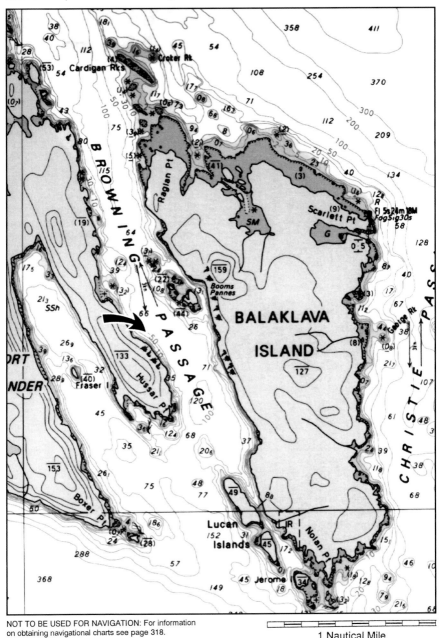

1 Nautical Mile

Skill: Intermediate and expert divers

Why go: "Tame" wolf-eels, Hunter and Huntress, and a myriad more wolf-eels live here. But the wolf-eel population is only one of the highlights at Hunt Rock. Incredible beauty is everywhere in the shallows where pastel lavender and pink brooding anemones cover the kelp stalks as well as the rocks. Deeper, look for octopuses and yelloweye rockfish. One yelloweye lives near the wolf-eels, but deeper. Divers estimate it weighs 44 pounds (20 kilograms).

When we first dropped on the bottom at Hunt Rock, I was horrified to see an enormous – probably 6-foot (2-meter) long – wolf-eel slither from behind our guide and up between his legs in front of him. Our guide didn't "miss a beat" – just kept feeding the other wolf-eel in front of him. He was obviously used to it. Six of them came to meet us that day. Hunter is 8 feet (2½ meters) long. He has a couple of bumps on his lip and divers have been hand-feeding him for years.

The alarming thing about it is the potential danger to the wolf-eels should a diver be startled by one. Expect this familiarity from wolf-eels at Hunt Rock. Lots more to see at Hunt Rock, too: fish are a big feature of the dive. We saw China rockfish, schools of black rockfish, kelp greenlings, white-spotted greenlings, a 15-pound (7-kilogram) lingcod and yelloweye rockfish. We also saw basket stars, huge rock scallops, yellow sponges and millions of small white plumose anemones.

Remember that Hunt Rock is locally considered a reserve – do not take any fish, shellfish or wolf-eels. Probably the best way to prevent the wolf-eels from becoming hurt is for all divers to be informed of the friendly greeting to expect when they dive Hunt Rock. Spread the word.

Bottom and Depths: At high tide, Hunt Rock is 30 feet (9 meters) deep. Hunter and Huntress's den is at 60 feet (18 meters) and more dens at 75 feet (23 meters). Bull kelp marks the spot.

Hazards: Current, small boats and bull kelp in summer. Dive on slack with a low tidal exchange. Slack is not always as predicted. Go early, watch the water and be prepared to pull out of the dive. Dive with a boat tender. Listen for boats, and ascend up your anchor line or in the bull kelp. Carry a knife for kelp.

Telephone: Cellular telephone or VHF radio on your boat.

Facilities: None at Hunt Rock. Air fills and charters in Port Hardy and God's Pocket.

Access: Hunt Rock is in Gordon Channel, ½ nautical mile (1 kilometer) offshore from Nigei Island. Far out – it is the farthest, most exposed site described in this guidebook. It is past the northwest end of Browning Passage and is 16 nautical miles (30 kilometers) northwest of Port Hardy.

Charter out of Port Hardy or God's Pocket and go to Hunt Rock. Or launch at Port Hardy and head out. Go to the green marker buoy at Hunt Rock. At slack water, kelp is visible on the surface. Anchor between two patches of kelp and Hunt Rock. Head down and look for the wolf-eel dens starting at 60 feet (18 meters) – if you can find them before they find you.

Leave a boat tender on board. Hunt Rock is too far out and too current-ridden to take a chance. Safest to dive from a charter boat whose operators know the area and from a boat equipped with loran and radar equipment. Fog can be a problem and it can come anytime, but usually there is less fog from May through September. The day we dived Hunt Rock radar was absolutely necessary from Browning Passage on. The day before we dived, five boats called for rescue because of the fickle weather.

Comments: No taking of any marine life from Hunt Rock. Local divers honor it as a reserve.

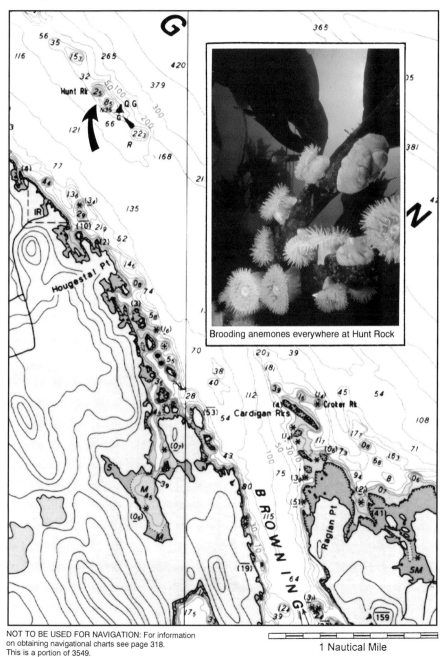

Brooding anemones everywhere at Hunt Rock

1 Nautical Mile

INDEX TO PLACES, MARINE LIFE AND DIVES, DIVING ACTIVITIES, CONDITIONS AND FACILITIES
including bottle dives, night dives, snorkeling sites, drop-offs, reefs, underwater parks and wreck dives

ILLUSTRATION CREDITS

Photographs
Front cover photograph, Jett Britnell

Back cover photographs, top left to bottom right: Gary McIntyre, Betty Pratt-Johnson, Jay Straith/Artificial Reef Society of British Columbia, Jett Britnell, Mike Richmond

"To the islands" opening photograph, by Airphoto '85

Photographs in this book were taken by the author except those credited below:
Debbie Anderson, pages 10 (bottom), 18
Alisen Brown, page 10 (top right)
Jett Britnell, pages 87, 157, 167, 183, 209, 221, 234 (top), 253, 279 (bottom right), 289
Brent Cooke, page 47
James A. Cosgrove, page 93
Exta-Sea Charters Ltd., page 279 (center right)
Rick Harbo, pages 91, 147, 277
Lou Lehmann, page 193
Gary Mallender, pages 131, 151, 227, 273, 275, 278 (bottom), 279 (top right), 305
Neil McDaniel, pages 65, 117, 129, 132 (bottom), 145, 181, 203, 261, 295
Gary McIntyre, pages 201, 207
Ministry of Small Business, Tourism and Culture/Kharen Hill Photography, page 46 (top)
Tony Nadelko, pages 133, 166 (top left)
Pacific Northwest Scuba Challenge Association, page 43
John Pratt-Johnson, pages 10 (top left), 30, 83, 223, 287, 320
Pauline Ptolemy, page 46 (bottom)
Mike Richmond, pages 165, 234 (bottom right), 235, 251, 259
Dale Sanders, pages 213, 225, 299
Selkirk Remote Sensing Air Photography, page 89
Jess Starnes, pages 13, 98 (bottom)
Photo from space by the LANDSAT satellite: distributed under authority provided by the Canada Centre for Remote Sensing and processed by Radarsat International Inc., page 99

Maps and Drawings
Maps by Eric Leinberger, pages 44-45, 49, 100-101, 134-135, 168-169, 236-237, 280-281

Marine life drawing by Greg Davies, pages 24-25

Drawing of *Barnard Castle*, courtesy of Jacques Marc/Underwater Archaeological Society of British Columbia, page 61

Logo and drawing showing public access, courtesy of Washington State Department of Natural Resources, pages 28 and 29

Nautical Charts
Reproduction of information from Canadian Hydrographic Service charts in this publication are for illustrative purposes only, they do not meet the requirements of the Charts and Publication Regulations and are not to be used for navigation. The appropriate charts, corrected up-to-date, and the relevant complementary publications required under the Charts and Publications Regulations of the Canada Shipping Act must be used for navigation. The NOAA charts are not to be used for navigation.

Contact the following to obtain information on local dealers and available charts and publications or to order charts and publications directly:

Chart Sales and Distribution Office
Canadian Hydrographic Service
Department of Fisheries and Oceans
Institute of Ocean Sciences, Patricia Bay
9860 West Saanich Road
Sidney BC V8L 4B2
(604)363-6358; fax (604)363-6841

Distribution Branch N/CG33
National Ocean Service, NOAA
6501 Lafayette Avenue
Riverdale MD 20737-1199
(301)436-6990; fax (301)436-6829

ACKNOWLEDGMENTS

A thread of shared experience over the years is woven into this guidebook. I will never forget the dives I enjoyed with so many people seventeen years ago when preparing the original *141 Dives*. During the past six years, while revising *141 Dives,* I have again experienced many new places and people. At the same time, *141 Dives* has expanded to become *99 Dives* and *101 Dives*. As noted, diving friends have multiplied, too.

With every dive I have a special memory of a diver or divers, as well as the dive. My thanks go to the following persons for happy times in the islands – for a wonderful collection of shared diving memories:

Thanks to Debbie Anderson for adventuring forth in a dive-kayak with me; to Ervin Carlier for sharing his first saltwater dive; to Kevin van Cleemput for sharing the first dive in this book, a jewel all by itself, and for extending our day and zigzagging all the way home to maximize the bonus of whale watching we lucked into; thanks to Hilary and Bryant Engebretson for their once-in-a-lifetime engagement dive with my husband and me; to Brian Cooper for introducing me to Big Red; to Lou Crabe for underwater antics and for introducing me to Beaver Cove tea after diving.The memories go on, but too little space on this page to share each one, so, simply "thanks" to Mike Flood, Ann and Randy Giles, Cheryl Gittens, Frank Graves, Carol Harding, Steve Le Casse, Gary McIntyre, Jim Mettler, Merilee Mitten, George Parson, John Pratt-Johnson, Ed Singer and Jason Terry for sharing rich diving experiences.

After diving comes the confirming of facts, the finding out of what was typical, what unusual. Many divers have generously shared their local knowledge and expanded my awareness of their home region so I can share it with readers; others have taken time to read and criticize my manuscript. While other persons have shared their expertise on tidal currents, marine life, geology, bottles, parks, medical aspects of diving, artificial reefs and wreck diving. For this help, thanks go to Andrew Bell, Jim Borrowman, Don Buchner, Ray Buckley, Kevin van Cleemput, Mike Clement, Joel Dovenbarger, Randy Giles, Rick Harbo, Tom Hemphill, Harry Kerr, Don Larson, Mike Lepawsky, Gary Mallender, Jacques Marc, Howard McElderry, Bill McKay, Gerry Millar, Peter Mustard, Peter Olesiuk, George Parson, Karen Pockett, Patrick Pringle, Mike Richmond, Wayne Rogers, Bob Simpson, Ed Singer, Nick Small, Jess Starnes, David Stone, Jay Straith, Jason Terry, Norman Todd, Geoff Townsend, Mel Turner, Tom Upton, Robert Vos, Fred West, Julie Wong and Bob Zielinski. Special thanks to Mike Woodward who reviewed the all-important tidal-current information; to Tim Ross and Marilyn MacPherson at the University of British Columbia map library, and Janet Collins at Western Washington University map library – all gave me invaluable help tracking down nautical charts; and thanks to Tim Niemier who launched me on kayak-diving. While tremendous thanks go to Neil McDaniel who, once again, read the entire manuscript and helped me with my observations of marine life.

Publisher and editor, Art Downs, read the whole thing, too. Thanks Art! Thanks for keeping a sharp eye on my use of hyphens and commas, thanks for keeping me laughing throughout book production – a major asset when the hard work comes. Your offbeat and always-present sense of humor is much appreciated. Grateful thanks also to Linda Davies who helped create the index; and to Doris Downs and Wendy van Oldenborgh, more sharp-eyed members of the book-production team who proofread and caught many errors. But if any errors remain in the book, I claim them as my own. Thanks to artist Byron Johnson and typesetter Dave Blair for working through a process that was often exasperating for all of us, as book production can be, to create a book design that I feel is not only attractive but also user friendly.

Finally, my biggest thanks go to my husband who did a multitude of important things like buying birthday presents for our seven grandchildren, who freed me up and gave me the time to do what I wanted to with this book, who waited patiently for me to complete it and re-enter the world. Thank you, John.

Betty Pratt-Johnson travels throughout the world, over it and under it. She loves exploring – scuba diving, hang gliding, caving, whitewater kayaking – then writing about it. Betty has enjoyed every dive described in this where-to-go guidebook. You can go with her on easy dives for new divers, as well as to more challenging sites to see sixgill sharks, wrecks, Steller sea lions and the largest octopuses in the world.

She is an award-winning photographer and writer. Her accurate, lively treatments of outdoor topics have appeared in *Diver, Skin Diver, BC Outdoors, Western Living, Reader's Digest, The New York Times.*